김
George Eliot U.S.

George Eliot U.S.

Transatlantic Literary
and Cultural Perspectives

Monika Mueller

Madison • Teaneck
Fairleigh Dickinson University Press

©2005 by Rosemont Publishing & Printing Corp.

All rights reserved. Authorization to photocopy items for internal or personal use, or the internal or personal use of specific clients, is granted by the copyright owner, provided that a base fee of $10.00, plus eight cents per page, per copy is paid directly to the Copyright Clearance Center, 222 Rosewood Drive, Danvers, Massachusetts 01923.[0-8386-4055-9/05 $10.00 + 8¢ pp, pc.]

Associated University Presses
2010 Eastpark Boulevard
Cranbury, NJ 08512

The paper used in this publication meets the requirements of the American National Standard for Permanence of Paper for Printed Library Materials Z39.48-1984.

Library of Congress Cataloging-in-Publication Data

Mueller, Monika, 1960-
   George Eliot U.S. : transatlantic literary and cultural perspectives / Monika Mueller.
      p. cm.
   Includes bibliographical references and index.
   ISBN 0-8386-4055-9 (alk. paper)
   1. Eliot, George, 1819-1880—Appreciation—United States. 2. American literature—19th century—Appreciation—England. 3. Eliot, George, 1819-1880—Knowledge—United States. 4. Eliot, George, 1819-1880—Knowledge—Literature. 5. Literature, Comparative—English and American. 6. Literature, Comparative—American and English. 7. American literature—English influences. 8. Eliot, George, 1819-1880—Influence. 9. English fiction—American influences. I. Title.
   PR4687.4.U6M84 2005
   823'.8—dc22
                                                                         2004017734

PRINTED IN THE UNITED STATES OF AMERICA

Für KK und für DFH

Her Losses make our Gains ashamed—
She bore Life's empty Pack
As gallantly as if the East
Were swinging at her Back.
Life's empty Pack is heaviest,
As every Porter knows—
In vain to punish Honey—
It only sweeter grows.
—Emily Dickinson on George Eliot

Contents

Acknowledgments	9
Introduction: Transatlantic Literary and Cultural Perspectives	13
George Eliot U.S.: Literary Relations 13	
Nineteenth-Century Social Discourses and their Literary Reflections 25	
1. George Eliot's "English" Novels and American Literature—Bringing It All Back Home?	51
The Scarlet Letter and *Woman in the Nineteenth Century* Revisited in *Adam Bede* and Co. 51	
The Microcosms of *Oldtown Folks* and *Middlemarch* 81	
2. Fuller's, Hawthorne's, Stowe's, and Eliot's Italy—Culture as Difference?	105
Nineteenth-Century American and British Travel Notes and Dispatches 105	
From "Faction" to Fiction: Italy in Eliot's Novels, Stowe's *Agnes of Sorrento,* and Hawthorne's *The Marble Faun* 124	
3. From *Uncle Tom's Cabin* to *Daniel Deronda*—and from Ethnicity to Identity?	151
Constructing "Race" 151	
From "Race" to (National) Identity 166	
Transcendental Soulmates 179	
4. Writing Beyond the Ending?: U.S. Adaptations of George Eliot	193
The George Eliot Heroine in the U.S. 193	
Culture in Need of Redemption? 204	
George Eliot—A "Classic" for the Twenty-First Century? 219	
Notes	235
Works Cited	271
Index	285

Acknowledgments

THIS STUDY EVOLVED FROM A POSTDOCTORAL THESIS (*HABILITATION*) submitted to the University of Cologne, Germany, Faculty of Arts. The project was conceived in Heidelberg, furthered in Potsdam, and finished in Cologne. I am grateful to the State of Brandenburg for supporting my work with a HSP III fellowship.

Along its way, this book has profited from the advice and encouragement of many people. The members of my *habilitation* committee—Heinz Antor, Hanjo Berressem, Paul Geyer, and Beate Neumeier—guided me through the arduous procedure. Special thanks goes to Beate Neumeier for overseeing the project and chairing the committee. I also wish to thank the anonymous reader from Fairleigh Dickinson University Press for his/her recommendations and the staff at Associated University Presses for their diligent work.

I appreciate the love, support, and advice I received from family, friends, and colleagues in and around Frankfurt/Heidelberg, Berlin/Potsdam, Cologne, and Birmingham, AL. I want to thank my parents, Gerda-Linde and the late Bruno Mueller (who unfortunately did not live to see this book finished) and my friends and colleagues Anja Bandau, Sharon DeVaney-Lovinguth, Norbert Finzsch, Dorothea Fischer-Hornung, Esther Fritsch, Karin Hirsch, Rüdiger Höffer, Andrea Kinsky-Ehritt, Christa Klein, Konstanze Kutzbach, Thomas Liesemann, Dagmar Schmitt, and Hubert Wurmbach.

Dorothea Fischer-Hornung and Konstanze Kutzbach went beyond the call of friendship by not only providing unflagging emotional support, but also reading the manuscript in its entirety and improving it through their invaluable suggestions. I dedicate this book to them.

❀ ❀ ❀

An excerpt from chapter three "From *Uncle Tom's Cabin* to *Daniel Deronda* —and from Ethnicity to Identity?" was published as "Nineteenth-Century Nar*race*ons: Harriet Beecher Stowe's *Uncle Tom's Cabin* and George Eliot's *Daniel Deronda*" in the December 2002 issue of the online journal *gender forum* <http://www.genderforum.uni-koeln.de>.

George Eliot U.S.

Introduction: Transatlantic Literary and Cultural Perspectives

GEORGE ELIOT U.S.: LITERARY RELATIONS

THE BEGINNINGS OF THIS STUDY ABOUT GEORGE ELIOT'S[1] (RECIPROCAL) relationship with American literature and culture can be traced to a moment in time a few years back, when I more or less accidentally picked up and read a copy of George Eliot's *Adam Bede* (1859). I was quite surprised by the obvious similarities between the plot of Eliot's first full-length novel and Nathaniel Hawthorne's *The Scarlet Letter* (1850); both novels feature young female protagonists named Hester (shortened to Hetty in *Adam Bede*) who bear illegitimate children as a result of having had an affair with a man named Arthur D.—D for Donnithorne in *Adam Bede* and D for Dimmesdale in *The Scarlet Letter*. Furthermore, both novels focus on the social consequences that these illegitimate births have for their female protagonists: Eliot's Hetty Sorrel kills her child for fear of social ostracism, whereas Hawthorne's Hester Prynne raises her daughter Pearl, proudly enduring her fate as an outcast in her Puritan community.

Intrigued by these parallels, I looked for evidence of Eliot's reading of Hawthorne's work, which I found in Edward Stokes's *Hawthorne's Influence on Dickens and George Eliot* (1985) and also in various shorter references to parallels between Hawthorne's and Eliot's novels, most notably *Adam Bede* and *The Scarlet Letter*. In *Hawthorne's Influence on Dickens and George Eliot*, which Stokes intended to be a classical "influence study," he painstakingly traces stylistic parallels between Hawthorne's and Eliot's novels; yet beyond his analysis of genre-related questions and the treatment of evil in Hawthorne and Eliot he does not inquire deeply into thematic parallels and differences—

differences which, considering the fact that both authors lived on different continents, might be culturally motivated and hence of significant interest to a comparative project. The obvious but intended limitations of Stokes's work encouraged me to look for more uncharted territory concerning Eliot's response to Nathaniel Hawthorne's work and the culturally motivated differences between their depictions of gendered, cultural, and racial issues.

Having detected further parallels between Hawthorne's and Eliot's approach to gender issues, as for example in Hawthorne's presentation of Hester Prynne's relationship with her much older (temporarily disappeared) husband, Roger Chillingworth, and Eliot's description of Dorothea Brooke's marriage to Edward Casaubon in *Middlemarch* (1871–72), I decided to turn to Hawthorne's and Eliot's Italian novels, *The Marble Faun* (1860) and *Romola* (1863), to investigate their respective constructions of cultural alterity. In her conception of her Italian novel, Eliot obviously followed Hawthorne's idea of incorporating a plot about evolutionary development, in which Italy and its inhabitants figure as representatives of an earlier historical stage. Thus, in *The Marble Faun*, Hawthorne's Donatello, the only Italian protagonist, experiences a "fortunate fall" from faun to human being, and from pagan to Christian, whereas in *Romola* Eliot's eponymous heroine undergoes several representative stages of Comtean social development from polytheism/paganism to positivism/altruism. But interestingly enough, Eliot clearly refused to emulate Hawthorne's politics of depicting Italian otherness as filthy, backward, and degraded.

Encouraged by the obviousness of Eliot's borrowings from Hawthorne, I decided to further explore Eliot's involvement with American literature in order to see if my efforts would yield enough material for a study which, by situating Eliot's work in an American cultural context, might shed some unusual, potentially disturbing light on both "typically British" and "typically American" literary and cultural perspectives. I discovered that while there are some monographs and articles that explore Eliot's relationship with American literature as well as some scholarly works that investigate "George Eliot and Europe,"[2] so far no book-length study situating George Eliot's œuvre in an American context has been published.

In their landmark publication *The Madwoman in the Attic* (1980), Sandra Gilbert and Susan Gubar have drawn attention to the fact that the romance elements in Eliot's fiction might at least partly be due to her study of American literature and that the oppositional impulses in her conception of gender can be traced to her favorable responses to both Margaret Fuller's view of gender, which encouraged women to transcend their gender boundaries by combining "female emotion" with "male intellect" (see Gilbert and

Gubar 1980, 479) and to Harriet Beecher Stowe's, which counseled women to stay within their traditional gender role, but encouraged men to develop the "female" virtue of nurturance (482). Gilbert and Gubar's work is extremely significant because of its pioneer insights into the "American" aspect of Eliot's gender politics, yet by focusing on the universality of nineteenth-century patriarchal ideology, it fails to engage with the subtler—and at least partly culturally conditioned—differences between Fuller's rather "self-reliant" deconstruction of gender roles and Eliot's more conservative conception of gender that shows the influence of contemporary European scientific discourses on gender.

More recently, Kimberly VanEsveld Adams has analyzed the Madonna as figure of female and feminist empowerment in nineteenth-century cultural discourse. Her analysis—especially in her 1996 article "Feminine Godhead, Feminist Symbol: The Madonna in George Eliot, Ludwig Feuerbach, Anna Jameson, and Margaret Fuller"—of the fictional Madonna-character (e.g. Dinah Morris from *Adam Bede*) as a single (working) woman empowered by a celibacy that guarantees independence from a man, sheds light on the beneficial escape from nineteenth-century gender ideology with which a celibate lifestyle could provide single working women. Yet like Gilbert and Gubar, who do not take into account cultural differences between Britain and the U.S., Adams does not devote much space to the cultural (and historical) incongruities between Eliot's British and Fuller's American "working Madonnas." But these differences undoubtedly account for the fact that Eliot's Dinah Morris, living at the turn of the nineteenth century and clinging to an archaic Methodism, seems historically and ideologically forced to get married and renounce her preaching, and thus cannot claim the freedoms available to a self-reliant Fullerian transcendentalist Madonna in mid-nineteenth-century New England.[3]

The construction of nationhood and race is the focus of Nancy Henry's unpublished 1994 dissertation "Originating Fictions: Harriet Beecher Stowe and George Eliot," in which she analyzes the many parallels between Stowe's and Eliot's presentation of race and national identity in *Uncle Tom's Cabin* (1852) and *Daniel Deronda* (1876). Concentrating on the two writers' depiction of their protagonists as racial and national leaders, she gives due recognition to the importance that one's cultural background has for the formation of both individual and collective identity. Yet while I acknowledge that Henry has done important work towards a better understanding of Eliot's reaction to Stowe's ideas about race and nationhood, I do not share her optimism in reference to the two authors' non-essentialist attitudes towards race and gender.

While there are several short publications about George Eliot's impact on twentieth-century U.S. authors,[4] longer publications about her influence on American literature have so far been restricted to discussions of Henry James's[5] and Edith Wharton's fiction. F. R. Leavis first called attention to Eliot's influence on James in *The Great Tradition: George Eliot, Henry James, Joseph Conrad* (1948) by observing that "Henry James wouldn't have written *The Portrait of a Lady* if he hadn't read . . . *Daniel Deronda*" (1950, 85). Leavis's work mainly focuses on similarities and differences between Eliot's and James's conceptions of their fictional characters and helped establish the view that James's novels show how innocent Americans are spoiled by a corrupt Europe. As its title indicates, Richard Freadman's *Eliot, James and the Fictional Self: A Study in Character and Narration* (1986) emphasizes the two writers' depictions of "human selves" in fiction—in the process of doing so it strongly attacks the poststructuralist notion that the self is culturally constructed. Like Leavis, Freadman does not pay much attention to Eliot's and James's construction of gender (a central focus of my analysis) and he also gives rather short shrift to the two authors' treatment of cultural identity and alterity. Mary Nyquist, in her article, "Determining Influences: Resistance and Mentorship in *The House of Mirth* and the Anglo-American Realist Tradition" (2001), finally adds Edith Wharton and gender concerns to the critical discussion. Yet her discussion, which traces the influence that Eliot's *Daniel Deronda* had on James's *The Portrait of a Lady* (1880, revised New York edition, 1908) and Wharton's *The House of Mirth* (1905), places a rather narrow focus on the presentation of mentorship in the three novels.

Engaging in a critical exchange with these important pioneer works on George Eliot and American literature, *George Eliot U.S.* will juxtapose Eliot's writing with American fiction from—mostly—the nineteenth century in order to show points of similarity as well as instances of (culturally motivated) difference. Moreover, it will present additional evidence of Eliot's readings in American literature, focusing on her dialog with American literature and culture in light of Eliot's and the American writers' reception of the most significant British/European and American nineteenth-century cultural discourses on scientific, social, gendered, and racial issues. It will, furthermore, highlight the culturally motivated differences between "typically British" and "typically American" reactions to cultural and racial alterity (particularly in reference to Italians and Jews) and present American reactions to and "rewrites" of the novels of George Eliot by Henry James, Edith Wharton, Elizabeth Stuart Phelps, Cynthia Ozick, and John Irving.

The affinities between Eliot's artistic sensibilities and those of the American writers whose works, as references in her letters indicate, she most frequently read and reviewed—Margaret Fuller, Nathaniel Hawthorne, and Harriet Beecher Stowe—are rather obvious, as is evident from the thematic inspiration reflected in her own fiction as well as from "reviews" in both her personal letters and literary journals. In spite of the fact that she had traveled all over Europe, Eliot never visited the United States; and of the contemporaneous American authors discussed in this study, she met only her young admirer Henry James, who first visited her in May 1869 and then again on a few occasions in 1878. James's biographer, Leon Edel, reports a significant event that happened during one of the visits: while James was looking on, Eliot's partner, George Henry Lewes, returned an edition of *The Europeans* (1878) that a friend of James's had lent them, with the words "Ah, those books—take them away please, away, away" (1985, 238). Henry James was rather disconcerted by the fact that Lewes apparently did not recognize him as the book's author. While Eliot's reactions to James's quite prolific criticism of her work are not known, her influence on him was profound, as Richard Freadman suggests: "James sought psychic and artistic individuality through comparison with his great precursor and peer. Needless to say, a vital part of this process was the creative reworkings of George Eliot's magnificent—but James thought, imperfect—aesthetic enterprise" (1986, 2).

In addition to getting to know Henry James, Eliot maintained a personal relationship by mail with Harriet Beecher Stowe, with whom she engaged in an ongoing dialog about literary and personal matters after Stowe had initiated contact in 1869 by means of a letter praising Eliot's work. In her letters to Eliot, Stowe at times broached rather bizarre subject matter. For example, she tried to convince Eliot that during a séance she had communed with the spirit of Charlotte Brontë, inquired if the figure of Casaubon was based on George Henry Lewes, and compared Theodore Tilton, whose wife her brother Henry Ward Beecher allegedly had an affair with, to Tito Melema from *Daniel Deronda* (see Fields 1898, 332–69). Considering Eliot's agnosticism and her very learned approach to religious matters, her extremely tactful replies to Stowe's at times rather outlandish remarks on religion (and several other topics) indicate that she must have valued Stowe's literary capabilities—which she had already praised in a favorable review of *Dred* (1856)—as well as her friendship very highly. And a neighbor of Stowe's, the American writer Elizabeth Stuart Phelps, also approached Eliot by letter. Phelps wanted her to write a "great novel" about a "Coming Woman" who rejects wifehood as vocation (see *George Eliot Letters* 1954–55, 5:388). Phelps's novel, *The Story of Avis* (1877), will be discussed as reaction to Eliot's poem "Armgart" (1873) in my final chapter, which deals with American reactions to Eliot.

Temperamentally, George Eliot was perhaps closer to Margaret Fuller and Nathaniel Hawthorne than to Stowe; even though she did not personally communicate with them, they both became very important to her literary work.[6] Her personal life showed astounding parallels to that of Margaret Fuller. Both authors were extremely erudite and often thought to be overly intellectual (at least for women); they both earned their livelihood as journalists and admired Goethe and German literature, and they both caused scandals through their "irregular" relationships with their lives' companions. It remains unclear whether or not Margaret Fuller got married to the impoverished Italian nobleman Giovanni Ossoli, by whom she had a son (see von Mehren 1994, 300). Eliot was prohibited from marrying George Henry Lewes because he could not obtain a divorce. Her heartfelt response to Margaret Fuller's untimely death by drowning in 1850 indicates that she recognized her as a kindred spirit: "It is a help to read such a life as Margaret Fuller's. How inexpressibly touching that passage from her journal—'I shall always reign through the intellect, but the life! the life! O my God! shall that never be sweet?' I am thankful, as if for myself, that it was sweet at last" (*George Eliot Letters* 1954–55, 2:15).

But Eliot's life also had parallels to Nathaniel Hawthorne's: due to rather difficult family situations both writers sequestered themselves at their families' homes for many years; they both used this time profitably for long literary apprenticeships, which enabled them to author very mature first fictions.[7] Moreover, they both had essentially conservative outlooks on life that kept them from embracing the causes of their day, such as the abolition of slavery in Hawthorne's and women's suffrage in Eliot's case. Hawthorne's and Eliot's temperamental and literary kinship is also palpable in the congruence of their literary topics. As the themes of their novels indicate, both were very interested in the past, in history and family history. They both created strong female characters, but due to their pessimistic views about the freedoms that women could actually achieve in nineteenth-century society, they customarily denied happy endings to their heroines' endeavors. And while both Hawthorne and Eliot had lost their faith in the religion of their forefathers, their works, nevertheless, inevitably focus on the function of religion in society—whether it be morally sustaining to the individual (as often in Eliot's works) or stifling (as often in Hawthorne's).

Religion is, of course, also at the center of Stowe's and Fuller's work—as is the case with most American writing from the nineteenth-century. Like Stowe's *Oldtown Folks* (1869), Eliot's *Middlemarch* (1871–72) investigates the role that religion plays in an "organic" society, but it nevertheless seems that Eliot engaged herself to a greater extent with Stowe's and Fuller's gender conceptions and social visions than with their ideas about religion. Thus, in addition to adopting aspects of Stowe's and Fuller's notions of gender, Eliot often follows them in comparing woman's lot to that of slaves; like the two American writers, she also stresses the importance of education to the fulfillment of women's lives. But, perhaps due to her negative assessment of the options available to "a leisured gentlewoman" in nineteenth-century patriarchal British society, she does not wholeheartedly support her American colleagues in their conclusion that educational success can and should necessarily lead to female vocational success and hence empowerment.

Moreover, as the following discussion will show, in addition to actively engaging in a dialog on questions of gendered, social, and racial issues with the works of the above-mentioned American writers, Eliot's work also intersects with their œuvres in its presentation of some more "cosmopolitan" nineteenth-century social and literary tropes, such as the popular philosophical conception of society as Grand Etre or oversoul, and the equally popular touristical notion of Italy as highlight of the Grand Tour. The American writers, who were inspired by Eliot, in their turn, appropriated topics and plots and "rewrote them with a difference." Elizabeth Stuart Phelps, like Stowe, urged Eliot to empower her female protagonists by letting them enjoy vocational success. Her protagonist, Avis, reflects character traits of Eliot's artist heroine, Armgart, (from the eponymous poem) and also brings to mind Eliot's most radically feminist protagonist, the Alcharisi. Henry James and Edith Wharton likewise seem to have tried to empower "the George Eliot heroine." They initially accord a good bit of agency to Isabel Archer and Lily Bart, their versions of Gwendolen Harleth, but, as their novels unfold, they show that, like Gwendolen, their own leisure class heroines also inevitably succumb to the constraints imposed by a global nineteenth-century ideology of gender.

Chapter 1 of this study, following this introduction, analyzes the impact that George Eliot's reading in contemporaneous American literature (Fuller, Stowe, and Hawthorne) had on her conception of gender and class in her domestic novels. It also addresses questions of genre modification and proposes that "American romance" changed the mimetic strategies of Eliot's "British realism." Chapter 2 focuses on how Eliot, Fuller, Hawthorne, and Stowe, who had all spent time in Italy during the country's struggle for unification, present Italian cultural difference in their notebooks, travel diaries, war dispatches, and fictional works. Proceeding from an inquiry into Stowe's and Eliot's construction of race and ethnicity as determinants of personal as well as collective identity, chapter 3 points out that, due to the Neoplatonic origin of the kabbalistic passages of Eliot's *Daniel Deronda*, the novel at times bears an almost uncanny resemblance to the transcendentalist writing of Ralph Waldo Emerson and Margaret Fuller. Chapter 4 concludes this study by analyzing how following generations of American writers appropriated and reworked themes from George Eliot's work. Elizabeth Stuart Phelps, Henry James, and Edith Wharton all indicated that the nineteenth-century gender hegemony criticized by Eliot functioned as a global ideology that enthralled America as well as Europe. Henry James, and Cynthia Ozick—roughly a hundred years apart—reaffirmed the call for cultural renewal that Eliot voiced in *Daniel Deronda*, where she juxtaposes the corrupt English leisure class culture with a conservative Jewish communal alternative. Gail Godwin, John Irving, and (at least to some extent) Cynthia Ozick, modern American writers who affirm Eliot's significance for the twentieth century, betray a surprising nostalgia for George Eliot's values and life by presenting her personal life with George Henry Lewes as worth emulating even at the turn of the twenty-first century.

Influence, Agency, and Intertextual Exchange

George Eliot U.S. traces the impact that American writers have had on George Eliot's work as well as the reflection of Eliot's writing in American literature and compares British and American reactions to gendered, cultural, and racial alterity. Since in her own work Eliot actively appropriated and reworked topics taken from American literature and socio-philosophical thought (in the same manner in which she engaged herself with historical and contemporary philosophical thought), it does not stretch the evidence to claim that she was "influenced" by American literature. In their introduction to *Influence and Intertextuality in Literary History* (1991), Jay Clayton and Eric Rothstein have very nicely elaborated the differences between the older—and therefore often deemed outmoded—idea of influence and the newer concept of intertextuality. They suggest that the most important difference between the two concepts is that "influence has to do with agency, whereas intertextuality has to do with a much more impersonal field of crossing texts" (Clayton and Rothstein 1991, 4).

Nineteenth-century writers, especially those associated with realism like Eliot, thought of themselves as "agents" writing about things that are real, or could be real, and—at least to some extent—chose who and what they were influenced by. In our own, postmodern times, however, the notion of "agency" has come under attack. Critics by now almost customarily call attention to two problems associated with it. Authorial agency is often associated with an appropriation of control on the part of the "realistic" writer who is trying to impose his/her personal view of life as "truth." Moreover, personal agency (and choice) is called into question by postmodern theories of identity, but agency might, nevertheless, still be needed in order to make significant statements about the politicized realms of gender, race, and class. Postmodern theorists have by now—not very successfully as some of them admit (see Shires 1992, 186-89)—tried to answer the often posed question of "How can we account for the fact that the subject is contradictory, in process, fragmented, produced by ideological hailings, but also able to constitute herself politically?" (Shires 1992, 186). Judith Butler, for example, who rejects "the figure of a choosing humanist subject" (1990, x), yet also wants to avoid "the trap of cultural determinism" (x), suggests that a certain degree of agency is still possible, even if the unified subject has come under attack. She thus argues in *Feminist Contentions* that "to claim that the subject is constituted is not to claim that it is determined; on the contrary, the constituted character of the subject is the very precondition of its agency" (Butler in Benhabib et al. 1995, 47).

Linda Shires, considering possible approaches to dealing with the biographies of nineteenth-century public figures, opts for reaching a compromise between radical constructionist and essentialist models of theorizing identity and agency and suggests to approach "life paradigms" by weaving together individual stories and by "showing how they are all constituted by culture" (1992, 187). Positioning myself on similar critical ground as Shires, I also view nineteenth-century writers as compromised agents, whose subjectivity is to some (not specifiable) extent culturally constructed. I therefore situate my understanding of the textual exchanges between Eliot and the American authors on the borderline between influence and intertextuality. A narrow definition of influence, according to Clayton and Rothstein, "should refer to relations built on transmission from one unity (author, work tradition) to another" (1991, 3) whereas intertextuality, which describes a more "impersonal crossing of fields,"

> might be taken as a general term, working out from the broad definition of influence to encompass unconscious, socially prompted types of text formation (for example, by archetypes or popular culture); modes of conception (such as ideas "in the air"); styles (such as genres); and other prior constraints and opportunities for the writer. (4)

Since in the cases of Eliot, Hawthorne, Fuller, Stowe, et al., the authors are not "dead"—at least according to a Barthesian understanding of the term—describing the flow of information between their texts in terms of a broad definition of influence, or a narrow definition of intertextuality, would allow us to take into consideration direct, acknowledgeable influence and inspiration along with "unconscious socially prompted types of text formation" and "modes of conceptions" and literary "styles."

My aim in setting Eliot's work in relation to American literature is a comparative one, which tries to highlight the "typically British" characteristics of Eliot's work and the "typically American" ones of the American authors, but also finds many points of convergence. Comparative works by American critics who deal with English and American literature have often tended to define American against British literature as an entirely new, separate undertaking, aimed at shaking off British cultural hegemony.[8] This is, for example, the approach of Robert Weisbuch in *Atlantic Double-Cross* (1986), which, as its subtitle says, deals with "American literature and British influence in the age of Emerson." Acknowledging his indebtedness to Bloom's landmark work, *The Anxiety of Influence*, and suggesting that it is transcendental spiritualism that finally sets off American from British literature, Weisbuch summarizes his findings as follows:

> The compulsive need to overcome British literary influence for reasons of pride or even for reasons of sufficient personal and national selfhood is real and strong; but it is absolutely accompanied by an American idea that, beyond all circumstances created by a social nexus, there is a permanent life, a being-in-the-world that is mysterious and fructifying. . . . British insults encouraged anew the Puritan derived idea of each individual as a microcosm of America and of America as the completion in secular reality of God's design for humanity. (1986, xvi-xvii).

As Paul Giles notes in *Transatlantic Insurrections* (2001), which, as also indicated by its subtitle, deals with "British culture and the formation of American literature, 1730-1860," Weisbuch and other critics have assumed that American literature matters less to British writers than British literature matters to American authors, with the consequence that "the conceptual parameters of British literature [are left] relatively intact" (2001, 9). Giles, however, calls for a different approach, putting less emphasis on questions of "monolithic" national identity because "a twenty-first century version of comparative literature needs to situate itself on a dangerous and uncomfortable boundary where residual assumptions about autochthonous identity are traversed by something different" (14). Also wanting to include an analysis of the effect of American on British literature in his study, he takes into consideration "various points of friction" where the discourses of British and American literature intersect and finds that "[f]rom this perspective, the cultures of Britain and America do not so much define themselves against each other as surreptitiously twist each other into strange, apparently unnatural forms" (14).

My project of finding areas of intersection as well as incompatibility between Eliot's works and those of the American writers, and of tracing American influences on George Eliot, will show that both of the intercultural dynamics described by Giles are at work there, too: Eliot at times defines herself against American literature and culture, and American literature writes back to Eliot in an effort to "teach her about gender or class" or correct her misreadings of American plots; yet at the same time both cultures, as depicted in the works of Eliot and the Americans, "twist each other into strange, apparently unnatural forms." Eliot's reactions to "typically American" viewpoints and approaches are apparent. In *Adam Bede*, her "British adaptation" of Hawthorne's *The Scarlet Letter*, she shows that even though Hayslope has not become entirely secularized, in Britain class difference supersedes the importance of religion as social determinant. In *Romola*, she defies Hawthorne's presentation of Italian alterity as "backward and filthy" and rejects his reactionary model of racial evolutionary development, which locates contemporary Italians on a lower evolutionary scale than contemporary Americans. And in *Daniel Deronda*, writing back at Stowe's *Uncle Tom's Cabin* and *Dred*, she indicates that, perhaps, all things considered, race does not matter as a marker of intelligence and social skills.

The American writers contemporary with Eliot, in spite of never having experienced British rule in their lifetimes, often act in a "postcolonial"[9] fashion, as their notebooks and literary works indicate: both Fuller and Hawthorne present Catholicism as "heresy" to a superior Protestantism; Fuller, moreover, in *At Home and Abroad* (1856) suggests that democracy is a quasi-American invention that the Europeans should finally adopt. In *Oldtown Folks* (1869) Harriet Beecher Stowe, reacting to Eliot's depiction of Maggie's gender woes in *The Mill on the Floss* (1860), not only tells Eliot how to empower women in a democratic society where women from all class backgrounds are allowed to make their lives meaningful through work; in a plot set in the aftermath of the American Revolution, she also extols democracy as a typically American trait and even depicts the rigidity of Puritan religion as a vestige of European feudalism.

But there are also a few plot twists in both the works of Eliot and the American writers which do not fulfill our expectations of national proclivities and contort and reverse our anticipations of what is typical of British and of American literature. Thus, a comparison of *Adam Bede* with *The Scarlet Letter* will show that Eliot's venerable British realism is not as different from Hawthorne's American romanticism as perhaps initially expected.

This impression will be corroborated by a juxtaposition of the romantic, kabbalistic scenes in *Daniel Deronda*, which focus on the kabbalistic "unity of the soul," with both Emerson's and Fuller's representations of the transcendentalist oversoul. The astounding similarities between the kabbalistic Jewish tradition, as presented by Eliot, and American transcendentalism can be traced to the Neoplatonic origins of both religious philosophies. And, as already indicated, a comparison of Eliot's works with those of her American contemporaries also suggests that the democratic American spirit is not always more inclusive of alterity than Eliot's "conservative," monarchical British Victorianism (which was often tempered by her adherence to a rather egalitarian eighteenth-century cosmopolitanism). While Stowe, for example, proposes racial separatism in her work, Eliot, in *Daniel Deronda*, opts for racial mingling and even intermarriage. Moreover, perhaps also a bit surprisingly, Eliot's conservative European "social organicism," at times seems no less inclusive than American models of social living that are based on Emersonian "self-reliance"—as, for example, the very "class conscious" model of communal living presented in Hawthorne's *The Blithedale Romance* (1851). In *The Blithedale Romance* Hawthorne's narrator implies that the educated community members participating in the Blithedale community found it very easy to look down on their more uneducated brethren.

The appropriation of fictional topics and plots by following generations of American writers who were influenced by Eliot (but, obviously, could not reciprocally influence her) also produced results that at times seem untypical of American literature and culture. Thus, Henry James and Edith Wharton point out in *The Portrait of a Lady* and *The House of Mirth*, their "rewrites" of *Daniel Deronda*, that American society at the turn of the twentieth century is far from classless. In their novels they present a U.S. that has emulated British class stratification to the point of not being able to counteract "European corruption." This has several consequences: a class-conscious gender hegemony sees to it that, as in Eliot's *Daniel Deronda*, the female protagonists of James's and Wharton's novels cannot transcend social constrictions that turn them into "female exchange objects" which please males by acting as "animated ornaments" rather than as assertive self-directed women. Because the heroines themselves adhere to the class and gender conventions that hamper them, they, unlike Stowe's female protagonists, cannot instrumentalize their "American" self-reliance in order to seek a fulfilling work life. Moreover, the American emulation of undesirable European social values keeps the U.S. from functioning as a cultural alternative to Europe. While in *Daniel Deronda* Eliot can still conceive of traditional Judaism with its conservative community life as a viable alternative to British upper class corruption, James cannot (or does not want to) present contemporary America as such because—at least in his fictional universe—it already resembles Britain too much. And Susan Cheever, Gail Godwin, John Irving, and Cynthia Ozick, as contemporary American writers, surprise with "anachronistic" appropriations of Eliot's plots and personal life. Cynthia Ozick, having published *The Puttermesser Papers* (1997) almost at the turn of the millennium, actually models the life of her heroine, Puttermesser, on George Eliot's, humorously suggesting that Eliot's "solutions" do not work in our postmodern age, whereas Gail Godwin, in the *The Odd Woman* (1979), and John Irving, in *A Widow for One Year* (1998), suggest that they still should.

Nineteenth-Century Social Discourses and their Literary Reflections

Nineteenth-Century Society: Etre Suprème or Oversoul?

Nineteenth-century social models are of particular importance to this study since they attempt to explain how different/ly gendered and "raced" bodies are arranged into one social body. Moreover, they provide a focus for the key arguments that recur throughout this book. With Comtean positivism and Emersonian transcendentalism, nineteenth-century philosophy from both sides of the Atlantic introduced important sociophilosophical theories that are reflected in and also perpetuated by the literary works discussed in this introductory chapter. Auguste Comte's theory conceived of humanity as an all-encompassing entirely secular *Etre Suprème* (or *Grand Etre*): "Humanity as the all-incorporating Being, simultaneously representing past, present and future" (Hesse 1996, 66). Ralph Waldo Emerson very similarly also saw humankind—past, present, and future—united in a *Grand Etre*, but his oversoul, as he called it, was suffused with divinity. Both Comte's and Emerson's model of viewing all of humankind as one social body (and soul, in Emerson's case) were complemented by other nineteenth-century "organic" social theories discussed below in this chapter, and are reflected in the writing of Eliot and Fuller, respectively.

Comte coined the term "sociology" and presented his social philosophy in his two multi-volume main works *Cours de philosophie positive* (1830–42) and *Système de politique positive ou traité de sociologie* (1851–54).[10] His social vision was not merely prescriptive, but aimed at actively instituting an altruistic "religion of humanity" based on brotherly love and scientific accomplishment.[11] Comte describes humankind as advancing in three stages towards "positive" altruism—the theological, polytheistic; the metaphysical, monotheistic; and the scientific, positivist stage (see [1853] 1896, 1:2). Once the positivist stage has been accomplished—according to Comte it had begun with thinkers like Bacon, Descartes, and Galileo (see [1853] 1896, 1:7)—all human knowledge will have been combined and humankind will have developed into a *Grand Etre* worthy of worship: "The *Grand Etre*, or *Etre Suprême* of Comtean religion is Humanity, and in its worship man expresses his complete synthesis of all knowledge, scientific, practical, and moral condensed in this central image" (Hesse 1996, 112).

Here, it is important to note that, in spite of his use of vocabulary from the realm of the spiritual, Comte's "religious worship" is entirely secular and that his "religion" does not attempt to solve the riddle of first causes. Comte, as Hesse points out, did not believe that "comprehension for the world itself . . . was within the realm of the human intellect. . . . Thus the *synthèse subjective* [of all knowledge] was guided by the needs and limited by the intellect of man" (84). By the same token, Comte, deliberately rejecting all metaphysical explanations, also disallows the idea that interpreting nature might lead to metaphysical insight; he therefore "considers (in common with Locke and Hume) the concept of Nature a mere abstraction, delusively conceived of by metaphysicians in an attempt by a finite, mortal being to penetrate into the real, the infinite being" (71).

Even though Comte's *Etre Suprême* is entirely secular, it still shows parallels to Emerson's depiction of the oversoul as a social being which encompasses all of humankind. In the following passage, Comte describes the characteristics of united (hu)mankind in a future positivist stage:

> We have yet to witness the moral superiority of a philosophy which connects each of us with the whole of human existence, in all times and places. The restriction of our expectations to actual life must furnish new means of connecting our individual development with the universal progression, the growing regard to which will afford the only possible, and the utmost possible, satisfaction to our natural aspiration after eternity. ([1853] 1896, 3:407)

Emerson describes his *Grand Etre*, the oversoul, as follows:

> The Supreme Critic on the errors of the past and the present, and the only prophet of that which must be, is that great nature in which we rest, as the earth lies in the soft arms of the atmosphere; that Unity, that Over-soul, within which every man's particular being is contained and made one with all other. . . . We live in succession, in division, in parts, in particles. Mean-

time within man is the soul of the whole; the wise silence; the universal beauty, to which every part and particle is equally related; the eternal ONE. ([1841] 1983, 385-86).

Unlike Comte, Emerson deifies his *Etre Suprême*, paralleling Ludwig Feuerbach's location of the divine in the human in *The Essence of Christianity*: "*Man has his highest being, his God, in himself;* not in himself as an individual, but in his essential nature, his species" ([1841] 1989, 281). Along with this apotheosis of man, Emerson also performs an apotheosis of nature. And also unlike Comte, he strongly believed that nature—as an integral part of the oversoul—gives humankind access to the infinite being of the divine by providing signs which the individual can learn to interpret correctly. As Jeffrey Steele points out, "[i]magining 'the whole of Nature' as 'a metaphor or image of the human Mind,' Emerson is lured by the psychological myth of a completely readable and accessible psychic text that would unlock its secrets for the individual who has learned the right key" (1987, 24).

The works of the nineteenth-century writers discussed in this study engage themselves with these religiophilosophical models of society as *Grand Etre* or oversoul by either endorsing or criticizing them. In one of her letters to Harriet Beecher Stowe, Eliot gives her own version of viewing humanity as a *Grand Etre* as "one comprehensive Church whose fellowship consists in the desire to purify and ennoble human life, and where the best members of all narrower churches may call themselves brother and sister in spite of differences" (*George Eliot Letters* 1954-55, 6:89). Moreover, permanently negotiating the place of the individual in society in her fiction, she features a plot of Comtean societal development from polytheism/paganism to positivism/altruism in her novel *Romola,* and incorporates aspects of Comtean philosophy in nearly all of her other works. In *Daniel Deronda,* based on the Jewish Kabbalah, she develops a model of the "self as a social relation within Divine Unity," which—due to the shared Neoplatonic origin of both philosophies—features astounding parallels to various Emersonian spiritual concepts, including that of the oversoul.

Margaret Fuller also tests the social applicability of transcendental philosophy in *Woman in the Nineteenth Century* (1845). While Emerson is mainly interested in instrumentalizing the power of the oversoul for the perfection of the individual through self-reliance, Fuller attempts to implement transcendental thought on a practical social level. Her presentation of marital relationships according to her ideal of the "marriage of true souls" serves as a very good example of her quest for more egalitarian social relationships. And, as Kimberly Adams astutely points out, Fuller assembled a "universal church" of her own: "Dante, Manzoni, the Seer of Prevorst, John Wesley, Mother Ann Lee, the Indian girl betrothed to the sun. These were the sources for her own religious ideas and her work on the Madonna; these were the members of *her* 'universal church'" (2001, 32).

Neither Harriet Beecher Stowe nor Nathaniel Hawthorne focuses on the Emersonian oversoul (as an American transcendental version of the *Grand Etre*) in their writing; they instead deal with individual and collective reactions to the social demands imposed by an earlier Calvinist Protestantism. Stowe shared a teleological view of social development with the other authors discussed, but for her—as the only conventionally religious person among these writers—the developmental goal was not the perfection of humankind and society but rather the return of Christ to earth, his "second coming." Following Jonathan Edwards, she believed that the second coming of Christ "would not occur until *after* the Church inaugurates a millennial reign of peace and prosperity" (Westra 1992, 143). Stowe's father, the minister Lyman Beecher, shared this belief and actually thought that "America would be the place as well as the instrument through which God would begin and establish his millennial kingdom throughout the earth" (147). Since Stowe reasoned that the millennium could not come about as long as the sin of slavery persisted on American soil, she made it the declared social goal of her novels *Uncle Tom's Cabin* and *Dred* to bring about the abolition of slavery. Her later work, *Oldtown Folks,* deals with individual rather than collective response to the social impact of religious doctrine. In *Oldtown Folks,* Stowe shows that the cruel Calvinist "doctrine of divine sovereignty" inspires unbelief and rebellion in church members who think that they might not be saved by God. Since this might even make them leave the Puritan fold, Stowe suggests infusing Calvinism with a portion of "feminine" love and abolishing the cruel doctrine.

Nathaniel Hawthorne, known for his opposition to transcendental optimism, takes a much more pessimistic view of the individual in relation to society. With *The Blithedale Romance* he suggests that communal living based on socialist and transcendentalist ideals cannot succeed because even a "small-scale" *Grand Etre* is not able to deal with the conflicts between the spiritual and the physical that arise from the personal relationships of the participants. With *The Scarlet Letter* he shows that, because of the irreconcilable incompatibility between Puritan (religious) law and the personal desires of his heroine, Hester, her rebellion must fail and she must remain an outsider to her Puritan community; and in *The Marble Faun* he intimates that cultural differences between Americans and "others" cannot be transcended. Developing John Franzosa's thesis that Hawthorne's notion of the self is indebted to Lockean and Scottish Common Sense philosophy (see Franzosa 1983, 1–6), Alison Easton draws attention to the circumstance that Hawthorne's (social) skepticism is largely due to the fact that he did not subscribe to transcendentalist conceptions of the self as both divine and autonomous:

> A key recognition for Hawthorne's work is that we exist not only in relation to, but also because of and through other people, institutions and the social meanings that they are shown to reproduce and to some extent produce. The Romantic failure to find that autonomous "self" led to this conclusion. Because a residual belief in independent being lingers on, Hawthorne's works do not wholly embrace an essentially social explanation of psychic processes. . . . There seems to be an understanding both that consciousness and the unconscious are to a great extent given a particular shape by the demands of the social network, and that by refusing positions within society, the individual would merely inhabit a void. (1996, 7)

Easton's insight is important because it points to a significant nineteenth-century paradigm shift from essentialist to constructionist explanations of both the "self" and the "other" as social relations. This paradigm shift not only accounts for Hawthorne's social skepticism but also explains the at times inconsistent attitudes (which vacillate between endorsing essentialism and constructivism) expressed by him and the other nineteenth-century writers regarding individual identity formations and collective social formations dealing with gendered, cultural, and racial "essentials."

Ideology and Difference

With his theory about the functioning of "Ideology and Ideological State Apparatuses" Louis Althusser has devised a model that is very useful in describing how ideology "produces" culture by constituting individual as well as cultural identity. Ideology makes subjects function as a part of a social body (such as nineteenth-century society as organic *Grand Etre*, for example) by means of "interpellation"—even if their race or gender might initially impede a perfect fit of "individual organ" and "collective body." Moreover, Althusser's theory provides an effective tool for analyzing the technologies—to borrow de Lauretis's terminology—of gender and identity formation. In the following, I will apply Althusser's insights to the nineteenth-century "technology of gender" and will also use them to investigate Eliot's presentation of the complex procedures of racial identification in *Daniel Deronda*. Althusser's original concept has been expounded on and modified by recent theorists; some of these offshoots will also be considered because they explain how his model provides an escape from its own mechanisms, thus allowing for a degree of resistance.

In his famous essay, which has immensely influenced contemporary theories of subjectivity, Althusser defines discourses which produce identity as ideology[12]—"the system of the ideas and representations which dominate the mind of a man or a social group" ([1970] 1984, 32). Ideology is his term for all ethical, legal, political, or religious worldviews, or "world outlooks" (36), as he calls them. He describes ideology as "the 'Representation' of the Imaginary Relationship of Individuals to their Real Conditions of Existence" (36) and stresses the illusory, fabricated character of ideologies as systems of belief:

> However, while admitting that they do not correspond to reality, i.e. that they constitute an illusion . . . we admit that they do make allusion to reality, and that they need only to be "interpreted" to discover the reality of the world behind their imaginary representation of that world (ideology = illusion/allusion). (36)

According to Althusser, the "interpellation" of individual subjects into ideology is effected as follows:

> [I]deology "acts" or "functions" in such a way that it "recruits" subjects among the individuals (it recruits them all), or "transforms" the individuals into subjects (it transforms them all) by that very precise operation which I have called *interpellation* or hailing, and which can be imagined along the lines of the most commonplace everyday police (or other hailing): "Hey, you there." (1984, 48)

The person addressed by ideology "recognizes that it was *really him* who was hailed" (48) into ideology and hence functions as a subject. (Chapter 3 shows how this works for Daniel Deronda's interpellation into Judaism).

Althusser's seminal essay first appeared in 1970; it has since been appropriated, commented on, and "improved" upon by theorists from various fields.[13] Thus, in *Technologies of Gender*, Teresa de Lauretis complains that Althusser and other Marxist critics have ignored gender in their description of how ideology constitutes subjects because "gender is located in the private sphere of reproduction, procreation, and the family, rather than in the public, properly social, sphere of the superstructural, where ideology belongs and is determined by the economic forces and relations of production" (1987, 6). De Lauretis, nevertheless, knowing that the personal is the political, claims Althusser's theory of the workings of ideology for feminism because it can be very profitably used to explain how gender constitutes "concrete individuals as men and women" (6).

Poststructural critics, interested in showing that Althusser's model allows for an at least partial "escape from ideology" and thus affords a possibility of subverting discourses of power, often downplay or disregard the essay's Marxist (and, therefore, truth-seeking) component. Instead, in order to explain the fragmentation of the postmodern subject, they call attention to the fact that identification might not proceed as smoothly as Althusser predicted because the specular relationship of the Subject of Ideology (e.g. God, the Law, etc.)[14] and its subject is expressed in and through language. G. M. Goshgarian points out that

> precisely because the dual mirror structure is this *linguistic* automaton—because one's ideological mirror image is reflected in mirrors made of *discourse*—the reassuring self-rapport ideology produces is never more than a fiction. Notoriously, the stuff of discourse slips, slides, perishes, will not stay still: caught up in the social struggles that divide and redivide it against itself, language spoils the dream of ideological stability it engenders and serves. Having torn a hole in the subject only to fill it with ideology's imaginary vision of wholeness, it tears a hole in the fabric of the ideological vision it weaves. (1992, 17)

Thomas Beebee, in *The Ideology of Genre*, points to Ross Chambers as a source of an earlier critical elucidation of Althusser which addresses a similar problem of ideological instability. According to Beebee, Chambers discovered the "ideological split" that accounts for instability within ideologies. Chambers—introducing power as a Foucauldian twist into his argument—explains this as follows:

> An ideology is not a doctrine to be accepted or not accepted but a discursive proposition that positions subjects in relations of power (power being itself a differential phenomenon, existing only through being unevenly distributed). Ideology necessarily produces these subjects relationally, and it is in the difference between them that the potential for ideological split resides, these subjects being differently positioned regarding the system that produces them. They "perceive" it, understand it, from different angles, so to speak and in different perspectives. (Chambers quoted in Beebee 1994, 15)

Following Chambers, Beebee thus views ideology as an organizing principle rather than some sort of machinery that turns out standardized subjects. Since ideology, as he says, is "never fully identical with itself anyway . . . it becomes something like the magnetic field that arranges a chaotic mass of iron filings into intriguing, ordered curves on a piece of paper" (1994, 18). It seems that Ross Chambers's work, at least to some extent, targets a problem that Stuart Hall identifies when he remarks that in Althusser's account, "there is no theorization of the psychic mechanisms or interior processes by which these automatic interpellations might be produced, or—more significantly—fail to be produced" (1996, 12). While Chambers's notion of "ideological split" still does not explain the exact way in which ideology works upon the unconscious, it at least seems to point toward a possible way in which interpellations might fail to achieve the desired effect, even if they never fail to be produced.

Hall, in his attempt to define identification processes, also seems to want to avoid the determinism of Althusser's model and therefore puts emphasis on the individual subject's active involvement in the process of being interpellated: "The notion that an effective suturing of the subject to a subject-position requires, not only that the subject is 'hailed,' but that the subject invests in the position, means that suturing has to be thought of as an *articulation*, rather than a one-sided process, and that in turn places *identification* . . . firmly on the theoretical agenda" (6). Here, his theoretical stance points towards that of Foucault in his introduction to *The Use of Pleasure*, where he describes his strategy of theorizing "the subject's" own involvement in the workings of power: "It appeared that I now had to undertake a third shift, in order to analyze what is termed 'the subject.' It seemed appropriate to look for the forms and modalities of the relation to self by which the individual constitutes and recognizes himself qua subject" (Foucault 1990, 6).[15]

Teresa de Lauretis, according to her understanding of Althusser and Foucault, likewise, resolutely stresses the subject's active participation and agency in constructing liberationist discourses about gender identity which have the potential to evade ideology:

> To assert that the social representation of gender affects its subjective construction and that, vice versa, the subjective representation of gender—or self-representation—affects its social construction, leaves open a possibility of agency and self-determination at the subjective and even individual level of micropolitical and everyday practices which Althusser himself would clearly disclaim. (1987, 9)

A similar argument regarding broader concerns of social identity is developed by Anthony Appiah in his account of the formation of collective identities in "Race, Culture, Identity." Perhaps as a result of reading too much agency into Judith Butler's theoretical stance on gender performativity and parody,[16] he regards this identification with collective identities as a possibility of individually or collectively "construct[ing] positive life scripts" to replace old "negative ones" (1996, 98):

> One form of healing the self . . . is learning to see . . . collective identities not as sources of limitation and insult but as a valuable part of what they centrally are. Because the ethics of authenticity requires us to express what we centrally are in our lives, they move next to the demand that they be recognized in social life as Women, homosexuals, blacks, Catholics. Because there was no good reason to treat people of these sorts badly, and because the culture continues to provide degrading images of them nevertheless, they demand that we do cultural work to resist the stereotypes, to challenge the insults, to lift the restrictions. (98)

Even though Appiah's ideas seem to present a good plan for influencing and directing individual and collective identification processes, many critics, such as Stuart Hall and Judith Butler, in spite of also focusing on the individual's participation in the identification process, would certainly not support positions which claim as much self-determination and agency as de Lauretis's and Appiah's actually do. Hall instead opts for an understanding of identity-constituting performativity—which to some extent resists discourses that interpellate into ideology—as contingent and "shorn of its associations with volition, choice, and intentionality" (1996, 14). (He, therefore, pleads for a different reading of Butler which she herself proposes in her later book, *Bodies That Matter,* and which focuses on a contingent performativity "understood not as a singular or deliberate 'act,' but rather as the reiterative and citational practice by which discourse produces the effects that it names" [1993, 12]).

As already indicated, Althusser's theory about the workings of ideology is useful in describing the mechanics of "technologies of gender," such as the nineteenth-century "Cult of True Womanhood"[17] which stipulated that "American woman" belonged in the home where "she could fulfill her dual feminine function—beauty and usefulness" (Welter 1966, 163). This ideology worked as a nineteenth-century "technology of gender" by interpellating individual "real" women into "True Womanhood" and forcing them to adopt the defining characteristics of the essence of femininity (or *Woman* in Althusserian terminology)—"piety, purity, submissiveness and domesticity" (152).[18] Moreover, due to their "natural" capacities for nurturing, it relegated women to the domestic sphere.[19] As Philippa Levine points out, this also worked for Victorian England, where "domestic ideology, or the ideology of the separate spheres" (1987, 12) "was highly effective in ordering people's values according to its precepts" (13).

In accordance with the prevailing nineteenth-century gender ideology, Margaret Fuller's writing, for example, posits many gender attributes as essential, assigning "energy," "power," and "intellect" to men and "harmony," "beauty," and "love" to women. But at the same time it also stresses the fluidity of gender characteristics by arguing that "the faculties have not been given pure to either [man or woman], but only in preponderance" ([1845] 1994, 326). This "ideological split" already points in the direction of an incipient paradigm shift towards understanding gender as constructed rather than essential. Quite similarly, George Eliot simultaneously challenges and inscribes essential gender difference. Thus, in her correspondence with Emily Davies, the founder of Girton, the first English women's college, she writes that "[w]e can [not] afford to part with that exquisite type of gentleness, tenderness, possible maternity suffusing a woman's being with affectionateness" (*George Eliot Letters* 1954–55, 4:468). In her fiction, Eliot, however, deconstructs this notion of biologistic maternity by devising extremely gentle, tender, and maternal men (Silas Marner, Adam Bede, Daniel Deronda) and at least two very unmaternal women (Armgart and the Alcharisi). Yet unlike Margaret Fuller who coined the famous phrase "let them be sea-captains, if you will" ([1845] 1994, 329), thereby demanding equal vocational rights for women, Eliot, in her letter to Davies, only demanded that women's "essential" gender traits should not be used to bar them from higher education.

In the mid- to late nineteenth century, contemporary sociobiological ideology still focused on the "biological inferiority" of women's "essential gender traits." Thus, Auguste Comte, for example, argued (similarly to Spencer and Darwin) in his *Cours de philosophie positive* that "biological analysis presents the female sex, in the human species especially, as constitutionally in a state of perpetual infancy, in comparison with the other" ([1853] 1896, 2:284). From this circumstance he inevitably concluded that women's only place is in the domestic sphere:

> [In the higher classes of society] we apprehend at once the law of social progression, as regards the sexes, which consists in disengaging women more and more from all employment that is foreign to their domestic functions . . . they should be universally, and more and more exclusively, set apart for their characteristic offices of wife and mother. ([1853] 1896, 3:121)

As chapter 1 will show, Fuller, Eliot, and Stowe, partly following contemporary sociobiological ideology and partly following their own "natural" instincts, which suggested that gender difference might be constructed rather than essential, vacillate between ideological poles that ascribed gender difference to either "nature" or "nurture." As a consequence, their works partially subvert and partially endorse the ideology of "True Womanhood." (Nathaniel Hawthorne, surprisingly, proves to be much less undecided in his masterpiece *The Scarlet Letter*, where he takes a radical deconstructionist stance regarding gender).

In addition to shedding light on nineteenth-century gender ideology, Althusser's theory of interpellation of the subject, which theorizes the constitution of personal and social identity, can also be employed to illuminate Eliot's explanation of identity formation in *Daniel Deronda*. The novel contains a philosophical meditation on the constitution of identity that seems to anticipate Louis Althusser's theory. Questions of how people arrive at a notion of personal identity have interested thinkers from the very beginning of philosophy. Transcendental philosophers like Plato, Aristotle, Descartes, and Kant[20] have assumed that ideas are innate and that human beings, according to the Cartesian "cogito ergo sum," possess something like a "unified self" which allows them to make coherent sense out of diverse external sense impressions. Yet other, more skeptical thinkers, as for example David Hume and Bishop Berkeley (who "invented" the notion of solipsism), have doubted that a "coherent internal self" exists and claim that the self ultimately is only a conglomerate of sense impressions received from the external world. As David Hawkes notes, Hume's notion of a "self" put forth in his *Treatise of Human Nature* (1739–40) already has a surprising affinity to postmodern notions of a fragmented self constituted in discourse: Hume went so far to claim that, since we have no sensual impression of our unified self—of what we would today call the "subject"—we have no knowable internal personality, and are in fact nothing but a bundle of random perceptions, on which we arbitrarily impose an ideal order and label it our "self" (see Hawkes 1996, 63).

While nineteenth-century theories of identity formation (such as the notion of personal and collective identity that is implicit in Emerson's and Fuller's philosophical thought and discussed at some length in chapter 3) often seem to proceed from the Cartesian idea of an essential core self which "unfolds" throughout an individual's life,[21] contemporary theories are often indebted to the insights of both Althusser and Foucault, and tend to view identity as non-essential and culturally constructed by the discourses that a society uses to make sense of itself and the world at large.

Anticipating Althusser's model of interpellation as technology of ideology in her novel *Daniel Deronda*, Eliot makes her protagonist Daniel realize on three occasions that he is being hailed by Judaism (and thus perhaps "called by his blood"): when he suddenly and strangely feels part of Jewish history during a synagogue service that he attended out of curiosity; when after the service a Jew asks him his mother's maiden name; and when Mordecai asks him in Mr. Ram's bookstore, "You are perhaps of our race?" ([1876] 1995, 387). Not being able to explain these strange occurrences to himself, Daniel remains reluctant, but somehow accepts being hailed into "Jewish religious ideology," and gladly becomes a Jewish subject after he has found out that he actually is Jewish. Even though she presents what seems like a discursive model of Daniel's identity formation, in *Daniel Deronda*, Eliot's concept of identity still waffles between a proto-Althusserian analysis that views Daniel's interpellation into Judaism as interpellation into ideology and a Cartesian conception of selfhood that does not equate faith with ideology—and belief with "false consciousness." While an Althusserian reading of Daniel's interpellation would have to rule out the authenticity of Daniel's racial/religious call, a proto-Althusserian reading that does not question that the spiritual power of Judaism would allow for a reading that views Daniel's interpellation as enabling him to find his "Jewish core self."

Moreover, by not making clear exactly how Daniel's identification with Judaism comes about, Eliot also seems to anticipate what Stuart Hall viewed as a shortcoming of Althusser's model of interpellation into ideology, namely the fact that there is no explanation for the complex psychic processes that are part of the identification procedure. Eliot addresses these complicated issues of identity formation when she investigates Daniel's identification with Judaism, which he actively pursues after he has become friends with Mordecai and Mirah. In doing so, she seems to encourage a reading that views Daniel's relationship with the siblings in terms of his emotional involvement with Mordecai (who is not only his spiritual leader, but for whom he also harbors a homoerotic infatuation) and Mirah, his sister (whom he later marries). Mordecai's relationship with Daniel is cast in terms of the kabbalistic marriage of androgynous souls in a divine "unity of the soul." Because both concepts share the same Neoplatonic roots, the kabbalistic concept of "divine Unity" bears a strong resemblance to the Emersonian oversoul—thus again linking Eliot's meditation on identity with American literature.

As chapter 3 will show, Daniel and Mordecai's "marriage of souls"— which also strongly resembles Margaret Fuller's concept of the "marriage of true souls"—is couched in a theory of identity formation that, like transcendentalism, explains humanity's fragmented condition as the "result of a fall from grace" and offers the "marriage of kindred souls in the unity of the soul" as solution to both individual and social identity crises. Thus, Eliot (who, as an agnostic, would perhaps like to but cannot insist on the religious dimension of the Jewish model) finally arrives at a conception of the self as a "social relation." But the fact that she never clearly indicates whether Daniel's tenuous Jewish identity has come about by interpellation (as "a call of the blood"), or as a result of his study of "preserved cultural memory," or even through (homo)erotic infatuation, shows that she remains torn between essentialist and constructivist notions of identity.

Nineteenth-Century Discourses on Cultural and Racial Alterity

INDIVIDUALS AND THEIR CULTURE(S)—DIFFERENT OR THE SAME?

Eliot shares an apparent reluctance to decide whether cultural and gendered identity is inborn or culturally constructed with her American colleagues. As the following discussion will show, this is also evident from the way in which the authors considered in this study deal with cultural, racial, and gender difference. Fuller's, Stowe's, Hawthorne's, and Eliot's vacillating between presenting difference between cultures, races, and genders as "natural" or socially constructed can at least partly be explained in terms of a paradigm shift from an eighteenth-century universalism—whose influence lasted well into the nineteenth century—which believed in the essential sameness and equality of all human beings (also including, at least in theory, women) to a nineteenth-century "scientific" particularism that postulated essential differences between cultures, races, and genders. As various critics have pointed out, it was late eighteenth- and early nineteenth-century biological and medical science that introduced the insight that there are significant physiological differences among humans and thus managed to supersede eighteenth-century notions of the basic sameness of humanity, which, based on Locke's observations, held that "the capacity to receive impressions was, had been, and was likely to be the same at all times and in all places among men" (Manuel 1991, 3).

In an article that mainly focuses on cultural development in France, Frank E. Manuel locates the beginnings of a new "doctrine of inequality" in Maurice de Talleyrand's assertion that "men are born with a variety of different faculties" (as Manuel observes, it is interesting to note that this statement was made in the midst of the French revolution with its demands for *egalité*) and P. J. G. Cabanis's early nineteenth-century scientific findings:

> In the Years IV and V Doctor Cabanis read before the Class of Moral and Political Sciences of the Institute [*Institut de France*] a series of papers on the interconnections between man's physical and moral being, in the course of which he developed a complete typology of character, as well as a series of

generalizations on how men were affected by differences in sex, age, temperament, states of morbidity, regimen, and climate. . . . Cabanis here modified the sensationalism of Locke, Helvétius, and Condillac at its very source, their presupposition that in general all human beings received identical impressions from nature. (8)

The insights of Cabanis and Marie François Bichat became important because they became an integral part of the works of "organicist" social theorists like Henri de Saint-Simon and Charles Fourier, who, in spite of advocating different versions of a socialist, egalitarian social order, accepted difference as "natural." Like their English successors John Stuart Mill, George Henry Lewes, and Herbert Spencer, to whose insights and organicism George Eliot was indebted, the French theorists viewed society as a "body" made up by individual(s as) "organs" and believed that organic, natural class stratifications would lead to an organic social order, untainted by the power conflicts deriving from the unnatural class stratifications of a society dominated by the aristocracy.

As Sally Shuttleworth observes, in nineteenth-century social organicism, as in biology and medicine, "the organism was no longer viewed simply as an association of organs" (1984, 3). Since scientists had come to believe that "[n]o element was autonomous; rather, each owed its form to its role and position with the development of the whole" (3), it was regarded as a complicated interdependent mechanism relying on individual components that could be very different from each other and were also subject to change. In England, as before in France, social organicism was soon instrumentalized to account for social change because, even though it viewed difference as a natural given, it could still be used to describe society as dynamic and mankind as malleable, as "an Organism, in which incessant movement accompanies constant stability of form" (Lewes [1853] 1996, 234).

The biological basis for the organicist idea that human nature is malleable—which was expressed by Comte, Spencer, and Lewes—is Lamarckian rather than Darwinian since it suggests that acquired characteristics can be transmitted genetically. Thus, even though Lamarck's theory eventually proved erroneous, it runs counter to what might be viewed as a deterministic thrust of Darwinism and supports the very important idea, endorsed by the writing of Fuller, Stowe, and Eliot, that education can be instrumentalized as a prime agent of social change. According to Eliot's partner, George Henry Lewes, whose theory allows for a rather anarchical (and therefore less harmonious) organicism, social organicism could initiate ideological change on practically every level of society. Therefore, it was also capable of affecting the social construction of the important categories of class, gender, and race. Organicism, according to Lewes's remarkably modern view of the role of language in the construction of social reality, invades language as the "chief vehicle of symbolic operation" (1874, 167): "The Language we think in, and the conceptions we employ, the attitude of our minds, and the means of investigation, are social products determined by the activities of the Collective Life" (174). And since language "both determines individual moral and cultural development and offers a symbolic system which functions, like scientific construction, to reveal connections and relations not evident to sense" (174), the language of organicism might indeed have been instrumental in initiating paradigm shifts like the important shift from essentialist to fluid conceptions of gender.[22]

In institutionalizing difference, organicism, which along with "Lamarckian malleability" also stressed physiological inequality and "Darwinian" chance development, was helped, as Manuel suggests, by Romantic ideology with its "new emphasis on the 'genesis' of national character as revealed by Herder, the new image of the unique personality as drawn by Goethe and Sénancour, [and] the general climate of opinion that fostered a new sensibility for diversity and plenitude rather than universality and oneness" (1991, 11). Eliot's essay "The Natural History of German Life" (1856), which talks about differing customs among the German peasantry while at the same time locating "the *national physique*" in the "long faces" and "straight noses" of Hessian farmers ([1856] 1894, 281), reveals this new sensibility for diversity and uniqueness.

Julia Kristeva, in *Strangers to Ourselves*, also calls attention to the significance of this incorporation of notions of particularity and uniqueness into the definition of (national) culture. According to her, it was indeed Herder who "extolled the originality of the German language" and introduced the extremely important concept of cultural alterity by inventing "the worship of the national spirit so dear to Romanticists" (1991, 178). Herder, according to Kristeva, thus significantly modified the older concept of universalism—while still "remaining deeply faithful to a Christian universalism" (178). Through his notion of a *Volksgeist*, he promoted the emergence of the concept of "foreignness":

> This *Volksgeist*, rooted in a language that is seen as a constant process of alteration and surpassing of itself, nevertheless becomes a conservative, reactional concept when it is extracted from the *Bildung*'s tempo and exalted of its original purity or consigned to the ineffable. Intrinsically, however, such an assimilation of language to *Bildung* and, conversely, this emphasis on na-

tional *speech* as the lowest denominator of identity—all this removed Christian or humanistic cosmopolitanism from its spiritual, natural, or contractural lack of precision; furthermore, it allows us to consider what is "foreign" under the logical, familiar aspect of language and culture. (179)

This shift from universalism to particularism and from equality to difference explains some of the problems that Margaret Fuller, Nathaniel Hawthorne, and George Eliot—and to some extent also Harriet Beecher Stowe—encountered when they tried to depict cultural alterity. (In *The Portrait of a Lady*, which is also partly set in Italy, Henry James did not even attempt to do so.) They all became aware of it in Italy because all of them spent time there during a thirteen-year span from 1847 to 1860, when Italy was trying to throw off Austrian and French rule and struggling for unification and nationhood. Fuller, Hawthorne, and Eliot recorded their impressions of Italy in travel diaries, while Stowe rendered her impressions of the country only indirectly in her Italian romance *Agnes of Sorrento* (1862). Hawthorne and Eliot kept conventional diaries of their travels (which they used as preparation for their Italian novels, *The Marble Faun* and *Romola*), whereas Fuller's travel notes were published as dispatches from Italy in Horace Greeley's *New York Tribune*.

They all looked at Italian culture and politics from a perspective that shows their own cultural formation; thus, for example, as representatives of Protestant cultures they all rejected at least some aspects of Roman Catholicism because they thought that it had a great "potential for superstition." Perhaps a bit surprisingly, Harriet Beecher Stowe, whose description of African Americans is often very biased, shows the greatest sympathies towards the alterity of Catholicism. Hawthorne's and Fuller's writing reveals that as American "postcolonials," who believed that they had come from a more advanced political system to the Old World their ancestors had left behind, they, at least at times, felt a certain political superiority towards the European countries. Fuller, having fallen in love with Italy and its population, wholeheartedly supported the Italian revolution; in her dispatches she set out to "reeducate" the Italians in democratic values: Europe—as the mother continent of Greece—was, after all, the true cradle of democracy. Hawthorne, however, in both his notebooks and his novel ignored the political situation for the most part and only projected his own xenophobic fears of "foreignness as filthiness" onto the Italian people. George Eliot neither embraced Fuller's enthusiasm about the country nor Hawthorne's rejection of it. In *Romola,* she only hints rather obliquely at the political situation in nineteenth-century Italy by presenting her readers with a similar situation in

Renaissance Florence, where Girolamo Savonarola struggled for the reestablishment of republicanism. And, unlike Hawthorne, Eliot, after having had recourse to stereotypes about Italians in her earlier writing, completely stays away from any evaluative and therefore potentially stereotypical statements about Italian culture.

In their evaluation of "foreign cultures" Fuller and Eliot profess their belief in the essential sameness of all human beings, whereas Nathaniel Hawthorne focuses on their difference. The reason for this difference in outlook might be found in the differing world views available to nineteenth-century intellectuals, who could either adopt or reject prevalent Enlightenment "universalist" or Romantic "transcendentalist" ideas. Eliot, adhering to an eighteenth-century universalism that stresses the similarity of all humans, asserts her disbelief in historical and cultural difference in the proem to *Romola*, where she has her narrator declare that "we are impressed with the broad sameness of the human lot, which never alters in the main headings of its history—hunger and labour, seed-time and harvest, love and death" ([1863] 1980, 43). In keeping with this view, she also incorporates a Comtean model of evolution in *Romola*. Romola's intellectual and emotional development—from her rejection of her father's learned Greek "paganism" via her adoption of medieval Catholicism to her implementation of advanced Comtean universalist altruism—sums up humankind's historical development. It points toward the final stage of positivism, when society will have reached a certain degree of perfection and all of humanity will have convened in an *Etre Suprême* that is worthy of worship.

Margaret Fuller's adherence to democratic values, which led to her support of the struggle for democracy in Italy, along with her belief in Emersonian transcendentalism, should also have virtually predestined her to adopt cultural universalism. However, in her dispatches, she did not follow the Italian revolutionary leader Mazzini in linking her transcendentalist "pantheism" with her democratic ideals. Mazzini, whom both she and Eliot supported, referred to "the unity of God, and therefore, of the human race" in an article that Eliot had commissioned for *The Westminster Review,* and thus announced his disbelief in "that narrow dualism which established an absurd antagonism between heaven and earth, between God and his creation" (1852, 447).

While both Eliot and Fuller did believe in the basic sameness of all human beings, they obviously could not ignore cultural alterity and were sometimes quite taken aback by it. Fuller, puzzled by what she perceived as the Italian "Catholic superstition," solves the problem for herself by predicting a "didactic" solution. In one of her dispatches, suspending her adherence to transcendentalism, she argues that the revolutionary implementation of the "right" (American) political system—republicanism—will also lead to the adoption of the "right" system of faith—Protestantism. Eliot, however, always unsure as to how to handle cultural difference (and in the case of Italian alterity unable to do so because she did not seek contact with Italians), often initially reverts to readily available stereotypes of the "culturally other," regardless of whether s/he is Italian, Jewish, or a Gypsy, for example, in order to almost completely disavow the cultural difference between individuals once the "common humanity" of the formerly "other" has been established.[23]

Among the writers discussed here, Nathaniel Hawthorne is the one who most unabashedly projects his fears of foreignness as abjection onto Italy. Not having evidenced any interest in getting to know Italians during his stay in Italy, Hawthorne, in both his Italian notebooks and in *The Marble Faun* (where he presents his Italian character Donatello as a racial atavism, an inferior, subhuman mixture between faun and human) persistently characterized them as superstitious, extremely filthy, and developmentally backward. Hawthorne's reasons for his unsympathetic depiction of Italians cannot be entirely known, but can perhaps be explained by his cocky "postcolonial" attitude towards the European parent continent—which he also exhibits on several occasions toward England, his "real mother country." In spite of having participated in the Brook Farm experiment in communal living, which was both transcendental and socialist in outlook, Hawthorne—unlike Fuller, Eliot, and Mazzini—apparently could not make himself believe in the essential sameness and equality of all human beings.

Many commentators have pointed out that bewilderment over cultural difference—as experienced by Nathaniel Hawthorne—often leads to a projection of the foreign spectator's fears of abjection onto the culturally other (see Mills 1991, 90; Spurr 1993, 77–78; Bhabha 1994, 72). This is, of course, particularly annoying for "the other" in a situation where power is distributed so unevenly that s/he has great difficulty in avoiding a self-definition that reflects the stereotypical judgment of the powerful colonizer (see Bhabha 1994, 75). The Italians depicted by Fuller, Hawthorne, and Eliot were, of course, not in a situation of colonial dependence, but they were, nevertheless, looked upon with a quasicolonial gaze by many "postcolonial" American tourists, such as Nathaniel Hawthorne. With the exception of Fuller's dispatches, which, every once in a while, try to show how Americans must have appeared to Italians, cultural dialog or exchange does not take place in these texts and Italy is viewed in terms of cultural difference from a position of cultural supremacy. As Homi Bhabha has observed, cultural supremacy exists chiefly in discourse as linguistic supremacy:

The concept of cultural difference focuses on the problem of the ambivalence of cultural authority: the attempt to dominate in the *name* of a cultural supremacy which is itself produced only in the moment of differentiation. And it is the very authority of culture as a knowledge of referential truth which is at issue in the concept and moment of *enunciation*. (1995, 34–35).

Bhabha, indebted to poststructural language theory, suggests that the subversion of cultural supremacy expressed in language is possible through language in a "Third Space" of enunciation "between the I and the You designated in the statement" (36). This Third Space "represents both the general conditions of language and the specific implication of the utterance in a performative and institutional strategy of which it cannot 'in itself' be conscious" (36). It enables an understanding of different cultural spaces because "though unrepresentable in itself . . . [the Third Space] constitutes the discursive conditions of enunciation that ensure that the meaning and symbols of culture have no primordial unity or fixity; that even the same signs can be appropriated, translated, rehistoricized and read anew" (37). But since the works of the authors discussed here often either ignore Italian alterity (Eliot, James) or present it as almost monstrous difference (Hawthorne), Italy does not function as a "social [space] where cultures meet, clash, and grapple with each other" (Pratt 1996, 530), a "contact zone" according to Mary Louise Pratt's well-known definition, but rather remains a foil for the projection of xenophobic stereotypes. More importantly, the notion of a Third Space that enables new readings does not take place within the texts themselves because—again with the exception of some passages in Fuller's dispatches—they do not encourage cultural dialog. Thus, the task of establishing new readings of these nineteenth-century texts that enable a resignification is left to academic critics operating from a Third Space created within their disciplines.[24]

RACE—DIFFERENT OR THE SAME? ESSENTIAL OR CONSTRUCTED?

The superseding of Enlightenment universalism by nineteenth-century particularism also accounts for the tensions palpable in nineteenth-century race theory. It explains the "racial confusion" that Fuller, Hawthorne (who treated the topic of race indirectly via the figure of Donatello, who is a mix between a human and a faun), Stowe, and Eliot experienced along with their above-described cultural confusion. Scientific theorizing about race with its attendant racial discrimination had already begun in the eighteenth century when, as Robert Young points out

> [T]he different varieties of human beings had been classed as part of the animal kingdom according to the hierarchical scale of the Great Chain of Being. Predictably the African was placed at the bottom of the human family, next to the ape, and there was some discussion as to whether the African should be categorized as belonging to the species of the ape or the human. (1995, 6–7)

Race theory expanded into a field of academic study in the nineteenth century. Eighteenth-century race theory (in spite of its obvious discrimination of Africans) was rather benign because it proceeded from a monogenetic view of human origin, according to which all human beings had a common ancestry and all human races were members of the same species. Racial difference—which was then believed to comprise variations in color, anatomy, intelligence, temperament, and morality—was attributed to environmental differences. During the first half of the nineteenth century, however, scientific opinion on race experienced a paradigm shift from the assumption of a monogenetic to the assumption of a polygenetic human origin. Polygenetic theories maintained that racial difference originated in the separate creation of different human species. In the United States this view was made popular by Josiah Nott, whose theories provided his country with a "scientific" apology for slavery.

This discussion about human origin opened up a new and powerful site for racial anxiety, which is reflected in nineteenth-century literature. Scientists started arguing about whether or not the "hybrid offspring" of different races—who were also different species according to polygeneticism—would be infertile like the offspring of horses and asses. The title of Nott's treatise, "The Mulatto a Hybrid—Probable Extermination of the Two Races if the Whites and Blacks are Allowed to Intermarry," bespeaks his fear that not only the "lower races," as was more generally believed, but all of humankind might be annihilated as a result of racial mixing. (It goes without saying that the alternative to this scenario, namely, complete amalgamation of the white and black races with its implied degeneration from the pure white race must have been equally frightening to many nineteenth-century theorists of race.)

The publication of Darwin's *On the Origin of Species* (1859) finally helped to end the scientific discussion about hybridity because Darwin showed that "whether different ethnic groups were classified as species or varieties, there was in any case no essential difference between them" (Young 1995, 13). With *On the Origin of Species,* Darwin reintroduced a monogenetic view of human origin into nineteenth-century evolutionary theory, but even if his findings paved the way for a more egalitarian view of the different races, they still could not eradicate racial determinism. By midcentury, Eliot's friend Herbert Spencer, one of the founders of modern sociology, had already shifted the site of racial difference from genes to culture. He reinstituted permanent difference between races by defining difference in terms of cultural habits—in this case "race habits"—that after having been gradually produced over time have become hereditary.[25]

Fuller's, Stowe's, and Eliot's writing clearly reveals the impact of nineteenth-century race theory, whereas Hawthorne's references to evolution and discourses about race are rather oblique. Nathaniel Hawthorne does not comment directly on race in *The Marble Faun* or elsewhere. More recent criticism has spent quite a bit of time either trying to find obscure hints about racial strife and slavery in Hawthorne's considerable body of work or deploring the fact that Hawthorne lacked such awareness.[26] Several critics have pointed out that in an entry in his French and Italian notebooks he associates Praxiteles's sculpture of a faun, which inspired his novel, with "an ugly, bearded woman, who was lately exhibited in England, and by some supposed to have been engendered betwixt a human mother and an orangoutang" (*French and Italian Notebooks* [1858-59] 1980, 174) and that by thus commenting on the possible effects of mixing different species, he revealed his anxieties about miscegenation (see Bentley 1995, 25–26; Martin 2002, 33). Recently, Kristie Hamilton has forged a connection between Hawthorne's description of Donatello as the last member of a vanishing race and "multiple narratives of extinction" (2003, 43) by comparing the doomed relation of Donatello and Miriam to the equally doomed love between the white Cora and Native American Uncas in James Fenimore Cooper's *The Last of the Mohicans* (50).

Interestingly, Margaret Fuller also comments on the phenomenon of "vanishing races"—and the implicit threat of degeneration and regression—in *Summer on the Lakes* (1844). Her writing clearly shows that she had studied the separatist influence of the race theories of her time; even though she did not seem to have wanted to, she had to question democratic universalist thought when it came to the subject of race. A closer look at her portrayal of Native Americans in *Summer on the Lakes* reveals that she developed an inclusive racial politics which defied at least some of the biases of contemporary race theory. In order to improve upon the—as she says—"unimproving" ([1844] 1994, 185) Native American race, Fuller adhered to a somewhat liberal race theory that allowed for racial mixing, but her writing suggests that her enthusiasm was checked by her knowledge of contemporary race theory. Hints at Native American "race habits" and at the childhood state of "savage" Native American civilization show that her ruminations about race in *Summer on the Lakes* are clearly influenced by its findings.[27]

Her belief in a monogenetic human origin and her trust in the common humanity of the "red" and the "white" races along with a wish to "better" the Native American race (whom she believed to be a vanishing race)—and also save it from extinction—caused her to advocate intermarriage between Native Americans and whites. She explores this idea in *Summer on the Lakes* by means of the fable "Muckwa, Or the Bear," which deals with the interspecies marriage between the Native American bear hunter Muckwa and a beautiful She-Bear. Muckwa and the She-Bear have two sons, "one of whom was like an Indian, and the other like a bear" (195), and live happily together until Muckwa, bored by his domestic life, goes bear hunting again and accidentally kills his sister-in-law. As a result of this, Muckwa and his human son have to leave the bear habitation. A carefully placed hint at the end of the story, "Perhaps the child of Norman-Saxon blood, no less than the Indian, finds some pulse of the Orson in his veins" (196), suggests that this fable is meant to be read as a story that not only dramatizes gender relationships and racial domination but also encodes Fuller's stance on racial hybridity.

Mid-nineteenth-century hybridity theory explains the fact that Muckwa and his bear wife have a bear child and a human child. Thus, F. W. Edwards suggested that "between proximate races, a union does not produce a mixture, but one or other of 'the pure primitive type'" (quoted in Young 1995, 79) and Herbert Spencer elaborated that "the current physiological test of distinct species is the production of a non-prolific hybrid" ([1854] 1996, 396) and that "the hybrids produced from two distinct races of organisms may die out in the first, second, third, fourth, fifth, &c., generation, according as the constitutional differences of the races is [*sic*] greater or less" (398). These observations had to be based upon experiments with animals, since nineteenth-century race theory was too young a discipline to produce conclusive results about human beings.

It might at first seem somewhat strange that Fuller, who was in favor of racial mixing or "amalgamation" would present a type of race mixing that leaves the separate species and all their differences intact, but in accordance with cutting-edge race science of her time she had to take this route if she wanted to suggest that Native Americans and bears—and by implication Native Americans and whites—are races that are proximate enough to warrant mixing. But it seems she found it hard to convince herself of this view. An earlier passage in *Summer on the Lakes* suggests that, commonsensical as she was, it was easier for her to believe that race mixing between Native Americans and whites would result in racially mixed types. Since this might indicate that the two races are of the more distant type that produces hybrids that will eventually become infertile, her tone betrays quite a bit of resignation: "[N]ature seems, like all else, to declare, that [the mixed] race is fated to perish. Those of mixed blood fade early. . . . They lose what is best in either type, rather than enhance the value of each, by mingling" (189–90). Fuller's astoundingly liberal racial politics—which are indeed commendable considering that her works still reveal vestiges of racial anxiety and prejudice concerning Native Americans[28]—can be understood in light of the ideological positions that she adopts as a transcendentalist and a feminist. As a result of her ideological allegiances, she seems to have realized that she had to practice politics that included marginalized groups.

Harriet Beecher Stowe's contested race politics, which Eliot does not emulate in her writings, initially proceed from a conservative, but rather "benevolent," stance on the origin of racial difference. As her statements in *Uncle Tom's Cabin* about African American slaves being "of one blood" with whites and also having immortal souls show (see [1852] 1981, 268), her Christian—and therefore necessarily creationist—outlook made her side with the evolutionary monogeneticists, who did not believe in the separate species theory.[29] In spite of having made the abolition of slavery her life's aim, Stowe consistently assigned what seem to be (often rather negative) essentialist notions of her own devising to her African American characters, whom she frequently pictures as "naturally religious," childlike, and feminized. While critics have deemed her feminization of African American males (Tom in *Uncle Tom's Cabin*; Tiff in *Dred*) a stroke of genius, which allowed her to debunk the stereotype of the black man as rapist (see Ammons 1986, 168), they have considered other aspects of Stowe's characterization of blacks as much less ingenious. African American critics in particular have voiced their outrage at her frequent presentation of small black children as petlike, her privileging of light-skinned black characters as more intelligent than dark-skinned ones, and her exclusive encoding of sexual desire between different races as transgression.

George Eliot, having liberally borrowed plotlines dealing with racial alterity from Stowe's work for *Daniel Deronda*, never commented on the "racialist" aspects of Stowe's depiction of blacks, which imply that race is an essential determinant of human behavior. But Eliot—most likely very deliberately—chose a less conspicuous race for her exploration of racial alterity. Much helped by the fact that the "racial difference" between English and Jewish people is not overly conspicuous, she avoided overtly "racialist" statements about Jews. And by clearly advocating intermarriage between Jews and Gentiles (e.g. Miss Arrowpoint and the musician Klesmer), she also disregarded Stowe's policy of eschewing racial amalgamation. In "The Modern

Hep! Hep! Hep!" (from her final published work, *Impressions of Theophrastus Such*), which presents her most theoretical statements on the subject of race, she argued that "[t]he tendency of things is toward the quicker or slower fusion of races. It is impossible to arrest this tendency" ([1879] 1894, 206).[30]

Daniel Deronda follows its pre-texts, *Uncle Tom's Cabin* and *Dred*, which deal with African American identity in terms of the need for nation-building, in exploring how individual and cultural identity are constituted. Eliot's presentation of Deronda's quest to become a national leader who readies a "homeland" for a Jewish nation whose members have never seen it was undoubtedly inspired by Stowe's "race plots," which tell the stories of George Harris and Dred, who also long to return to a national home that is only a distant ancestral memory. Both Stowe and Eliot investigate whether identification with one's race of origin is genetic, a "matter of the blood," or whether it rather is the result of voluntary affiliation[31] with one's ethnic group through the study of "preserved cultural" memory. While neither one of them reaches a definitive conclusion, it seems that Stowe prefers essentialist definitions of racial identity, whereas Eliot, after having thoroughly investigated the formation of racial identity, seems to conclude that racial identity can ultimately not be ascertained. Stowe's and Eliot's differing attitudes were immediately discerned by their respective critics and are also reflected in the reception of their works: from the publication of Stowe's novels, many critics—most notably African American ones—have viewed Stowe's fictional efforts at African American repatriation as an attempt to get rid of an "unwanted" race (see Yarborough 1986, 69), whereas Jewish critics almost unanimously welcomed Eliot's support of the foundation of a Jewish State (see Lewis 1996, 203).

By sending her Jewish protagonist, Daniel Deronda, on a quest for his Jewish identity, Eliot actually attempts to deal with cultural/racial alterity from within a marginalized ethnic group. But she does not resolve her protagonist's important pursuit of his racial identity: through his relationship with Mordecai and Mirah, Daniel identifies with Judaism, but his personality does not change in any significant way after he finds out that he is a Jew himself. Thus, the question remains, whether it is Daniel's genetic inheritance that influences his personal history or whether Daniel is an individual who is good at identifying with others and their otherness, i.e. has the power to "converge." In this context it has to be stressed that neither in *Daniel Deronda* nor in "The Modern Hep! Hep! Hep!," which presents a defense of Jewishness, does Eliot ever suggest that Jewishness is determined by race. In "The Modern Hep! Hep! Hep!," the narrator simply refers to "a common descent as a bond of obligation" ([1879] 1894, 188) without ever assuming a genetic "racial core."

Having studied the evolutionary theories of her time, Eliot did not necessarily adopt determinism. Her works show that she was very interested in the "chance elements" of Darwinian theory, "the multiplicity of possibilities, . . . coincidence as creative force . . . the absorbing unpredictability of what is to come," as well as the "acts of choice and will" that play an important part in sexual selection (Beer 1983, 191). Gillian Beer therefore argues that "[t]he theme, ordering and dialogue of *Daniel Deronda* all explore and question the genealogical view of time as descent and succession and bring into debate its adequacy as complete explanation" (193). As she points out, the novel thus leaves open the possibility that Daniel's identification with Judaism is a result of his ability to "converge" rather than the logical consequence of "racial essence." "Converging," defined by the Concise Oxford Dictionary as the tendency "of unrelated organisms . . . to become similar while evolving to fill a similar ecological niche" (CD-ROM edition, 1995), according to her, "creates one form of identity which does not require a study of beginnings and . . . is an important organizing principle of the novel which generates its own metaphysics" (1983, 194).[32]

Eliot's depiction of the basically unaltered Jewish Daniel has drawn criticism from commentators who have, for example, deplored the fact that Deronda is "transformed" only inasmuch as he sheds his Christianity and declares his Jewishness (see Press 1997, 324). In *Daniel Deronda* Eliot does, nevertheless, succeed in creating a (rather small) "Third Space" of possible hybridity and cultural exchange.[33] This exchange, which actually opens up an "*in-between* space . . . that carries the burden of the meaning of culture" and serves to function as "the 'inter'—the cutting edge of translation and negotiation" (Bhabha 1994, 38), takes place within the personal relationship of the English Daniel and the Jewish Mordecai and comes about as a result of Daniel's identification with Jewish culture and religion as well as his— perhaps even more important—homoerotic infatuation with Mordecai.

George Eliot's appropriation of and reaction to "American race plots" in *Daniel Deronda* suggests that, unlike Stowe and Hawthorne (and more in the vein of Fuller's liberalism), she held on to a pre-Romantic, universalist denial of "essential" cultural and racial alterity which precluded her from encoding race as significant difference. Thus, she adopted neither Stowe's example of postulating racial difference as essential nor Hawthorne's strange politics of depicting Italians as racially different and thereby inferior. Yet since she could not simply ignore "visible" difference, she devised a type of hybridization that paradoxically enabled a problematic universalism while simultaneously deconstructing it. Alicia Carroll calls attention to Eliot's "strategic hybrids" in *Dark Smiles: Race and Desire in George Eliot*: "Eliot is . . . drawn to both internalizing and externalizing images of Otherness, creating characters who are both 'Oriental' and English, both European and Gypsy, both experienced adult and innocent or primitive child, both English gentry and exotic other, both 'captive' and 'free,' and even both male and female" (2003, 7). She aptly concludes that in embracing "Other cultures, Other races, and even Other bodies and genders, Eliot ultimately expresses a troubled resistance to . . . contemporary illustrations of racial difference" (25).

1
George Eliot's "English" Novels and American Literature—Bringing It All Back Home?[1]

THE SCARLET LETTER AND WOMAN IN THE NINETEENTH CENTURY REVISITED IN ADAM BEDE AND CO.

FOLLOWING THE LEAD OF GILBERT AND GUBAR IN *MADWOMAN IN THE ATTIC* (1980), many critics have argued that important aspects of George Eliot's work—as for example, her characterization and gender conception—have benefited from her reading of American authors, such as Margaret Fuller, Harriet Beecher Stowe, and Nathaniel Hawthorne. My analysis of George Eliot's "domestic" English novels in relation to contemporaneous American works will corroborate these findings, centering on *Adam Bede* (1859) and *Middlemarch* (1871–72), but will go beyond these novels and a mere analysis of gender issues by also addressing questions concerning the cultural transferability of plots reflecting typically American social issues and religious and philosophical concepts.

Inspiration from American literature is often palpable in Eliot's work. Especially in her later novels, Eliot's literary realism was often tempered by an infusion of "American romance." Moreover, her conception of the "organic" social microcosm of Middlemarch depicted in the eponymous novel is astoundingly parallel to Stowe's rendition of harmonious small town life in *Oldtown Folks* (1869). But there are also significant differences between the American writers' approach towards the cultural determinants, class, gender, and religion, and Eliot's "British" take on these issues. In American writing from the nineteenth century the lives of fictional characters are often most profoundly influenced by their attitude towards religion, whereas in Eliot's novels class background is of utmost importance. These cultural differences between the U.S. and England had important consequences for the depiction of gender issues. Thus, the more democratic "classless" organization of American society seems to have enabled Fuller and Stowe (and, to a lesser extent also Hawthorne) to depict women as social agents, able to venture outside of the domestic sphere and into the work place.[2] This is a type of freedom and empowerment that Eliot does not accord her female characters. Like Fuller and Stowe, she deplored the lot of "woman in the nineteenth century," but, taking into account the position of women in British nineteenth-century society, she was still not able to follow the American example of creating strong, independent heroines who could find satisfaction in vocational success.

As many critics have pointed out, *Adam Bede*, George Eliot's second novel, is indebted to both Hawthorne's *The Scarlet Letter* (1850, mainly in its plot construction) and Fuller's *Woman in the Nineteenth Century* (1845, in its conception of gender roles).[3] Eliot had reread Hawthorne's novel before she started writing *Adam Bede*, and the fact that she drew inspiration from *The Scarlet Letter* cannot be overlooked. Both novels deal with the consequences that the birth of an illegitimate child in a highly traditional society has for the parents, and in particular the mother. In *The Scarlet Letter*, Hester Prynne, a young woman married to the much older Roger Chillingworth (assumed to be dead at the beginning of the story) has a child by the Puritan minister Arthur Dimmesdale, whose fatherhood remains unacknowledged throughout the novel. Hester gives birth to her child, Pearl, while she is in jail for having committed adultery. As additional punishment for her sin, she is sentenced to display a scarlet A on her dress. Even though she is free to leave her Puritan community after she has served her jail sentence, she decides to remain there and bear her shame.

In *Adam Bede*, the orphaned teenager Hetty Sorrel, raised by her tenant farmer aunt and uncle, becomes pregnant by the young country squire Arthur Donnithorne, whose grandfather is her family's landlord. After Arthur has ended the relationship for "class" and status reasons, but before Hetty discovers that she is pregnant, she becomes engaged to Adam Bede, the novel's hero, even though she does not love him. When she feels that she cannot hide her pregnancy any longer, she runs away from home in pursuit of Arthur Donnithorne, whom she does not find. She has her unwanted child—whose sex is not disclosed—and "kills" the child by not preventing its death from exposure to the elements. Hetty is sentenced to serve a jail sentence in Australia; shortly before her sentence is up, she dies, still far away from home.

By importing plot elements from *The Scarlet Letter* and by also naming the parents of the illegitimate child Hester (short "Hetty") and Arthur, Eliot openly acknowledges Hawthorne's influence. Yet there are also significant dissimilarities between Hawthorne's and Eliot's novels, which reflect differences between the two writers' philosophical and literary predilections as well as larger social and cultural differences between (Puritan) America and Great Britain at the turn of the nineteenth century. Eliot, for example, adds an interesting twist to Hawthorne's conception of characters: she splits Hawthorne's formidable, morally ambiguous heroine Hester into two characters. Hester, the "fallen woman," is represented by Hetty, the naïve and callous "child murderer," whereas Hester, the "Madonna," who becomes a nurse to her Puritan community, is embodied by the saintly Methodist preacher, Dinah. As Hetty's short-term fiancé, the equally saintly Adam fulfills the role of Hester's sinister satanic husband, Chillingworth, only as far as the novel's structure is concerned. By adding an additional character and substituting a "bad" with a "good" figure, Eliot replaces the morally ambiguous triangle of Hester, Chillingworth, Dimmesdale with a "bad" (Hetty/Arthur) and a "good" (Dinah/Adam) couple, thus offering the possibility for a happy ending to her novel.

British Realism vs. American Romance?

While this description of Eliot's character conception suggests that she might have wanted to idealize and perhaps even romanticize the bleak view of human relationships offered in *The Scarlet Letter*, her description of nature as indifferent rather than benevolent to her characters seems to mark—at least upon a first or cursory reading—another departure from Hawthorne's novel and reflect significant philosophical and cultural differences between Eliot's "realistic" English novel and its "romantic" American literary predecessor. In *The Scarlet Letter* nature provides Hester and her daughter Pearl, who are forced to live the life of recluses in the Puritan community, with the sympathy that they are denied by fellow human beings. Thus, from the "babbling brook" that seems to want to impart a secret to her to the "wild Indian . . . , [who] grew conscious of a nature wilder than his own" ([1850] 1986, 212) when seeing her, everything belonging to nature seems to have a special relation to Pearl who is the offspring and personification of a perfectly natural but socially illicit act. Moreover, nature even seems to understand the unlawful relationship of Hester Prynne and her lover Arthur Dimmesdale: "The forest was obscure around them, and creaked with a blast that was passing through it. The boughs were tossing heavily about their heads; while one solemn old tree groaned dolefully to another, as if telling the sad story of the pair that set beneath, or constrained to forebode evil to come" (170).

In *Adam Bede*, however, a novel set in rural England at the turn of the nineteenth century, Eliot completely rejects a pastoral interpretation and personifications of nature; "[n]ature's diffidence is a leitmotif to which Eliot returns again and again in the novel" (Corbett 1988, 295). This is exemplified by a comment on Arthur and Hetty's relationship. Immediately after a veiled reference, which uses imagery taken from nature and indicates that Arthur and Hetty have engaged in premature sexual relations ("If only the corn were not ripe enough to be blown out of the husk and scattered as untimely seed" [1859] 1985, 337), the narrator warns against all attempts to look for sympathy and forebodings of human fate in nature:

> For if it be true that Nature at certain moments seems charged with a presentiment of one individual lot, must it not also be true that she seems unmindful, unconscious of another? . . . There are so many of us, and our lots are so different: what wonder that Nature's mood is often in harsh contrast with the great crisis of our lives? We are children of a large family, and must learn, as such children, not to expect that our little hurts will be made much of—to be content with little nurture and caressing, and help each other the more. (338)

This plea to turn to human companionship rather than communion with nature indeed seems to be very different from Hawthorne's take on the subject in *The Scarlet Letter*, especially since, as Janice B. Daniel points out, Hawthorne seems to instrumentalize "the voice of nature" to provide another narrative perspective, intended to direct "the reader's . . . sympathy toward the novel's lovers" (1993, 314) because they do not meet with human sympathy. While Daniel adds an important insight by drawing attention to the narratological importance of the added perspective, she might be misinterpreting Hawthorne's intentions. In showing nature's benevolence, Hawthorne is not as wholeheartedly supportive of Hester and Dimmesdale as she suggests. A closer look at the following quotation shows that Hawthorne, like Eliot, implies that those who want to find sympathy in nature will eventually be disappointed because they might just have projected their own longings onto it: "Love, whether newly born, or aroused from a death-like slumber, must always create a sunshine, filling the heart so full of radiance, that it overflows upon the outward world. Had the forest still kept its gloom, it would have been bright in Hester's eyes and bright in Arthur Dimmesdale's" ([1850] 1986, 177). Moreover, Hawthorne's narrator, reflecting Hawthorne's rather conservative outlook on life, frequently draws attention to the dangers inherent in unchecked (human) nature. This indicates that the author of *The Scarlet Letter* did not endorse the discourse about nature's supposed understanding and support of the lovers as unequivocally as the narrative at other times seems to imply. One could, in fact, easily argue that Hawthorne, while hiding a highly critical attitude of uncritical nature worship behind sham idealizations of nature, presents an even harsher view of it than Eliot and thus clearly rejects the romantic organicism of nineteenth-century American transcendentalism.[4]

A related issue where differences between nineteenth-century "American romance" and "English realism" turn out to be much less significant than one would initially think (because Hawthorne's and Eliot's fictional conceptions are not as opposed as one might assume) is addressed by a larger "realism vs. romance debate."[5] Both writers have included statements about their theories of writing fiction in their works; Hawthorne gives his most important definition of romance in the preface to *The House of the Seven Gables*:

> When a writer calls his work a Romance, it need hardly be observed that he wishes to claim a certain latitude, both as to its fashion and material, which he would not have felt himself entitled to assume, had he professed to be writing a Novel. The latter form of composition is presumed to aim at a very minute fidelity, not merely to the possible, but to the probable and ordinary course of man's experience. The former—while, as work of art, it must rigidly subject itself to laws, and while it sins unpardonably, so far as it might swerve aside from the truth of the human heart—has fairly a right to present that truth under circumstances, to a great extent, of the writer's own choosing or creation. ([1851] 1986, 1)

In the often quoted "moonlight scene" of *The Scarlet Letter*, the narrator, who talks about meeting Hester's ghost, expands the above definition of the fictional leeway granted by the romance. He repeatedly refers to romance elements in terms of a different light thrown on everyday situations so that the extraordinary and secret hidden beneath the seemingly ordinary might appear. Thus, when in the novel Hester, Pearl, and Dimmesdale are reunited on the scaffold at night, a meteor lights up the sky so that their "family secret"—the secret that they are a family—is revealed. Dimmesdale—as a result of having an extremely guilty conscience—(mis)interprets the meteoric light by seeing it as a gigantic advertisement for the sin of adultery he committed, "looking upward to the zenith, [he] beheld there the appearance of an immense letter,—the letter A,—marked out in lines of dull red light" ([1850] 1986, 136). The A, however, is interpreted very differently by the sexton who hands Dimmesdale a glove the minister lost on the scaffold with the words "Satan dropped it there, I take it, intending a scurrilous jest against your reverence," and continues, "But did your reverence hear of the portent that was seen last night? A great red letter in the sky,—the letter A— which we interpret to stand for Angel. For, as our good Governor Winthrop was made an angel this past night, it was doubtless fit that there should be some notice thereof" (138). This issue of "seeing things in a different light" introduces an important narrative device that the romance affords Hawthorne: if reality is presented in an unusual light, it allows for different interpretations. The romance thus creates a space for Hawthorne's famous ambiguities which bring out the prematurely "postmodern" idea—often implied in Hawthorne's nineteenth-century fiction—that there is more than one version of reality and that therefore subjective interpretation(s) might be all that people looking for ultimate truth will actually find.

In contrast to Nathaniel Hawthorne, George Eliot in her famous "artistic program" outlined in chapter seventeen of *Adam Bede*, rejects romantic license in favor of realistic representation:

> Certainly I could, my fair critic [idealize my characters], if I were a clever novelist, not obliged to creep severely after nature and fact, but able to represent things as they never have been and never will be. . . . I aspire to give no more than a faithful account of men and things as they have mirrored themselves in my mind. The mirror is doubtless defective; . . . but I feel as much bound to tell you, as precisely as I can, what that reflection is, as I if I were in the witness-box narrating my experience on oath. ([1859] 1985, 221)

Even though Eliot here voices her refusal to depict "things as they never have been and never will be," and thus seems to reject Hawthorne's approach to novel writing, their artistic positions certainly are not as oppositional as they at first might seem to be. This becomes clear from Hawthorne's statement that "swerving aside from the truth of the human heart" would be an unpardonable offense if it were committed by the romancer, and from Eliot's admission that a novelist can only give his or her own subjective version of reality because the mirror provided by the individual mind will doubtless be defective and confused.[6]

Marxist critic Daniel Cottom, nevertheless, takes Eliot to be a diehard realist. He bases his argumentative strategy of *Social Figures: George Eliot, Social History, and Literary Representation* on his observation that "[i]n effect, Eliot argued that realism was the true author of her writing" (1987, 3) and claims that Eliot, fostering a liberal and highly "civilized" idea of social community, defined her writing against the romance because to her it represented "egoism . . . trashy literature, superstition, unenlightened religious enthusiasm . . . and sensual pleasure" (127). But even he has to admit that Hawthorne's art does not qualify as an exemplary oppositional pole:

> Whether one was Hawthorne saluting the claims of romance or Eliot those of realism, the choice was likely to be made one of morality and knowledge as well as style. Eliot's great admiration for Hawthorne and the fact that her own realism has often been analyzed for its romance elements may serve to indicate just what a slippery customer this truth over which everyone was arguing really was. (126)

Cottom's analysis of George Eliot's realism is particularly interesting because it is part of a larger debate on the effects of so-called "classic realism," a term coined by Colin MacCabe, who warned against realism's "pernicious effects" of telling the reader exactly what to think. MacCabe argues that Eliot does this by having her narrators employ a metalanguage that "refuses its own status as writing. . . . [T]he text outside the area of inverted commas claims to be the product of no articulation, it claims to be unwritten. This unwritten text can then attempt to staunch the hemorrhage of interpretations threatened by the material of language" (1978, 15).[7] Penny Boumelha has criticized this argument by referring to Eliot's subversive use of unrealistic elements in her fiction (see 1987, 20) and David Lodge, approaching the subject from a narratological angle by looking at the interplay of mimetic and diegetic elements in *Middlemarch*, makes a similar criticism. He concludes that "the distinction between mimesis and diegesis in George Eliot is by no means as clear-cut as MacCabe implies; . . . the diegetic element is much more problematic than he allows" (1992, 51). I agree with this critical position rather than McCabe's view and would like to add that Eliot's adoption of Hawthornian romantic indirection shows that, at least in her later fiction, Eliot does not manipulate her narratives in order to make them capable of imposing a single point of view as "reality." The obvious romance elements in her work, in similar fashion as the celestial A in *The Scarlet Letter*, serve the important purpose of introducing different perspectives on "reality." In *Daniel Deronda*, they usher in the ancient kabbalistic Jewish faith, and are used to explain why Deronda, an educated nineteenth-century Englishman—is called by an ancient religion to found a brand new nation on foreign soil. In her Jewish novel, Eliot adopts Hawthorne's mode of storytelling and his masterful use of indirection and artistic ambiguity: it never becomes clear whether Daniel's Jewish identity is a result of a "call of the blood," of his study of preserved Jewish cultural memory, or even of his homoerotic infatuation with Mordecai.

Yet Eliot's implementation of the Hawthornian romantic mode certainly does not imply that she suddenly gives up realism and social concern in order to opt for individualist arbitrariness and nihilism—Hawthorne himself, after all, prefers morality to immorality in his work, even if he does not clearly define these terms. Sacvan Bercovitch gives a convincing explanation of the purpose behind Hawthorne's ambiguities. He deems *The Scarlet Letter* "an interpreter's guide into perplexity" that, however, "is neither random nor arbitrary" (1991, 19). Quite contrarily, the novel incorporates "a strategy of pluralism" that issues "on the reader's part, in a mystifying sense of multiplicity—through which each set of questions and answers is turned toward the same solution: all meanings are partly true" (19). Eliot clearly emulates this "strategy of pluralism" in *Daniel Deronda* where she achieves very similar effects in her rumination on Jewish identity.

"American" Religion and "British" Class: Social Determinants and Agents of Punishment

Even though neither Eliot's nor Hawthorne's fiction provides the rigorous analysis of social processes that Marxist critics like Cottom seem to have wished for, the depiction of differences in social station in *Adam Bede* indeed presents an important point of departure from its American pre-text, *The Scarlet Letter*, where class difference does not seem to exist,[8] where nobody seems uneducated, and where everybody adopts the elaborate diction of the dignified church elders. In Hawthorne's novel, individual freedom is legislated and curtailed exclusively by Puritan religion, whereas in *Adam Bede*, this function is chiefly performed by "class" and tradition. Commentators usually agree that Eliot had a very uneasy relationship with the uneducated working classes, whom she apparently believed readily capable of gratuitous violence. Thus, the scene in *Felix Holt* where Holt tries to prevent the drunken multitude from committing physical violence towards other human beings during the election riot is usually read as instance of Eliot's distrust and fear of the working classes (see Ingham 1996, 111; Cottom, 41). And even though *Adam Bede*, set at the turn of the nineteenth century, precedes this period of revolutionary unrest in Europe, Eliot here also voices her fears of the drunken populace when she has Mr. Irwine exercise "crowd control" in this novel in a scene where he explains his reasons for not keeping Dinah from preaching in his parish.

The novel's "class issue"—or rather issue of social station, since *Adam Bede* is set during the period preceding industrialization[9]—is most importantly presented in Hetty's and Arthur Donnithorne's relationship. While

Hester Prynne and Arthur Dimmesdale cannot consider marriage because Hester's husband has disappeared, Hetty's and Arthur's marriage is precluded only for reasons of social status. As an aspiring social climber, Hetty loves the idea of reaching Arthur's social rank through marriage at least as much as she loves Arthur himself. Hetty has informed Arthur about the fact that she wants to marry him, but his reflections on the subject reveal that because of differences in rank between a gentleman and a farmer's daughter their union is simply impossible in their society:

> [T]his little thing would be spoken ill of directly, if she happened to be seen walking with him; and then those excellent people, the Poysers, to whom a good name was as precious as if they had the best blood in the land in their veins—he should hate himself if he made a scandal of that sort. . . . No gentleman, out of a ballad, could marry a farmer's niece. There must be an end to the whole thing at once. It was too foolish. ([1859] 1985, 184)

The Poysers's extremely harsh later reaction to the disgrace that Hetty has brought upon them implies that they seem to agree with Arthur about "pride in one's station," but the novel, nevertheless, indicates that Eliot did not think that class boundaries should be impermeable.[10] *Adam Bede* is set at a time when society witnessed "the gradual abandonment but not total atrophy of a picture of society vertically organized in a fixed hierarchy of *ranks* and *stations*" (Ingham 1996, 4).[11] This process of social change, which gradually made obsolete the idea of society resembling a divinely ordained "Great Chain of Being,"[12] is obvious in the novel. Even though Adam initially "was very susceptible to the influence of rank" ([1859] 1985, 208–9) as Eliot's narrator "confesses," he loses this susceptibility very quickly when he notices that he is morally superior to Arthur and then tells him to "stop a bit" in a "hard and peremptory voice" (343). Moreover, Eliot's presentation of Adam as a virtuous, upwardly mobile workman (who is extremely hungry for knowledge to boot) reflects her undying faith in education, rather than revolution, to bring about social change.[13]

While questions of social station are more important in *Adam Bede* than in *The Scarlet Letter*, religion plays a less important role in Eliot's novel than in Hawthorne's, but it still figures prominently. Even though there are some similarities between Hawthorne's and Eliot's presentation of religion as a social spectacle (e.g. the scenes in which the crowds witness Dinah preaching on the wagon or Hester standing on the scaffold), there are also very many differences. Unlike Hawthorne's seventeenth-century Salem, Eliot's 1890s Hayslope obviously does not represent a theocracy but features a variety of attitudes towards religion, which also reflect the village's social stratification. Dinah, for example, who, like Seth, comes from a simple farm background, "had the belief in visible manifestations of Jesus" (73) and adheres to a very fundamentalist Methodism: "They believed in present miracles, in instantaneous conversions, in revelations by dreams and visions; they drew lots, and sought for divine guidance by opening the Bible at hazard; having a literal way of interpreting the Scriptures, which is not at all sanctioned by approved commentators" (82). Adam, deriving from the same background, is also susceptible to the mystical aspects of faith, but as an incipient intellectual he takes a less doctrinal approach: "[T]hat mental combination which is at once humble in the region of mystery and keen in the region of knowledge . . . gave him his disinclination to doctrinal religion" (94). Mrs. Poyser, even more practical, flatly denies the spiritual direction that Dinah claims: "'When there's a bigger maggot than usual in your head you call it direction'" (124). And Hetty, presented as pretty but callous from the very beginning of the novel, finds it possible not to believe at all; even though she goes to church every Sunday, she "never appropriated any single Christian idea or Christian feeling" (430). Mr. Irwine, the representative of the Anglican Church, also seems to lack religious fervor. Apparently of noble origin, he sports a refined aristocratic look, prefers reading the classics to reading the Bible, feels "no serious alarm about the souls of his parishioners" (112) and refuses to castigate the Methodists because he is convinced that "'[w]e must "live and let live" . . . in religion as well as in other things'" (103). The minister, even though "his theology . . . was lax" (112–13), is presented in a predominantly favorable light through the narratorial comment that "he had that charity which has sometimes been lacking to the very illustrious virtue—he was tender to other men's failings" (113).

Mr. Irwine's and Dinah's sympathetic behavior is firmly grounded in Eliot's belief that religion should be a "religion of humanity" and that, in keeping with Comtean (and Feuerbachian) religious principle, it should have sympathy as its basis for action.[14] Thus, both Mr. Irwine and Dinah seem to act according to the Feuerbachian tenet that "[t]he highest and first law must be the love of man to man" ([1841] 1989, 271). Dinah, however, as an old-fashioned Methodist, would certainly not deny God's transcendence and divinity and thus would not be able to accept the philosophy underlying Feuerbach's statement about the "love of man to man": "[T]hat which in religion holds the first place—namely, God—is, as we have shown, in itself and according to the truth, the second, for it is only the nature of man regarded objectively; and that which to religion is the second, namely man—must therefore be constituted and declared the first" ([1859] 1985, 270). Both Mr. Irwine's and Dinah's practical ministering, however, reflects

Eliot's idea that religious feelings should be expressed as sympathy because sympathy is the prerequisite for community, as stated rather rapturously by Feuerbach:

> Feeling is sympathy; feeling arises only in the love of man to man. Sensations man has in isolation; feelings only in community. Only in sympathy does sensation rise to feeling. Feeling is aesthetic, human sensation; only what is human is the object of feeling. In feeling man is related to his fellow-man as to himself; he is alive to the sorrows, the joys of another as his own. Thus only by communication does man rise above merely egoistic sensation into feeling. ([1841] 1989, 283)

Sympathetic towards humanity's foibles, according to the principles outlined above, the ministers in *Adam Bede* always show mildness and understanding towards the sinners whom they counsel. This, as can easily be illustrated by the "judgment scenes" in *The Scarlet Letter* and *Adam Bede*, is the main difference between Eliot's and Hawthorne's presentation of religious officials, who are also state officials in Hawthorne's novel.

Hawthorne already makes it very clear from the first judgment scene, which shows Hester on the scaffold after she is released from prison, that the Puritan dignitaries are totally inadequate to their task of judging Hester: "[O]ut of the whole human family, it would not have been easy to select the same number of wise and virtuous persons, who should be less capable of sitting in judgment on an erring woman's heart, and disentangling its mesh of good and evil, than the sages of rigid aspect towards whom Hester Prynne now turned her face" ([1850] 1986, 60). The emotional inadequacy of the Puritan clergy becomes again very evident in another important judgment scene (whose emotional impact is only matched by the scene of Hetty's official trial) which takes place when Hester, because she has heard that the Puritan officials have made plans to take Pearl away from her out of their alleged concern for her own and Pearl's souls, seeks out (former) Governor Bellingham, and other Puritan officials present at his house. On the one hand, the Puritans reason that if Pearl, whose parentage is still not known to them and whose unruly behavior is a constant reminder of a broken law, is indeed demon offspring, begotten by Hester and the devil in the woods, they need to take the child away from her mother in order to protect Hester's mortal soul. On the other hand, they argue that if Pearl happens to be entirely human and therefore also endowed with a mortal soul, it might be advantageous for the well-being of Pearl's soul if she were removed from the sphere of Hester's bad influence.[15] Luckily, Dimmesdale, who also happens to be at the Governor's mansion, entreated by Hester's "Speak thou for me" (100), finally saves Hester and Pearl's "family unit" by pointing out the educational value that Pearl presents for Hester.[16]

The interference of highest state officials in matters that appear entirely private[17] might indeed seem very strange to a twenty-first century reader who might wonder why—even in a theocratic society—adultery and failure to disclose a child's paternity would constitute a particularly severe instance of breaking a law. Michael Colacurcio has tackled these questions using an argumentative strategy that almost seems to invoke the tenets of an "Eliotian organicism" which eschews social upheaval and violence. He hypothesizes that Hawthorne, having studied Winthrop's and Bellingham's journals, wanted to make clear that antinomian, "libertine" behavior as reflected in Hester's freedom of speculation did indeed pose a threat to Puritan society, which displayed much less "monolithic unity" (1985, 107) than one might assume. Therefore, judgment was extremely hard in cases of insurrection. Perhaps even more importantly, Colacurcio draws attention to the fact that adultery also might have presented a very grave breach of the law to the Puritans because—as in Dimmesdale's case—it could also be interpreted as an instance of idolatry: "[Dimmesdale] is consumed by his fear that his 'adultery' is really a classic case of 'idolatry'—that is, that he did once and does still love Hester more than God, preferring the creature to the creator in the one just definition of the unregenerate will" ([1850] 1986, 119).

The offense committed by Hetty and Arthur in *Adam Bede* evidently lacks the theological component of the "crime" in *The Scarlet Letter*. As a purely social offense in a comparatively secular society, their transgression initially does not have the dramatic moral implications that Hester Prynne's and Arthur Dimmesdale's adultery has within their Puritan universe. Only by having Hetty murder her child, and by giving very intense descriptions and testimonies of the days before and after Hetty's deed, can Eliot bring her drama up to par in *Adam Bede*. The trial scene makes it totally clear that Hetty's crime, which is judged by an appointed jury, is treated as a civil rather than religious offense and only derives its moral significance from its "unnaturalness": "[T]he prisoner was made to hold up her hand, and the jury were asked for their verdict. 'Guilty.' . . . [T]he sympathy of the court was not with the prisoner: the unnaturalness of her crime stood out the more harshly by the side of her hard immovability and obstinate silence" ([1859] 1985, 481–82).

Even though Hetty is sentenced "to be hanged by the neck till [she] be dead" (482), her immediate family is not able to show any compassion. But their almost Puritan sternness is neither religiously motivated nor a result of their horror at what a family member has been capable of doing. Their reasons for ostracizing Hetty are entirely status-related and social: "The sense of family dishonour was too keen . . . to leave room for any compassion towards Hetty. [Martin Poyser] and his father were simple-minded farmers, proud of their untarnished character . . . and Hetty had brought disgrace on them all—disgrace that could never be wiped out" (459). Hetty receives solace only from Adam, who still loves her in spite of what she has done, and from Dinah, who, truly concerned about Hetty's soul, manages to obtain a confession from her, thus opening the door to repentance and forgiveness for Hetty. Arthur Donnithorne, more of a hero in distress than Hawthorne's Arthur Dimmesdale, finally saves her life when he rides up like a knight in shining armor "carrying in his hand the hard-won release from death" (507).

The moral dilemma presented in *Adam Bede* is thus presented almost entirely as a secular affair; even Dinah's accomplishment in perhaps saving Hetty's soul out of true concern for Hetty's spiritual status seems to be a result of her ability to show compassion rather than a triumph of Methodist doctrine. Hetty's confession is not motivated by religious insight or fear, but rather by a "sympathetic" reaction to Dinah's sympathy (see Argyros 1999, 163). Similarly, Mr. Irwine's answer to Arthur's question if "'a man who struggles against temptation into which he falls at last [is] as bad as the man who doesn't struggle at all'" (217) is informed by commonsensical morality rather than religious doctrine:

> No my boy. I pity him, in proportion to his struggles, for they foreshadow the inward suffering which is the worst form of nemesis. Consequences are unpitying. Our deeds carry their terrible consequences, quite apart from any fluctuations that went before—consequences that are hardly ever confined to ourselves. And it is best to fix our minds on that certainty instead of considering what may be the best excuse for us. (217–18)

Mr. Irwine's advice to Arthur Donnithorne about avoiding "the inward suffering which is the worst form of nemesis" obviously reflects Arthur Dimmesdale's troubles throughout *The Scarlet Letter*, but it nevertheless fails to evoke the appropriate effective moral response in Arthur because of its (theological) mildness, and thus invites speculation as to whether or not Eliot displays a critical attitude regarding the spiritual and social effectivity of ministers who are just a bit too liberal.[18] Obviously lacking the fervor of Hawthorne's fire and brimstone Puritans—whose equally ineffective "religious" attitudes Eliot certainly would not have endorsed in any way—Mr. Irwine comes across as a figure who, in his sympathetic approach towards the sinners he counsels, neglects to inculcate accountability (and ultimately serves to delineate the limits of sympathy).

Gender/ed Issues

As with Eliot's presentation of religion in *Adam Bede*, her conception of gender and gendered behavior is less dramatic and bold than Hawthorne's in *The Scarlet Letter*. Hawthorne's Hester Prynne is perhaps the most memorable heroine in American nineteenth-century fiction; as a combination of "fallen woman" and "Madonna," she proudly accepts her fate. Having learned to live with the scarlet letter that advertises her adultery, she becomes a respected nurse and social worker within her community, even though she is still shunned by parts of it.[19] "[T]he scarlet letter had not done its office" ([1850] 1986, 145), as Hawthorne's narrator remarks, because it has failed to quell Hester's rebellious spirit. Even after seven years of displaying the scarlet letter on her chest, she still wants to run away with Arthur Dimmesdale and, as Hawthorne's narrator reveals in a very impressive passage, she harbors highly unusual thoughts (at least for a Puritan) about gender relations which culminate in a total deconstruction of the gender dichotomy. Arthur Dimmesdale, Hester's "partner in crime," pales by comparison. Unable to admit his deed because he is afraid of presenting a very bad example to his congregation and, even more importantly, because he fears for his social standing as a "shooting star" minister, he engages in spiritual and physical self-flagellation (which will eventually lead to his death) and feminizes himself in relation to Hester, whom he repeatedly asks to "'Think for me Hester'" because "'Thou art strong. Resolve for me'" (171). In *Adam Bede*, Eliot does not follow Hawthorne in creating a formidable heroine. Instead, she splits Hawthorne's character into two figures, Hetty and Dinah, representing the "fallen woman" and the "Madonna," respectively. The "fallen woman" character, Hetty, fails to live up to Hester in any way. Since she is a teenager, she necessarily lacks Hester's maturity. But Hetty is also gullible, vain, shallow, and a social climber. She represents one of those cases (like Rosamond Vincy), where Eliot's narrators react very unfavorably to women whose physical beauty does not indicate equal moral beauty. Their appearance not only provides yet another hint at the untrustworthiness of nature's language, but they also seem to be despicable cases of "false advertising" (see Mitchell 1994, 96).[20] Moreover, unlike Hester, Hetty is not a loving mother, but the murderer of her own child. As a villainous character, Hetty, however, is also not very convincing since she acts out of vanity and confusion rather than moral depravity. The fact that Tom Winnifrith discusses Hetty's and Arthur's relationship in terms of immature "teenage lust" that leads to "teenage pregnancy," also indicates that Hetty and her relationship with Arthur Donnithorne lack the maturity and moral significance of Hester Prynne and her relationship with Arthur Dimmesdale (see Winnifrith 1994).

Dinah Morris, Hester Prynne's second alter ego in *Adam Bede*, represents the Madonna side of Hester's personality. She serves her community as a minister and a nurse, thereby combining the vocations of both Arthur Dimmesdale and Hester Prynne. Like Adam Bede, whom Eliot characterizes at times as maternal and even Christlike, and who thus presents a positive version of Dimmesdale's feminization, Dinah is "too good" to be truly intriguing and therefore also pales compared to Hawthorne's character. Arthur Donnithorne, who represents Dimmesdale as a sexual transgressor, likewise, is less interesting because he lacks the depth of Hawthorne's character, who administers fatal self-punishment. As with Dimmesdale, who postpones fleeing with Hester because he wants to be praised for preaching the election day sermon, Arthur, out of concern for his good reputation, does not confess his seduction of Hetty to Mr. Irwine. Eliot's characters in *Adam Bede* are, overall, less compelling than Hawthorne's characters in *The Scarlet Letter*. This is certainly due to the fact that her individual figures as well as their relationships with each other, lack the depth, passion, and moral ambiguity that Hawthorne provides his characters with to guarantee their enduring power to fascinate his readers.

GENDER IN THE NINETEENTH CENTURY

Before considering the interesting question as to why Eliot, in her first full-length novel, refrained from creating equally captivating characters as Hawthorne, I would like to draw attention to the fact that Eliot's conception of gender and gender roles shows parallels not only to Hawthorne's but also to Fuller's and Stowe's examples. An investigation of the American writers' approaches towards gender—combined with a closer look at nineteenth-century (scientific) discourses of gender—will shed additional light on Eliot's gender conception in *Adam Bede* and her later novels. The writing of Eliot, Hawthorne, Fuller, and Stowe, like that of many other nineteenth-century authors, shows that their gender politics alternated between essentialist and constructionist positions. Their adherence to the sentimental ideal of "woman as (motherly) Madonna" (cf. Hawthorne's Hester, Stowe's Agnes of Sorrento, Fuller's "Virgin Mother," and Eliot's Dinah and Romola), for example, points in the direction of gender essentialism. But, at the same time, they all discarded essentialist attitudes and arrived at a fluid notion of gender. Thus, while Stowe, Fuller, and Eliot opted for "feminizing" men in order to sensitize them, Hawthorne presented male feminization in a negative light, yet still had his character Hester argue for a complete deconstruction of gender.

In *Woman in the Nineteenth Century*, the most important American nineteenth-century "feminist" manifesto, Margaret Fuller vacillates between upholding and deconstructing essentialist notions of gender. In one of her key passages, she offers a rather conservative, essentialist list of gender attributes (which already criticizes the "rude classification" that she feels unable to avoid):[21]

> The growth of man is two-fold, masculine and feminine.
> As far as these two methods can be distinguished they are so as
> Energy and Harmony.
> Power and Beauty.
> Intellect and Love.
> Or by some such rude classification, for we have not language primitive
> and pure enough to express such ideas with precision. ([1845] 1994, 326)

She nevertheless continues arguing that even though certain attributes prevail in either the masculine or the feminine they are not exclusive to one sex: "These two sides are supposed to be expressed in man and woman, that is, as the more and less, for the faculties have not been given pure to either, but only in preponderance. There are also exceptions in great number, such as men of far more beauty than power, and the reverse" (326). Furthermore, she famously demands that in spite of "essential" gender differences, the restraints on women's vocational choices be done away with, thereby indicating that she opts for abolishing the practical consequences of perceived gender difference: "But if you ask me what offices they may fill; I reply—any. I do not care what case you put; let them be sea-captains, if you will" (329).

An often quoted letter that George Eliot sent to Emily Davies, a leading Victorian feminist and founder of Girton, the first British women's college, shows that she had very similar—rather essentialist—ideas on gender difference:

> Spiritual wealth [is] acquired for mankind by the difference of function founded on the other, primary difference; and the preparation that lies in woman's peculiar constitution for a special moral influence.... And there lies just that kernel of truth in the vulgar alarm of men lest women should be "unsexed." We can no more afford to part with that exquisite type of gentleness, tenderness, possible maternity suffusing a woman's being with affectionateness, which makes what we mean by the feminine character.... The answer to those alarms of men about education is... to point out that com-

plete union and sympathy can only come by women having opened to them the same store of acquired truth or belief as men have, so that their grounds of judgment may be as far as possible the same. (*George Eliot Letters* 1954-55, 4:468)

Like Fuller, she demands that "female" characteristics should not be used to bar women from their right to education, but she also admits "primary gender difference" and the essentiality of feminine qualities like "gentleness" and "tenderness." (It is perhaps worth noting that in the above passage, she carefully shifts the point of view to a male perspective on the issue.)

Eliot's ambiguous stance on the question as to whether gender difference is innate or constructed can certainly be attributed to her engagement with contemporary natural and social sciences, i.e. her study of the writings of Auguste Comte, Charles Darwin, John Stuart Mill, and Herbert Spencer, which asserted innate gender difference. Apparently initially still indebted to an egalitarianism rooted in eighteenth-century philosophy, her close friend Spencer had argued in "The Rights of Women" (1851) that "[e]quity knows no difference of sex" and that it remains to be shown "why the differences of bodily organization, and those trifling mental variations which distinguish female from male, should exclude one half of the race from the benefits of [the] ordination [that human happiness is the Divine will]" ([1851] 1996, 155). But it seems that, with the help of his subsequent study of evolutionary theory, Spencer eventually found a reason to exclude "half of the race from human happiness." Evolutionary theory had shown him that the "mental variations" between the genders were more significant than he thought. By 1858 he wrote in his essay "Physical Training" that, "[a] girl develops in body and mind rapidly, and ceases to grow comparatively early" whereas "[a] boy's bodily and mental development is slower, and his growth greater" (391). This circumstance, according to Spencer, has dire consequences for the female brain:

> The abnormally rapid advance of any part in respect of structure involves premature arrest of its growth; and this happens with the organ of the mind as certainly as with any other organ. The brain, which during early years is relatively large in mass but imperfect in structure, will, if required to perform its functions with undue activity, undergo a structural advance greater than is appropriate to the age; but the ultimate effect will be a falling short of the size and power that would else have been attained. (391)[22]

Following this logic, he concluded in his section on "domestic institutions" in *The Principles of Sociology* (first published in 1870–72) that "[i]n domestic life, the relative position of women will doubtless rise; but it seems improbable that absolute equality with men will be reached" ([1898] 2002, vol. 1, part 3, 768). Due to the "natural" shortcomings of the female gender, women's proper place has to be in the home: "[A]ny extensive change in the education of women, made with the view of fitting them for businesses and professions, would be mischievous. If women comprehended all that is contained in the domestic sphere, they would ask no other" (769).[23]

Auguste Comte and John Stuart Mill, two social philosophers whose thought was also much valued by Eliot, likewise defended the ideology of separate spheres fostered by "The Cult of True Womanhood." Comte, having changed his initially negative attitude towards women,[24] reasoned in *A General View of Positivism* that woman is "undoubtedly superior to man" because of her "tendency to place social above personal feeling" (1865, 224). But he still held that women should be confined to the domestic sphere because "they are peculiarly qualified by the passive character of their life to assist in the action of the spiritual power in the family" (345) and, even more importantly, because "in all kinds of force, whether physical, intellectual, or practical, it is certain that Man surpasses Woman, in accordance with a general law which prevails throughout the animal kingdom" (225).

John Stuart Mill also relegated women to the domestic sphere, even though he argued vehemently in *The Subjection of Women* (1869) that "the principle which regulates the existing social relations between the two sexes—the legal subordination of one sex to the other is wrong in itself . . . and that it ought to be replaced by a principle of perfect equality" ([1869] 1983, 1). Throughout his essay, he repeatedly stressed that women's lesser social achievements were the product of their subjection and that their "true natures" could not really be known because they had been always been kept in a state of subjection. Yet Mill upheld the Victorian ideology of female domesticity in spite of his plea for equality and in spite of his conviction that women should be allowed to hold seats in the House of Commons (see [1869] 1983, 184-86). While he conceded that work is a tool of empowerment and that "[t]he *power* of earning is essential to the dignity of a woman if she has not independent property" (89), he still discouraged most women from exercising this power, arguing that "when the support of the family depends, not on property, but on earnings, the common arrangement, by which the man earns the income and the wife superintends the domestic expenditure, seems to me in general the most suitable division of labour between the two persons" (88).[25]

As Suzanne Graver points out, the scientists whose judgment Eliot valued the most—Comte, Lewes, and Spencer—repudiated essentialism in theory, but still retained vestiges of a metaphysical belief of natural law (including the law of gender) as immanent (see 1984, 157). It seems that Eliot adopted a similar stance because she was either not able or not willing to disregard "scientific evidence," which often appears to have deliberately ignored the fact that any alleged female inferiority might be the result of the historical subjection of women.[26] Yet in spite of her biological knowledge, Eliot often denounces essentialism in her fictional work as she deconstructs gender difference and demands equal rights. She focuses on women who are barred from education (Maggie, Dorothea) and vocational success (Dinah) and who suffer immensely from their relegation to the domestic sphere. In her later works, her heroines gradually invade the "male" sphere: Romola takes over her dead husband's role of breadwinner in his second family; and with the Alcharisi, in her last novel, *Daniel Deronda*, Eliot finally creates a heroine who completely defies the gender roles available to women in the nineteenth-century. It is obvious that from her first novel, *Adam Bede*, she apparently found it much less difficult to deconstruct male gender roles; like Stowe, she often feminized her male heroes. Through her presentation of gender-bending maternal and paternal love and nurturing, or lack thereof, she also persistently deconstructs gender essentialism and undermines the ideology of "separate spheres," which allots utmost importance to the female experience of motherhood.[27]

In addition to a discussion of nineteenth-century scientific discourses on gender, Karen Offen's identification of two different strains of early feminism (reflected in Eliot's work and Fuller's *Woman in the Nineteenth Century*) also helps to elucidate the seeming inconsistencies in Eliot's and Fuller's construction of gender—which can be explained in terms of early feminism's struggle with the prevailing gender ideology and scientific opinion on women. She argues that "relational feminism" (which represented a European tradition excluding Anglo-American feminist thought) "emphasized women's rights *as women* (defined principally by their childbearing and/or nurturing capacities) in relation to men" and "insisted on *women's distinctive* contributions in these roles to the broader society and made claims on the commonwealth on the basis of these contributions" (1988, 136). The Anglo-American "individualist feminist tradition," however, "emphasized more abstract concepts of individual human rights and celebrated the quest for personal independence (or autonomy) in all aspects of life" (136). It accomplished this mainly by downplaying "as insignificant all socially defined roles and minimizing discussion of sex-linked qualities or contributions, including childbearing and its attendant responsibilities" (136).

Offen concedes that in Anglo-American thought prior to the twentieth century, the distinction between these two traditions was not very clear cut, so that "in earlier centuries, evidence of both these modes can often be located in the utterances of a single individual" (136). The examples quoted above show that this certainly is the case in the writing of Fuller and Eliot, who might have helped initiate a paradigm shift from essentialist to constructionist thinking about gender. The essentialist passages of Fuller's and Eliot's writing, which stress the "naturalness" of female affection, gentleness, and maternal tenderness (whereas other passages deny these essentialist claims) can be traced to the (scientific) nineteenth-century gender ideology of the "true womanhood" of the "Angel in the House" which relegated women to the "unproductive" domestic sphere while the lucrative public sphere remained reserved to men.

In an article focusing on the "homoerotics" of Fuller's writing, Mary Wood calls attention to the fact that this division of the world into male and female spheres was carried over into the realm of literary production where women were also limited to writing about the domestic realm, whereas writing about philosophical topics remained a male prerogative. Fuller, according to Wood, challenges and deconstructs this split, but (as I have also shown above) still "vacillates between reinscribing and questioning the difference and complementarity that characterized the ideology of separate spheres" (1993, 7). This mechanism functions on the level of narrative voice as much as on the level of content. The narrator of *Woman in the Nineteenth Century* switches from an initially male to a female voice (as that of Eliot's narrators sometimes does)[28] as Fuller's essay progresses (see Wood 1993, 10–11).

The dynamics of Fuller's and Eliot's writing about gender both uphold and subvert essentialist gender ascriptions as well as the domestic ideology. They thus exhibit a quite obvious "de-naturalizing . . . [a] simultaneous inscribing and subverting of the conventions of narrative" (Hutcheon 1989, 49) which perhaps represents a "prophetic" version of what Linda Hutcheon has deemed (postmodern) complicity and critique. Since what Hutcheon writes about postmodernism actually mirrors the specifics of both Fuller's and Eliot's gender construction, it seems to me that Hutcheon's insights about postmodern literary characteristics do indeed shed some light on Fuller's and Eliot's sometimes unintendedly subversive challenging of dominant gender ideologies. Their writing, like "[t]he postmodern involves a paradoxical installing as well as subverting of conventions—including conventions of the representation of the subject. The complicitous inscribing is as evident as the subverting challenge" (14). Hutcheon argues that it is the paradox inherent in the critical positions of theorists such as Foucault and Lacan who remain "implicated in the notion of center they attempt to subvert" (14) which in fact makes them postmodern. And this postmodernity, according to Hutcheon, has a "de-doxifying" logic of its own. By the same token, one could maintain that Fuller's, Eliot's, and Hawthorne's presentation of gender very similarly, but less playfully because less aware of its subversive power, "de-doxifies" and denaturalizes nineteenth-century literary representations of gender,[29] such as "The Cult of True Womanhood."

Moreover, Teresa de Lauretis's less poststructural critical position sheds additional light on nineteenth-century constructions of gender. It is different from Hutcheon's in that it claims much more leeway and agency for "writing subjects." De Lauretis's question if discourses that "'implant' new objects and modes of knowledge in individual subjects" (1987, 16) need to "become dominant in order for social relations of gender to change" (17) asserts her belief in the power of discourse to effect a resignification of gender ascriptions. Thus she writes about the "contemporary subject emerging from debates about feminism":

> [U]nlike Althusser's subject, who, being completely "in" ideology, believes himself to be outside and free of it, the subject that I see emerging from current writings and debates within feminism is one that is at the same time inside *and* outside the ideology of gender, and conscious of being so, conscious of that two-fold pull, of that division, that doubled vision. (10)

Fuller and Eliot and other nineteenth-century writers, who obviously cannot be claimed as "contemporary subjects," were too deeply ensnared by their societies' "technologies of gender" to be able to intuit the paradox informing their gender politics (their works illustrate the "slippage" built into the Althusserian explanation of the workings of ideology) and therefore they never became fully conscious of the ways in which they revolutionized contemporary gender politics through changing its ideology. But one could, nevertheless, argue that Fuller's and Eliot's constructions of gender are like postmodernist ones in that they represent an early instance of a different kind of subversive gender performativity that effects modification and resignification of the technologies of gender in terms of a more contingently subversive reiteration and appropriation of the law of gender as theorized by Judith Butler in *Gender Trouble* (1990) and *Bodies That Matter* (1993).

Perhaps surprisingly, Nathaniel Hawthorne, who was otherwise known for his social conservatism, in a fascinating but most often overlooked passage from *The Scarlet Letter*, has his heroine voice innovative gender politics that are much more radical than those of Fuller or Eliot:

> Indeed, the same dark question often rose into [Hester's] mind, with reference to the whole race of womanhood. Was existence worth accepting, even to the happiest among them? . . . A tendency to speculation, though it may keep woman quiet, as it does man, yet makes her sad. She discerns, it may be, such a hopeless task before her. As a first step, the whole system of society is to be torn down, to be built up anew. Then, the very nature of the opposite sex, or its long hereditary habit, which has become like nature, is to be essentially modified, before woman can be allowed to assume what seems to be a fair and suitable position. Finally, all of her difficulties being obviated, woman cannot take advantage of these preliminary reforms, until she herself shall have undergone a still mightier change in which, perhaps, the ethereal essence, wherein she has her truest life, will be found to have evaporated. ([1850] 1986, 144)

In this passage, Hawthorne puts several revolutionary thoughts in Hester's mouth: she demands a complete restructuring of society so that "the very nature of the opposite sex . . . is to be essentially modified." In talking about "the very nature of the opposite sex" Hester, one can only speculate, possibly refers to "naturalized" female gender attributes including "beauty," "gentleness," "submissiveness," and other "typically female" personality traits and behavior patterns of the sort listed above by Fuller—and demanded by the "The Cult of True Womanhood."[30] By also referring to "the very nature of the opposite sex" in terms of "a long hereditary habit," Hawthorne, moreover, has Hester conceive of "gender habits" in the same way in which nineteenth-century scientists theorized about "race habits," which were seen as essentialized behavior patterns that, with some effort, could possibly be de-essentialized. But this—and here the narrative perspective of the passage seems to shift to a male perspective regretting this change—could only be achieved at the cost of "woman's ethereal essence, wherein she has her truest life," i.e., of what makes a woman a woman and keeps her, in George Eliot's words, from being "unsexed." Hawthorne thus has Hester voice highly exceptional thoughts on the future arrangement of gender relationships, ideas that are in fact so radical that he himself would and could not have endorsed them.[31]

The passage is particularly astounding in light of his private statements about women who had transgressed gender boundaries, especially if they did so by invading the male domain of authorship. His outburst to his publisher Ticknor about women authors, "America is now wholly given over to d——d mob of scribbling women" (*Letters 1853-56* 1987, 304) has become notorious. Jealous of the (financial) success that the female authors of sentimental romances enjoyed, Hawthorne sometimes could not help praise their work if he deemed it good (as, for example, Fanny Fern's *Ruth Hall*) but he always also had to point out that realistic, "honest" writing by women was inappropriate for reasons of gender propriety (see *Letters 1853–56* 1987, 177).[32] Considering that Hawthorne would have preferred to relegate all female writers to the domestic sphere, one might be inclined to conclude that the sympathy with the "transgressive woman" that he shows in *The Scarlet Letter* defied his own attitude towards sexual power and indicates that he lost control over his narrative. The fact that Hawthorne, as the only male among the authors discussed here, was able to express the most radical attitude toward gender in his fiction also might have to do with the time frame that he chose for *The Scarlet Letter*. Unlike the narrators and characters of the other writers discussed here, Hawthorne did not attempt to describe gender relations in his present or the more recent past. Instead, he used the genre of the historical romance to have a Puritan character project utopian statements into a remote and not really locatable future. George Eliot, however, could not renounce her conservative adherence to nineteenth-century discourses on gender and she also was much more concerned with giving advice to her contemporaries rather than future generations. Therefore, in *Adam Bede* (or anywhere else), she does not follow Hawthorne in his bold future-oriented deconstruction of gender presented in *The Scarlet Letter*; she instead decides to align herself with Fuller's and Stowe's gender perspectives, which are rather tame by comparison.

American Character/istic/s

Eliot's adoption of Fuller's and Stowe's perspectives also provides an explanation as to why, in *Adam Bede*, she decided to split Hawthorne's Hester character into two halves, a tainted "transgressive" and an untainted "domestic" one. The insights of the pioneering American feminist critics Sandra Gilbert and Susan Gubar, who were among the first to have significantly contributed to an understanding of George Eliot's conception of gender (especially in relation to American fiction) offer a clue for the necessity of "character splitting." Proceeding from the thesis that "Margaret Fuller and Harriet Beecher Stowe . . . seem to embody for her the warring impulses at work in her own art" (1980, 479), they argue that with Fuller Eliot had in common a desire to "transcend the limits of her sex" (479) and to "combine a man's mind with a woman's heart" (483) both in the "world of the intellect and action" (479). Yet at the same time, like Stowe, she wanted to "live a full life within traditional female roles" (532). Hetty and Dinah, the "split characters" from *Adam Bede* illustrate this "warring impulse"; Hetty transcends the limits of her sex (albeit in a very undesirable way), whereas Dinah, even though she initially enters the "world of intellect and action," finally succumbs to traditional domesticity. For Eliot's art this ambiguity, according to Gilbert and Gubar, had as a consequence that she did not heed Fuller's call of women "to the Minerva side" ([1845] 1994, 204). "Fuller had asserted the necessity of women acquiring 'masculine' powers of intellect," yet Eliot seems "to have preferred Stowe's emphasis on the need for men to develop 'feminine' receptivity, specifically that of female nurturance" (Gilbert and Gubar 1980, 482). But this does not necessarily mean that Eliot herself wholeheartedly agreed that her female characters, who more often than not are kept from developing their intellect and forced into submission (read marriage) in Eliot's novels, should happily acquiesce in their lot. Following Carol Christ's important lead that "the providential death [of oppressor characters] . . . allows Eliot both to avoid aggression by eliminating the situation that inspired hostility and to prohibit aggression by the recognitions that the deaths inspire in her characters" (1976, 131), Gilbert and Gubar reach the key conclusion about Eliot's gender politics that "the contradiction between feminine renunciation countenanced by the narrator and female (even feminist) vengeance exacted by the author—remains an important one in Eliot's fiction" (1980, 491).

More recently, Kimberly vanEsveld Adams has argued that, in reference to Eliot's relationship with U.S. literature in feminizing and apotheosizing male characters—as for example the Christlike *Adam Bede*—Eliot does not necessarily only emulate Stowe's maternal Christ figure, Uncle Tom, but also follows Feuerbach, who first proclaims the Virgin Mary part of the trinity but then ousts her after relocating the feminine element in the Son (see Adams 1996, 44–45). Eliot, similarly, first centers on Dinah's spirituality, but after stressing the feminine, maternal element in Adam Bede, makes him the central protagonist of her book. Adams views *Adam Bede*'s Dinah as a variant of an ideal of virginity—the Madonna as Virgin Mother. According to Adams, Fuller presents the Madonna in *Woman in the Nineteenth Century* as a feminist means to counteract the ideology of "true womanhood" through self-reliant empowerment of female characters. Dinah, however, "God-empowered as body-denying virgin" (57) exemplifies a newly emerging nineteenth-century ideal of a self-sufficient, self-reliant woman who (at least for a while in Dinah's case), devoid of any ties to a domineering man, is free to meditate about her God-given nature and her relationship with God.

I agree with Adams that Dinah's inability to achieve true Virgin Motherhood in *Adam Bede* (Dinah gets "conventionally" married and is subsequently silenced by the Methodist church and by Eliot) suggests, at least in some way, that "[t]he Madonna in Eliot . . . represents the state woman should but cannot yet achieve" (61). But I still want to point out that Adams's reading of Dinah as Fullerian Madonna is somewhat problematic if one considers the differences in the philosophies underlying Dinah and the Fullerian Madonna.[33] The most important problem with Adams's interpretation is that Eliot's presentation of the figure of Dinah as Madonna has other philosophical goals than those that Adams imputes to her: Dinah simply is not an American feminist transcendentalist Madonna who has a fortunate premature manifestation in English Hayslope at the turn of the nineteenth-century. Instead, she is Eliot's representative of an archaic Methodism, and as such her "feminist seeming independence" is more accidental and might at best hint at the future possibility of female self-realization through self-sufficiency. Fuller's Madonna, however, (which has to be put in relief against her creator's transcendentalist background—a background that is quite different from the brand of Methodism presented by Eliot because transcendentalism performs an apotheosis of the individual) is, in spite of the spiritual rhetoric, first and foremost a programmatic secular figure pointing towards the possibility of female empowerment through temporary celibacy which provides "a room of one's own" to think in.[34] But Eliot's depiction of Dinah as a Madonna figure, if not necessarily a Fullerian Madonna, is nevertheless important because it points toward another explanation for Eliot's decision to divide Hawthorne's Hester character into a "good" and a "bad" half. By purifying Hester as Dinah, Eliot might have wanted to gesture towards the important spiritual role that a strong female character like Hawthorne's Hester could have played in an extremely conservative theocratic society if she had not been tainted by sexual desire ("making an imperfect man her god") and adultery.[35]

Lori Lefkovitz, who describes Hetty and Dinah as "inseparable as body and soul, with overwhelming need for another" (1987, 92), ventures another thought-provoking explanation for Eliot's character splitting when she suggests that "she spares her heroine pain by again distinguishing between sexual and spiritual beauty (Hetty and Dinah, respectively), a distinction that Hawthorne blurs" (1987, 89). At this point, any critic familiar with Eliot's biography may perhaps be tempted to speculate that Eliot, who through her association with George Henry Lewes counted in at least some circles as a "fallen woman," might have stayed away for purely personal reasons from including a strong "fallen woman" character—especially one like

Hester, who proudly announces about her relationship with Dimmesdale that "what we did had a consecration of its own" ([1850] 1986, 170). Eliot's biographers stress that Eliot felt married to Lewes and did not view herself as a "fallen woman," but her public image must, nevertheless, have caused her a great deal of private pain, which she seems not to have wanted to address in her writing.

Contemporary feminist critics are often disappointed in Eliot's depiction of her women characters because she failed to create a heroine who, like herself, managed to successfully realize her desire on both a personal and a professional level. It certainly is a moot point to try to figure out whether Eliot did not create a heroine resembling herself because she felt that her success had come at too great a cost or whether she wanted to deny a similar success to "less exceptional" women. Critics, nevertheless, keep trying to find reasons for Eliot's failure to present a heroine who is passionate about her personal life and her vocation. As many commentators have noted, the desire that Eliot refuses her heroines need not necessarily be sexual desire, but can also be vocational desire. Thus, Dorothea Barrett complains about Dinah's lot that "the only heroine in any of the George Eliot novels who has a definite vocation . . . relinquishes her work without apparent pain, and subsides into the role of helpmate and mother" (1989, 42). But Barrett, nevertheless, belongs to the camp of Eliot critics who view Eliot's refusal to "properly" empower her heroines as reflection of insurmountable "social impediments" (43), which take the form of both internalized social norms and external restraints imposed by society. Unlike critics who, based on Eliot's female protagonists' lack of actual "feminist" accomplishments and her critical attitude towards the women's movement decide that Eliot was not a feminist (see Mitchell 1994, 87), Barrett, trying to reclaim Eliot for feminism, follows critical opinion that suggests that even though Eliot might have wanted to recommend female submissiveness, "the texts themselves subvert her intention" (1989, 42).

This critical unease about Eliot's depiction of gender issues also extends itself to her presentation of individual characters such as *Adam Bede*'s Hetty and Dinah, who, for various reasons—among them certainly Eliot's inability to have enough foresight to create heroines who conform to the expectations of "modern" feminists—fail to satisfy critics. And, I would like to argue, the vague sense of disappointment that the Hetty/Dinah pair leaves the reader with might also be due to that fact that Eliot creates two "diminished" characters by splitting Hawthorne's compelling figure Hester (who appeals even to twenty-first-century critics) into two separate figures. Many commentators feel that "Eliot harasses Hetty" (Karl 1995, 271) by presenting her as an almost entirely negative character who fails to evoke sympathy. The negative impression that Hetty leaves is created in particular by the fact that George Eliot—who according to all reports was physically rather plain —seems to imply that physical beauty must necessarily lead to murderous shallowness. Eliot's narrator, who deliberately steers the reader towards disliking Hetty, for example, implies at one point that Hetty loves Arthur less than the locket and the pretty earrings that he buys for her.

It might have been Eliot's fear of divulging details from her private life— as well as the fact that she could not simply copy Hawthorne's strong and ambiguous "scarlet woman"—that caused her to portray her own Hester as an extremely immature and self-serving teenager, incapable of experiencing the strong feelings that Hawthorne's passionate adult heroine Hester experiences. Eliot seems to have lost control over her character in spite of her strong attempt to give a very definite impression of Hetty; in the following quotation Karl provides a plausible explanation for Eliot's mean-spirited characterization of Hetty:

> In a sense, Hetty "gets away" from the author precisely because, while she is treated so unsympathetically, she still stands for so much Eliot has to deal with. Despite her harsh handling of her young beauty, Eliot could not quite control her: Hetty seeks to raise herself not by intellect but by physical wiles, and this does not fit easily into the author's frame of reference. As a fallen creature, Hetty, with all her posturing and simpering manner, becomes a subtle yet demonic double of Eliot's own desire to rise, achieve, emerge. (1995, 296)

By the same token, one could argue that Hawthorne's Hester, who calls for a complete deconstruction of the sex/gender system, similarly "got away" from her creator because Hawthorne invented her in spite of his social conservatism, which made him denounce the achievement of strong, accomplished women in his private writing and which, in his fiction, ultimately led him to deny triumph to Hester and made him kill off the equally strong "fallen woman," Zenobia, in *The Blithedale Romance*.

Like Hetty, Dinah also qualifies as a diminished version of Hester, who only fulfills Hester's role as selfless nurse to the community but is not invested with any of the engaging "revolutionary" ideas of Hawthorne's heroine. Thus, as already indicated above, Eliot follows neither Hawthorne nor Fuller in transforming the Madonna into a feminist. The pale, bloodless Dinah, and her seemingly passionless relationship with her future husband, Adam, often do not fare much better with contemporary critics than her counterpart Hetty. Modern commentators often criticize Eliot's conception of Dinah for her heroine's inability to show any passion other than religious passion and for even having to give that up—without a fight—together with her chosen vocation of a traveling minister after she gets married to Adam.[36]

Eliot's deconstruction of male gender roles by deliberately feminizing quite a few of her male characters (e.g. Adam Bede, Philip Wakem, Will Ladislaw, Daniel Deronda) has impressed feminist critics more favorably than her presentation of female gendered behavior. It seems that Eliot, like Stowe, had much less difficulty in "unsexing" males by attributing "female" qualities (gentleness, motherliness, etc.) to them, than she had in "masculinizing" females by investing them with "male" qualities other than "superior intellect" (e.g. aggressiveness, ambition, etc.). Hawthorne, conversely, apparently found "feminized" men very difficult to stomach.

The presence of *The Scarlet Letter* is most palpable in *Adam Bede*, yet Eliot's later work also shows that she often came back to issues presented in the novel. Thus, the characterization of Maggie, the protagonist of *The Mill of the Floss*, seems to be indebted to Hester from *The Scarlet Letter*, while the novel's plot structure is also reminiscent of *The Blithedale Romance*. Like Hester, the "inappropriately" tall and dark Maggie initially defies gender ascriptions: she outsmarts her brother in her academic work, cuts off her hair, and pushes her ultra feminine, blonde and pink cousin Lucy in the mud. In her young adulthood, Maggie, who "represents George Eliot's closest approximation of a female subject of desire" (1994, 107), actively desires a man who seems somewhat unworthy of her, as does Hester—Stephen comes across as vain and shallow; and Dimmesdale's loyalty to Hester does not match her loyalty for him. But while Hawthorne allows Hester to be the active partner in her love relationship with Dimmesdale and to show moral ambiguity in her actions, Maggie is denied such overtly subversive behavior. At first her actions seem ambiguous like Hester's because she desires a man who, as her cousin's fiancé, is off-limits. But it soon becomes clear that Maggie is denied Hester's freedom of making an immoral choice; thus, unlike Hester, who suggests to Dimmesdale that they run away together, Maggie does not take the active part in their planned escape. On a boat ride, it is Stephen who suggests eloping, but Maggie—after having had a dream in which both her almost fiancé, Philip, and her brother Tom act as "boatmen," steering her to act according to the Law of the Father—decides that she cannot make the "choice of the lower" and renounces her desire for Stephen:

> There was at least this fruit from all of her years of striving after the highest and best—that her soul, though betrayed, beguiled, ensnared, could never

deliberately consent to a choice of the lower. And a choice of what? O God—not a choice of joy—but of conscious cruelty and hardness; for she could never cease to see before her Lucy and Philip with their murdered trust and hopes? ([1880] 1979, 597)

Maggie is finally spared the lot of the "fallen woman" in more than one way; her morality and virginity are left intact and, by accidentally drowning, she does not have to suffer the shame of being treated like a fallen woman by a society that, after her escape with Stephen, would automatically have treated her accordingly.

One can only speculate why Maggie, like Hetty and Dinah, ultimately, becomes a "diminished," less ambiguous, and therefore less interesting, version of Hawthorne's passionate heroine Hester. For one, Eliot has Maggie face a more clear-cut choice than Hester, who committed adultery thinking that her husband was dead. Thus, she is necessarily left with much less room for moral ambiguity. And one also has to take into account the fact that Eliot's novels had a different objective than Hawthorne's. With his historical novels about Puritanism, Hawthorne meant to criticize both the narrow-minded religious theocracy of his forebears which discouraged individualism as well as a more universal egotistic individualism. Eliot, however, always saw herself as a moral teacher, whose aim it was to improve contemporary society by instructing her readership in a "religion of humanity" which advocated self-renouncing sympathy. Thus, Daniel Cottom is probably not too far off the mark in suggesting that it was Eliot's quasi-religious calling to promote incontrovertibly "moral" middle class values which made it simply impossible for her to create morally ambiguous protagonists (see 1987, 130).

Eliot's didacticism certainly played a major role in her conception of Maggie and other heroines. But in light of biographical criticism that claims that *The Mill on the Floss* (1860) reflected Eliot's own relationship with her brother Isaac, who broke off contact with her after she started to live with George Henry Lewes, one again is bound to wonder if her decision to have Maggie renounce Stephen—and thus "do the right thing"—might not again be an attempt to rework her personal biography. In addition to resembling Hester, Maggie also has much in common with Hawthorne's Zenobia from *The Blithedale Romance*. Like Zenobia, she is associated with demonic Medusa and Dark Lady imagery.[37] Dark and fair ladies from British and American romance tradition (in particular the novels of Sir Walter Scott and James Fenimore Cooper, respectively) apparently appealed to both Hawthorne and Eliot, who peopled their novels with many fair and dark characters such as Hetty and Dinah and Zenobia and Priscilla. In *The Blithedale*

Romance, the dark Zenobia becomes entangled with her fair half-sister Priscilla in a triangular relationship with the mesmerizer Westervelt. Later, both sisters vie for the love of the social reformer Hollingsworth. When Hollingsworth does not fall for Zenobia's advances and denigrates her feminism, she drowns herself, and Priscilla finally marries the reformer. In *The Mill on the Floss*, the Dark Lady Maggie[38] defies her beloved brother's patriarchism, runs off with Stephen Guest, renounces him—like a good girl— and then drowns while trying to save her brother's life. Lucy, the Fair Lady, eventually gets her fiancé back. The ending of *Mill on the Floss* resembles that of *The Scarlet Letter,* but with a twist: Hester, who defied authority, is finally reunited in adultery with her lover, Dimmesdale, and buried next to him: "On a field, sable, the Letter A. Gules" ([1850] 1986, 228). Maggie, however, who had given in to patriarchal authority, is buried next to her brother: "The tomb bore the names of Tom and Maggie Tulliver and below the names it was written 'In their death they were not divided'" ([1860] 1979, 657). And there is yet another resemblance to *The Blithedale Romance*: at the end of Hawthorne's novel, the narrator talks about Zenobia's grave being visited by Hollingsworth and himself, the two men who were in love with her. In *The Mill on the Floss* this is paralleled by a depiction of Maggie's tomb being visited by both Stephen and Philip (Maggie's deformed admirer who is feminized in relation to her as Dimmesdale is feminized in relation to Hester).

Eliot comes back to another aspect of *The Scarlet Letter*—the unhappy marriage of a vital young heroine to an older man who cannot live up to her expectations—in *Middlemarch*. In the case of both marriages, critics have speculated that part of the couples' marital problems is impotence. Both Hester's marriage to Chillingworth and Dorothea's marriage to Casaubon remain childless; but perhaps even more important than physical impotence is the emotional sterility of the scholars, who, as husbands, are much more inclined to "feed the hungry dream of knowledge" ([1850] 1986, 68) than to satisfy the needs of a much younger wife—even if these needs also turn out to be mostly educational as in Dorothea's case. Claudia Johnson has demonstrated very aptly that Hawthorne has set up an intricate argument which suggests that physical impotence equals creative impotence. This (creative) impotence attacks the principal male characters in the novel: Chillingworth is often seen gathering "herbs of potency" that are supposed to cure impotence, and the narrator of "The Custom House" essay preceding the novel complains about his creative fountain running dry. Ironically, it is the death-bound Dimmesdale, who, toward the end of the novel, perhaps by then suffering from sexual as well as creative dysfunction, reanimates the creative process by writing his highly imaginative election sermon.[39]

Eliot—who must have discerned Hawthorne's rather submerged argument about the connection of sexual and creative impotence—brings the matter much closer to the surface in *Middlemarch* by immediately associating Casaubon's possible sexual failure with the failure of his "Key to all Mythologies":[40]

> [H]e had reflected that in taking a wife, a man of good position should expect and carefully choose a blooming young lady—the younger the better, because more educable and submissive. . . . [I]n return, he should receive family pleasures and leave behind him a copy of himself which seemed so urgently required of a man—to the sonneteers of the sixteenth century. Times had altered since then, and no sonneteer had insisted on Mr. Casaubon's leaving a copy of himself; moreover, he had not yet succeeded in issuing copies of his mythological key. ([1871–72] 1994, 278)

When it dawns on Casaubon that Dorothea is not nearly as submissive as he would like her to be and that she has realized that his mythological key is not likely to open any doors, the already "shallow rill" (63) of his passion seems to dry up completely. His "religious faith wavered with his wavering trust in his own authorship" (280); he develops a heart condition and fails to "leave a copy of himself." Dorothea and Hester find their own way out of the predicament of being married to an older, possibly impotent man. Hawthorne has Hester welcome the false supposition that Chillingworth has perished during the passage from England to America and, therefore, allows her to commit adultery with the then still vigorous Dimmesdale. Eliot, however, again denies her heroine Dorothea (who in some ways is a more spirited version of Dinah from *Adam Bede*) Hester's moral ambiguity by giving her a respectable way out: Casaubon dies one of the frequent providential deaths in Eliot's fiction and Dorothea is free to marry the young and attractive Will Ladislaw. After *Middlemarch*, Eliot comes back once more to Hester, Dimmesdale, and *The Scarlet Letter* in her Italian novel, *Romola*, as will be shown in the next chapter.

THE MICROCOSMS OF *OLDTOWN FOLKS* AND *MIDDLEMARCH*

Gender, Religion, and Society

The "domestic" concerns of *Middlemarch* (1871–72) are paralleled by those of Harriet Beecher Stowe's *Oldtown Folks* (1869). The two novels not only show that Stowe and Eliot mutually inspired each other, but also indicate that they pursued a very similar aim: to portray everyday life in a small town which serves as a microcosm that reflects social issues which also regard the larger society that these towns are located in. In their rendering of small town life in the U.S. shortly after the American Revolution, and England at the time of the first Reform Bill, Stowe and Eliot, respectively, pay meticulous attention to the social and intellectual climate of the times their novels are set in. Eliot wrote *Middlemarch* as a centerpiece of her project of following cutting-edge scientists of her day in comparing society to a natural organism in which human beings function as more or less reliable individual "social organs"; Stowe, in *Oldtown Folks*, without explicitly invoking organicism, addresses very similar questions of how the individual fits into a society that is trying to establish a uniquely American identity after having thrown off British rule.

As gender relationships are among the most important social determinants in both novels, I will begin my analysis of social relations in the microcosms of Oldtown and Middlemarch by discussing the role of female education as a possible road to personal fulfillment and more satisfying gender relationships. Interestingly enough, Stowe's *Oldtown Folks* often reads as if she, after having studied *The Mill on the Floss*, decided to give Eliot advice about how to incorporate female educational and vocational success in her novels.[41] Eliot's *The Mill on the Floss* thematizes Maggie's educational dilemma but finds no solution to her problem of being too smart for her own good in a society that does not value the education of women. At the beginning of the novel, Mr. Tulliver already complains that "'a pleasant sort of woman may go on breeding you stupid lads and cute wenches, till it's like as if the world was turned topsy-turvy'" ([1871–72] 1994, 68–69). Even though he realizes that his daughter Maggie would "'ha been a match for the lawyers, she would'" (68), following social constraints, he has to waste the money he can afford for his children's education on his much less gifted son, Tom. Eliot uses her description of Tom's tenure as a pupil at Mr. Stelling's school (where his education unfortunately focuses on the classics instead of the drafting skills he could actually have used in his professional life) to showcase Maggie's intellectual gifts. Thus, for example, only through Maggie, who is denied access to the knowledge she covets, does Tom find out that Latin is a language that once was actually spoken by people in their everyday communications. Tom's teacher, Mr. Stelling, in spite of being impressed by Maggie's intellect, informs her that girls "'have a great deal of superficial cleverness: but they couldn't go far into anything. They're quick and shallow'" (221). Maggie, in spite of these disparaging remarks, once more attempts to find solace in Tom's schoolbooks after her father's bankruptcy. She tries to console herself by thinking that "Latin, Euclid and Logic would surely be a considerable step in masculine wisdom —in that knowledge which made men contented and even glad to live" (379–80).[42] Later, she desperately attempts to give meaning to her life by studying Thomas à Kempis's work in order to learn renunciation. But the knowledge Maggie is able to acquire by autodidactic means does not provide her with a way out of her conundrum since it will not help her find a vocation in her society. Having lost her stature as a commodity in the marriage market with her father's business failure, Maggie is denied a place in society. Eliot finally disposes of this "superfluous female" by having her drown after her unsuccessful elopement with her cousin Lucy's fiancé. In *Oldtown Folks*, Stowe, however, shows how education can actually help individuals lead satisfied lives, regardless of their social and class background, which can be transcended by means of it. *Oldtown Folks* tells the story of the coming of age of its narrator Horace Holyoke, a young boy living in somewhat impoverished circumstances after his father's early death, and his orphaned friends Harry and Tina Percival. In accordance with Horace's observation that "education might be said to be the ruling passion of the state" ([1869] 1982, 1102) of Massachusetts, the Oldtown folks and the wealthy Tory Boston relatives of one of the town's families see to it that the three children, in spite of having lost their fathers as providers, do not have to forfeit their seemingly inalienable right to a good education. Presenting a matrifocal universe run by capable women such as Horace's grandmother, a "female ruler" (1071), Stowe strongly focuses on the personal satisfaction that women can derive from education and vocation. Thus, the novel features quite a few "positive spinster characters," who, like Fuller's "virgins,"[43] are "self-reliant, self taught, self-fulfilled beings" (Adams 2001, 127) and who seem to have heeded Fuller's advice that "celibacy [is] the great fact of the time" ([1845] 1994, 295). Considering that Miss Minerva Randall (housekeeper to the school teacher brother of Tina's foster mother Miss Mehitable) actually is a sea-captain of sorts[44] one might wonder if Stowe perhaps conceived of her with Fuller's *Woman in the Nineteenth Century* in mind. At any rate, Stowe's narrator describes "Nervy" Randall as an absolutely satisfied, wholly self-reliant character:

> Study and work had been the two passions of her life, and in neither could she be excelled by man or woman. Single-handed, and without a servant, she performed all the labors of Mr. Jonathan Rossiter's little establishment . . . and found, also, time, to read Greek and Latin authors and to work out problems in mathematics and surveying and navigation, and to take charge of boys in reading Virgil. ([1869] 1982, 1292)

> She wore always a stuff petticoat of her own spinning, with a striped linen short gown, and probably all in her life never expended twenty dollars a year for clothing and yet Miss Nervy was about the happiest female person whose acquaintance it has ever been my fortune to make. She had just as much as she wanted of exactly the two things she liked best in the world,—books and work, and when her work was done, there were the books, and life could give no more. Miss Nervy had not sentiment,—not a particle of romance,—she was the most perfectly contented mortal that could possibly be imagined. (1293)

In reference to "domestic work" Stowe here actually does what Moira Gatens accuses most male writers and social philosophers of not doing (see Gatens 1991)—she allots to it the status of "real work" by valuing it as socially necessary and productive labor. Moreover, her narrator does not fail to point out that being an early feminist is another constituting aspect of Miss Nervy's contentedness: "[She] was one of those female persons who are of Sojourner Truth's opinion, that if women want any rights they had better take them, and say nothing about it. Her *sex* had never occurred to her as a reason for doing or not doing anything which her hand found to do" (1292).

If Miss Nervy can be seen as Stowe's example of a Fullerian "virgin," then Miss Mehitable, who adopts Tina (illustrating Stowe's and Eliot's conviction that "true" motherhood need not be grounded in biological motherhood) can be viewed as a Fullerian "Madonna" of sorts, a woman who is "self-centered," not "absorbed by any relation" to a man (even though Miss Mehitable certainly wishes she were), and a virgin mother like Mary. Unlike Miss Nervy, Miss Mehitable has a romantic, nurturing side to her character that complements her "masculine" intellect: "But in her quaint, uncomely body was lodged, not only a most active and even masculine mind, but a heart capable of those passionate extremes of devotion which belong to the purely feminine side of woman" (1106). It is this "female softness" that enables Miss Mehitable to open her heart to the orphan girl Tina and to adopt her.

One thing that becomes immediately evident from both Miss Mehitable's and Miss Nervy's description is that Stowe furbishes her "virgins" and "Madonnas" with "masculine" minds and unattractive physical characteristics. Thus, Miss Nervy is described as "ugly as Hecate" (1101) by Mr. Rossiter, who, apparently provoked by this female "ugliness," also assures "'I shall not fall in love with her'" (1102). Yet while Miss Nervy seems totally unconcerned about her lack of beauty, Miss Mehitable Rossiter puts an "extravagant valuation on personal beauty" and forever regrets being condemned to have "borne the curse of marked plainness" (1107). The aptly named Miss Asphyxia, the only disagreeable spinster in *Oldtown Folks*, from whose strict work regimen Tina is finally saved by Mehitable Rossiter, likewise features masculine bodily characteristics that keep men from developing an interest in her. Her utter unattractiveness, however, derives from the fact that, like her equally disagreeable married brother, she has internalized the Puritan work ethic to the point of turning herself into a machine.[45]

Like the other writers discussed in this chapter, Stowe apparently found it difficult to de-essentialize "gender specific" personality traits. In addition to also vacillating between constructionist and essentialist notions of gender identity, she does not separate conventional "internal" from conventional "external" gender characteristics. Thus, while she accepted that an intelligent woman could have a "masculine" mind, she could not conceive of this intelligent woman as also possessing "feminine" beauty. Conversely, she similarly associated extraordinary beauty, such as Tina's, with rather negative qualities of "female" slyness:[46]

> The girl . . . had in her all the elements of a little bundle of womanhood, born to rule and command in a purely womanly way. She was affectionate, gay, pleasure-loving, self-willed, imperious, intensely fond of appropriation. . . . She had, too, that capacity of secretiveness which enabled her to carry out the dictates of a strong will, and an intuitive sense of where to throw a tendril or strike a little fibre of persuasion or coaxing, which comes early to those fair parasites who are to live by climbing upon others, and to draw their hues and sweetness from the warmth of other hearts. (990–91)

But, since Stowe is not very steadfast about her essentialism, she concedes that Tina's inborn negative female characteristics can be altered—the adolescent Tina is described as "so intensely sympathetic with all social influence that she scarcely seemed to have an individuality of her own" (1326). Apparently lacking a "core self," Tina seems to be an entirely constructible proto-postmodern woman.

Stowe's obvious uncertainty about whether or not gender specific behavior modes are essential or socially constructed progresses as the novel advances. The following observation on Horace's part suggests that Stowe thought it entirely possible that gender specific behavior could be "unessential," merely "acquired" behavior:

> There is now a general plea in society that women shall be educated more as men are, and we hear much talk as if the difference between them and our

sex is merely one of difference in education. But how could it be helped that Tina should be educated and formed wholly unlike Harry and myself, when every address made to her from childhood was of necessity wholly different from what would be made to a boy in the same circumstances? (1275)

Moreover, Stowe has her narrator Horace thematize another gender problem—namely that of the "future social uses of the beautiful woman"—in the chapter "What Shall We Do with Tina?" Here, Horace and Tina's brother, Harry, deplore the fact that, unlike their own, Tina's education will ultimately not benefit her since, instead of taking a university degree or going to work, Tina only seems to have the beautiful woman's choice of getting married. In their discussion about "the uses of Tina," the boys realize that Tina really cannot do anything after her graduation except to "wait for the coming man" (1374) with whom, hopefully, she will have a relationship resembling a "marriage of true souls." As it turns out, Tina's first husband, Ellery Davenport, proves to be a bad choice (even though he does not manage to lead her astray), but she subsequently finds male guidance in Horace Holyoke. Unfortunately, Stowe does not volunteer her own opinion on Harry's helpful interjection that Tina is to wait for a man "who is to teach her what to do" (1374), so that the exchange between Horace and Harry remains very ambiguous in its presentation of gender relations. In *Oldtown Folks* Stowe thus presents three Fullerian solutions to the female gender conundrum: the plain, but highly intelligent self-reliant "virgin" (Miss Nervy) obtains satisfaction from books and her vocational experience; the also rather plain but more nurturing intellectual woman (Miss Mehitable) finds her calling in her role as adoptive mother and "Madonna"; and—last and perhaps least—the pretty and smart, but a tad less intellectual, woman (Tina, Esther) finds satisfaction along with "male guidance" in a "marriage of true souls."

George Eliot had read both *Oldtown Folks* and *Woman in the Nineteenth Century* before authoring *Middlemarch*, but there is no indication that she meant to follow the American example, devised by Fuller and Stowe, of positing "educated spinsterhood" as a viable alternative to "true womanhood." Thus, in *Adam Bede*, she refrains from fashioning Dinah as a Fullerian "feminist" Madonna and in *Middlemarch* she shies away from endorsing any of Stowe's vocational options for women. Also valuing education extremely highly, Eliot, furthermore, does not follow Stowe in making education a panacea to almost all social ills. Even though she presents gender relationships as a hindrance to personal fulfillment in *Middlemarch*, she does not apply the American remedy of putting women to work to the gender trouble she saw in her own society. This might, at least in part, be due to her conviction that English society, featuring a much more differentiated class system, would not support the integration of women from various backgrounds into the world of productive labor. Thus, it does not occur to Eliot to have the members of her "better society," such as Dorothea and Celia Brooke, stoop down to work as domestic companions or governesses rather than marry, and she often invests her clergymen with unmarried female relatives whom they have to support (e.g. Mr. Irwine, Mr. Farebrother). Eliot's female characters seem to dislike the idea of working outside of their own homes since female domestic labor—the only vocation then available to women besides teaching—does not seem to be valued as "real work" in their society as it is in Stowe's Oldtown. The "plain" but educated Mary Garth, for example, who does not have the privilege of being a member of the class of the landed gentry, prefers marriage to Fred Vincy (who is not a bit appalled by her "plainness"), to working as a private teacher. Moreover, Eliot's refusal to employ her heroines as domestic laborers might have to do with the fact that she, being a highly intelligent "plain" woman herself, had to do domestic work in her father's and her brother's households prior to becoming a writer. Having rejected for herself the role of the "bookish and mannish spinster" (who besides having to perform domestic chores is denied any expression of her sexuality) Eliot might not have wished it on her female protagonists, either.

Another explanation for her refusal to improve the lives of her female characters by means of vocational success might be that George Eliot, even though she might have wanted to, could not entirely ignore the "authoritative" voice of nineteenth-century (social) science when it made pronouncements about the subservient position women were to assume in society's private sphere because biology had given them the natural capacity of child bearing. In their sociological treatises Herbert Spencer and John Stuart Mill, for example, also addressed the inevitable question of how women—whom the new biological science of evolution viewed at least as different if not inferior—fit into the organic whole of society. As indicated above, Spencer, having supported women's equal rights in "The Rights of Women" (1851) had considerably changed his initially positive attitude by the 1870s and argued against any extensive change in the education of women because of their "natural" limitations.[47] And even Mill, who strongly endorsed the equality of women in *The Subjection of Women* (1869), advocated relegating women to the domestic sphere—ostensibly for the greater good of the family and society.

Eliot's attitude towards female submissiveness is quite ambiguous. She apparently found it very difficulty to discredit "scientific" opinion about "woman's (submissive) nature," yet the female characters featured in *Middlemarch*, nevertheless, consistently fail to submit to their husbands' expectations of submissiveness. By the same token, even though she joined the ranks that demanded higher education for women, and even though her novels provide a running commentary about the many ways in which women were disadvantaged by "The Cult of True Womanhood," she still sided with Mill in not opting for women to compete in the workplace, but rather wanted them to exert the positive moral influence that she repeatedly alluded to. Thus, in *Middlemarch*, Dorothea, who, of course, does not have access to higher education in spite of her intellectual resources which would have allowed her to be a scholar in her own right, is reduced to performing social work as another type of "socially unproductive labor."

Middlemarch does not offer any positive solutions whatsoever to the gender conundrum. Eliot rejects Fuller's and Stowe's suggestions regarding the social empowerment of women, yet at the same time she also shows that both science and the nineteenth-century ideology of gender will not improve gender relations and that personal intelligence is of no help in selecting a partner. Dorothea's pathetic and much commented upon marriage to Casaubon and Lydgate's equally frustrating marriage to Rosamond are good examples of this. Dorothea's choice of Casaubon for a husband is already tragic because to her it seems to be the only way of obtaining the education in the classics that she would like to have. British nineteenth-century gender ideology saw to it that—unlike Stowe's Miss Nervy—an intelligent woman of higher social rank could not easily satisfy her longing for books. Being denied access to the university as well as the workplace, a person like Dorothea Brooke could only fulfill her intellectual ambition in a "marriage of true souls." Unfortunately, in Dorothea's case the marriage ideal fails miserably; she and Casaubon never become soulmates. Moreover, the nineteenth-century gender ideology also falls short of its promises in that Dorothea's frequent submission to Casaubon does not deliver the effect of spiritual ennoblement of the male partner in the relationship. This, as Eliot's narrator points out, is due to the fact that Casaubon becomes highly unwilling to indulge Dorothea because he, likewise, suffers immensely from the marriage once he has realized that his young wife, having become aware of his intellectual failure, is not as submissive as he expects her to be. Having finally found her soulmate in Will Ladislaw, Dorothea becomes much happier in her second marriage. But, apparently due to the all pervasive ideology of female subservience, she still remains trapped in her role of helpmate to her husband, who, as a "public man," can help initiate some of the reforms that Dorothea hopes for.

The gender relations of the medical doctor and ambitious researcher, Tertius Lydgate, are similarly unfortunate, even though his search for a wife is informed by "scientific considerations" as well as the tenets of nineteenth-century gender ideology. As the novel advances, Eliot shows that the (male) privileges of education and scientific knowledge do not save Lydgate from selecting the wrong partner twice. Lydgate's life story exemplifies how a combination of individual and ideological "fate" can cause a person to fall short of his life expectations—in spite of a superior education. His rash temperament causes him to fall in love with the rather murderous French *femme fatale* Madame Laure; the same character trait, combined with an adherence to nineteenth-century gender conventions makes him marry Rosamond. When studying in Paris, he becomes infatuated with the actress Madame Laure, who murdered her fellow actor husband (by deliberately stabbing him on stage during a theatrical "stabbing scene") for the simple reason that he wanted to live in Paris rather than where she was from. As a consequence of this upsetting encounter with the abysses of female nature, Lydgate resolves that "henceforth he would take a strictly scientific view of woman, entertaining no expectations, but such as were justified beforehand" ([1871–72] 1994, 153). Yet, as Jacqueline Rose astutely points out, the male prerogative of access to the controlling discourse of science and his "scientific male gaze" do not necessarily help him control femaleness:

> Lydgate's research follows [the] paradigm [of new nineteenth-century science]: "he was ambitious above all to contribute towards enlarging the scientific, rational basis of his profession." But the very chapter which most clearly states this ambition—of character and writer alike—also reveals its opposite, that is, a form of looking at the woman that suddenly tips over into complicity with a sexual crime. Chapter 15 of *Middlemarch* suggests, therefore, that the controlling knowledge of science is threatened, but also guaranteed—upheld even—by the image of a female sexuality gone wild. (1986, 110)

I agree with Rose that with Madame Laure Eliot has—again—created a character who, in her vehement defiance of the female submissiveness required by the nineteenth-century ideology of gender, might have escaped her narrative control. But I do not agree with her suggestion that in this scene the controlling scientific knowledge is "upheld" by Eliot in an "image of a female sexuality gone wild." It rather seems to me that Eliot suggests that gender, and whatever its difference actually is, cannot adequately be described by nineteenth-century science. By arguing that "Eliot responded to and sometimes anticipated Spencer's most sexist and racist evolutionary arguments" (1991, 8), Nancy Paxton draws attention to the fact that in spite of not being able to refute the "scientific findings" of her time, Eliot, throughout her œuvre, engaged in a critical dialog with the pronouncements that nineteenth-century scientists made about the "nature of women." She especially targeted the insights of her former love interest, Herbert Spencer who, having studied evolutionary theory, came to revise his initial understanding that women were not inferior to men. By describing the catastrophic marriage of Lydgate to Rosamond, Eliot indeed shows that the rational discourse of science can neither contain nor restrain the irrational dangers arising from gender difference as it has been constructed by the nineteenth-century hegemony of gender (to which science gladly contributed). Therefore, science also cannot claim to control gender relationships—even when they seem harmless and domesticated.

Thus science, rationality, and adherence to contemporary notions about gender hinders rather than helps Lydgate, when "in spite of himself [he succumbs] to Rosamond's similar superficial charms . . . [and] marries a woman who, according to the most advanced scientific principles of evolutionary theory in the 1870s, is the perfect mate" (Paxton 1991, 176). To him Rosamond seems well suited not only because of her personal characteristics but also because of the education that has "finished" her:

> Lydgate thought . . . that he had found perfect womanhood—felt as if already breathed upon by exquisite wedded affection such as would be bestowed by an accomplished creature who venerated his high musings and momentous labours and would never interfere with them; who would create order in the home and accounts with still magic, yet keep her fingers ready to touch the lute and transform life into romance at any minute; who was instructed to the true womanly limit and not a hair's breadth beyond—docile, therefore, and ready to carry out behests which came from beyond that limit. ([1871–72] 1994, 352)

It is highly ironic that Lydgate never seems to comprehend fully that if he had been a bit less superficial in choosing a woman suitable to his tastes, he might have found an ideal wife in the ardent Dorothea, whose hunger for "real knowledge" would have made her the perfect helpmate in accordance with nineteenth-century gender ideology. Instead, he ruins his own life and possible professional success by falling for the pretty but utterly shallow social climber Rosamond Vincy. And Rosamond indeed proves to be a very bad choice: she loves Lydgate's social status and aristocratic family connections more than her husband, despises his vocation, and finally destroys his dream of becoming a famous medical researcher by making unreasonable financial demands which force him to compromise his integrity by getting involved in Bulstrode's business practices and work so hard that he has no time and energy left for his medical research. Lydgate, ultimately, can blame only himself (or his inability to transcend the contemporary ideology of gender) for his professional failure. Rosamond, however, completely succeeds in thwarting his professional ambition, as the narrator points out in this laconic comment: "He once called her his basil plant; and when she asked for an explanation, said that basil was a plant which had flourished wonderfully on a murdered man's brains" (835).

Social Organicism

The foregoing discussion has indicated that George Eliot puts great emphasis on gender relationships in her ambitious project of conceiving of society as an organism[48]; an analysis of Stowe's presentation of her less reflected organicism in *Oldtown Folks* will show that Stowe places equal emphasis on the importance of both gender and religion. Eliot's philosophy of social organicism is particularly evident in *Middlemarch*, where she describes the town's microcosm in terms of web imagery. It is indebted to her reception of cutting-edge scientists and philosophers of her time, such as Auguste Comte, Charles Darwin, John Stuart Mill, Herbert Spencer, and her partner, George Henry Lewes, whose social science treatise *Problems of Life and Mind* (1874) was written in the years before the publication of *Middlemarch*. Spencer lists the "evidence" that justifies "the comparison of societies to living organisms" ([1860] 1996, 306) in "The Social Organism," one of his first essays on the subject, in the following observation:

> That they gradually increase in mass; that they become little by little more complex; that at the same time their parts grow more mutually dependent; and that they continue to live and grow as wholes, while successive generations of their units appear and disappear; are broad peculiarities which bodies-politic display in common with all living bodies; and in which they and living bodies differ from everything else. (306)

Lewes, whose organicism reflects Comte's and Spencer's ideas and "infiltrated" Eliot's novels, situates (hu)man's position in that organism—and interaction with it—as follows: "Man is no longer to be considered as an assemblage of organs, but also as an organ in a Collective Organism. From the former he derives his sensations, judgments, primary impulses; from the latter his conceptions, theories, and virtues" (1874, 167). And he describes the relation of individual "organic" societies in relation to a social organism as follows:

> The organism is evolved . . . its organs are groups of minor organisms . . . all sharing in a common substance . . . ; precisely as the great Social Organism is a group of societies, each of which is a group of families, all sharing in a common life,—every family having at once its individual independence and its social dependence through connection with every other. (113–13)

In her "Address to Working Men, by Felix Holt," Eliot echoes Lewes in describing organic society in terms of "that wonderful piece of life, the human body, with all its various parts depending on one another, and with a terrible liability to get wrong because of that delicate dependence" ([1866] 1995, 489).[49] Eliot's description of society as a delicate "wonderful piece of life" perhaps already suggests that the social body has to be treated with care and that therefore radical social change—as proposed by radical political ideology—might be detrimental. Her elaboration of Lewes's metaphor points to the fact that philosophers interested in analyzing and promoting organicism had to address the relation of the individual to his/her society as well as the possibility of societal development and change.

Comte, describing history as logical progression from egoism/paganism to altruism/positivism, demanded the altruistic submission of individual desire to the good of society at large. Herbert Spencer, however, the author of one of the first sociological treatises, *Social Statics* (1851), stressed individual rights in *The Principles of Sociology* (1870–72), expecting individual desires to harmonize with societal ones according to his premise that "the society exists for the benefit of its members; not its members for the benefit of the society" ([1898] 2002, 1.2:461–62). Darwin, moreover, as Graver points out, by proposing that "competition and conflict are the fundamental conditions of existence" (1984, 166), fundamentally challenged Comte's and Spencer's organicist theories, which eschew random development and are concerned with the dynamic and ordered progression of society.

Since social change—such as the implementation of women's equal rights—and education proved to be inevitable and since, at least when it seemed teleological and progressive, it was sometimes even appreciated by the nineteenth-century scientists discussed, they had to find a way of accommodating change in their theories about organic society—even though they remained torn between essentialist and constructivist notions about humans and the society made up of them.[50] George Henry Lewes describes social change as a complicated dynamic process, which involves the adaptation of the individual organism (a person) to the external medium (society) as well as the adjustment of the social medium to possible change in "human feelings" about their social organization:

> No organ has a power of control; but the Organism will control an organ. The individual man is powerless against Society; but society can, and does, compel the individual. This does not prevent the individual from initiating a change, which may be passed on from one to another like yeast-cells growing in a fermenting mass; and in this sense Society is of course affected by the actions of individuals—since, indeed it is itself only the sum of individuals. (1874, 139)

He defines "the collective accumulations of centuries, condensed in knowledge, beliefs, prejudices, institutions and tendencies" (1874, 124) as the "Social Medium." The passages quoted indicate that he understands "the collective [societal] accumulations" in terms of Spencerian notions about "gender" or "race habits" which have ossified into (second) "nature." Lewes, theorizing about how change is possible within such an established system, adopted "Comte's belief that new institutions will 'arise . . . when a community of principles' introduces into 'existing institutions' new forces and new elements" (Graver 1984, 156). As already mentioned above, I view the paradoxical simultaneous upholding and subverting of "The Cult of True Womanhood" by Eliot, Fuller, Stowe, and Hawthorne as an insertion of "new forces and elements" into "existing institutions." As such, it is indicative of the uneasy beginnings of a paradigm shift which—based on the nineteenth-century writers' intuition about female intellectual equality rather than scientific finding—ultimately "de-doxified" the nineteenth-century ideology of gender.

George Eliot's fiction is indebted to the notions of organicism on both a philosophical and an organizational level. Thus, Eliot follows Lewes in presenting the social organism as a web. As Lewes writes in *Problems of Life and Mind*:

> Out of the general web of Existence certain threads may be detached and re-woven into a special group—the Subject—and this sentient group will in so far be different from the larger group—the Object; but whatever different arrangement the threads may take on, they are always threads of the original web, they are not different threads. The elements of the sentient Organism are the elements detached from the larger group; the motions of the sentient Organism are the motions of these elements. (1874, 189)

Gillian Beer has isolated the main characteristics of Eliot's presentation of society as a web and the individual's place in it in *Darwin's Plots*:

> Threads remain themselves, though part of a total fabric. (1983, 168)
>
> The web exists not only as interconnection in space but as succession in time. (169)
>
> The web is not a hierarchical model. It can express horizontality and extension, but it does not fix places, as on the rungs of a ladder or "in single file." (170)

In *Middlemarch* Eliot, as Beer notes, "seeks out ways beyond the single consciousness" (172) and focuses on the web's most important "knotting," or connecting devices that determine the community's social make-up. Social connections are to a rather large extent predetermined by the positions that gender, class, and (ethnic) origin ascribe to individuals in society. All of the novel's characters have to find or maintain their place in society and some of them, as for example Lydgate, who, as a medical doctor, tries to locate the "primary organic tissue," or Casaubon, who wants to find the "Key to all Mythologies," even look for but cannot find the "common basis" for the entirety of (human) life. They fail because according to Eliot's scientific knowledge (based on Lewes's belief in diverse origins of life rather than Darwin's belief in a single progenitor of organic life) "there is not one 'primitive tissue,' just as there is not one 'key to all mythologies'" (Beer 1983, 154). By the same token, Eliot presents social development as development that is changeable rather than fixed. She bases her insights on two generally agreed upon scientific precepts, namely that "[t]he power of nature is the power of motion" and that "[e]volution is the universal process" (155). *Middlemarch* thus poses as one of its most important philosophical queries the opening question of "how the mysterious mixture [of mankind] behaves under the varying experiments of Time" (3).

In an important passage at the beginning of chapter 11, Eliot, cleverly foreshadowing and summarizing the entire novel's most important plotlines and also foregrounding the work's organic structure, describes how the characters' individual lots mutually intersect with and influence larger social movement:

> Old provincial society had its share of this subtle movement: had not only its striking downfalls, its brilliant young professional dandies who ended by living up an entry with a drab and six children for their establishment, but also those less marked vicissitudes which are constantly shifting the boundaries of social intercourse, and begetting new consciousness of interdepen-

dence. Some slipped a little downward, some got higher footing: people denied aspirates, gained wealth, and fastidious gentlemen stood for boroughs; some were caught in political currents, some in ecclesiastical, and perhaps found themselves surprisingly grouped in consequence. . . . Municipal town and rural parish gradually made fresh threads of connection—gradually, as the old stocking gave way to the savings-bank, and the worship of the solar guinea became extinct, while squires and baronets, and even lords who had once lived blamelessly afar from the civic mind, gathered the faultiness of closer acquaintanceship. Settlers, too, came from distant counties, some with an alarming novelty of skill, others with an offensive advantage in cunning. In fact, much the same sort of movement and mixture went on in old England as we find in older Herodotus, who also, in telling what had been, thought it well to take a woman's lot for his starting point. ([1871–72] 1994, 95–96)

As I have already demonstrated, *Middlemarch*, with its initial comparison of the young Dorothea to St. Theresa, not only takes "woman's lot" as a starting point for a description of a society in which unequal and incompatible gender relationships are of utmost importance to the protagonists' lives, but makes gender a central agent in the social locationing of individuals.

Moreover, the novel also deals with the positioning effected by other social determinants such as class and communal or religious affiliation. Even though the political issues surrounding the second Reform Bill seem to play a lesser role in the protagonists' lives compared to the gender issues, they nevertheless point towards other important facets of social change in a formerly rather static "higher" society that now has to deal with the foreignness of outsiders as well as that of the formerly ignored lower classes. Like Lydgate, the newcomer who can maintain his standing in Middlemarch society only by repeatedly compromising and finally giving up his initial aims, Will Ladislaw, an outsider of doubtful origin, has to fight for his footing in Middlemarch. Likened by Mrs. Cadwallader to "'an Italian carrying white mice'" (492), he is suspicious by virtue of his mix of English, Polish, and Jewish blood, as Mr. Hawley points out:

> So our mercurial Ladislaw has a queer genealogy! A high-spirited young lady and a musical Polish patriot made a likely enough stock for him to spring from, but I should never have suspected a grafting of the Jew pawnbroker. However, there's no knowing what a mixture will turn out beforehand. Some sorts of dirt serve to clarify. (719)

Having worn out his welcome with his jealous older cousin, Casaubon, Will, the social outsider, decides to stay in town because he is secretly attracted to Dorothea. He involves himself in the political scenery and works as a secretary for her uncle, Mr. Brooke, who, in spite of actively counteracting reform by treating his own tenants badly, electioneers for the Reform Bill. Mr. Brooke serves as an important catalyst figure for the novel's social plot as Eliot uses him and his connection with Ladislaw to show that Middlemarch society undergoes significant change towards democratization. Thus, Mr. Brooke's being put in his place by his tenant Dagley (and later by the ventriloquist, who humiliates him in the marketplace by providing a parodic echo of the inebriated Mr. Brooke's already ludicrous speech) suggests that the gentry are rapidly losing power: "'An' I made out what the Rinform were—an' it were to send you an' your likes a-scuttlin'; an wi' pretty strong-smellin' things too. An' you may do as you like now, for I'm non afeard on you'" (397).

Besides indicating the instability of the existing social system, the figure of Mr. Brooke serves yet another purpose. By familiarizing the polite Middlemarch society with the "foreign Ladislaw" through comparing Will to "a sort of Burke with a leaven of Shelley" (499) and also hiring him, he is instrumental in establishing Will as an accepted member of society. And Will is there to stay, despite Mr. Brooke's later opposition to his marriage with his niece Dorothea. Thus, even though Mrs. Cadwallader keeps maintaining that "'his blood is a frightful mixture! The Casaubon cuttle-fish fluid to begin with and then a rebellious Polish fiddler or dancing-master'" (819), Will's alterity is finally accepted and safely contained, as is indicated by Mr. Cadwallader's short reaction: "'Nonsense, Elinor'" (819). Will's accomplishment of becoming "an ardent public man, working well in those times when reforms were begun with a young hopefulness of immediate good" (836) actually shows that, in spite of his initial difference from it, Will is the character who at the end of the novel is most successfully integrated into the social organism surrounding him. However, in her description of the microcosm of *Middlemarch*, Eliot avoids the trouble of dwelling on types of alterity that are more difficult to deal with, such as Madame Laure's murderous alterity. Even though the narrative does not particularly focus on her Frenchness, it is clear that the actress's murderousness is French rather than English. Madame Laure obviously constitutes another example of the female impulse towards violence in George Eliot's writing. After confessing to Lydgate—who had come to propose marriage to her—that she really meant to kill her husband, she tells him, "'You're a good young man. . . . But I do not like husbands. I'll never have another'" (153). Exuding a fatal sexuality and murderous agency directed against the male as an already structurally inscribed oppressor in marriage, this French *femme fatale* is much more dangerous than the domestic English murderess of the ilk of Hetty Sorrel, who dispassionately consents to premarital sex only because she wants to rise in social stature and kills her child out of confused desperation. (Hetty is quite similar in character to Lydgate's wife, Rosamond, who loses her unborn first child because she values a ride on horseback with Lydgate's high class cousin, the smart Captain Lydgate, more highly than her child's safety.) The Middlemarch community fortunately does not have to deal with women like Madame Laure; Eliot sees to it that her murderous alterity remains in her own country across the channel.

Middlemarch expunges other equally socially undesirable characters, such as the criminal extortionist, Raffles, and the morally corrupt banker, Bulstrode, once they have worn out their welcome in the community. The alcoholic Raffles dies conveniently after Bulstrode more or less accidentally gives him an overdose of brandy; Bulstrode, in his turn, is shamed into leaving town after having made some amends to the people he wronged. Bulstrode, a stern pillar of his community, is one of the characters that Eliot uses to show that Christian religion has lost most of its vital function of sustaining the social fabric of Middlemarch with moral guidance and purpose—this socially important function has been taken over by a more secular sympathy of the sort enacted by Mr. Farebrother, the rather unenthusiastic minister. In his religious practice, Bulstrode is much more ardent than Casaubon, who is a dried up religious scholar rather than a good shepherd. He is also more zealous than Mr. Farebrother, to whom being a "fair brother" (in accordance with Eliot's ideal of the "religion of humanity") to his parishioners is much more important than religious zeal. The banker Bulstrode, by contrast, is zealous, but his heart-felt religiosity still does not keep him from being morally corrupt. Thus, as a young accountant, Bulstrode had already developed a habit of devising "biblical" excuses for his misdeeds of selling stolen goods for his equally pious church-going employer (who later became his wife) and cheating her daughter, Will Ladislaw's mother, out of her inheritance:

> The profits made out of lost souls—where can the line be drawn at which they begin in human transactions? Was it not even God's way of saving His chosen? "Thou knowest,"—the young Bulstrode had said then, as the older Bulstrode was saying now—"Thou knowest how loose my soul sits from these things—how I view them all as implements for tilling Thy garden rescued here and there from the wilderness." (616)

Bulstrode is punished for his deeds by the appearance of his nemesis, Raffles, but his just punishment is not sufficient to the purpose of restoring much needed authenticity and fervor to religious practice in *Middlemarch*.

As a "contemporary Saint Theresa,"[51] Dorothea Brooke actually has the religious fervor that both Casaubon and Farebrother lack, combined with a burning desire to do good and reform society, but this will not get her far in Middlemarch, where "[t]he religion which inspired Antigone and Saint Theresa to perform their heroic deeds alone is gone" (Edwards 1977, 690) and where a young woman's idealism and ambition are thwarted from the very beginning by her sex. Thus, Eliot's narrator already makes it clear in the prelude to *Middlemarch* that Dorothea is one of those "many Theresas" who because of "meanness of opportunity" (having been born with the wrong sex) were not able to live an "epic life wherein there was a constant unfolding of far-resonant action" ([1871–72] 1994, 3). As quite a few frustrated female commentators have pointed out, in *Middlemarch* Eliot thus leaves all purposeful and effective social action to her male characters; she apparently could not conceive of "those later born Theresas" being helped by "coherent social faith and order which could perform the function of knowledge for the ardently willing young soul" (3). Thus, George Eliot "either would or could not create an alternative universe in her fiction" (Edwards 1977, 687).

Without having devised an equally elaborate framework of social organicism as Eliot did in *Middlemarch*, Stowe had embarked on a parallel project with *Oldtown Folks*, published two years before Eliot's novel. In her most ambitious "novel of ideas,"[52] she addresses very similar questions of how the individual fits into his/her society. As her biographer Joan Hedrick observes, "*Oldtown Folks* might be read as a search for the perfect form of family or human community" (1994, 343). That George Eliot noticed this, too, is indicated by an encouraging letter to Stowe about the novel, in which she praises the American writer for both her accurate depiction of provincial life and her religious tolerance:

> I think few of your many readers can have felt more interest than I have felt in that picture of an elder generation, for my interest in it has a double root: one is my love for our old-fashioned provincial life which had its affinities with a contemporary life even all across the Atlantic, and of which I have gathered glimpses in different phases . . . [as through] my experimental acquaintance with some shades of Calvinistic orthodoxy. I think your way of presenting the religious convictions which are not your own except by indirect fellowship, is a triumph of insight and true tolerance. A thorough comprehension of the mixed moral influence shed on society by dogmatic

systems is rare even among writers, and one misses it altogether in English drawing-room talk. (*George Eliot Letters* 1954–55, 5:48)

Eliot's *Middlemarch* foregrounds gender and class relations as having the greatest influence on the social organism in her early to mid-nineteenth-century England. As has been demonstrated, Stowe's *Oldtown Folks*, set in the 1790s, a decade and a half after the American Revolution, also deals with gender and class in that it proposes rather egalitarian (at least for its time) gender and class relationships. Stowe, moreover, in *Oldtown Folks* focuses strongly on the relationship of the individual to his/her faith and presents a "postcolonial" American reaction to the otherness of Europe. Like Eliot in some of her novels, she depicts Europe as a spiritually sterile and morally depleted place.[53]

In Oldtown—unlike Eliot's Middlemarch—religion is still a vital force in everyday life. Stowe's protagonists think and talk about religious issues all the time; they discuss the doctrines of Calvinism, the rituals of Anglicanism, and the pernicious influence of irreligious French thought. As in her other New England novels, in *Oldtown Folks* Stowe seems to both support and subvert (and thus "de-doxify") conservative Calvinism, which, in spite of its shortcomings, she believes to be vastly superior to European forms of religious practice. Stowe particularly targets the cruelty of a Calvinism that states that only very few of its believers have been chosen by God to be saved from eternal condemnation as his elect. She abhorred the rather cruel "doctrine of divine sovereignty," which she found highly contradictory because it implied that while it is entirely up to God whom he chooses to save (he might arbitrarily choose not to save an ardent believer), the proper kind of submission to God's will can still bring about a conversion experience in the individual which then indicates that he or she is a member of the elect. In her youth, Stowe agonized over the possibility of not having been saved (see Hedrick 1994, 144–45); in *Oldtown Folks* she aims to expose the "schizophrenic" nature of the Puritan doctrine by having the minister's daughter, Esther, who later becomes Harry's wife, relive her own painful experience:

> [Esther's] love of the absolute right was almost painful in its excess of minuteness, and yet, in her own view, in the view of the Church, in the view even of her admiring and loving father, she was no Christian. Perfectly faultless in every relation so far as human beings could observe, reverent to God, submissive to his will, careful in all outward religious observances, yet wanting in a certain emotional experience, she judged herself to be, and was judged by the theology which her father taught, utterly devoid of virtue or moral excellence of any kind in the sight of God. The theology of the times

also taught her that the act of grace which should put an end to this state, and place her in the relation of a forgiven child with her Heavenly Father, was a voluntary one, momently in her power, and that nothing but her own persistent refusal prevented her performing it; yet taught at the same time that, so desperate was the obstinacy of the human heart, no child of Adam ever would, or ever could, perform it without a special interposition of God,—an interposition which might or might not come. ([1869] 1982, 1330)

In all of her New England novels, Stowe's outrage about this "unfair" doctrine is directed in particular at the eminent Puritan minister, Jonathan Edwards (1703–58) who had reintroduced the "doctrine of divine sovereignty" after his equally eminent forebears John Winthrop (1587-1649) and Cotton Mather (1663–1728) had already abolished it.[54] In *Oldtown Folks*, Stowe, by means of her narrator, accuses Edwards of "completely upsetting New England from the basis on which the Reformers and the Puritan fathers had placed her, and casting out of the Church the children of the very saints and martyrs who had come to this country for no other reason than to found a church" (1233). Taking a decidedly postcolonial, antiroyalist stance, she further argues that "the doctrine of Divine sovereignty" and "similar theologies" are not American because they "were not formed by the Puritans; they were their legacy from past monarchical and mediaeval ages" (1245–46), and she likewise claims that "[i]f any should ever be so curious as to read . . . most of the writings of Jonathan Edwards, they will perceive with singular plainness how inevitably monarchical and aristocratic institutions influence theology" (1244). Stowe thus charges Edwards with a counterrevolutionary "European" anti-Americanism that she, interestingly enough, reserves for various types of religious belief that she did not agree with.[55]

Arguing that "[t]heology being human and a reflection of human infirmities, nothing is more common than for it to come up point-blank in opposition to the simplest declarations of Christ" (1247), she decides to rectify what she perceived as man-made doctrinal wrongs by debunking the "doctrine of divine sovereignty" through an infusion of (feminine) Christian love. She thus grants her protagonist Esther a somewhat "irregular"—possibly even "false" (at least by Edwardsian standards)—conversion experience, in which human love and divine love relate to each other metonymically:

The hour of full heart union that made them one placed her mind under the control of his. [Harry's] simple faith in God's love was an antidote to her despondent fears. His mind bore hers along on its current. His imagination awakened hers. She was like one carried away by a winged spirit, lifted up and borne heavenward by his faith and love. She was a transfigured being. . . . Mr. Avery was in raptures. The long agony was past. . . . But now, when the dove that had long wandered actually bent her white wings at the window of the ark, he stretched forth his hand and drew her in with a trembling eagerness. (1333)[56]

One could argue that in "rewriting" religious doctrine, Stowe actively tries to change aspects of the religious belief of her society through an infusion of "typically female" love; she thus instrumentalizes female agency—as a legitimate and workable strategy, according to de Lauretis—to bring about ideological change.

The subsequent development of the plot of *Oldtown Folks* explains Stowe's reasons for wanting to change Puritan doctrine. By means of the religious fates of her characters Emily Rossiter and Ellery Davenport, she intends to show that unless Puritan doctrine can be modified, Calvinism will lose its clientele and society its ordering principle. According to Stowe, Calvinism needs to be preserved, however, because for her, as a believer, it is the one "true religion," and as such it is vastly superior to the empty rituals of Anglicanism and dangerous "French moral relativism." As the mainstay of society, the Calvinist faith also performs the indispensable social function of enabling true community in Oldtown, Stowe's microcosm for a young U.S. society trying to establish a unique identity after the American Revolution. Stowe is aware of the fact that in order to keep functioning, a vital social organism like Oldtown, or even the big city of Boston, cannot lose to afford its individual members. She exemplifies this insight by means of the figures of Emily Rossiter and Ellery Davenport, who are alienated from society by the cruelty of Calvinist religious doctrine and morally endangered by the alterity of European religious relativism.

Having lost her parents, Miss Mehitable's younger sister, Emily, is brought up by Dr. Stern, a minister whose name reflects his educational program. In his household "she had passed through two or three of those seasons of convulsed and agonized feeling [sic] which are caused by the revolt of a strong sense of justice and humanity against teachings which accuse the great Father of the most frightful cruelty and injustice" ([1869] 1982, 1256). As a consequence, she turns to French literature and is ensnared by its religious and moral relativism. After studying Rousseau's *La Nouvelle Héloïse*, and identifying with his statement "'I should prefer the Bible falsified or unintelligible to believing God unjust and cruel'" (1259), Emily runs off to France. She is accompanied by Ellery Davenport, a grandson of Jonathan Edwards, who, as a result of his grandfather's attempt to inculcate in him the "doctrine of divine sovereignty," has completely lost his faith and adopted a cynical moral relativism. Years later, after their unofficial, "illicit" relationship has almost ended, Ellery turns up in the Boston household of Miss Mehitable's high-class Tory relatives, who have agreed to oversee and finance the education of the three Oldtown orphans, Tina, Harry, and Horace. In spite of the American Revolution, Miss Mehitable's Boston family has retained their loyalty to the English king and the Anglican Church—they are mildly ridiculed by the novel's narrator for displaying a painting of Charles I in their house, including the Royal Family in their prayers, and adhering to "empty" rituals, such as "'readin' prayers out of book'" (1197).

Interestingly enough, Stowe uses the intelligent cynic Ellery Davenport to point out to the Tory family (and, of course, also to her readers) that the social problems resulting from the cruelty of the "doctrine of divine sovereignty" cannot be solved by reverting to European ways and the Anglican faith. Thus, Ellery Davenport (who seems to compare Calvinist doctrine to the evolutionary tenet of "survival of the fittest" by arguing that "'Nature herself is a high Calvinist'" [1187]), tells the Kitterys: "'[I]f I set out to be religious at all, it would oblige me to carry the thing to as great lengths as did my grandfather Jonathan Edwards. . . . [A]nd as to all these pleasant comfortable churches, where a fellow can get to heaven without it, I have the misfortune of not being able to believe in them, so there you see precisely my situation'" (1187). Ellery Davenport, moreover, in a passage that George Eliot would probably at least partly agree with, reasons that, in addition to featuring a theology that is too lax to provide moral guidance, the Anglican Church is spiritually depleted and fosters a class difference that is detrimental to the spiritual well-being of the lower classes:

> If you had been in England, as I have, where the true Church prevails, you'd see that pretty much the whole of the lower classes there are predestinated to be conceived and born in sin, and shapen in iniquity; and come into the world in such circumstances that to expect even decent morality of them is expecting what is contrary to all reason. This is your Christian country, after eighteen hundred years' experiment of Christianity. The elect, by whom I mean the bishops and clergy, and upper classes, have attained to a position in which a decent and religious life is practicable, and where there is leisure from the claims of the body to attend to those of the soul. These, however, to a large extent are smothering in their own fat. (1187–88)

Stowe thus wants to show that the Old World alterity of the Boston Tories is simply "wrong." Nevertheless, it is an otherness that can be accommodated in the New England social organism because it does not threaten "true" Christian belief and morality.[57] Thus, as Stowe's narrator observes, the Boston Episcopalians are doctrinally generous in that they believe that Calvinists can be saved, too—even if that has to happen by "'uncovenanted mercies,'" as Miss Deborah Kittery states.

However, as in Eliot's *Middlemarch*, there exists one type of otherness that has to be expunged from the social body: morally dangerous French alterity (like the murderous French feminist alterity of Madame Laure in *Middlemarch*) cannot be contained in a New England that for the most part, like Miss Debby, believes that "'God made two kinds of nature,—human nature and French nature'" (1379). Rousseau's liberalism is dangerous to Stowe because it is highly seductive since it is both right and wrong at the same time. It is right because it doubts God's cruelty, but it is also wrong because its antiauthoritarian stance threatens to destroy the moral fiber of New England by introducing an antireligious moral relativism. Thus, Rousseau's ideas seduce Emily Rossiter into believing in the false idea of "free love" and making herself vulnerable to the truly "unregenerate" cynic Ellery Davenport, who exploits her emotionally and sexually and endangers the spiritual well-being of her soul.

After much suffering, Emily Rossiter finally repents for her adherence to the false French ideas which make the sacred institution of marriage only a "choice of the individuals." As the mother of Ellery Davenport's illegitimate child, she warns Tina, who meanwhile has become married to Ellery, about her husband's true character. This scene suggests that she might be the model for Grandcourt's disenfranchised mistress, Lydia Glasher, in *Daniel Deronda*. Emily is finally forgiven and readmitted to the social organism of New England only because Horace provides the voice of reason by asking Miss Mehitable, "'Should we not make a distinction between errors that come from a wrong belief and the mere weakness that blindly yields to passion?'" (1415), and thus talks her into making her sister a part of her household again. Davenport, however, repents only partially; he tries to make amends for his conduct with Emily and treats Tina decently, but then falls prey to madness. As a still disruptive social element, he, like the "undesirables" in *Middlemarch*, is eventually expunged from New England, and the novel, by dying in a political duel.

In *Oldtown Folks*, Stowe presents the U.S. shortly after the American Revolution in a very unique socioreligious crisis brought about by adherence to the cruel Calvinist "doctrine of divine sovereignty." In a postcolonial spirit, she makes it very clear from the beginning of the novel that this crisis cannot be overcome by turning to Europe for guidance because Europe is morally corrupt. She thus traces the cruelty inherent in the doctrine, which presents God as a wrathful, punishing, and unforgiving father, to a European monarchical political spirit that Puritan religion could not free itself from and exposes Anglicanism, the religion of the mother country that America had just rebelled against, as sterile and elitist. Turning to the more liberal ideas of French philosophers, who criticized patriarchal religion, provides no alternative for Stowe, either, since French literature abounds with "dazzling, unsettling theories with regard to social life" (1415), which lead the individual to the dangerous conclusion that s/he is "free to construct her own system of morals" (1446). She finally comes up with a "feminist" solution to the crisis of faith: Calvinism is the appropriate religion for the U.S., but it needs to be infused with a dose of "typically female" New Testament love. Thus, Stowe, unlike Eliot, who in *Middlemarch* presents a sterile and ossified Anglicanism that cannot be revitalized by young female religious enthusiasts like Dorothea, envisions a bright future for a reformed Calvinism in the Oldtown community.

2
Fuller's, Hawthorne's, Stowe's, and Eliot's Italy—Culture as Difference?

NINETEENTH-CENTURY AMERICAN AND
BRITISH TRAVEL NOTES AND DISPATCHES

MARGARET FULLER, NATHANIEL HAWTHORNE, HARRIET BEECHER STOWE, and George Eliot all spent more or less extended periods of time in Italy and manifested their interest in Italy in their writing about this foreign culture. While Stowe and Eliot, who had begun to study Italian as early as 1840 "with the intention of reading the literature" (Thompson 1998, 30), only visited Italy as tourists, Fuller and Hawthorne actually lived in Italy during times of political unrest. Fuller had traveled to Europe in 1847 with Marcus and Rebecca Spring, a couple who she was friends with. To support herself during her stay abroad, she worked as a foreign correspondent for Horace Greeley's New York *Tribune*, earning ten dollars per dispatch (von Mehren 1994, 228). In England, her first stop in Europe, Fuller met the Italian revolutionary leader Giuseppe Mazzini and henceforth supported his cause of Italian unification, suddenly finding herself in the middle of the 1848 revolution against Austrian (and later French) occupation and for unification of the separate Italian duchies and republics. Fuller recorded her impressions of the ultimately unsuccessful Italian revolution in her dispatches, which were posthumously published in 1856 by her brother Arthur B. Fuller, in a volume entitled *At Home and Abroad, or Things and Thoughts in America and Europe*. Her manuscript for a *History of the Italian Revolution* had perished in the fatal shipwreck that claimed her own life and the lives of her family just off the shores of New York on their voyage back from Italy.

Roughly ten years later, Fuller's reluctant admirer Nathaniel Hawthorne spent sixteen months in Italy (and sailed home on the same ship as Harriet

Beecher Stowe, who had spent half a year in Italy). After Hawthorne's appointment as American consul in England had ended, the Hawthorne family decided to live in Italy for a while and arrived in Rome in January 1858 at an equally heady period in Italian history when through the political and military efforts of Giuseppe Garibaldi, a leader in the 1848 revolution, and the Piedmontese politician Camillo Benso di Cavour, Italian unification was significantly furthered.[1] While Hawthorne meticulously recorded many of his impressions of Italy in his Italian notebooks and even set his last novel *The Marble Faun* (1860) in Italy, he—curiously enough—never directly mentioned the political situation, but only obliquely alluded to the presence of French soldiers at various points in his novel, which mainly deals with the lives of members of the American expatriate community in Rome.

Eliot's "Recollections of Italy. 1860," entirely coincidentally, read like Hawthorne's Italian notebooks in many places, and a closer look at her Italian novel *Romola* (1863) reveals that she had keenly absorbed both Fuller's *At Home and Abroad* and Hawthorne's *The Marble Faun*—and also seems to have been familiar with Stowe's *Agnes of Sorrento* (1862)—by the time she started to write her own novel set in Italy. In her conceptualization of *Romola*, she shared Fuller's and Stowe's interest in Italian culture and Italian national politics by transposing political concerns of the nineteenth century onto a fifteenth-century plot involving Girolamo Savonarola's struggle for a return to republicanism in Florence. More obviously, by including a Comtean positivist allegory of teleological human development in her novel, she seems to have adopted Hawthorne's idea of choosing Italy as a testing ground for ideas about evolutionary development. In Hawthorne's *The Marble Faun*, Donatello, the only Italian protagonist, experiences what is called "a fortunate fall" from faun to man, whereas in *Romola* the eponymous heroine of Eliot's novel goes through various stages of Comtean development while she is surrounded by characters who also represent different developmental stages.[2]

The fact that Eliot's decision to write about Italy resulted from her intellectual curiosity about Italy rather than an interest in its people and its culture is also palpable in her writing. In her "Recollections of Italy. 1860" —like Hawthorne in his Italian notebooks—she does not record any contact with the Italian population.[3] Literary critics often complain about the contrived quality of *Romola*. J. B. Bullen, for example, states "[t]he failure of *Romola* is usually attributed to George Eliot's inability to breathe life into the dry bones of her researches in the Florentine archives" (1975, 434). Hawthorne's *The Marble Faun* exhibits a similar problem in spite of his vivid (and often rather depreciatory) notebook comments about Italians and

Italian life. Donatello, the protagonist among the few Italian characters, is a faun, a mixture of human and goat, and as such he immediately comes across as a very contrived character who certainly does not resemble a "normal" young Italian. Eliot's writing about Italy shows that she was interested in Italian culture primarily in its historical importance. There are almost no references to contemporary Italian life to be found in either the notebooks or her novel; only her depiction of Catholicism reveals the cultural bias of an intellectual Englishwoman who regarded medieval Catholicism as merely a stage in historical progress. Religion is also the site where the cultural biases of Fuller and Hawthorne become obvious; they also denounce what they perceive as the superstitious aspect of Catholicism. Perhaps surprisingly, Harriet Beecher Stowe gives the most sympathetic and in-depth analysis of Catholicism in her Italian novel, *Agnes of Sorrento* (1862), which was serialized in *Cornhill Magazine* immediately before *Romola*,[4] and which also deals with a young woman who is affected by Girolamo Savonarola's struggle for religious reform.

Among the American writers discussed in this chapter, Fuller is the one who embraced Italian life the most enthusiastically (Stowe also shows a positive attitude but since she did not maintain a travel diary, this attitude can only be gleaned from her novel). As a "postcolonial" American, Fuller seems to have had entirely positive feelings towards Europe even before she went there. Her biographer Joan von Mehren states that she traveled to Europe with the purpose of "bring[ing] back some fresh ideas to hasten progress in the New World" (1994, 229). Nathaniel Hawthorne, however, who, as a professional fiction writer, had always been in dire need of money, mainly went to Europe because he wanted to better his financial situation.[5] After his college friend Franklin Pierce, for whom he had written a campaign biography, became President of the United States, Hawthorne was appointed by Pierce to the prestigious and lucrative position of consul to Liverpool. Even before going to England, the Hawthornes decided to fulfill Sophia Hawthorne's "lifelong dream" of spending an extended period of time in Italy so that "she would be able to see the artistic masterpieces that she had learned to love and live with through inadequate reproductions" (Miller 1991, 392). As his notebooks indicate, Hawthorne's response to England remained ambivalent; at times he praised England as the home country of his ancestors, yet at other times—especially when he felt in any way threatened by English response to the United States—he betrayed an urge to annihilate England in a postcolonial rage.

Through the texts that they authored about Italy, Fuller, Hawthorne, Stowe, and Eliot evaluated Italian culture, inscribed—and in a way even created—its meanings from the perspective of their own cultural backgrounds. Fuller and Hawthorne viewed the Old World of Italy from a postcolonial point of view that compared Old and New World accomplishments, whereas Stowe cast a critical but sympathetic eye on religious worship in Italy. Eliot, however, as a fellow European, seems to have aimed at providing a more global European perspective that often tries to negate cultural differences within Europe, but still reveals Eliot's cultural biases. As travel writers they all became amateur anthropologists and "cultural translators" for their readers and as such—whether or not they were aware of it—these authors wielded quite a bit of cultural power: "[I]f the anthropological translator, like the analyst, has final authority in determining the subject's meanings—it is then the former who becomes *the real author* of the latter. In this view, 'cultural translation' is a matter of determining implicit meanings" (Asad 1986, 162). Thus, Fuller, Hawthorne, and to a lesser extent, Eliot and Stowe, serve as translators of the meanings of human as well as cultural subjects. By using their descriptive powers they assert their agency as viewing and speaking subjects. Their texts also reveal what Marie Louise Pratt, referring to Eurocentrism in travel writing,[6] has called "the hegemonic reflex" (1992, 15)—a cultural bias, which betrays an unstated belief in the cultural superiority of one's native country. Fuller's, Hawthorne's, Stowe's, and Eliot's assessments sometimes converge in their evaluation of Catholicism—as the most obvious marker of cultural difference in Italy—and there are also additional common denominators in their opinions of other aspects of cultural life, such as Italian art. Interestingly enough, these convergences do not necessarily arrange themselves according to national origin. Thus, Eliot shares an interest in and a similar assessment of Italian politics with Fuller and does the same regarding Italian art with Hawthorne.

The prose texts discussed in this chapter (as well as Hawthorne's, Stowe's, and Eliot's novels) can all be viewed as variants of travel writing. Since "writers can hardly break free from the basic cultural presuppositions that give their work meaning" (Spurr 1993, 189), these texts give insight into their writers' cultures of origin while they also produce a culturally biased textual "version" of the foreign culture they describe and translate.[7] For their evaluation of the travel journals, readers also need to keep in mind the generic differences between the three prose texts (by Fuller, Hawthorne, and Eliot), which account for some differences among the many similarities. With her dispatches to the New York *Tribune* Margaret Fuller primarily sought to educate the American public about the political situation in Italy as well as specific points of Italian culture, whereas Nathaniel Hawthorne kept a private journal of his impressions of Italy—partly as preparation for his Italian novel

The Marble Faun. And George Eliot wrote her journal of her trip to Italy after she was back in England; later she recounted a fictionalized version of her experiences in the Roman museums in *Middlemarch*. In conceptualizing the journal of her Italy trip, she observed generic constraints, as Margaret Harris and Judith Johnston point out in their introduction to *The Journals of George Eliot*: "Writing in retrospect, GE constructs her Italian journey as a version of the Grand Tour inflected by English Romanticism" (1998, 329). By calling attention to the controlled nature of Eliot's journal, Harris and Johnston provide an important clue that should be taken into account when analyzing the differences in the three writers' portrayals of Italy in their prose texts: Fuller authored a public text whereas Hawthorne kept an entirely private journal that became famous for its (sometimes inappropriately) irreverent tone; Eliot's studied "recollections" take a middle position between public and private, even though according to Harris and Johnston "[t]here is nothing to suggest that these journals were composed for publication" (xviii).

Considering Margaret Fuller's experiences in Italy, it does not come as a surprise that her account of Italy in *At Home and Abroad*—the narrative that helped to spark Eliot's interest in Italian politics which she later fictionalized in *Romola*—is the text that is the most enthusiastic and positive about Italian culture. Fuller's experiences in Italy provided her with excitement on both an intellectual and a personal level. The—albeit failed—"Italian revolution" afforded her a chance to indulge in reveries about an improved social order under socialism; Fuller also found personal happiness in her relationship with the Italian Marchese Giovanni Ossoli whom she might have married in 1848, shortly before their son was born.

From the very beginning Fuller's journal-style dispatches—collected in *At Home and Abroad*—"translate" Italian culture and politics for Americans in the United States.[8] Fuller stated that she had come to Europe in order to look for lessons to teach to America; she accordingly initially presents herself as a "colonial subject" to the readership at home: "Although we have an independent political existence, our position toward Europe, as to literature and the arts, is still that of a colony, and one feels the same joy here that is experienced by the colonist in returning to the parent home" (1856, 250). But in spite of her deferential attitude, it seems that it is not the Americans, but the Europeans whom Fuller wants to teach a lesson about what she recognizes as a great European idea fully realized only on American soil.[9] This idea is, of course, democracy, and Fuller is proud of the American accomplishment. Throughout the volume she, nevertheless, criticizes inappropriate behavior by Americans abroad who show a lack of awareness of cultural otherness along with insufficient interest in Italy and its struggles for democracy and independence from Austrian rule: "Absorbed at home by the lust of gain, the love of show, abroad they see only the equipages, the fine clothes, the food,—they have no heart for the idea, for the destiny of our own great nation: how can they feel the spirit that is struggling now in this and others of Europe?" (240).

Having recognized parallels between the American and the Italian revolution, she identifies Europe as the cradle of democratic culture and bemoans its state of corruption when she writes that "the public failure [in Europe] seems amazing, seems monstrous" (253). Throwing overboard her deferential posture in a move anticipating the United States' appropriation of leadership in global politics, she calls on her own country to take the lead in Italy's struggle for unification and democracy:

> I earnestly hope for some expression of sympathy from my country toward Italy. Take a good chance and do something; you have shown much good feeling toward the Old World in its physical difficulties,—you ought to do still more in its spiritual endeavor. This cause is OURS, above all others; we ought to show that we feel it to be so. At present there is no likelihood of war, but in case of it I trust the United States would not fail in some noble token of sympathy toward this country. The soul of our nation need not wait for its government; these things are better done by individuals. . . . I have been ardently desirous to judge fairly, and had no prejudices to prevent; beside, I was not ignorant of the history and literature of Italy, and had some common ground on which to stand with its inhabitants, and hear what they have to say. In many ways Italy is of kin to us; she is the country of Columbus, of Amerigo, of Cabot. . . . Please think of this, some of my friends, who still care for the eagle, the Fourth of July, and the old cries of hope and honor. (249)

Later, she castigates slave-holding America for having betrayed the democratic spirit, but nevertheless attributes cultural superiority not only to the American achievement of democracy, but also to the American brand of religion, in spite of her initial posture of deference to the mother continent.

By the time she came to Italy, Fuller already sympathized with radical politics, as Larry Reynolds points out in *European Revolutions and the American Literary Renaissance*. Reynolds speculates that Fuller was radicalized when she became an eyewitness "to the starvation in the winter of 1846–47 and blamed the king" (1986, 61). As intellectual sources of her radicalism, he names the novelist George Sand, the Polish poet and exiled revolution leader Adam Mickiewicz, and well known French followers of Fourier (see

Reynolds 1986, 60). In her dispatches from Italy she mainly champions the Italian revolutionary leader Giuseppe Mazzini, whom she met in England and who upon their very first meeting in his English exile had asked her to act as a courier for him (see von Mehren 1994, 247). During her time in Italy she had to witness the failure of the Italian revolution but supported its cause until the very last. In her vivacious and passionate dispatches to the readers of the New York *Tribune,* she gave detailed up-to-the-minute reports of the current political situation, including complete quotations of Mazzini's letter to the Pope (who finally betrayed the revolutionary's republican cause)[10] and also the Triumvir's[11] letter to Ferdinand Lesseps, the French leader, who in 1849 had come as a self-declared "friend and a brother" (1856, 390) to the Romans. Lesseps ultimately sided with the Austrians and finally ordered his forces to attack—and defeat—the insurgent Republican troops and restored the Pope who had fled the city. Fuller, even though she was pregnant at the time and later the mother of a small child, literally threw herself in the midst of action, joining Ossoli at the battle line and later becoming *Regolatrice* of the Hospital of Fate Bene Fratelli.

Thus having "gone somewhat native," Fuller keeps defending the Italian revolutionary valor from Anglo-Saxon prejudice, which she locates in an American and British inability to deal with cultural otherness:

> I met an American. He had "no confidence in the Republic." Why? Because he "had no confidence in the people." Why? Because "they were not like *our* people." Ah! Jonathan and John,—excuse me, but I must say the Italian has a decided advantage over you in the power of quickly feeling generous sympathy, as well as some other things which I have not time to particularize. (358)

Having noticed that in his cultural ignorance "the American . . . attaches some value to his crude impressions and frequent blunders" (359), she gives her own advice for understanding other cultures: "It is necessary to speak the languages of these countries, and know personally some of their inhabitants, in order to form any accurate impressions" (360).

Whether or not Fuller herself always understood Italian culture well enough to form "accurate impressions" remains debatable since a closer look at her attitude towards Catholicism reveals her own cultural biases—which reflect common Anglo-American biases. Diego Saglia lists a few of those stereotypical preconceptions about Italianness: "[T]he institutional threats then ascribed to Italianness were cumulatively spiritual (superstition), sexual (lechery), and moral (murder)" (1998, 25). Whenever Fuller mentions the Catholic faith, she seems to be taken aback by at least one of its aspects, and the reader can sense a strange impulse on her part to remedy the situation. To her, the sight of a young novice is "revolting and painful to the last degree" because she feels that "monastic seclusion" is not always voluntary (1856, 272); having witnessed a believer kiss the Pope's foot she comments "the act seemed to me disgustingly abject" (276)—this statement will gain significance in light of my discussion (below in this chapter) of Hawthorne's description of Italy as paradigm of human abjection. Fuller's overall evaluation of Catholicism as degenerated, pagan, and ultimately substanceless is devastating:

> How any one can remain a Catholic—I mean who has ever been aroused to think, and is not biassed [sic] by the partialities of childish years—after seeing Catholicism here in Italy, I cannot conceive. There once was a soul in the religion while the blood of its martyrs was yet fresh upon the ground, but that soul was always too much encumbered with the remains of pagan habits and customs: that soul is now quite fled elsewhere, and in the splendid catafalco, watched by so many white and red-robed snuff-taking, sly-eyed men, would they let it be opened, nothing would be found but bones. (299)

Her ultimate indictment of Catholicism—and also increasing political radicalization—is obvious from her last *Tribune* dispatch, when the revolutionary cause was already lost for the time being (her brother, perhaps due to their "apocalyptic socialism," as Reynolds speculates [1988, 72] omitted her last three letters from *At Home and Abroad*):

> The seeds for a vast harvest of hatreds and contempts are sown over every inch of Roman ground, nor can that malignant growth be extirpated, till the wishes of Heaven shall waft a fire that will burn down all, root and branch, and prepare the earth for an entirely new culture. The next revolution, here and elsewhere, will be radical. Not only Jesuitism must go, but the Roman Catholic religion must go. (quoted in Reynolds 1988, 73)

While, perhaps surprisingly, she does not once in her dispatches refer to her transcendentalist convictions,[12] Fuller decides to present Protestantism as a cure for Catholic ills. She does this in a very revealing passage which implies that the democratic political protest, which made the Pope flee Rome, has caused Italy to become "Protestant":

> *The work is done*; the revolution in Italy is now radical, nor can it stop till Italy becomes independent and united as a republic. Protestant she already is, and though the memory of saints and martyrs may continue to be

revered, the ideal of woman to be adored under the name of Mary, yet Christ will now begin to be a little thought of; *his* idea has always been carefully out of sight under the old *régime*; all the worship being for the Madonna and saints, who were to be well paid for the interceding for sinners,—an example which might make men cease to be such, was no way coveted. Now the New Testament has been translated into Italian; copies are already dispersed far and wide; men calling themselves Christians will no longer be left entirely ignorant of the precepts and life of Jesus. (1856, 381)

Presenting herself to her American readership as a staunch descendant of the Puritans, who puts all of her faith in Christ—rather than an iconoclastic transcendentalist—Fuller here implicitly argues that the "right" democratic ideals will necessarily lead people to adhere to the "right" religious faith—Protestantism. Since the values of democracy and Protestantism are quintessentially American, it should not come as a surprise that, in a passage in which she again turns to reluctant America for support, she suggests that Italy's ills are to be providentially cured by an American remedy:

Yet even now it is not too late. If America would only hail triumphant, though she could not sustain injured Rome, that would be something. . . . I have also a lurking confidence in a providential order of things, by which brute force and selfish enterprise are sometimes set at naught by aid which seems to descend from a higher sphere. Even old pagans believed in that, you know; and I was born in America, Christianized by the Puritans,—America freed by eight years' patient suffering, poverty, and struggle,—America so cheered in dark days by one spark of sympathy from a foreign shore, America, first "recognized" by Lafayette. . . . It is natural that I should have some faith. (387)

At this point, Fuller makes a very interesting move in her interpretation of cultural specifics. Via her dispatch she assures her American audience of the superiority of their very own American political and religious values, while at the same time reminding them of the fact that these values necessarily originate in Europe and could not have flourished in the United States without European assistance. Carried away by her idealism (and perhaps also her rhetoric), she even suggests in a rather bizarre passage that democratization has cured Rome from "cloak and dagger-crime," the most (stereo)typical of the Italian vices:

The order of Rome, thronged as it is with troops, is amazing. I go from one end to the other, and amid the poorest and most barbarous of the population, (barbarously ignorant, I mean), alone and on foot. My friends send out their

> little children alone with their nurses. The amount of crime is almost nothing to what it was. The Roman, no longer pent in ignorance and crouching beneath espionage, no longer stabs in the dark. His energies have true vent; his better feelings are roused; he has thrown aside the stiletto. (388)

Even though one might wonder to what extent Fuller deliberately catered to her American readership, passages like the ones quoted above indicate that in spite of her undeniable sympathies for Italy, she retains many cultural stereotypes and prefers American values and customs—or rather the accomplishment of American values on European soil—over Italian ones.

Harriet Beecher Stowe, who in *Agnes of Sorrento* projects the observations of her own travels in Italy onto a fifteenth-century plot dealing with religious unrest preceding the execution of Girolamo Savonarola, shows greater sensitivity in dealing with Italian Catholicism than the other American writers discussed in this chapter. This is particularly surprising since—as the next chapter will indicate—her depiction of African Americans in *Uncle Tom's Cabin* (1852) and *Dred* (1856) lacks the cultural sensitivity that she shows in her presentation of Italian Catholic alterity. Stowe addresses the usual issues that seem to bother nineteenth-century Protestants about Catholicism: monastic life, celibacy, Catholic prayer rituals, "idolatrous worship of saints," and the institution of the Pope, but her comments show that she, for one, is aware of her own cultural biases. For example, she remarks on the occasion of Agnes performing her "Hail, Mary!":

> However foreign to the habits of a Northern mind or education such a mode of prayer may be, these forms to her were all helpful and significant, her soul was borne by them Godward . . . but the Northern mind of Europe is entirely unfitted to read and appreciate the psychological religious phenomena of Southern races. ([1867] 1967, 97)

She similarly explains the worship of saints, which Fuller and Hawthorne simply disqualify as "pagan habits," as historically necessary syncretism needed to supersede Roman paganism: "Christianity, when it entered Italy, came among a people every act of whose life was colored and consecrated by symbolic and ritual acts of heathenism. The only possible way to uproot this was in supplanting it by Christian ritual and symbolism equally minute and pervading" (96). And she also points out the social significance of Italy's religious "institutions that guaranteed to each individual a livelihood" (166)—convents often served as refuge for women who had no means to support themselves and monasteries provided shelters for artists who could not have made a living for themselves.

But in spite of stressing what Stowe perceived as positive aspects of Catholicism, *Agnes of Sorrento* ultimately endorses Protestantism rather than Catholicism. Stowe's heroine Agnes gradually learns to pray directly to God instead of his potentially corrupt human representatives and Stowe also makes sure to stress the Protestant qualities of her "good" Catholic characters. Savonarola, for example, "whose reforms gave no quarter to right or left" (168), is among the Republican Florentine statesmen and monks who are graced with what seems to be a proto-American democratic spirit:

> A republic, in the midst of contending elements, the history of Florence, in the Middle Ages, was a history of what shoots and blossoms the Italian nature might send forth, when rooted in the rich soil of liberty.... Its statesmen, its merchants, its common artisans, and the very monks in its convents, were all pervaded by one spirit. The men of Florence in its best days were men of a large, grave, earnest mould. What the Puritans of New England wrought out with severest earnestness in their reasonings and their lives, these early Puritans of Italy embodied in poetry, sculpture, and painting. (257)

Thus, ultimately, Stowe, even though she also foregrounds what she perceives as the positive aspects of Catholic modes of worship, proposes the same thing that Fuller proposes regarding religious worship in Italy: Catholicism is not utterly devoid of good qualities, but Italy must be "Protestantized" in order to fend off both religious and political chaos and corruption.

From the outset of his stay in Europe, Nathaniel Hawthorne took a much cockier "postcolonial" stance than both Harriet Beecher Stowe and Margaret Fuller. His attitude towards England, his "mother country," waffled between identification and total rejection. In his *English Notebooks, 1853-56*, he identifies with his English roots via his ancestor who left England:

> My ancestor left England in 1635. I return in 1853. I sometimes feel as if I myself had been absent these two hundred and eighteen years—leaving England just emerging from the feudal system, and finding it on the verge of Republicanism. It brings the two far separated points of time very closely together, to view the matter thus. (*English Notebooks, 1853–56* 1987, 138)

Yet in 1855, when tensions over British recruiting practices in the United States (which threatened to violate the United States' neutrality) led to a political conflict, Hawthorne, responding to rumors of impending war between England and the United States (see *Letters 1853–56*, 1987, 400n) erupted in postcolonial rage and wanted the United States to attack immediately. He declared: "We hold the fate of England in our hands, and it is time we crushed her—blind, ridiculous, old rump of beef, sodden in strong beer, that she is; not but what she has still vitality enough to do us a good deal of mischief; before we quite annihilate her" (397).

Toward Italy, which was part of the "parent continent," but not his "mother country," Hawthorne had less strong feelings, but his cultural evaluation is nevertheless marked by the same pattern of attraction and repulsion. During the sixteen months that they spent in Italy, the Hawthornes —as they had already done in England—visited nearly all the famous tourist sights and looked at countless museums, churches, and galleries. Hawthorne's Italian notebooks focus mainly on descriptions of Italian buildings and art and record his interactions with other English-speaking people in Italy. There is almost no evidence of any contact with Italians[13] except for a few casual remarks about conflicts with servants[14] and attempts to discourage beggars. Nearly all direct comments on the Italian population in the Italian notebooks leave the reader with the impression that nineteenth-century Italy was populated with beggars and drowned in filth.[15] Hawthorne vented his disgust at what he perceived as typically Italian habits very eloquently and impressively in a notebook entry about a visit to the town of Bolsena. The entry is highly representative of Hawthorne's writing about Italy and encompasses a one-and-a-half-page long passage of entirely negative description of Italian hereditary habits:

> I wonder whether the ancient Romans were as dirty a people as we everywhere find those who have succeeded them. . . . I think it must be an hereditary trait, probably weakened and robbed a little of its dirty horror by the influence of milder ages; and I am much afraid that Caesar trod narrower and fouler ways, in his path to power, than those of modern Rome, or ever of this disgusting town of Bolsena. . . . Rotten vegetables, thrown everywhere about, musty straw, standing puddles, running rivulets of dissolved nastiness—these matters were a relief amid viler objects. The town was full of great black hogs, wallowing before every door. . . . Donkeys (of which there were many) likewise accosted us with braying; children (little imps engendered of dirt, and growing nastier every day they lived,) pestered us with begging; men stared askance at us as they stood in corners or turned against a housewall, and women endangered us with dirty slops which they were flinging from doorways into the street. No decent words can describe—no admissable image can give an idea—of this noisome place. (*French and Italian Notebooks* [1858–59] 1980, 480–81)

Hawthorne mollifies this outburst (which is echoed by similar descriptions of Rome in both the notebooks and *The Marble Faun*) immediately by adding, "And yet, I remember, the donkeys came up the height loaded with fruit, and with little flat-sided barrels of wine; the people had a good atmosphere . . . and there seemed to be no reason why they should not live a beautiful and jolly life" (480). He continues, "I did not mean to write such an ugly description as the above, but it is well, once for all, to have attempted conveying an idea of what disgusts the traveller, more or less, in all these Italian towns" (481).[16]

This passage, which perhaps tells more about Hawthorne's own fears and hang-ups than about Italy, is characteristic of his way of dealing with cultural, class based, ethnic or sexual otherness. His reaction to "Italian filth" in particular brings to mind Julia Kristeva's psychoanalytic theory of abjection as individual and collective fear of otherness that surfaces in "loathing an item of food, a piece of filth, waste, or dung" (1982, 2). The abject frightens when it manifests itself as bodily excretion because it is not the body itself, yet still a part of it. It must be expelled to keep intact the border between inside and outside and to prevent corporeal decay. The abject always suggests annihilation and meaninglessness:[17]

> A massive and sudden emergence of uncanniness . . . now harries me as radically separate, loathsome. Not me. Not that. But not nothing, either. A "something" that I do not recognize as a thing. A weight of meaninglessness, about which there is nothing insignificant and which crushes me. On the edge of non-existence and hallucination, of a reality that, if I acknowledge it, annihilates me. (2)

Every encounter with the abject is reminiscent of the initial abjection of the maternal body that the subject has to perform in order to acquire language and to establish the border between self and (m)other. Kristeva describes the process of separation as "a violent, clumsy breaking away, with the constant risk of falling back under the sway of a power as secure as it is shifting" (13). What is expelled continues to be perceived as attractive and as a threat to the separated self.

Encounters with the abject jeopardize personal and collective identity because they threaten the border of the subject and are accompanied by feelings of loss and loneliness (which might occur more frequently if one is away from one's usual surroundings).[18] To escape the attraction of this dangerous otherness[19] that is represented by decay, filth, and excrement—but still signifies a "desired" dissolution of bodily boundaries because of the continuing attraction of the maternal body—the individual (for example, Nathaniel Hawthorne in Italy and in "maternal" England) must reject the abject in order to be able to define and defend the boundaries of identity. By calling the abject and abjection "safeguards" and "primers of my culture" (2), Kristeva points out that this mechanism works for entire cultures as well as for individuals. Her theory provides a structural model for the social construction of abjection, but it does not explain why certain cultures label certain individuals or groups as abject—historically, "foreign others" have often been labeled abject along with racial and sexual minorities. Interestingly, George Eliot also describes this mechanism of labeling racially others as abject—of course without being able to employ postmodern critical terminology. In "The Modern Hep! Hep! Hep!" Eliot identifies the habit of projecting undesirable physical qualities onto minorities in order to facilitate ethnic discrimination: "There is understood to be a peculiar odour from the negro body, and we know that some persons, too rationalistic to feel bound by the curse on Ham, used to hint very strongly that this odour determined the question on the side of negro slavery" ([1879] 1894, 208).

Kristeva stresses, in *Powers of Horror,* that cultures also invent strategies for purifying the abject. She suggests that the sacred, which also figures prominently in nineteenth-century Italy, is a cleansing of the abject: "The various means of *purifying* the abject—the various catharses—make up the history of religions, and end up with that catharsis par excellence called art, both on the far and near side of religion" (1982, 17). This point of her theory is nicely illustrated by both Hawthorne's continual juxtaposition of religion and filth in his Italian notebooks and his wife Sophia's religious worship at the shrine of high art. And, as we will see in the next chapter, it is also illustrated by the sublimation of what Eliot's fictional character Daniel Deronda perceives as the "filthy" aspects of everyday Jewish life; Deronda evades these by focusing on the esoteric aspects of Jewish religion.

As David Spurr observes on the subject of abjection, presenting the culturally other as debased and savage is characteristic of the colonial situation, in which "misery and abjection are presented as two faces of the same condition . . . so that the physical suffering of indigenous people can be associated with their moral and intellectual degradation" (1993, 77–78). The colonizer—just like Hawthorne, the "harmless" American traveler—has developed mechanisms that allow him/her to view him/herself as "less backward" and culturally superior because "modern colonial discourse has produced . . . on the level of ideology, a projection of anxiety onto the racial and cultural Other that has always been part of the human imagination" (77).

The stereotyping that is part of the strategy of debasing the culturally other in colonial discourse (and, as I would argue, also in the dialog presented between various diachronic stages of Western culture in this chapter—e.g., Hawthorne's "filthy Old World Italians") is often seen as the result of very similar psychological projections, which betray a failure to confront one's own "phobias and fetishes," as Homi Bhabha argues when he proposes "to read the stereotype in terms of fetishism" (1994, 72):

> [t]he scene of fetishism functions similarly as, at once, a reactivation of the material or original fantasy—the anxiety of castration and sexual difference—as well as normalization of that difference and disturbance in terms of the fetish object as the substitute for the mother's penis. . . . [F]etishism is always a "play" or vacillation between the archaic affirmation of wholeness/similarity—in Freud's terms: "All men have penises"; in ours: "All men have the same skin/race/culture"—and the anxiety associated with lack and difference—again, for Freud "Some do not have penises"; for us "Some do not have the same skin/race/ culture." (74–75)

As a consequence of this scenario, the "fetish or stereotype gives access to an 'identity' which is predicated as much on mastery and pleasure as it is on anxiety" (75). This cultural anxiety can easily be seen in Nathaniel Hawthorne's writing.[20]

In spite of incipient U.S. cultural imperialism, it would certainly be utterly absurd to argue that in the nineteenth century the United States' relationship to Italy was in any way like that of colonizer and colonized, yet I nevertheless want to suggest that Hawthorne's attitude towards Europe can be deemed "postcolonialist." He positions himself in the role of a rebellious son, who, out of an acquired cultural superiority to his "mother continent," sets out to "civilize the brutes."[21] At various points in his notebooks, he asserts that American culture is superior because of its egalitarian democratic political and social system. Thus, he touts the American political system in a very revealing passage about why he does not feel at home in Italy:

> It would only be a kind of despair, however, that would ever make me dream of finding a home in Italy; a sense that I had lost my country through absence or incongruity, and that earth is not, at any rate, an abiding-place. I wonder that we Americans love our country at all, it having no limits and no oneness; and when you try to make it a matter of the heart, everything falls away except one's native State;—neither can you seize hold of that, unless you tear it out of the Union, bleeding and quivering. . . . I think the singularity of our form of government contributes to give us a kind of patriotism, by separating us from other nations more entirely. If other nations had similar institutions—if England, especially, were a democracy—we should as

readily make ourselves at home in another country as now in a new state. (*French and Italian Notebooks* [1858–59] 1980, 464)

Nathaniel Hawthorne's positions on the virtues of American democracy might not be all that far removed from those of Margaret Fuller, yet this passage still shows amazing differences. While in 1848 Fuller supported Italy's struggle for democracy with all her might, Hawthorne, living in Italy ten years later at a time of similar political unrest, does not even take notice of the political situation which had escalated during the month of his arrival—January 1858—when Felice Orsini, an Italian nationalist, had attempted to assassinate the French emperor Napoleon III. As a result, France had started to negotiate with Piedmont about finally removing the Austrian troops from Italy and dividing territorial spoils.[22] Hawthorne occasionally mentions the presence of French soldiers in Italy, in one case commenting how "well behaved and courteous" (141) they were to his family, yet does not once treat current political conflicts at greater length. While this attitude fits in with his general avoidance of political statements (critics have commented for quite some time about the fact that in his writing he almost never referred to the salient problem of slavery in his own country, and suggested that "time and providence," rather than human involvement, would put an end to it),[23] it might also perhaps be due to the fact that both Hawthorne's interest in contemporary Italian culture and his "cultural competence" did not match Margaret Fuller's.

But in his Italian notebooks, Hawthorne surprisingly shows a much greater tolerance of Roman Catholicism than Fuller, reserving his criticism of the Catholic faith for his novel *The Marble Faun*. Alternating between negative and positive statements about Catholicism, such as voicing his opinion "that a great deal of devout and reverential feeling is kept alive in people's hearts by the Catholic mode of worship" (*French and Italian Notebooks* [1858–59] 1980, 98), he locates his criticism of church-related matters in the "venal Italian character" rather than the tenets of Catholicism, as the following statement shows:

> We saw nothing of my wife and Miss Shepard; but found afterwards that they had been much annoyed by the attentions of a priest who wished to show them the Cathedral, till they finally told him that they had no money with them, when he left them without another word. The attendants in churches seem quite as venal as most other Italians, and, for the sake of their little profit, they do not hesitate to interfere with the great purposes for which their churches were built and decorated; hanging curtains, for in-

stance, before all the celebrated pictures, or hiding them away in the sacristy, so that they cannot be seen without a fee. (1903 b, 28)[24]

In another notebook entry, he also praises the generally religious atmosphere of Italy, where "[t]he cool, dusky refreshment of these holy places . . . probably suggests devotional ideas to the people" (*French and Italian Notebooks* [1858–59] 1980, 357), but doubts that this atmosphere suffices to counteract the "character" of the Italian Catholics: "If we could only see any good effects in their daily life, we might deem it an excellent thing to be able to find incense and a prayer always ascending, to which every individual may join his own. I really wonder that the Catholics are not better men and women" (357).

Whereas Fuller accepted the Pope as an authority figure and even wrote him a letter beseeching him to further the unification and democratization of Italy, Hawthorne presents him as just another rather curious tourist attraction (but he, at least, refrained from commenting on the Italian toe-kissing habit):

> His face was kindly and venerable, but not particularly impressive. . . . The Pope bent his head upon the desk, and seemed to spend three or four minutes in prayer; then rose, and all the purple Cardinals, and bishops, and priests, of whatever degree, rose behind and beside him. Next, he went to kiss St. Peter's toe, at least I believe he kissed it, but I was not near enough to be certain; and lastly, he knelt down and directed his devotions towards the high altar. . . . I am very glad to have seen the Pope, because now he may be crossed out of the list of sights to be seen. (150)

Hawthorne's somewhat flippant but seemingly benign discussion of Roman Catholicism reveals another important difference between his and Fuller's attitude towards Italy: Fuller cared so deeply about the Italian population that she wanted to "save them from themselves," whereas Hawthorne viewed Italians in Italy as a more or less amusing nuisance to be put up with when visiting the country's cultural treasures (which, after all, had been the Hawthornes' main incentive to coming to Italy).

As the English notebooks already indicate, Hawthorne left out hardly any tourist sight to be seen in the parts of Europe that he visited. Like Eliot after him, he treated Italy as a gigantic art museum; ample evidence of this is, of course, also to be found in the Italian notebooks. While the endless descriptions of famous artworks and how to get to them are rather tiresome, Hawthorne's irreverent tone—which often becomes rather insulting when applied to people—is refreshing when used to describe more or less famous works of art.[25]

In the Italian notebooks, Hawthorne clearly shows signs of being fed up with traveling to all the artworks that his wife wanted to see and he even more clearly shows his dislike for the Italian population. Thus, his final assertion that he never wants to see the beautiful familiar sights of Rome again does not come as a surprise (especially when considering the important fact that during his last year in Italy he also had to go through the agony of almost seeing his daughter Una die from malaria):

> I walked to the Pincian, and saw the garden and the city, and the Borghese grounds, and St Peter's, in an earlier sunlight than ever before. Methought they never looked so beautiful, nor the sky so bright and blue. I saw Soracte on the horizon, and I looked at everything as if for the last time; nor do I wish ever to see any of these objects again, though no place ever took so strong a hold of my being as Rome, nor ever seemed so close to me and so strangely familiar. (524)

Compared to both Fuller's and Hawthorne's accounts of Italy, George Eliot's "Recollections of Italy. 1860," which consist simply of a string of observations about places visited and works of art looked at, provide a rather unsatisfactory reading experience—which apparently is also true of most of her other travel writing. This seems chiefly due to the fact that in her journals, as also later in *Romola*, Eliot—perhaps in an effort to sanitize the aspects of Italy that Hawthorne found abject—appears to deliberately ignore most aspects of Italian cultural alterity. Postponing her evaluation of Catholicism until the publication of her novel, Eliot, unlike the American writers discussed in this chapter, does not comment on the impression that Italian religious worship left her with, thus forgoing a chance to provide an interesting reading experience in her journals. Henry James, dissatisfied with Eliot's journals, gives a good description of the first impression that Eliot's accounts of foreign places leave: "She enumerates diligently all the pictures and statues she sees, and the way she does so is proof of her active, earnest intellectual habits; but it is rarely apparent that they have, as the phrase is, said much to her" (quoted in Harris and Johnston 1998, 329). A rather typical passage from "Recollections of Italy. 1860" might serve to illustrate James's observation:

> I forgot to mention, at Santa Maria Novella, the chapel which is painted with very remarkable frescoes by Simone Memmi and another artist whose name will not occur to me at this moment. The best of the frescoes is the

one in which the Dominicans are represented by black and white dogs—*Domini Cane*. The human groups have high merit for conception and lifelikeness, and they are admirable studies of costume. At this church, too, in the sacristy, is the Madonna della Stella, with an altar step, by Fra Angelico—specimens of his minuter painting in oil. The inner part of the frame is surrounded with lovely angels, with their seraphic joy and flower-garden colouring. ([1860] 1969, 357)

Tom Winnifrith furthermore complains that despite her interest in historical Italy, "Eliot refers very little to contemporary Italy" (1997, 169). And, indeed, the only reference to the Italian population in her journals—which open with the rather stiff statement of purpose that Eliot had looked forward to the journey "rather with the hope of the new elements it would bring to my culture than with the hope of immediate pleasure" (Harris and Johnston 1998, 336)—is the following unspecific description of people she saw in Genoa:

A drive in the direction of the Campo Santo along the dry pebbly bed of the river, showed us the terraced hills planted with olives, and many picturesque groups of the common people with mules or on carts;—not to mention what gives beauty to every corner of the inhabited world—the groups of children squatting against walls or trotting about by the side of their elders, or grinning together over their play. (338)

The emotional paucity of Eliot's Italian journals is certainly due to the fact that they are recollections, and as such lack both the immediacy and factual detail of Fuller's dispatches and Hawthorne's journals. In their introduction to *The Journals of George Eliot*, Margaret Harris and Judith Johnston argue that it would, however, "be erroneous to assume that [Eliot] turned aside from [current affairs]. She more frequently displays concern about national and international events in letters than in her journals, and that concern finds complex expression in her fiction" (1998, xx-xxi). This tendency is indeed noticeable when it comes to Eliot's Italian experience. Even though Italian unification was at hand in 1860,[26] and even though Eliot had already evidenced her interest in Italian politics by reviewing Margaret Fuller's *Letters from Italy* in the May 17, 1856, edition of *The Leader*, she does not really comment on the political situation in her journal, except for a short remark about the significance of the city of Turin and Benso de Cavour:

[N]ow . . . [Turin] is the centre of a widening life which may at last become the life of Resuscitated Italy. At the Railway station as we waited to take our departure for Genoa, we had sight of a man whose name will always be connected with the story of that widening life—Count Cavour—"imitant son portrait" which we had seen in the shops, with unusual closeness. (337)

Eliot explained her apparently subdued interest in politics during her trip in her correspondence from Italy. Even though she announces in one letter that she herself would like to remove the French from Italy ("I feel some stirrings of the insurrectionary spirit myself when I see the red pantaloons at every turn in the streets of Rome" [*George Eliot Letters* 1954–55, 3:288]), she admits in another letter that during her trip she was more interested in sightseeing than in politics: "On a first journey to the greatest centres of art, one must be excused for letting one's public spirit go to sleep a little" (294). Harris and Johnston speculate that "the almost complete suppression of reference to current affairs" in "Recollections of Italy. 1860" is due to Eliot's adherence to constraints imposed by the genre of travel writing (1998, 330).[27] While this might—at least to some extent—explain the absence of political references in the Italian journal, it still does not explain why Eliot almost completely refrains from any kind of observation about contemporary Italian culture in her journal. "Recollections of Italy. 1860," with its endless lists of Italian sights and museums visited by Eliot and Lewes (which led one critic to complain that "Italy was little more to her than a vast museum" [Lord Acton quoted in Harris and Johnston 1998, 328]) describes many of the sights depicted by Hawthorne and reads like a shorter version of his Italian notebooks, completely stripped of any kind of evaluative description of Italian culture. But while Hawthorne often vents his postcolonial rage at Italians as Europeans, Eliot—perhaps making an effort to present herself as a cosmopolitan European rather than an Englishwoman, or perhaps trying to avoid negative, "abject" descriptions—remains completely silent on the subject of Italianness. In *Recollections of Italy. 1860*, Eliot does not even mention that, during the trip, Lewes suggested writing a novel about Savonarola: "[I]t occurred to me that his life and times afford fine material for an historical romance. Polly [Lewes's nickname for George Eliot] at once caught the idea with enthusiasm" (quoted in Thompson 1998, 70).

From "Faction" to Fiction: Italy in Eliot's Novels, Stowe's *Agnes of Sorrento*, and Hawthorne's *The Marble Faun*

While Lewes undoubtedly provided Eliot with the initial idea for *Romola*, I would nevertheless suggest that Eliot was also inspired by the American authors discussed above. The plot elements dealing with religion and human development echo Hawthorne's treatment of similar themes in *The Marble Faun* and *The Scarlet Letter*, whereas parallels between Fuller's and Eliot's discussion of political leadership hint at the fact that Eliot also drew some inspiration from Fuller's Italian dispatches. Even though the plot of *Romola* bears resemblances to Stowe's *Agnes of Sorrento*, it can only be assumed—but not established—that Eliot's Italian novel provides a reaction to Stowe's Italian novel.

References to Italy appear in all of Eliot's writing after her 1860 trip. Thus, she depicts an "English" inability to truly enjoy Italian art via her character Dorothea in *Middlemarch*, transposes concerns of the *Risorgimento* onto Savonarola's Florence in *Romola* (which also contains a critique of Catholicism), and alludes to Giuseppe Mazzini in her presentation of the Jewish quest for nationhood in *Daniel Deronda*. Yet, as in "Recollections of Italy. 1860," contemporary Italy remains conspicuously absent from all of these works. This might be due to the fact that Eliot, like Hawthorne, found it very difficult to tackle cultural otherness and—at least after "Mr. Gilfil's Love Story"—felt uncomfortable dwelling on stereotypical representations of "abject" Italianness.

David Lodge notices about Caterina, the Italian female protagonist of "Mr. Gilfil's Love Story" (from *Scenes of Clerical Life*), what critics usually notice about her non-English characters, namely that "she is all too obviously a character deriving from 'fiction' rather than 'actual life'" (1973, 51). In Caterina's case this might be understandable since "Mr. Gilfil's Love Story," Eliot's first story to focus on a foreign character, was published in 1858, before she spent an extended period of time in Italy. She thus presents Italianness in light of the usual stereotypes about Italian filth, poverty, and superstition and also seems to ascribe Caterina's "uncontrollable passion"—which in the story leads to mock murder—to her national origin. But, to be fair, one nevertheless has to point out that in "Mr. Gilfil's Love Story" Eliot also casts enough aspersion on what seems to be English national character.

Caterina is the child of Sarti, a "small, meagre man, sallow and dingy" ([1858] 1973, 148), who used to be "the *primo tenore* of one short season" (149), but now, due to first losing his voice and then his wife, lives in abject poverty in dirty surroundings with his little daughter Caterina. When Sarti dies, Lady Cheverel, an English lady who is on the verge of leaving Italy after having spent a few years there, decides to take Caterina, "a tiny child, apparently not three years old" (151), back to England with her for humanitarian reasons. But, as the narrator of Mr. Gilfil's love story makes clear from the beginning, English charity has its limits: "It would be a Christian work to train this little Papist into a good Protestant, and graft as much English fruit as possible on the Italian stem" (152), but neither Lady Cheverel's husband, Sir Christopher, nor the childless lady herself "had any idea of adopting her as their daughter, and giving her their own rank in life. They were much too English and aristocratic to think of anything so romantic" (152).

Caterina, who is described as a tiny "yellow bantling" (159) and often addressed in pejorative sexist fashion by pet animal names ("'There's a clever black-eyed monkey. Now bring out the table for picquet'" [143]),[28] is accepted as a family member of sorts only after it becomes clear that she has inherited her father's gift for singing. Yet along with this stereotypical Italian virtue,[29] she also seems to have inherited the stereotypical Italian vice (also hinted at by Fuller and Hawthorne) of a too passionate nature, as becomes clear early on:

> [T]he little Southern bird had its northern nest lined with tenderness and caresses, and pretty things. A loving sensitive nature was too likely, under such nurture, to have its susceptibility heightened into unfitness for an encounter with any harder experience; all the more, because there were gleams of fierce resistance to any discipline that had a harsh or unloving aspect. For the only thing in which Caterina showed any precocity was a certain ingenuity in vindictiveness. When she was five years old she had revenged herself for an unpleasant prohibition by pouring the ink into Mrs Sharp's workbasket; and once, when Lady Cheverel took her doll from her . . . the little minx straightway climbed on a chair and threw down a flower-vase that stood on a bracket. (158)

While this might seem a rather slight example for demonstrating the innate qualities of Caterina's "Italian stem," there is some evidence throughout "Mr. Gilfil's Love Story" that still rather amateurishly suggests (since this was George Eliot's first published work of fiction) that Eliot, at least to some extent, seems to have believed in "inborn Italianness." Thus, Caterina, who, as an adult, presumably does not speak any Italian since she came to England as a three-year-old, keeps addressing Sir Christopher as *Padroncello* throughout the story and keeps prints of Naples on the wall in her room. Caterina's passionate Italianness finally culminates in the attempted murder in Italian fashion (by dagger) of the faithless Captain Wybrow, who had romanced her along with a beautiful English socialite. Wybrow escapes her rage only by providentially dying of heart failure even before their actual meeting.

Andrew Thompson, in spite of critically remarking that in this scene "Eliot's text degenerates into the cloak-and-dagger stuff of Italian melodrama based on medieval and Italian melodrama" (57), develops a rather complicated argument suggesting that Eliot incorporates hints at Italy's political lot in "Mr. Gilfil's Love Story." Thompson takes a brief quotation from Filaccia's sonnet, *Italia mia,* to suggest that "an allegory of the subjection and oppression of Italy is being played out on the domestic stage of Cheveral Manor" (62-63) and "that Caterina's rebellion 'against her destiny' is of course intended to mirror the violent overthrow of the *Ancien Regime* in France" (63) and thus cast light on the Italian situation. His attempt at saving Eliot from stereotyping Italians seems a bit far-fetched, especially since Eliot herself eventually tones down Caterina's rampant Italian passion by having Maynard Gilfil, her morally upright clergical suitor, explain to her that even though she brandished the dagger, her "(Italian) nature" is not murderous:

> Tina, my loved one, you would never have done it. God saw your whole heart; He knows you would never harm a living thing. He watches over His children, and will not let them do things they would pray with their whole hearts not to do. It was the angry thought of a moment, and He forgives you. (234)

While Eliot did not shy away from characterizing Italians in "Mr. Gilfil's Love-Story," they are conspicuously absent from *Middlemarch,* Eliot's first novel after her trip to Italy. In Rome, her heroine, Dorothea, sees the same sights as Eliot did: the Vatican, St. Peter's, various palaces and villas, and an artist's studio. Already completely disenchanted with her new husband, Casaubon, on her wedding trip, Dorothea fails to enjoy Rome and can only focus on what seems negative and even traumatizing. The Catholic faith is a mere superstition to her Protestant sensibilities and the Roman ruins invite thoughts of decay, and death—as they did in Nathaniel Hawthorne—and thus also vaguely hint at "Italian abjection":

> Ruins and basilicas, palaces and colossi, set in the midst of a sordid present, where all that was living and warm-blooded seemed sunk in the deep degeneracy of superstition divorced from reverence, . . . the long vistas of white forms whose marble eyes seemed to hold the monotonous light of an alien world: all this vast wreck of ambitious ideals, sensuous and spiritual, mixed confusedly with the signs of breathing forgetfulness and degradation. . . . Forms both pale and glowing took possession of her young sense, and fixed themselves in her memory even when she was not thinking of them, preparing strange associations which remained through the after-years. ([1861–62] 1994, 193)

Casaubon's typically inadequate reaction to Italian art, captured by Eliot in a hilarious dialogue between Casaubon and Dorothea, does not exactly help Dorothea to a better appreciation of what Rome has to offer:

"Should you like to go to the Farnesina, Dorothea? It contains celebrated frescoes designed or painted by Raphael, which most persons think it worth while to visit."

"But do you care about them?" was always Dorothea's question.

"They are, I believe, highly esteemed." (197)

Since Eliot's "Recollections of Italy. 1860" only lists all the artworks that Eliot saw in Rome without revealing much about Eliot's emotions about them, one can only guess whether or not with this exchange Eliot might have ridiculed her own inability to appreciate the visual arts without any previous instruction. Joseph Wiesenfarth seems to corroborate such a view by arguing that Ruskin did for Eliot what Will Ladislaw does for Dorothea, namely teach her the "language of art," which ultimately enabled both to appreciate art (and Rome): "[J]ust as Ladislaw taught Dorothea, Ruskin taught George Eliot" (1982, 374).

Eliot's next work about Italy, *Romola*, perhaps does not address "Italianness" much more adequately, but it nevertheless hints rather obliquely at the political situation in contemporary Italy. While I suspect that Eliot might have shied away from dealing with Italianness in *Romola* because she was taken aback by Hawthorne's inadequate and ultimately xenophobic rendering of Italian culture in *The Marble Faun*, the novel that *Romola* was inspired by, her reluctance to fictionalize Italianness might also be explained by her belief in the essential sameness of all human beings, regardless of spatial or temporal concerns. In the proem to *Romola*, her narrator asserts the "broad sameness of the human lot":

> The great river-courses which have shaped the lives of men have hardly changed; and those other streams, the life-currents that ebb and flow in human hearts, pulsate to the same needs, the same great loves and terrors. As our thought follows close in the slow wake of the dawn, we are impressed with the broad sameness of the human lot, which never alters in the main headings of its history—hunger and labour, seed-time and harvest, love and death. ([1863] 1980, 43)

Eliot here positions herself in the Enlightenment tradition of viewing human nature as unchangeable. In *The Interpretation of Cultures*, anthropologist Clifford Geertz—who attacks the notion of a constant human nature from the vantage point of late twentieth-century anthropology[30]—cites the eighteenth-century philosopher Mascou with a very similar view of human nature: "The stage setting [in different times and places] is indeed, altered, the actors change their garb and their appearance; but their inward motions arise from the same desires and passions of men, and produce their effects in the vicissitudes of kingdoms and peoples" (quoted in Geertz [1973] 1993, 34). While this *consensium gentium* approach, "the notion that there are some things that all men will be found to agree upon as right, real, just or attractive" (38–39), has come under attack by modern anthropology, which looks at cultural diversity rather than universality and thus prefers to study the various "control mechanisms—plans, recipes, rules, instructions" for the "governing of behavior" (44), it was still more or less received knowledge in the nineteenth century.

Hans Ulrich Seeber argues in an article on "Cultural Synthesis in George Eliot's *Middlemarch*" that Eliot was a cosmopolitan. Indebted to a Goethean notion of *Bildung* that assumes that "[u]nknown alien cultures and experiences are accessible by acts of hermeneutic understanding" (1997, 19), she had a thoroughly European outlook and believed in "cultural synthesis."[31] According to Seeber,

> [a]lthough Eliot makes use of national stereotypes for purposes of characterization and classification . . . nationalism does not rank high on her list of priorities. Both in her novels and in her essays she looks at Continental Europe with remarkable sympathy. Being perfectly confident of her English identity she is bent upon widening her horizon, appreciating the achievements of continental cultures and depreciating their defects. (20)

I would certainly underwrite Seeber's claim that "Eliot continues an eighteenth-century transnational discourse of humanitarian values and cultural endeavour" (21), but I do not share his optimistic assessment of Eliot's overall cultural competence which, according to him, allows her to depreciate the "defects" of other cultures and "look at German life with a completely unprejudiced eye" (21). I would rather argue that Eliot sometimes shied away from assessments and representations of foreign cultures precisely because she knew the limits of her abilities as a cultural critic. This idea can perhaps be corroborated by David Hollinger's insight that cultural critics realized only in the second half of the twentieth century what Eliot could not realize during her own time—that in order to understand another culture from a cosmopolitan point of view one must take into account the fact that cosmopolitanism always also has local roots which cannot be ignored.[32]

Eliot's awareness of the limits of her descriptive powers regarding foreign cultures might have influenced her decision to conceptualize Romola as a highly educated heroine from a wealthy background—who very much resembles all of her other heroines—and to choose a historically and culturally remote Renaissance setting for her Italian novel. By commenting upon the

Risorgimento through her fictional presentation of fifteenth-century Florentine politics, Eliot nevertheless also shows her interest in current political affairs. Thus she pays tribute to both Margaret Fuller as a literary precursor and to Giuseppe Mazzini as a political leader. For a long time before actually traveling to Italy in 1860, Eliot had been supportive of the *Risorgimento*. Eliot's interest in Mazzini was sparked by the fact that George Henry Lewes knew him personally and was rekindled when she reviewed Fuller's dispatches from Italy. When she worked as a journalist for *The Westminster Review*, she commissioned an article from Mazzini, which was published in the April 1852 issue as "Europe: Its Conditions and Prospects." In this article, Mazzini, who "was a leading proponent and, to some extent, the creator of political nationalism" (Riall 1994, 66), outlined his philosophy, which, as the following quotation shows, bears remarkable resemblance to both Fuller's transcendentalism and Eliot's secular "religion of humanity":

> This war-cry which rises from the ranks of the Proletaire is the cry of our fathers, the Hussites: *The cup for all, the cup for all!* It is the logical consequence of the doctrine common to us all, the unity of God, and, therefore, of the human race. . . . Yesterday, we worshipped the priest, the lord, the soldier, the master; to-day we worship MAN, his liberty, his dignity, his immortality, his labour, his progressive tendency, all that constitutes him a creature made in the image of God. . . . We believe that every man ought to be a temple of the living God. . . . We believe no more in that narrow dualism which established an absurd antagonism between heaven and earth, between God and his creation. (1852, 447)

In his article, Mazzini apparently locates the theological origin of this "pantheism" or "transcendentalism" in Hussite belief, whereas he grounds its social component in the revolutionary egalitarianism represented by the cry for liberty, egality, and fraternity. Mazzini viewed the French Revolution as a culmination of all progressive and liberationist ideas and believed that within an organic society which is struggling for democratic unity each individual "in the great common workshop of Humanity" has to labor incessantly "towards a common end,—collective perfectionment, the discovery and progressive application of the law of life" (450). Eliot and Fuller must have admired Mazzini for both the same and different reasons. Both writers certainly appreciated his teleological view of social progress (Eliot, after all, incorporated a Comtean teleological model of history in *Romola*); yet while Fuller presumably preferred Mazzini's combination of transcendentalism and revolution to his insistence on duty,[33] Eliot most certainly preferred his insistence on the individual's duty to submit to societal goals.

Eliot showed her support of Mazzini's ideas throughout her writing. Impressed by his leadership, she voiced her support of the Italian and French revolutionary causes on several occasions, even though she usually remained cautious about political statements. In an often-quoted letter to John Sibree from March 8, 1848, she not only praised the French Revolution, but also wrote: "I should not be sorry to hear that the Italians had risen en masse and chased the odious Austrians out of beautiful Lombardy. But this they could hardly do without help, and that involves another European war" (*George Eliot Letters* 1954–55, 1:255). Moreover, she also shows her respect for the *Risorgimento* and Margaret Fuller's treatment of it in her review "Margaret Fuller's Letters from Italy" (May 17, 1856), where she commends Fuller for having understood that Catholicism and political reform do not agree with each other, "she had from the first no faith in the permanence of such paradoxes as a liberal Pope and a reforming Romanism" (1856, 475). Eliot also expresses her approval of Fuller's stance towards English people and Americans who do not support the revolutionaries:

> In her remonstrances with her countrymen for their want of sympathy for the struggling Italians, she mentions an appeal which ought to go home to the English conscience as well as the American: "Some of the lowest of the people," she says, "have asked me, 'Is it not true that your country had a war to become free?' 'Yes,' 'Then why do you not feel for us?'" ([1876] 1995, 475)

In light of this positive assessment of Italian revolutionary activities it does not come as a surprise that Eliot chose Mazzini as a role model for her future national leader, Daniel Deronda. In the Hand-and-Banner scene in *Daniel Deronda*, Daniel praises Mazzini and presents Italian unification as a model for Jewish nationhood:[34]

> Look into Mazzini's account of his first yearning, when he was a boy, after a restored greatness and new freedom to Italy, and of his first efforts as a young man to rouse the same feelings in other young men, and get them to work towards a united nationality. Almost everything seemed against him: his countrymen were ignorant or indifferent, governments hostile, Europe incredulous. Of course the scorners often seemed wise. Yet the prophecy lay with him. (536)[35]

Moreover, a little later in the novel, Daniel's future wife, Mirah, sings Leopardi's ode to Italy, "*O patria mia*," and Daniel feels one "with the grandeur of the whole, which seemed to breathe as inspiration through music" (558).

Yet Eliot nevertheless refused to contribute to the Mazzini fund in 1865. The reason she gave in a letter to a British Mazzini supporter does make sense from her conservative point of view:

> As it is, the application of the desired fund is only intimated in the vaguest manner by the Florentine committee. The reflection is inevitable, that the application may ultimately be the promotion of conspiracy. . . . Now, though I believe there are cases in which conspiracy may be a sacred, necessary struggle against organised wrong, there are also cases in which it is hopeless, and can produce nothing but misery. . . . [I]t seems to me that it would be a social crime to further conspiracy even by the impulse of a little finger, to which one may well compare a small money subscription. . . . I trouble you and Mr. Taylor with this explanation, because both Mr. Lewes and I have a real reverence for Mazzini, and could not therefore be content to give a silent negative. (*George Eliot Letters* 1954–55, 4:199-200)

Like Nathaniel Hawthorne, who preferred waiting for providential means to solve the slavery conflict in his native country, Eliot was always afraid of social change in England.[36] Welcoming revolutionary activity in France and Italy in her March 8, 1848, letter to John Sibree,[37] she nevertheless thought that England needed different measures because: "Our working classes are eminently inferior to the mass of French people" and "[o]ur little humbug of a queen is more endurable than the rest of her race because she calls forth a chivalrous feeling, and there is nothing in our constitution to obstruct the slow progress of *political* reform. This is all we are fit for at present" (*George Eliot Letters* 1954–55, 1:254). Her reluctance to address topical issues—especially those relating to her personal situation or that of her own country—might be yet another reason why Eliot chose to deal with revolutionary matters so obliquely in *Romola*. Tom Winnifrith, apparently quite dissatisfied with Eliot's equivocating attitudes towards revolution, calls *Romola* "a rather detached answer to those who saw an easy answer to Italy's nineteenth-century problem" (1994, 169). As he and Andrew Thompson have pointed out, the political plot of *Romola* resembles the political developments of the *Risorgimento*.[38] Thompson briefly sums up the most obvious parallels:

> Savonarola came to power on the death of Lorenzo, and substituted a Republic for the (albeit enlightened) despotism of the Medici. He was of the Church but "antipapal" in resisting the authority of Rome and he revealed himself to be a great leader of men. To write about *this* particular period of Italian history in 1861-3 was necessarily to engage with some of the main issues of the *Risorgimento*: the kind of government (despotism, monarchy or

democracy) which was best for Italy; the role of the Church and the Pope; and the role of great leaders of men as prophets and visionaries. (70)

Eliot's depiction of Romola's relationship with Savonarola is undoubtedly inspired by her reading of Fuller's dispatches. Romola's desperate attempts to keep her spiritual guide Savonarola from letting his politics corrupt his formerly unimpeachable morals echo Fuller's—albeit unheard—pleas to the weak Pius IX to resist the pressure exerted on him by counter-revolutionary forces. Interestingly enough, both leaders relied on the French as political allies: Fuller reports that Pius IX did not have enough backbone to withstand political pressure from the powerful French[39]—who thanked him by restoring him—whereas Eliot shows that Savonarola, who, in Eliot's novel, disappoints Romola by succumbing to political corruption, availed himself of French military power for his own political and religious purposes: "The French army was that new deluge which was to purify the earth from iniquity; the French king, Charles VIII, was the instrument elected by God . . . and all men who desired good rather than evil were to rejoice in his coming" ([1863] 1980, 273). The scene in which Romola addresses Savonarola during their final disagreement almost seems to reflect Fuller's anger at Pope Pius IX and employs a tone that is very similar to that of Fuller's dispatches:

> Do you, then, know so well what will further the coming of God's kingdom, father, that you will dare to despise the plea of mercy—of justice—of faithfulness to your own teaching? Has the French king, then, brought renovation to Italy? Take care, father, lest your enemies have some reason when they say, that in your visions of what will further God's kingdom's you see only what will strengthen your own party. (578)

The discussion of plot elements from *Romola* has shown that Eliot relied on Fuller's dispatches, but a comparison of the plots of Stowe's *Agnes of Sorrento* and *Romola* suggests that Eliot—who in all likelihood was familiar with Stowe's novel—might also have drawn inspiration from the figure of Agnes of Sorrento. Upon a first reading of the two novels, there are quite a few similarities between their plots and between Stowe's and Eliot's heroines; Italy and its landscape are described very similarly by both writers; both Agnes and Romola are nearly flawless human beings who never waver in their attention to (religious) duty; as their stories unfold both of them become romantically involved with the men they eventually marry; they both become part of the religious conflict surrounding Girolamo Savonarola's ascent to power and execution; and in both cases their gender also thwarts their ability to participate fully in the politicoreligious drama that unfolds around them. But the many differences between the two novels' plots do suggest that Eliot might have used *Agnes of Sorrento* as a foil rather than a model for *Romola*. Thus, perhaps most importantly, Savonarola remains an incorruptible religious and political leader in Stowe's novel, whereas he is corrupted by the adverse effects of power in Eliot's novel. In Stowe's novel anger at religious leadership is directed only at the Pope and his corrupt cardinals and priests—Agnes's future husband Agostino, for example, angrily remarks about the Pope's (undeserved) omnipotence, "'What then? Is the Holy Ghost indeed alone dispensed through the medium of Alexander and his scarlet crew of cardinals? Hath the power to bind and loose in Christ's church indeed been given to whoever can buy it with the wages of robbery and oppression?'" ([1892] 1967, 106). Moreover, there are remarkable differences in the two authors' conceptions of gender. Throughout Stowe's novel, Agnes, a devoutly religious orange vendor from Sorrento, who later finds out that she is of noble origin, remains helpless and in need of (male) support. Unlike the highly educated Romola, who finally loses her faithless husband and then usurps his traditional role of head of household and breadwinner after she has "adopted" his "other wife" and her children, Agnes remains within traditional gender bounds and can fully rely on the personal integrity of both Agostino and his (and her uncle's) religious leader Girolamo Savonarola. In her depiction of males as both faithless and corrupt, Eliot radically departs from Stowe's conception of the male gender in *Agnes of Sorrento*. Whereas the men in Agnes's life show their respect for her by either bravely protecting her from her religious enemies—as Agostino does—or successfully subduing their sexual urges towards her—as her confessor Francesco finally manages to do—Romola cannot rely upon "traditional" male protection as she is brutally betrayed by the two men she loves and respects: her husband reveals himself to be a traitor whose sexual and political unfaithfulness is paralleled by Savonarola's spiritual and political corruption. (While it is evident that in *Romola* Eliot did not hesitate to depart from most aspects of Stowe's gender conception, it might be less obvious that in devising the gendered character of Romola, she, in spite of allotting to Romola a wider range of power of action, remained faithful to the two "basic models" she found in Stowe's and in Fuller's writing: Stowe's "feminized savior" [from *Uncle Tom's Cabin*] and Fuller's "virgin madonna.")

Eliot's involvement with Italy in *Romola*, as to some extent also Stowe's in *Agnes of Sorrento*, does not go much beyond the discussion of the religiopolitical situation in fifteenth-century Florence and the fact that all place names and protagonists' names are Italian. Joan Bennett astutely observes that the novel's artificiality partly stems from an inability to hear or reproduce the way in which Florentines speak:

> There is an obvious, conscious effort to find appropriate metaphors (such as cheese and macaroni) and to introduce a few Italian words (*oimè* and *ecco*) and to suggest the time by archaic grammar or idiom. . . . But, when all is done, Nello speaks a language no one ever spoke and whose rhythms are not familiar to the author's ear as are the rhythms of English speech. We have only to compare a few sentences of an Englishman of similar social class, Mr Chubb, the inkeeper of Felix Holt, to recognize the devitalizing effect of Nello's language. (1948, 143)

Readers of *The Marble Faun*, the Hawthorne novel that partly inspired *Romola*, are faced with a similar situation. Italy fails to come to life in Hawthorne's novel because—with the exception of Donatello, who as a mixture of man and faun is a very strange young Italian, and Miriam's model who does not speak to anybody,—there are no Italian characters in the novel. Rome merely serves as a picturesque backdrop for a story that mainly deals with the relationships of American expatriates among themselves. As if anticipating such criticism of his depiction of Italy, Hawthorne placed a disclaimer in his preface to *The Marble Faun*, stating that

> The author proposed to himself merely to write a fanciful story, evolving a thoughtful moral, and did not purpose attempting a portraiture of Italian manners and character. He has lived too long abroad, not to be aware that a foreigner seldom acquires that knowledge of a country, at once flexible and profound, which may justify him in endeavouring to idealize its traits. ([1860] 1990, 3)

Since he certainly did not "idealize Italy's traits" in *The Marble Faun*—as the subsequent discussion of his treatment of Catholicism will show—Hawthorne's "gentle reader" might rather be inclined to believe that Hawthorne's disclaimer might have been intended to deny "malignant intent." While Hawthorne failed to provide insights about quotidian Italian culture, he did not shy away from presenting Italy's religious culture, even though the only priest who is given a chance to represent Catholicism is an American. Hawthorne's evaluation of Catholicism, like Fuller's, is biased by his perception of the unreformed, "pagan" nature of the Catholic faith[40]—one often cannot help but think that Hawthorne, who presents Italian "racial" and religious characteristics as earlier stages in human development, wished Donatello could have evolved from faun via Catholic man to Protestant New Englander. In *The Marble Faun*, both Hawthorne's spokesperson, Kenyon, and his narrator echo many of the critical attitudes that Hawthorne, who became famous for his pervasive criticism of Puritan theology, already expressed in his notebooks towards Italy and Catholicism.

Hawthorne's presentation of the differences between Catholicism and Protestantism—which is much more candid than Eliot's rather "theoretical" analysis of medieval Catholicism in *Romola*—is most prominent in the chapters "Altars and Incense" and "The World's Cathedral," which focus on Hilda's need to confess having witnessed Donatello's murder of Miriam's model and include a disagreement about the spiritual tenets of New England Protestantism and Catholicism. In a scene echoing a passage from the Italian notebooks, in which Hawthorne discusses being drawn towards the Catholic ritual of confession himself because of the psychological benefits it offers, Hilda, in dire need of spiritual help, senses the psychological appeal of confession, but meets with Catholic resistance against "Protestant heresy." Once she has confessed, the American priest, having noticed that Hilda is not a Catholic, confronts her by asking "'on what ground, my daughter, have you sought to avail yourself of these blessed privileges (confined exclusively to members of the one true Church) of Confession and Absolution?'" (359). Entering a doctrinal argument, Hilda tells him point blank that she did not seek absolution because only "'our Heavenly Father can forgive my sins'" (359). The priest, noticing that this Protestant woman knows how to argue her point, threatens her "with somewhat less mildness in his tone" (359) that since her confession was made in a secular way, he is not bound to keep secrecy about "a great crime against public justice" (360). After Hilda has resisted his plea to come "into the true fold" (362) in spite of his threats, the scene ends with an ambiguous truce, quite typical of Hawthorne, which leaves undecided which one of the "true believers" will go to heaven—or if, perhaps, even both might make it.

Hawthorne's attitude toward Catholicism at times reflects his cultural bias[41] but is not significantly different from his attitude towards Puritanism. Apart from the historical burden that he had to bear as a descendant of the Puritans, Hawthorne seemed rather unimpressed by denominationalism. Agnes McNeill Donohue concludes, a bit optimistically, from Hawthorne's presentation of religious issues in *The Marble Faun* that Hawthorne became very sympathetic towards Catholicism in Italy.[42] Yet the fact that Hawthorne continually exploited religious themes in his art, even though he was a possible agnostic and never went to church, does not necessarily reflect a penchant for organized religion of any denomination. He did this perhaps for the same reason that William Myers attributes to Eliot's interest in religious doctrine: "George Eliot valued religious doctrine, ceremony and discipline, not for the general contribution they made to furthering the abstract principle of altruism, but for their capacity to register in detail the specific potentialities of man, good and evil" (1984, 25).

In *The Marble Faun*, Hawthorne, focusing on Italianness as alterity, combines his "religion plot" with a plot about human development that highlights foreignness by presenting it as racial difference signifying backwardness and abjection. By means of his description of Donatello as a "primitive" stuck in an earlier historical stage, Hawthorne assumes a position of narrative control that usually is reserved to the European gazing at the "native." Reversing a discriminatory mechanism, he again assumes a cocky postcolonial stance vis-à-vis the "primitive and backward" mother continent since, as Nancy Bentley observes:

> In nineteenth-century primitivism, the operative traits are not physical but moral and temporal: to be primitive was to belong to a particular place in time, though that same temporal identity might well determine one's proper homeland. Conceived in this way, the concept of primitive culture could be transferred from colonized peoples to European societies as an instrument to gauge the advancement of a given nation or social class. (1995, 51)

To complicate matters, both the "religion" and the "race" plot are interwoven with a story of fated love between the culturally and racially other protagonists of the novel. Miriam is an expatriate woman of ambiguous racial origin. Donatello, as implied by the narrator of *The Marble Faun*, is an Italian nobleman whose allegedly pointed furry ears indicate not only that he is the result of transspecies mating between a forest creature and a human, but also suggest that Hawthorne in keeping with nineteenth-century sensibilities seems to have harbored fears about the possibility of regression from human to animal.

Donatello falls in love with the almost equally racially mysterious Miriam when her life is already burdened by a terrible secret from the past—perhaps incest—that has made her an accomplice to a terrible deed—perhaps murder. Miriam is followed by a nemesis who knows something about her past and frightens her by appearing wherever she might be. Donatello eventually cannot bear to watch her suffer any longer. A desperate encouraging look from Miriam finally entices him to murder her follower by throwing him over a precipice. The narrative of *The Marble Faun* reflects the fears about cultural (and in this case also racial) alterity that Hawthorne had already uttered in his European notebooks. It implies that Donatello's murder of the model—which ultimately precipitates his "fortunate fall"—could be racially motivated and might not have taken place if the somewhat childlike Donatello and his girlfriend Miriam had not, unfortunately, belonged to a "lower order" of human being. Before the murder takes place, Kenyon, the male part of the "civilized" American couple whose ultimately successful love story serves as a backdrop to Miriam and Donatello's story, warns his love interest, Hilda, that Miriam cannot be trusted because of her uncertain national and racial origin: "'And your delicate instincts say all this in her favor?—nothing against her? . . . But she is such a mystery! We do not even know whether she is a countrywoman of ours, or an Englishwoman, or a German'" ([1860] 1990, 108–9). Her perhaps even more dangerous "drop of burning African blood" (23) is not even mentioned here. At the end of the novel, the readers are finally told what it is that accounts for Miriam's otherness; she is "from English parentage . . . but with a vein likewise of Jewish blood" (429).

In this context it is worth mentioning that in his English notebooks Hawthorne gives a revealing description of a "prototype" for Miriam—a Jewish woman whom he met at a banquet in London and observed with great curiosity. Hawthorne's characterization of her (which for no apparent reason deems her capable of murder) shows that the otherness of this "oriental woman" both fascinated and repulsed him:

> She was slender, and youthful . . . and looking at her, I saw what were the wives of the old patriarchs, in their maiden or early married days—what Rachel was . . . —what Judith was; for womanly as she looked, I doubt not she could have slain a man, in a good cause. . . . I never should have thought of touching her, nor desired to touch her; for whether owing to distinctness of race, my sense that she was a Jewess, or whatever else, I felt a sort of repugnance, simultaneously with my perception that she was an admirable creature. (*English Notebooks* 1941, 320–21)

Even more interesting is Hawthorne's extremely anti-Semitic comment on the subject of the beautiful woman's husband:

> But, at the right hand of this miraculous Jewess, there sat the very Jew of Jews: the distilled essence of all the Jews that have been since Jacob's time; he was Judas Iscariot; he was the Wandering Jew; he was the worst, and at the same time, the truest type of his race . . . and he must have been circumcised as much as ten times over. I never beheld anything so ugly and disagreeable, and preposterous and laughable, as the outline of his profile; it was so hideously Jewish, and so cruel and so keen. . . . And yet his manners and aspect, in spite of all, were those of a man of the world, and a gentleman. (321)

This description of the "ugly and disagreeable" Jew who seems to "have been circumcised ten times over" betrays Hawthorne's irrational fear of the sexual prowess of an/"other" man. He reacts by depicting him as bodily abject because of a "sexual deviance" that he deems the result of racial otherness.

In *The Marble Faun*, Miriam is associated with the murderous penchants of the Jew's wife. Miriam's drawings and sketches hint negatively at her murderous heritage since they show Jewish women in the act of committing murder. Thus, one sketch depicts "Jael, driving the nail through the temples of Sisera" (43), whereas another one features Judith contemplating the stare on the cut-off head of Holofernes with "the startled aspect that might be conceived of a cook, if a calf's head should sneer at her, when about to be popt [*sic*] into the dinner-pot" (44). And since Miriam's friend and love interest Donatello is the result of mixing between different species, it is even more obvious that the cards must be stacked against him. The narrator explains that Donatello's racial background brings out positive qualities in his youth but predestines him for evil deeds like murder with advancing age:

> [A] son of Monte Beni gathered into himself the scattered qualities of his race.... Beautiful, strong, brave, kindly, sincere, of honest impulses ... he was believed to possess gifts by which he could associate himself with the wild things of the forest ... and could feel a sympathy even with the trees, among which it was his joy to dwell. On the other hand, there were deficiencies both of intellect and heart, and especially, as it seemed, in the development of the higher portions of man's nature. These defects were less perceptible in early youth, but showed themselves more strongly with advancing age. ([1860] 1990, 235)

But since Donatello also has admirable qualities, he is given a second chance. The civilizing influence of Roman Catholicism makes him repent his deed and experience it as "a fortunate fall" saving him and his suddenly quite human soul from spiritual death and transforming him from beast to man.[43] Yet, while the fall might have saved his soul, the trajectory of the narrative shows that death in the form of extinction of his race is exacted as payment for his sin. The narrative of *The Marble Faun* implies that even the "childlike" Donatello knows that he belongs to a "vanishing race"; due to evolutionary changes he is the last of his breed and therefore no longer in tune with nature:[44]

> The young Count found it impossible, now-a-days, to be what his forefathers had been. He could not live their healthy life of animal spirits.... Nature, in beast, fowl, and tree, and earth, flood, and sky, is what was of old;

but sin, care and self-consciousness have set the human portion of the world askew; and thus the simplest character is ever the surest to go astray. (239-40)

Sin has thus caused Donatello to go astray and has made it impossible for him to become the progenitor of a rejuvenated race of Monte Benis, even though his relationship with Miriam survives against all odds. But their relationship is one "cemented with [their victim's] blood" (175), as Donatello realizes, and it will inevitably suffer from "the ever-increasing loathsomeness of a union that consists in guilt" (175). As a consequence of their deed he and Miriam are not together anymore at the end of the novel. Donatello is in prison for murder and Miriam has become a Roman penitent. Thus, the "abject," racially other couple that seems to threaten the borders of civilization is not given a chance to procreate; the American couple is luckier: Kenyon and Hilda finally return to America, and therefore to civilization, to live happily ever after.

In his article "*The Marble Faun* and American Postcolonial Ambivalence," Mark Kemp proposes a reading of the novel which suggests that Hawthorne—like Eliot after him—incorporated an "encoded" narrative about the political situation in nineteenth-century Italy in his novel. Kemp focuses on postcolonial issues rather than race, but, curiously enough, does not take into account Hawthorne's own postcolonialist stance. By murdering Miriam's model, who happens to be a monk, Donatello, as Kemp argues, throws off his colonial fetters—represented almost imperceptibly in the novel by references to Austrian and French occupation as well as the Catholic clergy. Donatello as "colonized Other" (228), decolonizes himself through his "fortunate fall" which makes a new man out of him and thus, according to Kemp's reading, corresponds to Fanon's view of "decolonization [as] the veritable creation of new men" (228). However, this decolonization cannot be accomplished because "[w]hen Donatello metamorphoses from presocial, prepolitical 'faun' into historicized, political *man*, he is by Hawthorne's reckoning *fallen* and must therefore pay for his sin by being subordinated to the state's power, even if that power is Catholic and despotic" (229).

While this reading of Donatello as an Italian revolutionary seems at times self-contradictory (how can Donatello redeem himself through the Catholic "fortunate fall" if the fall is the result of throwing off Catholicism?) and unconvincing (Hawthorne does not in any way link Donatello with the revolutionaries),[45] I still agree with Kemp that it is possible to read *The Marble Faun* as a postcolonial text. But I would argue that the postcolonial subject in the process of decolonizing himself is not Donatello throwing off

Catholicism but rather Hawthorne expressing his oedipal wish to throw off Europe. As already indicated throughout this chapter, Hawthorne considered both his "mother country," England, and Italy as politically and socially backward because they adhered to outmoded hierarchical social systems and, at least in the case of Italy, were also unhygienic. Casting himself in the postcolonial role of the rebellious son who has acquired cultural superiority over the abject backward parent continent, he showed his contempt for it not only in his European notebooks but also in *The Marble Faun* where Italian women are associated with "witch-like ugliness" ([1860] 1990, 290) and the female version of the usual cloak-and-dagger crime—stabbing "with the steel-stiletto that serves them for a hair pin" (407). Hawthorne's love-hate relationship to Europe finds its best expression in the narrator's long and often quoted paradoxical tirade both against and in favor of Rome which is likened to an abject maternal corpse:

> When we have once known Rome, and left her where she lies, like a long decaying corpse, retaining a trace of the noble shape it was, but with accumulated dust and a fungus growth overspreading all its more admirable features . . .—left her, sick at heart of Italian trickery, which has uprooted whatever faith in man's integrity had endured till now, and sick at stomach of sour bread, sour wine, rancid butter, and bad cookery needlessly bestowed on evil meats—left her, disgusted with the pretence of Holiness and the reality of Nastiness . . . we are astonished by the discovery, by-and-by, that our heart-strings have mysteriously attached themselves to the Eternal City, and are drawing us thitherward again, as if it were more familiar, more intimately our home, than even the spot where we were born. (326)

This invective goes well beyond whatever postcolonial rage Hawthorne might have harbored and reflects the usual attraction and repulsion he experienced whenever he was confronted with ethnic, cultural, or sexual otherness.

Nathaniel Hawthorne's problem with foreigners and foreignness seems to be addressed by a well-known section from Julia Kristeva's *Strangers to Ourselves* (which, as the subsequent discussion of *Romola* will show, also targets concerns raised by Eliot about the "stranger within us"). Kristeva applies Sigmund Freud's deconstruction of the *heimlich* vs. *unheimlich* dichotomy in the German language to the figure of the stranger as well as to cultural strangeness—*heimlich* means "homey" but also "concealed"; the dichotomy is rendered less ambiguously as "uncanny strangeness" (1991, 182) in the English translation. She thus expounds that Freud locates a pervasive foreignness in the individual psyche:

> [T]hat which *is* strangely uncanny would be that which *was* (the past tense is important) familiar and, under certain conditions (which ones?), emerges. A first step was taken that removed the uncanny strangeness from the outside, where fright had anchored it, to locate it inside, not inside the familiar considered as one's own and proper, but the familiar potentially tainted with strangeness and referred (beyond its imaginative origin) to an improper past. The other is my ("own and proper") unconscious. (183)

Accordingly, she formulates her essay's main question: "How could one tolerate a foreigner if one did not know one was a stranger to oneself?" (182).

At first it appears as if Nathaniel[46] Hawthorne's problem with "tolerating a foreigner" could be located in his inability to confront the stranger and strangeness within himself, yet the ending of the above quoted passage about Rome, where Hawthorne writes "our heart-strings have mysteriously attached themselves to the Eternal City, and are drawing us thitherward again, as if it were . . . more intimately our home, than even the spot where we were born," suggests that he has intuited the meaning of the bon mot "Wir nennen das unheimlich, Sie nennen's heimlich"[47] (Freud 1999, 57) quoted by Freud in his essay.

Hawthorne's works indicate that he did not know how to deal openly with this intuitive insight or perhaps simply did not want to. What Hawthorne perceived as "uncanny strangeness" in Italy corresponds to the indicators of the uncanny listed by both Freud and Kristeva: death, fear of castration, loss of boundaries, etc. Castration anxiety might indeed have been the motivator of Hawthorne's oedipal rebellion against his parent continent Europe, whereas a fear of the dissolution of (corporeal) boundaries might have motivated his projection of his own fear of abjection onto "Italian filthiness." Yet Hawthorne seems to have remained ultimately unable to confront his own strangeness; the American protagonists of *The Marble Faun* react likewise when they turn their back on the uncanny, "filthy" strangeness of Italy with all its licentious implications.[48]

In *The Marble Faun*, Hawthorne conceived of Europe as an Old World remaining in an earlier historical stage than the New World of the United States. In his Italian novel and his European notebooks, he demonstrates his conviction that Italy suffered from atavistic social mores and an almost "pagan" superstitious religion; that England and Italy's undemocratic governments were inferior to American democracy, and that their inhabitants were coarser and at times even stuck in an earlier developmental stage of the human race and racially "other."[49] Focusing particularly upon the religious dimension of the story of development in *The Marble Faun*, Elissa Greenwald remarks that "in Rome, the transition from Judaism to paganism, paganism to Christianity, turns religion into a narrative history in which faith depends on historical links between forms of worship" (1991, 131).

George Eliot's incorporation of a developmental plot in *Romola* indicates that she was particularly inspired by this aspect of Hawthorne's novel. Eliot who, as a European had no reason to assume a "postcolonial" posture of assumed superiority over Italy, does not follow Hawthorne's depiction of Italians as savagely murderous and racially primitive and therefore does not focus on race and ethnicity in her developmental narrative. While Hawthorne bases his plot on what seems to have been his rather vague knowledge of evolutionary theory, as a cursory reference to Cuvier in *The Marble Faun* suggests,[50] Eliot, having studied Higher Criticism (Baruch Spinoza, David Friedrich Strauss), evolutionary theory, and Comte's social theories, presents a very informed "quasi-religious" Comtean model of social progress in *Romola*. Having gone through an ardent evangelical phase in adolescence, Eliot renounced her belief in God after having experienced her own "Victorian crisis of faith" in her early twenties, but remained fascinated by religion and continued to present "religious" solutions to the philosophical and emotional problems addressed in her works. Her presentation of Catholicism in *Romola* differs quite a bit from Hawthorne's—and also Stowe's and Fuller's—in that her descriptions of Catholic religious practices seem much less impassioned than Hawthorne's and more disinterested than Stowe's. Unlike Hawthorne, who as an American "postcolonial" rendered his experiences with Italy in terms of racial, cultural, and religious alterity, and unlike Stowe, who, as a true believer in Christianity had to endorse the Christian faith, Eliot does not present Catholicism as necessarily "less primitive" and "more advanced" than the "pagan Hellenism" her foreign characters Tito and Baldassare are associated with.

Romola, having been reared by her Neoplatonist father, Bardo, is introduced to Catholicism through her dying brother Dino's prophecy that the man she married in his dream (a figuration of her Greek husband Tito) "had the face of death" and was "the Great Tempter" ([1863] 1980, 215). Necessarily biased against Christianity because of the education she received from her father, she still feels that she has to accept the warning, but is appalled at what has become of Dino: "There was an unconquerable repulsion for her in that monkish aspect; it seemed to her the brand of the dastardly undutifulness which had left her father desolate—of the grovelling [*sic*] superstition which could give such undutifulness the name of piety" (209). Thompson reads Romola's reference to "groveling superstition" as proof of an anti-Catholic bias on Eliot's part (73), but I do not quite agree with his view because Romola's statement simply seems to reflect her background. Moreover, Eliot does not write about medieval Catholicism in order to criticize it; the aim of her fairly dispassionate presentation of the prevalent form of worship is rather to present medieval Catholicism as a stage in a developmental process leading to an improved society informed by "more advanced" Comtean social ideology. This is also evident from the way in which Romola converts to Catholicism. Savonarola keeps her from leaving Florence for the first time by reminding her that her wifely and patriotic duties continue to exist even though her marriage has ended for her. Romola accepts his morality and is won over to his Catholicism because of Savonarola's charismatic personality. Romola's conversion is in keeping with the philosophy of Comte, who believed that religion should appeal to the affections as much as to the intellect. As David Maria Hesse observes, "Comte primarily sought to stimulate the emotions of man as a means of procuring morality" (1996, 110). Romola, whose personality resembles that of Hester Prynne from *The Scarlet Letter* rather than that of any of the female characters in *The Marble Faun*, follows Hester in submitting to duty and a law that she cannot accept. She heeds Savonarola's advice to stay in Florence because "[a]s the anger melted from Romola's mind, it had given place to a new presentiment of the strength there might be in submission, if this man, at whom she was beginning to look with a vague reverence, had some valid law to show to her" ([1863] 1990, 430). In this scene Eliot makes sure that her readers understand that it is not Catholicism itself, but rather Savonarola's charismatic personality and Romola's inborn altruism and sense of duty that makes her accept the tenets of the faith: "Romola was so deeply moved by the grand energies of Savonarola's nature, that she found herself listening patiently to all dogmas and prophecies, when they came in the vehicle of his ardent faith and believing utterance. No soul is desolate as long as there is a human being for whom it can feel trust and reverence" (465). Even though Romola is suspicious of and appalled by the visionary Catholicism of the Florentine seeress Camilla Rucellai[51] and even though she notices about her confessor and some of Savonarola's disciples "with a sickening sense that these people were miserably narrow" (463), she goes along with it because it leads her towards the practice of altruism: "[S]he found herself recovering a firm footing in her works of womanly sympathy" (463). In keeping with the fact that her response to and acceptance of religion is chiefly emotional, she finally turns her back on Catholicism after Savonarola fails to prevent the killing of his political enemy, her godfather Bernardo del Nero, because she feels that the Frate has been seduced by his political power and has succumbed to corruption:

Was it that the expression of serene elevation and pure human fellowship which had once moved her was no longer present in the same force, or was it that the sense of his being divided from her in her feeling about her godfather roused the slumbering sources of alienation, and marred her own vision? Perhaps both causes were at work. (571–72)

After Savonarola dies in the trial by fire and thereby also fails his martyrdom, Romola leaves Florence, drifting away in a boat—presumably in order to end her life—and wakes up in the vicinity of a plague-stricken village. There, like Hester Prynne, who voluntarily takes up charity work among the Puritan community that hates her, she takes care of the sick, recovers from the traumatic experiences she has had, and reflects on what critics identify as her newly found Comtean "religion of humanity":

> The experience was like a new baptism to Romola. In Florence the simpler relations of the human being to his fellow-men had been complicated for her with all the special ties of marriage, the State, and religious discipleship, and when these had disappointed her trust, the shock seemed to have shaken her aloof from life and stunned her sympathy. But now she said, "It was mere baseness in me to desire death. If everything else is doubtful, this suffering that I can help is certain; if the glory of the cross is an illusion, the sorrow is only the truer. While the strength is in my arm I will stretch it out to the fainting; while the light visits my eyes they shall seek the forsaken." (650)

Having come to this acceptance, Romola, like Hester, who returns to New England after her stay in England and again takes up the burden of the scarlet letter, goes back to Florence to take up her duties there.[52]

In keeping with this characterization of Romola as utterly self-effacing female, critics have also read Romola's altruistic personality in light of the figure of the Comtean "madonna." As such she is "the secular equivalent of the Virgin Mary—but more deserving of adoration for her acts of humanity" (Bullen 1975, 434) and exemplifies Comte's idea of woman as "the spontaneous priestess of Humanity" (1865, 276) and the principle of love since "she excels Man in love, as Man excels her in force" (250). Feminist critics in particular have been dissatisfied with Romola's depiction as a meek Madonna (as opposed to an empowered Fullerian "virgin") because they feel that this association causes her passive obedience to her father and later to Savonarola, but a closer look at some of her subversively rebellious actions shows that, modeled on Hester Prynne, she is, in fact, much less passive and obedient than the novel seems to suggest at times.[53] Romola's rebellion against patriarchal domestic relations goes beyond a mere rejection of gender conventions by echoing Hester's rebellious "freedom of thought" regarding gender roles. While Hester becomes what might be the first successful single mother in American literature, Romola decides to become the "head" of a very unusual family—even by "modern" standards—consisting of two mothers and two children. Therefore, I do not agree with those critics who argue that Romola's decision to take over Tito's place in the family indicates that Eliot meant to "degrade" Romola to the conventional role of mother and "Angel in the House,"[54] but would rather suggest that her heroine's actions, which culminate in her usurping his place, bespeak a great deal of feminist aggression against her faithless husband and the patriarchy he represents.[55]

In addition to modeling her heroine on Hawthorne's Hester, Eliot, as already indicated, also takes inspiration from the American writer in linking questions of religious faith and human development, yet her focus is different from Hawthorne's. Perhaps because Eliot indeed believed in European cultural transnationality, she focuses on cultural similarity within Europe and teleological development of intrinsically valuable European idea(l)s in her Italian novel, which is told from a European perspective. She thus presents medieval Catholicism within her larger scheme of showing Comtean social progress from polytheism (Bardo's philosophy) over monotheism (Savonarola's Catholicism) to positivism (Romola's altruism). Inspired by Hawthorne's development narrative, which shows how Donatello by means of his "fortunate fall" is transformed from an unredeemed half-creature into a redeemed man, Eliot incorporates two narratives of personal development in *Romola*.

Romola's exemplary advance through various stages of humankind's historical development—first paganism, then Catholicism, and finally positivism/altruism—tells a story of positive personal development. But Eliot also included a story of negative development by revealing how Tito, her foil for Donatello, becomes more and more corrupt and passes up every opportunity of personal redemption. There are many parallels in the initial description of both characters, as Edward Stokes notices: "[T]he constant emphasis, in the early portrayal of both Donatello and Tito, is on their beauty, vitality, gentleness, spontaneity, naturalness, and apparently eternal freshness of youth" (1985, 185); in addition to that, both men have dark curly hair and foreign looks. Yet while Hawthorne inevitably blames Donatello's personal shortcomings on his racial otherness, Eliot neither establishes a connection between the Greek Tito's "developmental retardation" (his "pagan" foreignness) and his corruption, which first makes him deny his stepfather Baldassare and then betray his wife Romola, nor does she relate Baldassare's vengeful murder of Tito to his origin. But Eliot's rendition of Romola's first impression of Tito nevertheless provides an almost uncanny echo of Hawthorne's description of Donatello in the first chapter of *The Marble Faun*:

> George Eliot's remark that "Romola's astonishment could hardly have been greater if the stranger had worn a panther-skin and carried a thyrsus . . ." almost inevitably recalls Hawthorne's comment: ". . . if a lion's skin could have been substituted for his modern talma, and a rustic pipe for his stick, Donatello might have figured perfectly as the marble faun." (1985, 184)

But the initial parallels soon give way to radically divergent character development; unlike Donatello, who experiences a "fortunate fall," Tito just experiences a regular fall from grace.

In her conception of her development plot Eliot forgoes Hawthorne's race plot which links "primitive development" with "murderous racial characteristics." She develops only the notion—which also seems to exist as an unspoken idea in *The Marble Faun*—that Catholicism and "Italianness" are earlier stages in teleological human development. Yet while it is difficult to find a reason for Hawthorne's treatment of contemporary Italians as "developmentally backward" and "racially other" in comparison with their American peers, one can argue with greater ease that Eliot's Comtean model of social progress required her to position *Romola*'s fifteenth-century Florence at an earlier stage on her scale without necessarily implying that the earlier developmental stages—such as Hellenism—are necessarily primitive.

Eliot was introduced to Auguste Comte's philosophy about human development in the early eighteen-fifties, after she had already translated Strauss's *The Life of Jesus* (1835–36) and Feuerbach's *The Essence of Christianity* (1841). George Henry Lewes published a book on *Comte's Philosophy of the Sciences* in 1853, providing Eliot with additional information on Comtean positivism. While Feuerbach and the Higher Critics, like the American transcendentalists, in spite of having rejected the idea of an afterlife, performed an apotheosis of humanity by claiming mankind's god-like status and by referring to Jesus as "the ideal man," positivism introduced the idea of an absurd universe that does not care about humanity, but immediately alleviated the possibly negative aspects resulting from such a world view by postulating a "religion of humanity" which reintroduced Christian values in secularized form.

Eliot's interest in Comte has been recognized by many critics who agree that in *Romola*, Eliot, by means of the life story of her heroine, follows

Comte in showing that "[i]nterpreted correctly, history was the record of the progress of humanity from egoism to altruism" (Bullen 1975, 425). Throughout her own life, Romola experiences the three Comtean developmental phases in her personal development, while the people around her—in keeping with the nineteenth-century developmental notion that ontogenesis is parallel to phylogenesis—also represent different developmental stages. The three phases of Comte's model (the theological, polytheistic; the metaphysical, monotheistic; and the scientific, positivist stage) "correspond broadly to ancient polytheism, medieval Catholicism, and modern Positivism" (428). In the final stage of positivism, society will have reached a certain degree of perfection because by then all the knowledge of humanity will have been synthesized and humankind will have convened in an *Etre Suprême* that is worthy of worship. Comte was convinced that the third stage of modern positivism was progressing in the early nineteenth century and that "[h]is own philosophy would repair the ravages of centuries of anarchic individualism and, by returning to the forms and institutions of primitive Catholicism, would build a new religion" (429).

In Romola's universe, as various critics have pointed out, her scholarly father Bardo (who worships "pagan" Greek and Roman scholarship) as well as her Greek husband Tito, represent "the foreign": pagan polytheism. Her brother Dino and Savonarola stand for medieval and "modern" Catholicism, respectively, and Romola herself, who finally rejects Savonarola's corrupted Catholicism, becomes a true representative of the "religion of humanity" in her function as voluntary nurse and "head" of Tessa's family. Thus Eliot, "through the ingenious device of setting the action in the Florentine Renaissance" (432) with its pagan revival, manages to move—at least philosophically—from the fourth to the nineteenth century in a historical novel set in the Renaissance.

But unlike Hawthorne, who in *The Marble Faun* associated earlier historical development with foreignness as both atavistic and murderous, Eliot does not imply in *Romola* that representatives of the earlier historical stages tend towards abjection or have a racially and developmentally necessary penchant towards violence. In her study *The Triptych and the Cross*, Felicia Bonaparte suggests as part of a complicated argument about Tito's Bacchian roots that with *Romola* Eliot, in fact, aimed to improve her readers' understanding of cultural alterity and "the stranger within us." Focusing on Romola's association with Ariadne and Tito's with Bacchus, Bonaparte argues that in her Italian novel Eliot does not privilege Christianity over Hellenism—and therefore, as one might conclude, also does not automatically privilege "domestic progress" over "atavistic foreignness." In a reversal of roles, Romola, who is often associated with Ariadne in the novel, is not the "passive" Ariadne who is saved by Dionysos on Naxos and given "the promise of immortality, of life in death," (1979, 92) but the "active" Ariadne "who gave Theseus the thread that led him safely out of the Cretan labyrinth" and who "is the savior, a reversal of roles that lurks with prophetic irony between Tito's instructions to Piero [to paint him as the hero]" (93). Bonaparte presents Romola as torn between the hedonistic vision of the pagan painting that Tito/Bacchus had commissioned in her honor and the vision of the cross given to her by her dying brother Dino, which also represents the Christian faith of her spiritual leader Savonarola.

Perhaps inspired by Hawthorne's *The Marble Faun*, Eliot indeed situated her "pagan" foreign character on a lower developmental scale within her Comtean scheme, but there is an important difference in Hawthorne's and Eliot's discussion of developmental difference that should not be overlooked: unlike the Italian Donatello, who needs to undergo a fortunate fall in order to develop his higher faculties,[56] the Greek Tito Melema is as intelligent as his Florentine hosts and also seems far less "foreign" to begin with. Interestingly enough—and without referring to Kristeva—Bonaparte suggests that through the figure of Tito/Bacchus Eliot attempted to make her readers understand "the stranger within us":

> Indeed, what Bacchus offers is very precious. "Precious gift," or more strictly, "precious object," is what Tito's name, Melema means in Greek. Eliot knew as well as Euripides that we deny Bacchus at our peril, for he is always, as the Greeks said, the stranger within us. . . . All we can choose is whether we will accept Bacchus willingly or unwillingly; one way or another, accept him we must. It is not in man's nature to rescind the laws of nature, not even the laws of his own nature. (83–84)

Yet while I appreciate Bonaparte's clever insight, in light of Eliot's reluctance to deal with Italianness, I do not think that Eliot—if she intended to make that point at all—was very successful in alerting her readers to recognize the "stranger within us." Perhaps because she truly believed in Enlightenment cosmopolitanism (but perhaps also because she tried to avoid reciprocating Hawthorne's xenophobic presentation of Italians) Eliot, after having had recourse to stereotypical presentations of otherness in her earlier work, shied away from dealing with foreignness in *Romola*. Like Fuller, Eliot often professed her belief in the essential sameness of all human beings, but her notion of universalism apparently made it difficult, if not impossible, for her to register cultural alterity, as the next chapter, which focuses on Jewish alterity in *Daniel Deronda* will also show. Even in her later work she was not able to project a vision of the "rooted cosmopolitanism" (endorsed by David Hollinger for the twenty-first century) that would have enabled her to portray Italians, and later Jews, as similar but, nevertheless, different.

Thus, even though Eliot avoided some of the pitfalls that Hawthorne succumbed to in his portrayal of Italy, her Italy at the threshold from paganism to medieval Catholicism—just like Hawthorne's nineteenth-century Italy as tourist spot—functions neither as a contact zone where "cultures meet, clash, and grapple with each other" according to Pratt's definition (1996, 530) nor as a "Third Space of enunciation" that would enable new cultural readings in Homi Bhabha's sense. While Hawthorne's narrator and characters often make derogatory comments about Italian culture and Catholicism in *The Marble Faun*, the foreign characters featured in *Romola* (Tito, Baldassare) do not comment on Italy and therefore also do not provide a unique perspective on the cultural alterity of Italy. Moreover, even though *Romola* is told by a narrator who looks back on fifteenth-century Florence and is aware of the difference in historical time, the narrator seems to be telling the story from the point of view of a cultural insider who (for whatever reasons) does not reveal many specifics of his/her culture and, even more importantly, does not criticize this culture in any way. The result, as suggested above, is a presentation of Italy in *Romola* as "cultural wasteland" and museum at the same time, which, in spite of obvious differences, resembles Hawthorne's depiction of Italy in *The Marble Faun*.

3
From *Uncle Tom's Cabin* to *Daniel Deronda*— and from Ethnicity to Identity?

Constructing "Race"

Daniel Deronda (1876), George Eliot's final novel, which explores aspects of Jewish life, also shows quite a few affinities with contemporaneous American literature. Eliot's presentation of the interplay of race and religion, as well as her exploration of gender, reveals traces of her readings in American literature and echoes many thematic aspects of the works of Harriet Beecher Stowe and the transcendentalists. Stowe's exploration of "race" in *Uncle Tom's Cabin* (1852) and *Dred* (1856) motivated Eliot's inquiry into racial origin as determinant of identity. Eliot's continued interest in how individual and social identity is constituted led her to an exploration of the teachings of ancient Jewish Kabbalah in *Daniel Deronda*. Due to the shared Neoplatonic origin of Kabbalah and transcendentalism, the kabbalistic passages in *Daniel Deronda* show a similarity to transcendentalist spiritual concepts developed by Ralph Waldo Emerson and Margaret Fuller.

Shortly after its publication and long before writing *Daniel Deronda*, her "race novel," George Eliot had reviewed Harriet Beecher Stowe's novel *Dred*. In her review, she credits Stowe with having "*invented* the Negro novel" (1990, 380) and she praises *Dred* as "a novel inspired by a rare genius—rare both in intensity and in range of power" (379). She furthermore commends Stowe for presenting "a people to whom what we may call Hebraic Christianity is still a reality, still an animating belief," for addressing the "conflict of races," which is "a great source of romantic interest," and for what Eliot thinks is a fairly realistic depiction of African Americans: "Though she paints her negroes *en beau*, they are always specifically negroes" (380). Eliot's only criticism of the novel addresses the "absence of any proportionate exhibition of the negro character in its less amiable phases" (381). She seems to think that Stowe should have more fully exploited the dramatic potential inherent in the story about Dred, the "swamp prophet," who is killed before he receives a sign from God telling him to start a slave revolt. Eliot argues that by giving away that opportunity, "Mrs. Stowe loses . . . the most terribly tragic element in the relation of the two races—the Nemesis lurking in the vices of the oppressed" (381). But she concludes rather prophetically that with her novels about African American life, Stowe has made her mark as a major American writer: "But whatever else she may write, or may not write, *Uncle Tom* and *Dred* will assure her a place in that highest rank of novelists who can give us a national life in all its phases—popular and aristocratic, humorous and tragic, political and religious" (380).

In writing *Daniel Deronda*, Eliot shared some of the same concerns. She also decided to address the subject of racial otherness and to depict—in her case English—"national life in all its phases" and, at least according to Jacob Press, she might even have "invented the Jewish novel" (1997, 300). By focusing on Jews as an ethnic group which has a common religion at the very core of its "racial" identity, Eliot ensured that her characters, like Stowe's, would benefit from a religious practice that is "still a reality, still an animating belief." To stress the romantic element that she apparently also deemed a necessary ingredient in writing about racial strife, Eliot borrowed a number of ideas from Stowe for her novel about race. With her character Mordecai, she introduces a Jewish prophet who hands down ancient kabbalistic wisdom, and prophesies the founding of a Zionist state. Eliot explained her rationale for writing a novel about Jews in one of her letters to Stowe: she meant to work towards the rectification of a racial wrong by "treat[ing] Jews with such sympathy and understanding as my nature and knowledge could attain to" because she felt that "towards the Hebrews we western people who have been reared in Christianity, have a peculiar debt and, whether we acknowledge it or not, a peculiar thoroughness of fellowship in religious and moral sentiment" (*George Eliot Letters* 1954–55, 6:301–2).

Harriet Beecher Stowe's aims in writing *Uncle Tom's Cabin* and *Dred* also went much beyond the romancers' interest in writing an engaging story about racial strife and the lives and customs of black people. In Stowe's antislavery novels the political purpose of abolishing slavery takes precedence over any aesthetic considerations; for her the liberation of African American slaves was absolutely necessary on religious grounds since she viewed slavery as a dangerous impediment to the advent of the millennium which would precede Christ's second coming (see Westra 1992, 156). Therefore, in her novels the subject of race always ties in with religion. As with Eliot's *Daniel Deronda* and *Romola*, *Uncle Tom's Cabin*—like many other nineteenth-century novels—is concerned with questions of development and progress. Throughout her book, Stowe explores the meaning of gender difference along with issues of religious, cultural, and racial progress. Whether sexual and racial difference is natural or whether it is culturally constructed are main concerns of her novel—and, of course, of *Daniel Deronda*. Stowe never takes a definite essentialist position, yet her description of her black characters as mostly childlike, together with her persistent linkage of superior intelligence (such as George Harris's) with lighter skin color, suggests that she viewed blacks as evolutionary and culturally less developed. Since it was her life's aim to abolish the enslavement of human beings, she actively tried to debunk the stereotypical presentation of Africans as naturally savage and brutal by endowing them with the best "white qualities" such as "natural religiousness" and motherliness. She also took great care to present her outstandingly intelligent African American protagonist George Harris as capable of academic success and intellectually on a par with any white person.

Daniel Deronda, like *Uncle Tom's Cabin* and *Dred*, also serves a purpose that combines religion and politics. While *Uncle Tom's Cabin* proposes both to solve America's slavery problem and to further millennialism in America by relocating free blacks to Liberia, Eliot's *Daniel Deronda* advocates the establishment of a Jewish nation in Palestine. Beyond these obvious parallels, there are quite a few other similarities in Stowe's and Eliot's thematic conceptions and strategies of characterization. In *Daniel Deronda*, Eliot evidently follows Stowe's lead in strategically feminizing some of her male protagonists as well as stressing the "natural religiousness" of her "racially other" protagonists. Mordecai, Daniel's spiritual leader, adheres to an old form of religious faith like Stowe's Dred. Daniel Deronda, whom one commentator describes as "Jesus the Jew [with] the manners of a nineteenth-century Englishman" (Cave 1995, xxxii), is very much like Stowe's feminized black males, the Christlike Uncle Tom and the maternal Tiff, in that he likes to console young women in distress by talking religion and ethics with them. By turning Daniel into a "stereotypical Victorian heroine"—to borrow Elizabeth Ammons's description of Tom (1986, 167)—Eliot makes her Jewish main hero, Daniel, a harmless, "normal" person much in the same way in which Stowe automatically forecloses the possibility that Tom might be viewed as a savage native male. "Victorian heroines" simply cannot be equated either with stereotypically "savage black males" prone to violence and rape or with "swarthy, cunning, unsavory Jewish pawnbrokers." But Daniel also has something in common with the mulatto George Harris, whose masculinity and initial rebelliousness, according to Stowe, stem from his white father. George is deprived of his birthright because he is the illegitimate black son of a white man; he seeks and finds a racial identity by becoming one of the founders of a free black nation in Liberia. Daniel, who has been deprived of his Jewish birthright, establishes his personal identity as racial identity and becomes the cofounder of a Zionist state.

Through the incorporation of this nationalist plot, *Daniel Deronda* ends on a similar note as *Uncle Tom's Cabin*: those who are racially other leave the West of their own volition and decide to move to other countries. Nearly all of the surviving African American characters from *Uncle Tom's Cabin* move to the paradisiacal Liberia, whereas Daniel Deronda and his wife Mirah emigrate to Palestine in order to help establish a Jewish colony. Incidentally, these endings which propose emigration of the "other race" have been received quite differently by Stowe's and by Eliot's public; Jewish commentators welcomed George Eliot's support of the foundation of a Jewish state (see Lewis 1996, 203), whereas at least some of Stowe's black contemporaries did not appreciate her possible hint that Africans should live in Africa (see Yarborough 1986, 69).

Stowe's presentation of blacks drew immediate protest and thus established a long tradition of criticizing Stowe for her portrayal of African Americans as racially inferior. From the publication of *Uncle Tom's Cabin* on it has been obvious to critics that Stowe, in spite of her commitment to the abolition of slavery and in spite of her professed sympathy for blacks, actively promoted racial stereotypes. In his landmark article "Strategies of Black Characterization in *Uncle Tom's Cabin* and the Early Afro-American Novel," Richard Yarborough has meticulously detailed aspects of Stowe's characterization of blacks that have met with critical disapproval—from her tendency to endow mulatto characters with more intelligence than pure black ones over her use of "comical darky" figures, to her annoying presentation of little black children "mopping and moving and grinning all between railings, and tumbling over the kitchen floor" ([1852] 1981, 353).[1] A tradition of criticizing Stowe for what appears to be a racist presentation of blacks was established early on. As Yarborough points out, black male commentators immediately noticed that Tom seems to lack masculine virtues: "To blacks like Allen and George T. Downing, Harris is 'the only one that really betrays any other than the subservient, submissive, Uncle Tom spirit, which has been the cause of much of the disrespect felt for the colored man'" (1986, 69).

The fact that twentieth-century critics were usually somewhat put off by Stowe's conviction that there are essential racial characteristics[2] can be explained by changes in attitudes towards race that have taken place since the mid-nineteenth century. Nineteenth-century race theory, whose views influenced popular attitudes towards race, usually held the belief that there are differences between races, that there is a gradation from "lower" to "higher" races, and that racial differences are innate and essential. Liberal late twentieth-century scientific theories about race, however, usually proceed from the hypothesis that if there are any differences between races—other than obvious morphological differences—these differences are culturally constructed.

Early race theory still believed in race and skin color as a marker of essential difference; and, curiously enough, not only Africans, who looked different, but also Jewish people, whose skin tone does not serve as a marker of racial difference from gentiles, were subjected to its biases. Ivan Hannaford writes that the identificatory badge that was first used in thirteenth-century Spain to set apart Spanish Jews and that "distinguished people who could not be set apart by their physical appearance in later times became the mark of Cain and then absorbed by logic and association of ideas into the mark of race" (1996, 126). Sander Gilman, however, reintroduces (skin) color by arguing in *The Jew's Body* that "the general consensus of the ethnological literature of the late nineteenth century was that the Jews were "black," or at least, "swarthy" (1991, 171). Not surprisingly, essentialist views of race have frequently been deemed wrong in recent writing about race. Thus, in "Race, Culture, Identity" Anthony Appiah "deconstructs" race by reasoning that "biological variation in skin color does not correlate (a whole lot) with other characteristics" (1996, 70) and Hannaford introduces a similar argument in *Race: The History of an Idea in the West*:

> Those who cling to the old view argue that there is still some evidence of genetic, sociobiological, or clinical differentiation that may be termed "racial." Those who contest that premise argue that advances in high-speed data processing permit the quantification of such vast numbers of biological characteristics of individuals and groupings that no generalized evidence of raciation can be discerned. (1996, 7)

While there is no evidence in *Daniel Deronda* that George Eliot might have been aware of the nineteenth-century view that Jews were "black," there is no doubt that she was familiar with race theory through her interest in Darwin and her friendship with Spencer. And even though there is no indication that Harriet Beecher Stowe also studied race theory, it is still obvious that her ideas about race reflect contemporary attitudes about race. As a devout Christian, Stowe had to side with monogenist race theory, which held that blacks and whites were of the same species, in order not to contradict the Bible's version of human creation. Miss Ophelia, one of the "religiously correct" characters in *Uncle Tom's Cabin,* thus declares Stowe's view "that the Lord made them of one blood with us" and that "they've [also] got immortal souls" ([1852] 1981, 268). But this did not necessarily mean that Stowe thought that America was the best place for African Americans. In keeping with nineteenth-century race theory, Stowe enthusiastically depicts a golden future for Africans in Africa:

> If ever Africa shall show an elevated and cultivated race,—and come it must . . . life will awake there with a gorgeousness of which our cold western tribes faintly have conceived. In that far-off mystic land of gold and gems, and spices, and waving palms and wondrous flowers, and miraculous fertility, will awake new forms of art, new styles of splendor; and the negro race, no longer despised and trodden down will, perhaps, show forth some of the latest and most magnificent revelations of human life. (275)

The flowery language of this passage might at first conceal the dark subtext that runs through it and tries to make palatable the idea that Africans, who are environmentally adapted to the African continent, should live in Africa. Immediate protest against Stowe's colonizationist stance made Stowe revise her politics. According to Yarborough, Stowe "reportedly regretted her decision, explaining that she would end the novel differently if given the opportunity to write it over again" (1986, 69).

Dred, Stowe's second antislavery novel, avoided some of the pitfalls of *Uncle Tom's Cabin.* Instead of sending black characters to Liberia, Stowe projects integrated utopian communities of black grandparents and "white, black, and foreign" ([1856] 1970, 333) grandchildren in Northern cities and in Canada. Moreover, Stowe's main hero, after whom the novel is named, proves that a purely black character can exhibit masculine valor and intelligence. But with the character of Tiff, who instead of wearing pants sometimes wears two aprons—one in front and one in back—and who constantly worries about what he can do to inculcate religion in the two white children he takes care of, Stowe again portrays a black male as maternal and devoutly religious. In an often quoted passage from *A Key to Uncle Tom's Cabin,* she gives her rationale for such depictions: "The negro race is confessedly more simple, docile, childlike, and affectionate, than other races; and hence the divine graces of love and faith, when in-breathed by the Holy Spirit, find in their natural temperament a more congenial atmosphere" ([1854] 1968, 41).

Anthony Appiah notes that this myth of the "naturally religious African" (which is mirrored by Eliot's also "naturally religious" Jews) was also common among missionaries who had come back from Africa impressed with the Africans' "natural religiosity" and "the yearning of the native African for a higher religion" (1992, 23). According to Appiah this supposed naturalness of religious worship among Africans was fabricated in the minds of those who observed the behavior of enslaved African Americans through a "racialized" lens:

> It is tempting to see this view as yet another imposition of the exile's distorting vision; in the New World, Christianity had provided the major vehicle of cultural expression for the slaves. It could not be denied them in a Christian country—and it provided them with solace in their "vale of tears," guiding them through "the valley of the shadow." Once committed to racialist explanations, it was inevitable that the rich religious lives of New World blacks should be seen as flowing from the nature of the Negro—and thus projected onto the Negro in Africa. (23)[3]

For Stowe, this "natural religiosity" always ties in with "childlikeness." Both in *Uncle Tom's Cabin* and in *Dred*, individual African Americans and also "the race as a whole" are described as childlike and dependent. In *Dred*, the narrator sermonizes, "The Negro race, with many of the faults of children, unite many of their most amiable qualities in the simplicity and confidingness with which they yield themselves up in admiration of a superior friend" ([1856] 1970, 46). Her character Clayton, who compares "the Ethiopian race" to "a slow-growing plant," predicts that "if they ever become highly civilized, they will excel in music, dancing, and elocution" (74). Even though, as I think, these descriptions veer away from what Appiah defines as "racialist" views into what one might have to label "racism,"[4] it is evident that Stowe believed in a certain dynamism within the Great Chain of Being. Apparently, she had internalized the popular belief that "lower races," like children, could actually "grow up."

In this context, it is interesting to note that throughout her novels dealing with race, Stowe consistently equates women with children and black men—thus, in *Dred* Harry Gordon, Nina's slave brother, never addresses his wife, Lisette, by her first name, but always calls her "child" instead. From a twenty-first-century point of view one might certainly wonder what kind of self-image Stowe had if she associated women with children. Did she mean to imply that their intelligence was "less developed" than that of white males? If this was the case one could almost exonerate Stowe from the reproach of racial discrimination because in the light of this conviction, she would put herself on par with black males. But by the same token one could, of course, also argue that Stowe's socialization necessarily made her adopt racist and sexist viewpoints.

During the mideighties of the twentieth century, white female critics—who wanted to save Stowe from the charge of racism—called attention to the fact that by making Tom "soft like a woman," Stowe introduced a matrifocal vision into American literature. Elizabeth Ammons, for example, very astutely identified what Stowe accomplished when she created Tom:

> Stowe's Tom *is* soft. He personifies the motherly Christ. . . . That Tom is not classically masculine—that he does not fight for his life but instead puts the lives of others first, that he refuses to meet violence with violence, that he remains compassionate, giving, and emotional to the end—illustrates Stowe's political genius in *Uncle Tom's Cabin*. What better way to inflame the culture against slavery than by characterizing her hero as a stereotypical Victorian heroine: pious, home-centered, self-sacrificing, nonviolent? (1986, 168)

Stowe expands this strategy of turning black men into harmless "Uncle Toms" by also presenting the spirituality of women in terms of the childlikeness that she attributes to some black men.[5] Her insistence that women have no sexual desire[6] and that most—or at least some—black men are like women might be viewed as an ingenious move because it allows her to sidestep the issue of sexual desire between white women and black men. Her presentation of Tom evokes the image of an aged avuncular black male, even though at the beginning of her novel her narrator describes him as the father of small children and "a large powerfully-made man" ([1852] 1982, 68). In *Dred*, Tiff even becomes "doubly maternal" by virtue of the two aprons he always sports. Stowe's narrator comments on the scene of Tiff sleeping between his two white stepchildren—whom he has saved from their licentious alcoholic stepmother—with the words: "How innocent, soft and kind are all of God's works" ([1856] 1970, 170). Sarah Smith Ducksworth and Hortense Spillers, two recent critics who identify themselves as African American, have nevertheless remained unconvinced by Stowe's description of innocent relations between old black men and young white children and discover subtexts of sexual deviance behind Stowe's presentation of Tom as a motherly savior[7] (a role that, arguably, Daniel Deronda also fulfills in reference to Gwendolen). The fact that contemporary black critics have such powerfully negative reactions to Stowe's depiction of relations between black men and little white girls shows that, even in the late twentieth century, the intersection of gender and race—which is always an intersection of power relationships as well—still seems to be considered dangerous territory.

Stowe's presentation of sexual desire between adult members of different races in terms of violence or transgression has to be understood in light of nineteenth-century race theory, which harbored fears of degeneration and annihilation as the result of the mixing of "higher" and "lower" races and tried to establish whether or not the hybrid progeny of different races—who according to polygenism were also different species—would be infertile like mules. Stowe's narrative strategy clearly entails ruling out any desire between different races; in those cases where she deems it necessary to hint at biracial sexual relations, she presents sexual desire between adult members of different races in terms of violence or transgression. Most of the mixed race characters in Stowe's work indicate that they are either the product of sexual violence perpetrated against their mothers by their white fathers or at least the offspring of a very uneven relationship between a white father and a dependent black mother. If sexual relations between different races seem to be in any way motivated by sexual desire, this desire is marked by transgression rather than love. Thus, biracial sexual attraction must necessarily lead to repulsion and Stowe's ideal of domesticity cannot flourish in mixed race relationships. In *Dred*, Stowe cites the negative example of Anne's uncle who "lived with a quadroon woman, who was violently tempered, and when angry ferociously cruel and so the servants were constantly passing from the extreme of indulgence to the extreme of cruelty" ([1856] 1970, 47). And in *Uncle Tom's Cabin* she depicts the sexually exploitative relationship between Cassy and Legree which ultimately brings about Legree's doom since Legree does not dare to alienate Cassy completely because of the sexual hold that the memory of their relationship still exerts over him.

In spite of Stowe's debatable attitudes about race, there is no doubt that both her and Eliot's novels are political novels which seek to expose the corruptness of the dominant cultures of the countries that they are set in. Stowe's objective of denouncing slavery in *Uncle Tom's Cabin* and *Dred* is more than obvious, whereas Eliot's purpose of uncovering the decadent aimlessness of the British gentry by juxtaposing it with a healthy Jewish communal alternative that busily devises the building of a Zionist nation is a little more difficult to detect. Eliot very obviously seems to have wanted to present the Jewish race in a sympathetic light in *Daniel Deronda*.[8] Here, I think, it is only fair to point out that it may well have been easier for Eliot to depict Jews as a cultural asset for England than for Stowe to present Africans as an integral part of American society. To Eliot, Jews must have seemed physically and culturally much less "other" than people of African descent appeared to Stowe. Eliot might have chosen Jews as the particular ethnic group for her fictional evaluation of "race" not only because Jewish people presented the only large racially other group in Britain, but also because they do not necessarily look physically different from English people. By studying a racial minority that can mingle undetectably with the majority, Eliot might have felt better equipped to explore whether or not race is an essential determinant of human behavior or whether it really is only skin-deep.

As Jan Nederveen Pieterse observes, there are some similarities between antiblack racism and anti-Semitism in spite of the difference in the ability "to pass for white":

> [B]oth groups were regarded as non-Christian. The early medieval tripartite division of the world based on Sem, Ham and Japhet, as the ancestors of Asia, Africa and Europe respectively . . . portrayed Semites and Hamites, although both were descendants of Noah, as peoples "external" to Christendom, and later as external to "Europe." The nineteenth-century theory of Aryan race, from the Comte de Gobineau to Houston Stewart Chamberlain, again excluded both "Semites" and "Africans" from the hallowed ground of the Nordic, or Indo-European race. "Africans" were placed at the foot of the human ladder and "Semites" were cast in the role of historical counterparts to the Aryans. (1992, 218)

But Pieterse argues that there were also some differences in the ways in which these different racial groups were discriminated against. Jews, unlike blacks, were "envied for their success at money-making" and "hated for their religion and their clannishness" (218). Ivan Hannaford points out that in medieval times the particular branch of Jewish believers who are the ancestors of Mirah and Mordecai in *Daniel Deronda*, namely, the Sephardic Spanish Jews, became something like a separate "caste" in Spain because they were discriminated against by both Muslims and Christians, and because they themselves did not want to "lose a distinct identity not as an expression of racial difference but as a passionate desire to preserve a noble spiritual lineage" (1996, 106). The trajectory of the Jewish plot of *Daniel Deronda*, and especially its identity-theme, suggests that Eliot's own idea of Jewishness does not rule out such a definition of Jewishness as clan, or caste, which tries to preserve its unique identity. She certainly does not agree with nineteenth-century race theory which defines Jews as a separate, inferior race.

Her presentation of Jews in *Daniel Deronda* is very different from Stowe's presentation of blacks in *Uncle Tom's Cabin* and reflects the same reluctance—or even inability—on Eliot's part to deal with cultural and ethnic difference that she already exhibited when dealing with Italianness in *Romola*. Her wavering between giving slightly stereotypical or highly idealized descriptions of her Jewish characters recalls her depiction of Italianness in *Romola*. Unlike Stowe's African Americans, her Jewish characters are obviously not enslaved and for the most part highly educated; if they want to, they can easily deny their Jewish origin. Quite a few of them are even socially on a par with the purely English characters. While Stowe does not seem to be able to let a "comical darky" go unnoticed, Eliot, for the most part, does not single out behavior patterns as essentially Jewish (for example, she takes great care to present "stereotypically Jewish" greed as stereotypically English as well) and she does not make intelligence dependent on her characters' degree of "whiteness" or Englishness. She also does not dwell much on physical descriptions of her Jewish characters. The musician Herr Klesmer is described as an amalgam, "a felicitous combination of the German, the Sclave [*sic*], the Semite" ([1876] 1995, 47), but beyond this description, he is a stereotypical musician rather than a stereotypical Jew, just as the Alcharisi is a stereotypical diva rather than a stereotypical "Jewish mother." The English-Jewish brother and sister, Mordecai and Mirah, are also not primarily defined by racial markers. Mirah comes across as an almost generic frail woman in need of male protection and Mordecai is depicted as a consumptive, sick-looking workman with "wasted yellow hands" and "a consumptive glance" (495). It is primarily this description of him that stays with the reader. His face is initially described as "a finely typical Jewish face" (386), but there are so few physical descriptions of him throughout the hundreds of pages of the novel that readers might easily forget this initial description. Daniel Deronda's ethnic background does not seem readily discernible, either. Eliot presents him as a very handsome, only slightly foreign looking man, who does not have any of the typically English features of his "uncle," Sir Hugo Mallinger, and whose face is "not more distinctively oriental than many a type seen among the what we call the Latin races: rich in youthful health, and with a forcible masculine gravity in its repose" (495–96). Because Jewish racial origin is rendered as rather inconspicuous, Eliot—unlike Stowe—can present various ways of dealing with it. Unlike Stowe's protagonists, Eliot's characters, as, for example, Daniel and his mother, seem to have the freedom of accepting or denying their racial identification.

Terence Cave devotes several pages of his introduction to the Penguin edition of *Daniel Deronda* to stressing that at the time of *Daniel Deronda*'s publication, Jewish response to the novel (unlike black response to *Uncle Tom's Cabin*) was unanimously favorable (see Cave 1995, xv–xvii) and that especially Eliot's envisioning of the "dream of a national home" for Jews was much appreciated (xvii-xviii).[9] Eliot's presentation of Jews in the novel, however, has been implicitly criticized for being overly idealistic, by Amy Levy in her novel *Reuben Sachs*, which was conceptualized as a reaction to *Daniel Deronda*.[10] It has also come under attack by critics who take a postcolonial approach to *Daniel Deronda* and often simultaneously criticize Eliot for making her Jewish characters either too stereotypically Jewish or not Jewish enough. Reina Lewis and Susan Meyer, for example, take offense at her preference for refined Jews, her presentation of Mirah's father as a thief, and her dwelling on the Cohens' stereotypical greed (see Lewis, 219; Meyer 1996, 180). But Lewis has to concede that David Kaufman, of the Jewish theological seminar of Budapest, "[felt] that her treatment of negative qualities in Jews is fundamental to the book's task of making Jews real" (1996, 223). She mainly criticizes Eliot for insisting on Judaism's role as "other, not centre of the text" (207). Eliot, according to Lewis, marginalizes and "others" Judaism by focusing on nationalistic rather than assimilationist Judaism, by thus "represent[ing] Judaism as a living example of an ancient culture that owes more to developments in its past than its present" (208), and by "relocat[ing] nineteenth-century Jews in a spiritually glowing medieval past, thereby bypassing any of the difficulties associated with contemporary Jews with all their flaws" (210). Susan Meyer, who argues that in *Daniel Deronda* Eliot presents a man of "alien racial identity" as a very tenuous solution "to the original problem of the tension between women and a constraining society" (1996, 160), views George Eliot's fictional Zionism as a proto-Zionism designed "to create, at least in the novel's fictive space, an England purified of people of other races and purified of the energies of women's discontent at their secondary social status" (191). As with those critics who accuse Stowe of wanting to remove blacks from the American continent, Meyer blames Eliot for following a proto-Zionist impulse which was sparked "by English gentiles in this period . . . who were fascinated with the idea of the Jewish return" (183), and which "arose in part from a desire for imperialist expansion and racial domination, and in part from a desire to have the Jews elsewhere" (187). She concludes that "[t]he proto-Zionism of *Daniel Deronda* is of a piece with its time. When the novel is considered in its historical context, its simultaneous anti-semitism against ordinary Jews and idealization of refined Jews burning with desire to leave England for Palestine no longer seems incongruous" (187). Susan Meyer's discovery of Eliot's proto-Zionism seems to be contradicted by Terence Cave's observation that Chaim Guedalla, a leader of the London Jewish community, "enclos[ed] a pamphlet summarizing recent discussions of the possibility of raising Turkish finance for a Jewish colony in Palestine" and that "Eliot was delighted to find that these discussions had been taking place at about the time she had been composing the *Hand and Banner*-scene" (1995, xv). But even apart from this possible factual error in Meyer's criticism of *Daniel Deronda*, I disagree with both her and Lewis's assessment of the novel because I think that Eliot's exploration of race pursues aesthetic and philosophical aims much different from those outlined by these two critics. In her recent book, *George Eliot and the British Empire*, Nancy Henry refutes Meyer's and Lewis's criticism of Eliot's "imperialist" leanings by calling attention to the ideological blind spots of postcolonial criticism (see Henry 2002, 113–15; 123–26) and by pointing out that critics who attack Eliot's "Zionist" (and by implication imperialist) views often confuse the statements of her fictional character Mordecai with those of his creator (see Henry 2002, 138). Moreover, her in-depth analysis of Eliot's complex presentation of colonial issues in *Daniel Deronda*, *Impressions of Theophrastus Such*, and various letters succeeds in substantiating her claim that "even at the height of her success did her fiction not lose its concern for the displaced and marginalized" (116).[11]

Eliot uses her Jewish novel, *Daniel Deronda*, to investigate possible meanings of "race" and racial identification through a dialogic presentation of the subject which encompasses short comments that characters make about "race" as well as complex issues of racial identification. This investigation of racial identification is made possible by the fact that Eliot's Jewish characters do not seem to look much different from her gentile characters. The issue of "race" is a topic of discussion within the Jewish community of *Daniel Deronda* as well as in the English community after it has come into contact with Jews. As soon as Mirah has become an adopted member of the Meyrick family, "race" starts to matter within the Meyrick family circle. Comments range from Mrs. Meyrick's anxious wish that Mirah convert to Christianity over Mirah's apologies for being Jewish and therefore possibly "bad" to Hans's plea for racial amalgamation which, of course, results from his desire for Mirah who, after all, might not want to convert.

Eliot's presentation of Jews, like her presentation of gentiles, includes sympathetic as well as unsympathetic depictions and introduces her readers to a wide range of Jewish personalities. As already mentioned above, her somewhat deprecatory characterization of the greedy and rather vulgar, yet still kind, Cohens has met with recent criticism because it invokes a negative racial stereotype. But, as she also frequently does in regard to stereotypes regarding Italians in "Mr. Gilfil's Love Story," Eliot debunks the Jewish stereotype almost as soon as she has invoked it. Thus, she compares the greedy behavior of a member of the marginal group to "hegemonical" English greed: "[N]o shadow of a Suffering Race distinguished his vulgarity of soul from that of a prosperous pink-and-white huckster of the purest English lineage" ([1876] 1995, 39).

The—perhaps a bit too aptly named—Jewish musician Klesmer, whom Cheyette describes as "an assimilated 'Wandering Jew'" (1993, 51), however, is an entirely positive figure of racial integration. The fact that he refuses to tell Gwendolen any lies about her artistic capabilities, combined with his refusal to give up his love for his English fiancée when faced with her parents' resistance to their union, stresses his independence from his (potential) employers and attests to his personal integrity. As a person whose racial origin is already described as mixed, he actively pursues racial amalgamation through his marriage to the "purely English" heiress Catherine Arrowpoint.

Besides the example of Klesmer, there are various other Jewish characters whose yearning for assimilation into the gentile population is opposed to Mordecai's romantic kabbalistic Jewish nationalism. In the *Hand and Banner* scene Pash and Gideon, members of the Jewish Philosophers' Club, argue that Jewish nationalism is dead. Gideon holds that because it is "the order of the day in point of progress" Jews should assimilate into the gentile population and "'[get] rid of all . . . superstitions and exclusiveness. There's no reason why [Jews] shouldn't melt gradually into the populations we live among. . . . I would as soon my children married Christians as Jews. And I'm for the old maxim, "A man's country is where he's well off"'" ([1876] 1995, 527). Mordecai, however, who believes that "'nationality [has to be] a feeling'" (525) in order to function as an idea, argues that Jews, precisely because of their position as exiles, need to "'[l]ook towards a land and polity'" so that they may preserve their cultural memory and "'share the dignity of a national life which has a voice among the peoples of the East and the West'" (532).

By violently denying her Jewish heritage throughout most of her adult life, Daniel's mother, the Alcharisi, even goes one step beyond the assimilation postulated in the *Hand and Banner* scene. She rejects all racial and gendered ascriptions applied to her, and at one point, she actively chooses not to be Jewish any longer: "'I made myself like the people I lived among'" (635). As she explains to Daniel, her reason for rejecting her race—along with her gender—can be located in her father's sexism which reflects the overall sexism of Jewish patriarchy: "'To have a pattern cut out—"this is the Jewish woman; this is what you must be; . . . a woman's heart must be pressed small, like Chinese feet; her happiness is to be made as cakes are, by a fixed recipe." That was what my father wanted. . .'" (631). Ardently pursuing her goal of making her own life differ from this "fixed recipe," the Alcharisi decided to pursue her stage career as a singer at the expense of her son:

> Every woman is supposed to have the same set of motives, or else to be a monster. I am not a monster, but I have not felt exactly what other women feel—or say they feel, for fear of being thought unlike others. When you re-

proach me in your heart for sending you away from me, you mean that I ought to say I felt about you as other women say they feel about their children. I did *not* feel that. I was glad to be freed from you. (628)

Eliot's decision to present a woman who does not feel any "natural" love for her child has met with critical disapproval well into the late twentieth-century. Bonnie Zimmerman suggests that the figure of the Alcharisi shows that "the rejection of the traditional female role . . . would entail the loss to society of love, sympathy, tenderness, affection and nurturance" and that "George Eliot . . . identified this hatred and intolerance, as well as the rejection of feminine sympathy and nurturance, as a potential danger in the emerging feminism of her day" (1986, 235). Even though I assume that the characterization of Daniel's mother as an "unmotherly mother" might also have been inspired by Stowe's unsympathetic description of the unloving Marie St. Clare from Stowe's *Uncle Tom's Cabin*, I do not think that Eliot meant for the Alcharisi to be viewed in an entirely negative light. Like Klesmer, Daniel's mother is honest and upright and remains true to herself under pressure.

The Alcharisi who boasts "'I am not a loving woman. . . . I was never willingly subject to any man. Men have been subject to me'" ([1876] 1995, 666) fits into Eliot's larger project of showing that, provided that they are willing to pay a price for it, women can, at least for some time, escape their gender along with their patriarchal interpellation as subjected female.[12] Strangely enough, as soon as Eliot seems to have asserted the Alcharisi's independence from the current ideology of gender she apparently reinserts her into the ideology of race—if not gender—and seems to force her to confess the truth about Daniel's racial inheritance to him:

It is illness, I don't doubt that it has been gathering illness,—my mind has gone back; more than a year ago it began. . . . Then a great horror comes over me: what do I know of life or death? and what my father called "right" might be a power that is laying hold of me—that is clutching me now. Well, I will satisfy him. I cannot go into the darkness without satisfying him. I have hidden what was his. I thought once I would burn it. . . . I thank God I have not burnt it! (636).

Ultimately, it cannot be known whether it is feelings of guilt, her bad health, or a strange "call of the blood" that motivates the Alcharisi's confession, or whether her father's friend Joseph Kalonymous coerced her into her confession: "'My father may have God on his side. This man's words are like lion's teeth upon me'" (638). But what can definitely be said is that the motif of being interpellated by "Race" is also closely connected with Daniel's recovery of his racial identity.

FROM "RACE" TO (NATIONAL) IDENTITY

Daniel heeds Mordecai's call to become a Jewish national leader as soon as he finds out that he really is of Jewish origin. Eliot's decision to focus on Jewish nationalism in her novel on "race" was certainly inspired by Stowe's portrayal of an incipient African American nationalism in *Uncle Tom's Cabin* and *Dred*. Her characterization of George Harris as a future national leader and the eponymous Dred as a race prophet serve both as models and foils for Eliot's Daniel and Mordecai. But there are also some important differences in Eliot's and Stowe's presentation of race-based national (and also individual) identity. Stowe assigns a mostly extrinsic Western cultural identity to her characters by disregarding their ethnic and cultural origins. George's vision of Liberia reflects a biblical paradise just as Dred's spirituality is based primarily on the Old Testament. Even though Stowe was aware of African American folk traditions, her Christian world view kept her from validating non-Christian African spiritual practices. George Eliot, however, romanticized the ancient kabbalistic Jewish tradition that she presents in *Daniel Deronda* after having meticulously researched it.[13]

In her unpublished 1994 dissertation "Originating Fictions: Harriet Beecher Stowe and George Eliot," Nancy Henry has investigated the many parallels between Stowe's and Eliot's depiction of race and national identity in *Uncle Tom's Cabin* and *Daniel Deronda*. Thus she points out that "Eliot and Stowe differ from other nationalist movements of the period because members of the Diaspora community define themselves by 'returning to a place where they have never been'" (1994, 18) and that George's and Daniel's "returning to other lands" (64) is part of a process of recovering "absent parental ties" (67) and an unfamiliar personal past. All of this, she argues, is embedded in a larger argumentative strategy which the two authors employ to suggest "that individual identity could be reconstructed on the basis of an origin transmitted to the individual person through textually preserved cultural memories" (62–63). Henry's main thesis is that while "the second origin . . . looks to be essential, racial, fixed" the return to this "homeland" where George and Daniel have never been is a matter of intellectual choice rather than a genetic "call of the blood." At several instances in her dissertation she argues that the genetic "binding ties in these novels are not imposed or inescapable" (77):

Stowe's and Eliot's interpretations of returning underlie a similar critique of fixed geographic and racial origins. George, the mulatto, French-educated former slave and Daniel, the Oxbridge-educated gentleman Jew, embody a comparable mixture of cultural inheritances and experiences. George's choice to identify himself as African and Daniel's to identify himself as Jewish represent a self-conscious, retrospective positing of origins. (18)

Henry identifies important similarities in Stowe's and Eliot's depiction of race and nationality, but I disagree with her about the freedom of choice she assigns to an—albeit fictitious—African American character in choosing his national and racial affiliation. In the above quote, Henry obviously alludes to George Harris's "letter to one of his friends" in which he proclaims his refusal "to pass for an American, or to identify myself with them" ([1852] 1981, 608). While it might have been possible for George, whose "shade of color" is "slight" to "mingle in the circle of whites" (608)—where societal power is located—this would not have been the case for most other former slaves who could not have chosen to become "white Americans" in the same manner in which the racially inconspicuous Daniel chooses to become the Jew that he actually is.

Contradicting her above statement about the ready availability of "textually preserved memories" for the characters of *Uncle Tom's Cabin*, Henry further expounds her understanding of Harriet Beecher Stowe's racial politics by explaining that "[i]n Stowe's imagined Liberian nationalism, the cultural basis of the community which wants to return, reverts to 'race' because it seems to have no coherent alternative culture—in the sense of textually or orally transmitted practices, rituals and beliefs to unify and distinguish it" (1994, 73). Anthony Appiah's discussion of W. E. B. DuBois's difficulties in finding a nonracial rationale for Pan-Africanism to some extent corroborates this difficulty in formulating a nonracial basis for community,[14] yet I still think that it does not fully explain Stowe's attitude about race and "repatriation." Stowe actually seems to have actively suppressed whatever knowledge she might have had about "orally transmitted practices" and "a coherent alternative culture" within the African American community because these spiritual practices derive from non-Christian African belief systems.[15]

As part of her optimistic evaluation of Stowe's racial politics, Henry maintains that Stowe contests "the attribution of behavior to essential or biological characteristics" (1994, 10). She also concludes that "there is no ambiguity in [Eliot's] conviction that bonds of obligation by which we understand such terms as 'blood' and 'race' are the product of habit" (5).

While Henry might not be too far off the mark in her assessment of Eliot's racial politics in *Daniel Deronda*, I cannot agree with her statement about Stowe's stance, since in Stowe's novels as well as in her explanatory essay, *The Key to Uncle Tom's Cabin,* enough evidence of her conviction that race is a decisive determinant of human behavior, intelligence, and identity can be found.[16]

While many critics conclude that Stowe's overall dubious racial politics culminate in a scheme for African repatriation, Henry argues that Stowe's investigation of national identity finally made her revise her racial politics and present the result of this in *Dred*:

> For Stowe, national identity follows from national origin and in *Dred*, it is precisely the concept of America's origins that she must revise. *Dred* emphasizes a continuous revolutionary process rather than a fixed and exclusively white democratic ideal. . . . The trajectory from *Uncle Tom's Cabin* to *Dred* is the move from Africa for Africans and America for Anglo-Saxons to America as a process for achieving a coherent national character with people possessed of different cultural memories. (1994, 104)

Even though Dred, the swamp prophet, cannot bring about racial integration by means of a revolution, Henry celebrates *Dred* as a novel featuring a "utopian vision" in "the final resolutions of plot in *Dred* which imagine a radical disregard for national, racial, and gender roles" (124–25). Since, as I have pointed out earlier, Stowe carefully avoided any hint at the possibility of racial amalgamation within her utopian community of mixed-raced grandparents and grandchildren, I cannot agree with this optimistic conclusion about the trajectory of Stowe's racial and national politics. A closer examination of the race theme in *Daniel Deronda* shows that Henry's statement that Eliot "unambiguously took Stowe as a literary model" (20) is untenable. But there are, nevertheless, some similarities in the ways in which both authors romanticize race in conjunction with religion. Eliot seems to have borrowed plot elements from both *Uncle Tom's Cabin* and *Dred* and incorporated them into a single plot in *Daniel Deronda*. She heightens the effect of the race/religion theme taken from Stowe's novels by combining the European Zionist movement's "dream of a national home" and the "race prophecy" from *Uncle Tom's Cabin* and *Dred*, and by making Daniel fulfill Mordecai's prophecy (thus showing that nation-building can indeed be accomplished when it is based on religious "feeling").

Eliot elaborates on the investigation of cultural and racial identity that Stowe introduces in *Uncle Tom's Cabin* and *Dred*. Henry optimistically suggests that in Stowe's as well as Eliot's novels individual identity is constituted through the study of "preserved cultural" memory. As I have already pointed out, I think that this is the case in Eliot's novel rather than in Stowe's works. Unlike Eliot, Stowe does not look for a long-engrained cultural memory (which in the nineteenth-century was often labeled a "race habit") in the African American population, but instead, having postulated that Africans are naturally religious, she invests them with a cultural identity based on Christian religion because that is where she locates absolute truth for all people. Thus, George Harris, referring to blacks as "they," expresses his hopes for a Christianization of Africa: "I trust that the development of Africa is to be essentially a Christian one. If not a dominant and commanding race, they are, at least, an affectionate, magnanimous and forgiving one" ([1852] 1981, 611). Similarly, Stowe's narrator introduces the African American prophet Dred with a statement about the "naturalness" of his Christian prophecy: "It is remarkable that, in all ages, communities and individuals who have suffered under oppression have always fled for refuge to the Old Testament, and to the book of Revelation in the New" ([1856] 1970, 214–15). In *The Key to Uncle Tom's Cabin*, Stowe similarly expounds the idea that Africans are naturally "given to visions":

> The African race, in their own climate, are believers in spells, in "fetish and obi," in "the evil eye," and other singular influences, for which probably there is an origin in this peculiarity of constitution. . . . Considering these distinctive traits of the race, it is no matter of surprise to find in their religious histories, when acted upon by the powerful stimulant of the Christian religion, very peculiar features. We are not surprised to find almost constantly, in the narrations of their religious histories, accounts of visions, of heavenly voices, of mysterious sympathies and transmissions of knowledge. ([1854] 1968, 46)

While Stowe basically views spiritual inclinations in a positive light, she stresses that they have to be practiced within the proper Christian framework. Even though Dred is a self-taught Christian, he remains culturally deprived and therefore dangerous: "It is difficult to fathom the dark recesses of a mind so powerful and active as his, placed under a pressure of ignorance and social disability so tremendous" ([1856] 1970, 23). Because of the dangerous and revolutionary potential emanating from such a character as Dred, whose well-chosen name already is "a portent of dread," Stowe disposes of him by having him killed by a racist mob. Henry argues that the aborted revolution of *Dred* suggests that Stowe favors historic gradualism (see 1994, 106–07), yet her decision to forgo a revolution and to dispose of another truly "masculine" black male in favor of the "feminized" avuncular

Tiff could also be read as a continuation of the politics of "repatriating dangerous blacks" that she pursued in *Uncle Tom's Cabin*. This strategy was criticized by Eliot in her review because she thought that it wasted the potential for novelistic drama inherent in the race plot.

In her Jewish adaptation of Stowe's African American race plot, Eliot avoided some of the "racial pitfalls" that Stowe could not avoid. By focusing on highly cultured Jews rather than "uncultivated" black swamp dwellers, Eliot sidestepped not only the problem of dealing with protagonists who are "other" because of skin color, but also evaded the class issue that exacerbates the race issue of *Uncle Tom's Cabin* and *Dred*. And by presenting Jews as representatives of an already combined racial and religious alterity, Eliot, unlike Stowe, did not have to invent a rationale for a racial propensity for religiousness. Her careful study of Jewish life—which was perhaps sparked by her realization of shortcomings in her previous depiction of Italianness—enabled her to investigate the meaning of racial/cultural identity and to draw a historically correct, but still rather researched, picture of the Jewish faith and Jewish customs.

In her edition of *George Eliot's* Daniel Deronda *Notebooks*, Jane Irwin calls attention to Eliot's enormous research of Jewish history which investigated an abundance of information about historical and contemporary aspects of Jewish life and law, ranging from food regulations to discriminatory gender laws to questions of heresy. She points out that Jews were amazed at Eliot's knowledge of their faith: "As Sigmund Freud was to remark, George Eliot knew of things 'we [Jews] speak of only among ourselves'" (1996, xxx). Irwin also stresses that it is this research "which extended far beyond what might have been useful for color in her novel and gave her an entry into the inner life of Judaism" (xxxiii) that makes her protagonists believable, otherwise "these characters might have been only vessels of pathos, comparable to Riah in *Our Mutual Friend*" (xxi). This observation can also be used to explain what makes Eliot's presentation of the race plot so much more sophisticated than Stowe's—in spite of the fact that her depiction of Judaism and Jewish characters sometimes seems as "over-researched" and sterile as her Renaissance Florence and its Italian characters. Eliot conceived her figures very carefully before authoring *Daniel Deronda*,[17] whereas Stowe wrote her *Key to Uncle Tom's Cabin* (1854) after the publication of the novel in order to provide a rationale for her racial politics and her characterization of African Americans. Thus, Eliot's visionary Mordecai, for example, puts forth very well researched kabbalistic prophecy whereas Stowe's African American prophet, Dred, spouts spiritual gibberish reflecting his ignorance and cultural deprivation. An example of this can be seen in the following conversation between Dred and his white friend Clayton about Dred's gift of vision:

> "And the Lord showed unto me that even as a ship which is forsaken of the waters, wherein all flesh have died, so shall it be with the nation of the oppressor." "How did the Lord show you this" said Clayton, bent upon pursuing his inquiry. "Mine ear received it in the night season," said Dred, "and I heard how the whole creation groaneth and travaileth, waiting for the adoption; and because of this he hath appointed the tide." "I don't see the connection," said Clayton. "Why because of this?" "Because," said Dred, "every day is full of labor, but the labor goes back again into the seas. So that travail of all generations has gone back, till the desire of all nations shall come, and He shall come with burning and with judgment, and with great shakings; but in the end thereof shall be peace." ([1856] 1970, 293)

Initially, Mordecai's explanation—to Daniel—of where his own gift of prophecy comes from might sound similarly strange:

> "A spiritual destiny embraced willingly—in youth?" Mordecai repeated in a corrective tone. "It was the soul fully born within me, and it came in my boyhood. It brought its own world—a medieval world, where there were men who made the ancient language live again in the new psalms of exile. They had absorbed the philosophy of the Gentile into the faith of the Jew, and they still yearned toward a centre for our race. One of their souls was born again within me, and awaked amid the memories of their world." ([1876] 1995, 498)

Yet while Stowe's home-spun spirituality has no philosophical basis, Mordecai's elucidation of his spiritual gift contains information about the kabbalistic transmigration of souls (his own body holds the soul of a medieval Sephardic Jew) as well as the Neoplatonic sources of the Kabbalah.[18] Eliot herself, as if she were indeed writing back to Stowe, stresses the fact that Mordecai is not an "ignorant dreamer":

> I speak not as an ignorant dreamer—as one bred up in the inland valleys, thinking ancient thoughts anew, and not knowing them ancient, never having stood by the great waters where the world's knowledge passes to and fro. . . . English is my mother-tongue . . . . But my true life was nourished in Holland, at the feet of my mother's brother, a Rabbi skilled in special learning; and when he died I went to Hamburg to study and afterwards to Göttingen. (497)

As Irwin points out, in *Daniel Deronda*, "George Eliot has set herself the daunting task of bringing the revelations of Old Testament visionary prophecy into conjunction with the mundane world of contemporary London—in a context where the prophetic mode of William Blake's *Jerusalem* would be inappropriate" (1996, 163).

Eliot validates the race/religion plot and heightens its romantic effect by allowing Mordecai—who, like Stowe's Dred, knows that he will not be able to carry out his vision himself—to choose his own successor through charming him with his gift of prophecy. Daniel, who does not know that he is Jewish when he first meets Mordecai, heeds Mordecai's call without really knowing why. The "Jewish part" of the novel focuses on Daniel's decision to follow this "call of the blood"—or love—and seems to forsake the "objective" realms of realism and science in favor of the "personal" ones of romance and religion. The story of Daniel's response to Mordecai's plea to join him in his crusade for Jewish nationalism is one of the most fascinating episodes of *Daniel Deronda* as it examines the meaning of "race" and explores the constitution of individual as well as collective identity.

Daniel's encounters with his racial origin are mystifying from the beginning. After having met Mirah, but before he even knows that he is Jewish, just at the point at which he is fed up with the idle existence of an English gentleman and greatly desires "either some eternal event, or some inward light, that would urge him into a definite line of action, and compress his wandering energy" (365), Daniel is mysteriously drawn to Judaism. He attends a service at a synagogue in Frankfurt and suddenly feels personally addressed:

> The Hebrew liturgy . . . the chant of the *Chazan's* or Reader's grand wide-ranging voice with its passage from monotony to sudden cries . . . the devotional swaying of men's bodies backwards and forwards, the very commonness of the building and shabbiness of the scene where a national faith, which had penetrated the thinking of half the world, and moulded the splendid forms of that world's religion, was finding a remote, obscure echo—all were blent for him as one expression of a binding history, tragic and yet glorious. He wondered at the strength of his own feeling; it seemed beyond the occasion—what one might imagine to be a divine influx in the darkness, before there was any vision to interpret. (367–68) [19]

After the service Daniel is approached by a Jew who asks him about his mother's maiden name. Realizing that the man might think him a fellow-Jew, "Deronda . . . said coldly, 'I am an Englishman'" ([1876] 1995, 368). This is the first of two occasions on which he is identified as a fellow Jew by Jewish men. The second occasion occurs when Daniel first meets Mordecai in Mr. Ram's bookstore and Mordecai grasps his arm and excitedly asks him "'You are perhaps of our race?'" (387). Deronda—still not knowing his racial origin—again denies being Jewish: "Deronda coloured deeply, not liking the grasp, and then answered with a slight shake of the head, 'No.'" (387). Even though Daniel initially tries to resist being hailed, this identification of Daniel as Jewish strangely anticipates Louis Althusser's interpellation into ideology which contemporary cultural theory views as an important model for the construction of the social subject.

It seems that Judaism both as racial ideology and as a system of religious belief or religious ideology (according to Althusser's Marxist definition, "ideology" is "the system of the ideas and representations which dominate the mind of a man or a social group" [(1970) 1984, 32])[20] sends forth the "call" that Daniel does not just yet heed. Daniel's interpellation into Judaism unfolds in accordance with the processes outlined by Althusser roughly a hundred years later. Judaism works not only as a biological, racial determinant but also as a religious ideology because it fulfills Althusser's postulate that there be a proper Subject ("a Unique, Absolute, *Other Subject*, i. e. God" [52]) "in whose Name the religious ideology interpellates all individuals as subjects" (52-53). Daniel is hailed by this Subject and like the "suspect" from Althusser's example, who is hailed by the policeman's "Hey, you there" (48), he turns around.[21] From then on everything proceeds in accordance with Althusser's plan:

> [T]he hailed individual will turn round. By this mere one-hundred-and-eighty degree physical conversion, he becomes a *subject*. Why? Because he has recognized that the hail was "really" addressed to him, and that "it was *really him*" who was hailed" (and not someone else). Experience shows that the practical telecommunication of hailings is such that they hardly ever miss their man: verbal call or whistle, the one hailed always recognizes that it is really him who is being hailed. And yet it is a strange phenomenon, and one which cannot be explained solely by "guilt feelings," despite the large numbers who "have something on their consciences." (48)

Initially, Deronda, like a person who "has something on his conscience," who could be "found out," wants to shake Mordecai's grasp and not be of the Jewish race. Why is this so? The question is whether Daniel colors because he, as a presumable Englishman, suddenly confronted with what he views as the "abject" aspects of Judaism "had lately been thinking of vulgar Jews with a sort of personal alarm" ([1876] 1995, 366) since they have "that look of ma[king their] toilet with little water" (387) or because he interprets Mordecai's grasp as an unwanted advance.

It looks as if—just like the Alcharisi cannot for all time deny her race—Daniel cannot escape his interpellation, his "call of the blood." On the second occasion of meeting Daniel, Mordecai, "a frail incorporation of the national consciousness" (517), tells him that he is his successor: "'But I have found you. You have come in time. . . . You will take the sacred inheritance of the Jew'" (500). Daniel remains skeptical because he does not know what to make of Mordecai's visionary conviction that he is the perfect carrier of the torch: "A . . . plausible reason for putting discipleship out of the question was the strain of visionary excitement in Mordecai, which turned his wishes into overmastering impressions and made him read outward fact as fulfilment" (513). At the same time Daniel, whose musings about his relationship with Mordecai employ "nationalist" vocabulary, speculates that Mordecai might be his chance to overcome his sense of unbelonging and to find his "citizenship":

> Nay, it was conceivable that as Mordecai needed and believed that he had found an active replenishment of himself, so Deronda might receive from Mordecai's mind the complete ideal shape of that personal duty and citizenship which lay in his own thought like sculptured fragments certifying some beauty yearned after but not traceable by divination. (512)

Daniel finally suspends his pronounced skepticism by meditating upon the speculative nature of all knowledge:

> And since the unemotional intellect may carry us into a mathematical dreamland where nothing is but what is not, perhaps an emotional intellect may have absorbed into its passionate vision of possibilities some truth of what will be—the more comprehensive massive life feeding theory with new material, as the sensibility of the artist seizes combinations which science explains and justifies. At any rate, presumptions to the contrary are not to be trusted. (414)

Gillian Beer establishes a connection with Darwinian thought and argues that Darwin's theory of biological descent is often speculative rather than deterministic and that *Daniel Deronda* "moves into that central problem focused by Darwinian theory: is there a foreknown or an ultimate plan? Is teleology itself a fiction?—do we self-protectively interpret as providence that which is chance?" (1983, 191). She poses a string of rhetorical questions in order to reveal the speculative nature of Eliot's ruminations about biological descent: "Are beginnings to be identified with origins? Is it possible to search out the primal repose of the original? Is there a necessary connection between the idea of the source and the idea of development—or is this habitual connection itself ideological and polemical?" (188). Interestingly enough, late twentieth-century cultural theory asks very similar questions about the origins of individual as well as collective and even national identity.

Carroll, Beer, and other commentators—with the exception of Nancy Henry, who remains on the surface of the identification problem by deciding that cultural identity in Stowe's and Eliot's novels is "simply" passed on through preserved textual memory—hint at the complex mechanisms of identification in *Daniel Deronda*, but do not thoroughly investigate them. Eliot's text poses the question of whether or not a Jew who has not been socialized as a Jew can assume his Jewish heritage and identification solely on the strength of his racial affiliation.[22] As we have seen, Mordecai is convinced of this; Daniel himself also seems to believe in the power of "Race." He tells his mother, "'I consider it my duty—it is the impulse of my feeling—to identify myself, as far as possible, with my hereditary people'" ([1876] 1995, 661). He further elaborates that he has indeed been called by "the stronger Something" ("Race," Judaism, or love) to carry on his grandfather's legacy: "'But that stronger Something has determined that I shall be all the more the grandson whom also you willed to annihilate'" (663).

Since discourse on racial identity in *Daniel Deronda* is highly indeterminate, Daniel's discovery of his racial origin and the subsequent constitution of his Jewish identity is presented as a very complicated issue. On the one hand it seems as if Eliot proceeds from a Cartesian concept of selfhood which supposes that every human being has a core self which s/he needs to discover, yet on the other hand she appears to anticipate modern theories proposing a discursive constitution of cultural identity through interpellation into ideology. The way in which race and religion are conflated in Eliot's depiction of Judaism allows for a reading that—strangely mixing proto-Althusserian analysis with a Cartesian conception of selfhood—suggests that "Race" functions as "the stronger Something" that interpellates Daniel and helps him "dig out" his authentic Jewish self that had previously been buried beneath his false Englishness.[23]

Thus, Eliot's conception of identity and its constitution works according to both definitions of identification described by Stuart Hall. According to the older, commonsensical definition, "identification is constructed on the back of a recognition of some common origin or shared characteristics with another person or group, or with an ideal and with the natural closure of solidarity and allegiance established on this foundation" (1996, 2). Hall explains that the newer "discursive approach" sees identification as "a construction, a process never completed—always 'in process'" (2) because identities are "points of temporary attachments to the subject positions which discursive practices construct for us" (5-6). These discursive procedures are described by Anthony Appiah as an ongoing dialogue with far reaching consequences. To illustrate this, he provides the following answer to his rhetorical question "If, in understanding myself as an African American, I see myself as resisting white norms . . . why should I at the same time seek recognition from these white others?" (1996, 95):

> [I]t is in dialogue with other people's understanding of who I am that I develop a conception of my own identity . . . but also because my identity is crucially constituted through concepts (and practices) made available to me by religion, society, school, and state, and mediated to various degrees by the family. . . . Dialogue shapes the identity I develop as I grow up: but the very material out of which I form it is provided, in part, by my society. (95)

Appiah views individual people's identities as "made up" of two dimensions: "There is a collective dimension, the intersection of her collective identities and there is what I will call a personal dimension, consisting of other socially or morally important features of the person—intelligence, charm wit, cupidity—that are not the basis of forms of collective identity" (93). Collective identities supply the dialogues that shape personal identities (which are not to be confused with the older notion of "authentic" core selves): "[They] . . . provide what we might call scripts: narratives that people can use in shaping their life plans and telling their life stories" (97).

Eliot's Daniel Deronda, whose initial cultural identity is that of a young English gentleman, explores Sephardic Judaism for an alternative collective identity offering him "a traditional society," with "shared beliefs, values, signs and symbols as the common culture" (see Appiah 1996, 86). Since until adulthood he does not find out that he is Jewish and therefore knows almost nothing about the "common origin" he supposedly shares with his race, he wills himself into the Jewish community by joining their dialogues, as for example in his study of Hebrew.[24] He even devises for himself a strategy of dealing with anti-Jewish sentiment (including his own): After experiencing "certain ugly little incidents" ([1876] 1995, 366) in the Jewish quarter, such as encountering a Jewish youth who "cheated him like a pure Teuton, only with more amenity" (366), he reacts by neutralizing negative ascriptions through "comparison":

> But a little comparison will often diminish our surprise and disgust at the aberrations of Jews and other dissidents whose lives do not offer a consistent or lovely pattern of their creed; and this evening Deronda, becoming more

conscious that he was falling into unfairness and ridiculous exaggeration, began to use that corrective comparison: he paid his thaler too much, without prejudice to his interests in the Hebrew destiny. (366)

Daniel's strategy here parallels Appiah's self-help scheme for improving the life scripts of those that are discriminated against: "In order to construct a life with dignity, it seems natural to take the collective identity and construct positive life scripts instead" (1996, 98).[25]

The question remains whether or not Daniel—in whom fears of an illegitimate birth have instilled a feeling of sympathy towards those who are "othered" by society (minorities, women)—can actually become the Jew that he already is by trying to perform the ascriptions of his racial identity. Contemporary commentators, as for example Jacob Press, do not seem to think so. Press contends that "Deronda willingly divests himself of the identity category of 'Christian,' declares his 'identification' with the Jews—and that is where his transformation stops. Jewish nationalism becomes a way of reframing an otherwise intact ideology of self" (1997, 324). Carolyn Lesjak who maintains that only a "slim notion of hybridity" can be attached to the figure of Daniel, however, argues that

> Daniel is . . . figured as both a *Jew* and an Englishman. In this sense, then, despite the narrative's trust toward a history of pure nationality, Deronda is symptomatic of a hybrid national reality, of an expression of "Englishness," which undermines that of his uncle, Hugo Mallinger, precisely because it marks the presence of difference *within* it. (1996, 35)

Daniel's lack of "authentic Jewishness" at the end of the narrative allows for two explanations: 1) Eliot, who did not know how to present believable Italian characters, also did not know how to turn an Englishman into a Jew, even if he has got the "right blood,"[26] or 2) she did believe in convergence and social constructivism rather than "racial essentialism" in spite of invoking the interpellative powers of "Race" as a possible "call of the blood."

Appiah discusses W. E. B. DuBois's difficulties in finding common ground for pan-African solidarity in *In My Father's House* and suggests that, ultimately, DuBois had to concede that race-based rationales for solidarity ("common history," "long memory," "the social heritage of slavery" [1992, 41]) simply do not work: "The logic of his argument leads naturally to the final repudiation of race as a term of difference to 'speaking of civilizations where we now speak of races.' The logic is the same logic that has led us to speak of gender—the social construction out of the biological facts—where we once spoke of sex" (45). Eliot appears to have made a similar discovery about the arbitrariness of essentialist attitudes towards race and sex which she does not seem to be able to formulate clearly in *Daniel Deronda*. Nevertheless, in the exchange between Daniel and his mother, the Alcharisi hints at a "nature," which here seems to be some notion of self beyond race and sex, when she insists: "'I had a right to be an artist, though my father's will was against it: My nature gave me a charter'" ([1876] 1995, 664). *Daniel Deronda* thus builds up an unresolved tension between essentialist and constructivist conceptions of identity, stressing that in some way identity is always a fiction of the self.[27]

Timothy Brennan shows that the same questions of origin that are raised concerning the construction of individual identity are also valid in regard to national identity. Like older theories about individual identity, older theories of national identity stress what seems to be the unchanging, essential basis of national identity. Thus, nationalist theory often invokes Old Testament mythology which relies on "the idea of a chosen people, the emphasis on a common stock of memory" (1990, 59) and which assumes a "collective personality of 'the people,' the unity and common destiny of a 'community'" (52). Yet, as Brennan stresses, even more so than individual identity, national identity also has a fictional element because "the rise of the modern nation-state in Europe in the late eighteenth and early nineteenth centuries is inseparable from the forms and subjects of imaginative literature" (48). Thus, the novel "was crucial in defining the nation as an 'imagined community'" (48). This assumed fictitiousness of any kind of national beginning can be invoked to give a positive answer to the question of whether or not Daniel Deronda as a Jew who has not been socialized as one—or Stowe's George Harris as an African who has never been to Africa—can actually build a nation based on racial affiliation. If Zionism, as Carolyn Lesjak argues, is by definition a hybrid and if the linguistically and territorially "'borrowed nature' of its programme . . . dramatises the acquired processes whereby a sense of national identity was created" (1996, 30), then there is nothing essential about Zionist identity. Therefore, Daniel, as an intelligent, responsible individual, might be as good a national leader as any.

Jacob Press, however, who discusses *Daniel Deronda* and Jacob Herzl's *Altneuland* as Zionist novels concerned with nation-building, seems to be bothered by the fact that both George Eliot and the Jewish nationalist Herzl apparently do not know how to render Jewish difference in an adequate manner, and therefore "articulate a vision of separateness that replicates that from which it has separated" (1997, 325).[28] Describing the mechanism of identification that Beer has named "convergence," he reluctantly concludes that there might be no alternative to assimilation simply because there is no "racial core":[29]

> For what is "assimilation" but an organization of the self so as to foreground those personal characteristics that will enable one to become a member of the group with which one wishes to be associated? In this sense, both Herzl and Deronda are Jewish assimilationists in two senses: they assimilate themselves into Jewishness, and they assimilate Jewishness into themselves. There is no simple sense in which their projects can be discredited on this account. (325)

Here, Press identifies what seems to be the dilemma in theorizing about racial identity once the notion that there is no such thing as an individual or collective core self has been accepted. George Eliot, unlike Harriet Beecher Stowe, to some degree seems to have been aware of the fact that racial identity ultimately cannot be established. Her characterization of her Jewish figures shows that this partial awareness had consequences for her depiction of her "racially other" characters. While Stowe assigns her own essentialist notions about blacks to her African American characters, Eliot, by meticulously researching Jewish cultural history and then inventing a Jewish character who remains an Englishman (which reflects an inability to render convincing descriptions of cultural alterity already known from her depictions of Italianness), finds a less discriminatory but still rather evasive solution to the problem of locating racial identity.

Transcendental Soulmates

Perhaps because of these difficulties in defining racial identity, Eliot's novel also allows for a reading that views Daniel's identification with Judaism as a result of his emotional relationship with Mordecai and Mirah rather than as a result of a "call of the blood." Daniel's mother hints at this when she suspects that what motivates Daniel might be "love" rather than "Race":

> "You are in love with a Jewess." Deronda coloured and said, "My reasons would be independent of any such fact." "I know better. I have seen what men are," said the Princess; peremptorily. "Tell me the truth. She is a Jewess who will not accept anyone but a Jew. There *are* a few such," she added with a touch of scorn. ([1876] 1995, 661)

Daniel himself later on acknowledges the fact that his love for Mordecai and Mirah is instrumental in boosting his enthusiasm about his newly discovered Jewishness: "If this revelation had been made to me before I knew you both, I think my mind would have rebelled against it. Perhaps I should have felt then—'If I could have chosen, I would not have been a Jew'" (750). But while the Alcharisi has correctly identified Daniel's motivation, she is not altogether right about the gender of Daniel's object of love, for, although he eventually marries Mirah, the emotional bond that motivates his decision to acknowledge his Judaism is chiefly between him and Mordecai.

The language used to describe the relationship of Mordecai and Daniel is erotically charged from the beginning of their acquaintance: "In ten minutes the two men, with as intense a consciousness as if they had been two undeclared lovers . . . turned face to face, each baring his head from an instinctive feeling that they wished to see each other fully" (495). Their friendship is so dominant that Daniel continues to emphasize the impact of his relationship with Mordecai even after he has told himself and others that he is in love with Mirah. Thus, he explains to Gwendolen about his discovery of his Jewishness: "I had been prepared for it by becoming intimate with a very remarkable Jew" (802). The scene in which Mordecai tells Daniel that Daniel will inevitably help him fulfill his Jewish destiny—even against his will—is saturated with sexualized vocabulary:

> "You would remind me that I may be under an illusion—that the history of our people's trust has been full of illusion. I face it all." Here Mordecai paused for a moment. Then bending his head a little forward, he said, in a hoarse whisper, "*So it might be with my trust, if you would make it an illusion. But you will not.*" [emphasis in original] The very sharpness with which these words penetrated Deronda, made him feel the more that there was a crisis in which he must be firm. (502)

Eliot here uses language that is typical for seduction scenes in nineteenth-century literature. The word "crisis," for example, was "a common nineteenth-century euphemism for sexual excitation" (Kolodny 1984, xix). Eliot's wording suggests that she, being familiar with *The Blithedale Romance* (see Stokes 1985, 93), might have used the homoerotic "seduction scene" from the *Blithedale* chapter "A Crisis" as a literary model. Hawthorne's narrator Miles Coverdale, who remembers withstanding seduction at the hands of the philanthropist Hollingsworth, recounts his experience in words that sound very much like Eliot's: "'Coverdale,' he murmured, 'there is not the man in this wide world, whom I can love as I could you. Do not forsake me!' . . . Had I but touched his extended hand, Hollingsworth's magnetism would perhaps have penetrated me with his own conception of all these matters. But I stood aloof" ([1851] 1984, 133–34).[30] Perhaps even more important than a similar use of language is the fact that in both novels desire is presented in the language of idealism and spirituality. In *The Blithedale Romance* the philanthropist Hollingsworth unsuccessfully attempts to seduce Coverdale to his transcendentalist social reform scheme ("Hollingsworth once more brought forth his rigid and unconquerable idea" [131]), whereas in *Daniel Deronda* Mordecai successfully lures Daniel into Jewish nationalism.

And Elinor Shaffer elucidates Eliot's possible theological inspiration for the sexualization of spirituality: "The work of both Feuerbach and Renan underlies her analysis of the sexual basis of religion, Feuerbach in his theoretical formulation of the I-thou relation and his systematic equation of theology and pathology, Renan in his psychological and literary studies of the sources of religious experience" (1975, 234). Shaffer thus locates the source for Eliot's depiction of the emotional (and sexual) dependence of "man on man" (or woman) in Feuerbach's realization that God is no longer at the center of religion because in the nineteenth century "the concrete empirical dependence of a man [is] on nature and other men" (245) and that the I-thou relationship has evolved from a relationship between a human being and his or her creator to a relationship between humans.[31] Unlike Hawthorne's Coverdale, who turns down Hollingsworth's advances, Daniel is receptive to Mordecai's plea. Thus, after Daniel has acknowledged to himself that "Feelings had lately been at work within him which had very much modified the reluctance he would formerly have had to think of himself probably as a Jew" ([1876] 1995, 515), he willingly takes up his lot as Mordecai's disciple.

Even though the homoerotic content of the novel is too obvious to be ignored, only a few critics have paid attention to it. Press, for example, focuses exclusively on the novel's Jewish part, yet he does not position the relationship of Daniel and Mordecai within the kabbalistic Jewish tradition. He points out that the sexually charged metaphors betray a desire "to penetrate" on Mordecai's part and a desire "to submit" on Daniel's part and projects late twentieth-century attitudes toward homosexuality onto the two characters as, for example, when he writes that "Mordecai has a thing for high-class types" (1997, 307). Laura Callanan, however, puts the homoerotic content of Daniel Deronda in historical perspective. She speculates that Eliot—at a time when homosexuality was barely known as a sexual orientation—was aware of homosexuality because she personally knew Dr. Carl Friedrich Otto Westphal, who became famous for his research on "contrary sexual feelings" (1996, 180).[32]

Both Press and Callanan, however, ignore the important fact that Eliot has added another spiritual level to the homoerotic relationship of Daniel and Mordecai which, following Christian David Ginsburg's account of the Kabbalah, presents them as exiled androgynous souls waiting for the great Jubilee when all souls will come back to "the bosom of the Infinite Source—in the Palace of love, where the heavenly King is united with all souls by a kiss" (Irwin 1996, 452). As Mordecai explains to Daniel about their upcoming kabbalistic "marriage of souls":

> In the doctrine of the Cabbala, souls are born again and again in new bodies till they are perfected and purified, and a soul liberated from a worn-out body may join the fellow-soul that needs it, that they may be perfected together, and their earthly work accomplished. Then they will depart from the mortal region, and leave place for new souls to be born out of the store in the eternal bosom. It is the lingering imperfection of the souls already born into the mortal region that hinders the birth of new souls and the preparation of the Messianic time.... When my long-wandering soul is liberated from this weary body, it will join yours, and its work will be perfected. ([1876] 1995, 540)

Since according to Ginsburg these souls are androgynous the "latent paradoxes" inherent in this situation make for a rather strange gender triangle in Daniel's marriage situation (Irwin 1996, 452).[33] Thus, in chapter 63 when Daniel goes to see Mordecai and Mirah after he has found out that he is Jewish, and when he has just made up his mind to propose to Mirah, personal pronouns, which would immediately reveal the sex of the beloved he is thinking about, are carefully avoided.

Saleel Nurbhai and K. M. Newton argue that Mordecai's and Daniel's "marriage of souls" is routed through Mirah:

> Mirah, who can be—and in Baker's *George Eliot and Judaism* has been—identified with the soul of Judaism, is first united with Mordecai: "He has recovered the perfect sister." Mordecai now has the perfect soul which he wants to reunite with Deronda—the perfect vessel for his ideas. . . . The marriage of Mirah to Deronda marks the movement of the soul from Mordecai to Deronda, thus it cannot be properly fulfilled until Mordecai is dead. (2002, 44–45)

However, evidence of the fact that the passive, quiet, and unintellectual Mirah functions as "the soul of Judaism" seems to be rather scant to me. Moreover, the erotically charged vocabulary of the metempsychosis scenes also suggests that the marriage is a direct one between Daniel and Mordecai. In the emotional scene in which Daniel reveals his Jewishness to the siblings, his relationship with Mordecai is also prevalent: "The two men clasped hands with a movement that seemed part of the flash from Mordecai's eyes, and passed through Mirah like an electric shock" (748). In accordance with the predominance of Daniel's relationship with Mordecai, Daniel's marriage (of souls) with Mordecai begins in this chapter, whereas his "legal" marriage to Mirah takes place later. His marriage with Mordecai is "consummated" in the novel's final scene when Mordecai dies:

> It was not till late in the afternoon, when the light was falling, that he took a hand of each in his and said, looking at Deronda, "Death is coming to me as the divine kiss which is both parting and reunion—which takes me from your bodily eyes and gives me full presence in your soul. Where thou goest Daniel, I shall go. Is it not begun? Have I not breathed my soul into you? We shall live together." He paused, and Deronda waited, thinking that there might be another word for him. . . . He sank back gently into his chair, and did not speak again. But it was some hours before he had ceased to breathe, with Mirah's and Deronda's arms around him. (811)

Thus, Daniel's marriage to Mordecai results in eternal unity, whereas his marriage to Mirah seems to have produced a corpse whom both of them hold as if he were a newborn baby. The discussion of the relationship of *Daniel Deronda*'s main male protagonists has shown that love for a person who happens to be Jewish is the chief force behind Daniel Deronda's identification with Jewishness. Whereas Daniel's love for Mordecai focuses—at least in the beginning—on Mordecai as an individual, Mordecai's love for Daniel cannot be viewed separately from his social and religious vision which places his relationship with Mordecai within a general design to end Jewish exile on both a spiritual and a geographical level.

The idealized marriage of Daniel's and Mordecai's souls brings to mind the marriage ideal of another eminent nineteenth-century American author, namely Margaret Fuller, who also evaluated the concept of marriage within a "social program" that aimed at an empowerment of women along with raising a transcendental spiritual awareness of democracy. Daniel and Mordecai's "male/male marriage" (more so than his legal marriage with Mirah) fulfills all the criteria that Margaret Fuller postulates for her marriage ideal presented in *Woman in the Nineteenth Century* where she discusses the marriage unions of rather diverse couples ranging from Mary and Percy Bysshe Shelley via the Count and Countess Zinzendorf and several examples from classic mythology to a Native American marriage.[34] According to Fuller's high standards, ideal marriages transcend death and—more often than not—are "instances of marriage as intellectual companionship" ([1845] 1994, 270). She writes that marriages of such caliber "speak of aspiration of soul, of energy of mind, seeking clearness and freedom. . . . [T]he two minds are wed by the only contract that can permanently avail, of a common faith and a common purpose" (270).

The relationship of Mordecai and Daniel, which is an integral part of Mordecai's vision of ending the exile of the Israelites, fits all of these examples and might even exceed them because it belongs to "[t]he fourth and the highest grade of marriage union . . . the religious, which may be expressed as pilgrimage towards a common shrine" (272). Fuller's poem "The Secret Marriage," from Appendix H of *Woman in the Nineteenth Century* seems to sum up what Eliot had in mind when she conceptualized the union of her two male protagonists:

> If, near this other life, thy inmost feeling
> Trembles with fateful prescience of revealing
> The future Deity, time is still concealing.
> . . . .
> Hide never the full presence from thy sight
> Of mutual aims and tasks, ideals bright,
> Which feed their roots to-day on all this seeming blight.
> Twin stars that mutual circle in the heaven,
> Two parts for spiritual concord given,
> Twin Sabbaths that inlock the Sacred Seven;
> Still looking to the centre for the cause,
> Mutual light giving to draw out the powers,
> And learning all the other groups by cognizance of one another's laws:
> . . . .
> A world whose seasons bloom from pole to pole,
> A force which knows both starting-point and goal,
> Home in Heaven,—the Union of the Soul.
>
> (361–62)

Fuller's poem captures the dynamics of the relationship between Eliot's protagonists, which is characterized by Mordecai's strong effort to win Daniel for his spiritual project and thus accomplish what is required of a relationship featuring a spiritual "union of the soul" as stated in the poem. Strangely enough, when Eliot depicts the onset of Mordecai and Daniel's blessed state, she has Mordecai repeat the word "fuller" three times in his description of the ecstatic consummation of their spiritual union.[35]

Mordecai and Daniel's relationship has to be seen as part of Eliot's larger vision of a divine unity of all souls in *Daniel Deronda*. Mordecai explains this concept to Daniel as follows:

> [T]he *Shemah,* wherein we briefly confess the divine Unity, is the chief devotional exercise of the Hebrew; and this made our religion the fundamental

religion for the whole world; for the divine Unity embraced as its consequence the ultimate unity of mankind. See, then—the nation which has been scoffed at for its separateness, has given a binding theory to the human race. Now, in complete unity a part possesses the whole as the whole possesses every part: and in this way human life is tending toward the image of the Supreme Unity: for as our life becomes more spiritual by capacity of thought, and joy therein, possession tends to become more universal, being independent of gross material contact." (734)

Once *Daniel Deronda*'s affinities with Fuller—and thus with American transcendentalism—have been established, it becomes impossible to ignore the fact that Mordecai's "divine Unity" has a strong resemblance to the transcendentalist oversoul as "that Unity, that Over-soul, within which every man's particular being is contained and made one with all the other" (Emerson [1841] 1983, 385–86).[36] Moreover, Mordecai himself is able to interpret the "occult relation" between mind and nature derived from the material world according to a mental process that strongly resembles Emerson's idea of "correspondence" between mind and nature (see Steele 1987, 24).[37] Jeffrey Steele argues that, according to Emerson's ideal, "[a]iming toward an illumination that has not yet been fully achieved, the individual must learn to interpret signs that reveal one's assimilation of spiritual power. As a consequence, self-understanding becomes a hermeneutic process in which one is committed to interpreting the self" (25). Mordecai explains to Daniel how even before he actually came to know Daniel as "[t]he prefigured friend [who] had come from the golden background" ([1876] 1995, 493), he was gradually enabled to understand Daniel's future appearance as the fulfillment of his plans: "As thoughts move within us darkly, and shake us before they are full discerned—so events—so beings: they are knit with us in the growth of the world. You have risen within me like a thought not fully spelled: my soul is shaken before the words are all there. The rest will come—it will come" (501). According to Mordecai's interpretation, Daniel typologically fulfills the promise of spiritual restoration that began with his own existence: "'My life is nothing to me but the beginning of fulfilment. And yet I am only another prayer—which you will fulfil'" (576–77).

The similarities between kabbalistic and Emersonian transcendental spiritual concepts can be explained in terms of the fact that both religious philosophies have their roots in Neoplatonism, the school of thought developed by Plotinus.[38] Kenneth Walter Cameron has painstakingly traced Neoplatonic thought in *Nature*, focusing on the dynamics of spiritual emanation and flow in Emerson and in the Neoplatonic system which "is one of necessary Emanation, Procession, Aspiration and Reversion to source" and in which "[a]ll existence flows from the Divinity and strives to return to its origin and there remain" (1971, 47).[39] Neoplatonism always operates on the level of trinities: "One of these is the trinity of Divine principle—the Absolute, spirit, and soul; the other is tripartite division of man into Spirit, Soul, and Body" (Carpenter 1930, 79). Emerson, according to Frederic Ives Carpenter, "took over the general idea that man may live on any of the three different planes of being, but he did not keep the strict formalism of the triads of Plotinus" (79). Emerson's philosophy, however, does not really explain the origin of the oversoul, and Kabbalah also strays from the path outlined by Neoplatonism because it does not describe emanation as an activity proceeding out of God, but rather as a process taking place within God (see Bloom 1975, 25). In addition, Kabbalah—unlike Emersonian philosophy which explains evil in terms of distance from God in the lower emanations—accounts for the existence of evil through the inclusion of Gnostic elements within God. Harold Bloom, following Hans Jonas, describes this Gnostic element as the struggle of "God against creation, spirit against matter, good against evil, soul against the body" (20) in the "breaking of the vessels" which attends the creation of man and which comes about because of "a plethora of rigor in God himself" (41). Bloom emphasizes the Kabbalah's indebtedness to Neoplatonism as strongly as Carpenter stresses the Emersonian oversoul's affinity to it, when he writes: "Classical Kabbalah begins with a Neoplatonic vision of God. God is the *Ein-Sof* ("without end"), totally unknowable, and beyond representation" (1975, 19). According to Neoplatonic thought,

> [t]he All-Soul or Over-Soul emanates from the Divine Mind and is a reflection. It likewise has two functions or principles: (a) It contemplates the Divine Mind above it; (b) it looks forward to Nature and generates the lower and material universe according to the models (or "ideas") of the divine Mind. The Over-Soul is the eternal cause of the existence of the *cosmos* or sense-grasped universe. . . . It contains all souls. The sphere of the Over-Soul is "intelligible light." Time begins in the Over-Soul. (Cameron 1971, 49)

Thus, the sometimes almost uncanny resemblance between the kabbalistic concepts presented in *Daniel Deronda* and the transcendentalist oversoul can be traced to the Neoplatonic origin of both spiritual concepts.

Eliot had met Emerson personally and kept reading his work as late as 1870.[40] Nevertheless, it is very difficult to establish whether or not she actually harked back to American transcendentalism when she conceptualized the kabbalistic passages in *Daniel Deronda*. Epigraphs from works of the English romantic poets and the German Heinrich Heine suggest that Eliot meant to draw attention to parallels between kabbalistic and romantic thought.[41] American transcendentalism, which shares many of the sources of English and German romanticism, is hinted at through the inclusion of a stanza from Walt Whitman's short poem "Vocalism." The lines from "Vocalism"—"Surely whoever speaketh to me in the right voice, / him or her I shall follow, / As the water follows the moon, silently, / with fluid steps anywhere around the globe" ([1876] 1995, 326)—introduce the chapter in which Daniel becomes Gwendolen's spiritual guide and prefigure his discipleship to Mordecai. They anticipate the theme of finding one's own identity through identification with spiritual leadership which pervades the second half of the novel. Nurbhai and Newton, who focus less on Daniel's identification with Mordecai, view the relationship between the two men as that between a creator and his creation—in their interpretation of the novel, Daniel becomes a golem who will carry out Mordecai's plans (see Nurbhai and Newton 11; 170); the kabbalistic figure of the golem will be discussed at greater length in the section of Cynthia Ozick in the following chapter.

As previously mentioned, Gilbert and Gubar have argued that it was to some extent due to her readings in nineteenth-century American writing that Eliot on some occasions veered away from her customary realism (1980, 471–73). While I certainly do not want to contradict their findings that writers like Hawthorne, Fuller, and Stowe inspired Eliot, I nevertheless think that the nonrealistic mode of *Daniel Deronda*, which many commentators have drawn attention to, cannot be attributed directly to American romanticism, but is rather the consequence of Eliot's very similar philosophic beliefs. However, the reference to Whitman suggests that she was aware of the correspondences between Kabbalah and transcendental thought.

In *Daniel Deronda* Eliot has recourse to Kabbalah—and to a lesser extent to transcendentalist thought—because these philosophies provide explanations of the individual and the social self that are congenial to her own world view and her ideas about identity and identification. It seems that Eliot—in a nostalgic frame of mind—invoked Neoplatonic philosophy, Kabbalah, and transcendentalism in *Daniel Deronda* because they provide similar explanations for humanity's fragmented condition as resulting from a "fall from a state of grace" and because they also offer solutions to this "identity crisis." Cameron explains this "crisis" for Neoplatonism as follows:

> Individuality pre-exists in the soul-world. All things there are together, yet distinct. . . . Before descent into the world of Nature and after reascent to the Over-Soul, each one's thoughts are revealed to other souls in direct vision,

> though without discourse. Although it would seem better for souls to remain above, yet self-will (i.e., the individual nature of the unincarnate soul) makes it want to venture forth to birth and become separated from the whole. Coming down is one fault; entering into bodies is another. If the soul returns quickly, it usually suffers no hurt. (1971, 49)

Gershom Scholem, the eminent Kabbalah scholar, describes the kabbalistic equivalent of the soul's "fall from grace" as an accident during the creation process when *Adam Kadmon,* the god who created the world, was filling vessels with light emanating from his eyes. These vessels, which were supposed to contain aspects of the creation, broke because the light was too strong and subsequently fell down to earth where they created chaos. On earth the—in the process of creation—disassembled "first man" *Adam Kadmon* (who, in a strange way, seems to anticipate the "fragmented state of the postmodern subject" in contemporary discussions about "identity") had to be reconstructed as an image of the original god *Adam Kadmon* in the shape of five figurations or faces (*partsufim*) of the original creator-god. The fragmented "first man" had to begin the restoration of creation by gathering the fallen divine sparks and putting them back in the right place (see Scholem [1960] 1996, 112–15). The "restoration of creation must be carried out by the religious acts of individual men, of all Jews struggling in the Exile, and indeed of all men and women struggling in the exile that Luria [one of the originators of written Kabbalah] saw as the universal human existence" (Bloom 1975, 42–43).

Interestingly enough, in *Nature,* Emerson also uses the image of man as "a god in ruins" ([1836] 1983, 44), reminiscent of *Adam Kadmon,* to describe man's potential fragmentation and his fall from his state as a creator-god,[42] and in "The American Scholar" he uses the example of the "One Man"[43] to point out the deficient, divided nature of man:

> The old fable covers a doctrine new and ever sublime; that there is One Man,—present to all particular men only partially, or through one faculty; and that you must take the whole society to find the whole man. Man is not a farmer, or a professor, or an engineer, but he is all. . . . In the *divided* or social state, these functions are parcelled out into individuals. . . . The state of society is one in which the members have suffered amputation from the trunk, and strut about so many walking monsters,—a good finger, a neck, a stomach, an elbow, but never a man. ([1837] 1983, 53–54)

Emerson calls for the "American scholar" to counteract this fragmentation. The scholar, as "Man Thinking" should lead the world in its "main enterprise, . . . the upbuilding of a man" because "a man, rightly viewed, comprehendeth the particular natures of all men" since "[i]t is one soul which animates all men" (67). Steele comments that the transcendent image of "One Man" is a model of identification which "represents the joining together of isolated particles of energy, the scattered drops of the original 'fountain of power.' It recalibrates the individual being by aligning the disorder of random actions against an archetype of wholeness" (1987, 37).[44]

Eliot, apparently still clinging to her organic ideal, presents a similar attempt at putting together a dispersed social body in *Daniel Deronda* through identification of individuals with kindred spirits in a "marriage of souls." Yet unlike Emerson, who focuses on the "de-fragmentation" of the individual, Eliot stresses social unity along with individual unity. Harold Bloom points out regarding social reconstruction via the re-membering of *Adam Kadmon* that "Luria seems to have taught that there were families of souls, united by the root of a common spark. Each person can take up in himself the spark of another soul, of one of the dead, provided that he and the dead share the same root" (1975, 44). This takes place in the relationship of Daniel and Mordecai, in which love, both as the mating of fraternal souls and erotic feeling, constructs individual and social identity. Their relationship even instigates nation-building since Daniel's identification with Mordecai leads to his identification with Judaism in the "divine Unity." When he puts the rhetorical question "Unless nationality is a feeling, what force can it have as an idea?" ([1876] 1995, 525) to his philosopher's club, Mordecai voices the realization that feeling—rather than a shared racial background—is the prime motivator in social relations. In his lesson to Daniel on the importance of "divine Unity" he also points out that Judaism, because it has "given a binding theory to the human race," will eventually transcend its boundaries because it "is the fundamental religion for the whole world; for the divine Unity embraced as its consequence the ultimate unity of mankind" (734).

In addition to the Neoplatonic connection, Eliot's world view shared some other aspects of Emersonian thought that are related to questions of the self. As mentioned before, Eliot's views of the social function of religion were heavily influenced by Ludwig Feuerbach's *The Essence of Christianity*, which she had translated into English. Emerson and Feuerbach had an almost identical socioreligious agenda. "Anticipating Feuerbach's understanding of theology by a decade," Irena Makarushka argues, "Emerson asked 'What is God? The most elevated conception of character that can be performed in the mind. It is, the individual's own soul carried out to perfection'" (1994, 1–2). Feuerbach expresses this idea very similarly: "But if it is only in human feelings and wants that the divine 'nothing' becomes something, obtains qualities, then the being of man is alone the real being of God—man is the real God.... The true statement is this: man's knowledge of God is man's knowledge of himself, of his own nature" ([1841] 1989, 230).

Emerson—and by implication also Feuerbach—thus extends to everybody the promise of salvation which Puritanism had reserved for the elect (see Makarushka 1994, 6; Urbanski 1980, 99). Yet by locating the divine within each human being, neither Emerson nor Feuerbach wants to reduce God to man; unlike Auguste Comte who conceives of society as an entirely secular *Grand Etre*, they both aim at raising man to the level of the divine. This apotheosis of man obviously has to have consequences for individual conduct. Emerson connects "the divine within . . . with a call to action" (Makarushka 1994, 7) which obligates the individual to reclaim his or her divinity. Thus, everybody would be required to raise him- or herself from "a god in ruins" to "One Man." But while Emerson views this assumption of divinity chiefly as an individual act that each man or woman has to perform solitarily, Feuerbach stresses the communal aspect of religion:

> *The mystery of the Trinity is the mystery of participated, social life—the mystery of I and thou* . . . [emphasis in the original]. Not only consultations, but compacts take place between the chief persons in the Trinity, precisely as in human society.... And as the essential bond of the Divine Persons is love, the Trinity is the heavenly type of the closest bond of love—marriage. ([1841] 1989, 293)

It is obvious that this concept of a socioreligious compact—minus focus on the trinity—informs *Daniel Deronda* (as well as Fuller's marriage ideal in *Woman in the Nineteenth Century*):

> The mystical basis of the I-thou unity is the gnostic-cabbalistic notion of Adam as the soul that contained all souls.... The moral task of man in the Jewish cabbala [*sic*] is to restore his primordial spiritual structure, and so contribute to the restoration of the spiritual structure of mankind. This was combined with a doctrine of metempsychosis, facilitating the passage of souls. In *Daniel Deronda*, the mystical substratum is expressed directly through the fraternal relation of the master and his disciple, Mordecai and Daniel. (Shaffer 1975, 255)

In her *Daniel Deronda* notebooks Eliot describes this kabbalistic restoration process very similarly.[45] Even though the concept of "divine Unity" in *Daniel Deronda*, which is meant to result in the "ultimate unity of mankind," seems very close to the Emersonian oversoul, the social outlook provided by its "transcendental" vision seems to be much closer to Fuller's ideal. While Fuller does not formulate a socioreligious theory of communal life in a society based on transcendentalist thought in *Woman in the Nineteenth Century*, her programmatic essay—whose main focus is on gender relationships—nevertheless indicates that she aimed at the implementation of transcendental thought on a social level. Emerson, however, even though he furnishes a philosophical basis for communal life through the concept of the oversoul, does not exploit the social potential of divine unity in the oversoul, but rather stresses man's solitary task of uncovering the divine within his own being.[46] Packer, who explains Emerson's rather antisocial "curious position" towards friendship in terms of the loss he sustained when his brother Charles died (50), even deems Emerson's broodings on his relationships with others "psychotic," as for example, when Emerson writes, "the roots of my relation to every individual are in my own constitution & not less the causes of his disappearance from me" (Emerson quoted in Packer 1982, 51).[47] Considering Emerson's attitude towards friendship and love, it does not come as a surprise that he argues vehemently against the ideal of a "marriage of kindred souls" presented in *Woman in the Nineteenth Century* (and by implication *Daniel Deronda*) when he writes: "Love is only phenomenal, a contrivance of nature. . . . The soul knows nothing of marriage, in the sense of a permanent union between two personal existences. The soul is married to each new thought as it enters into it" (quoted in Schulz 1997, 15).[48] Fuller's view of the self, which might thus be described as "relationally visionary," and Emerson's view of the self, which is "contemplatively visionary," provide two rather different models of a transcendental understanding of identity (see Schulz 1997, 147). Eliot's concept of the self has affinities to both Emerson's and Fuller's thought yet is much closer to Fuller's outlook in its concern with the self as social relation.

She arrives at this conception of the self as "social relation" after taking Harriet Beecher Stowe's exploration of "race" as a determinant of both individual and social identity as a point of departure. While at times she seems to have reached the conclusion that it is acquirable, non-essentialist "cultural memory" rather than "race" which determines a person's identity, she nevertheless remains torn between essentialist and constructivist conceptions of identity. Perhaps in order to counteract her realization that a unified, "essential" self is not possible, she partially aligns herself with transcendental thinkers such as Fuller and Emerson who present models of an integrated, unified self. Steele contends that Emerson presents as an alternative a much more optimistic model of the self, which allows the individual to get in touch with the "God within" who will lead him or her towards "progressive mastery of one's world" (1987, 25).[49] He reasons that in light of tendencies to "deconstruct" the self, "Emerson presents his interpretation of the self as a patch for the collective psyche" (31). One might be tempted to conclude that in her final novel, *Daniel Deronda*, George Eliot, by telling the successful story of Daniel's identification with Judaism through his relationship with Mordecai, the visionary, aimed at presenting an Emersonian "self-aware individual . . . in control of his or her destiny" (176). Yet, in view of the earlier discussion of the complex psychic processes attending Daniel's identification, it seems more likely that Eliot's exploration of how identity is constructed remains inconclusive and oscillates between concepts of the fragmented and the unfragmented self.

4
Writing Beyond the Ending?: U.S. Adaptations of George Eliot

THE GEORGE ELIOT
HEROINE IN THE U.S.

THE PREVIOUS CHAPTERS HAVE SHOWN THAT GEORGE ELIOT OFTEN DREW inspiration from American literature. Not surprisingly, she, in her turn, influenced American writers such as Harriet Beecher Stowe, Elizabeth Stuart Phelps, and, perhaps most thoroughly and notably, her younger admirer, Henry James.[1] As the following discussion will indicate, these contemporaneous American authors—as well as younger generations of writers, including Edith Wharton and our own contemporaries Susan Cheever, Gail Godwin, John Irving, and Cynthia Ozick—all sought literary inspiration in *Middlemarch* (1871–72), *The Mill on the Floss* (1860), and, most often and importantly, in her challenging final novel, *Daniel Deronda* (1876).[2]

George Eliot's American "adaptors" were interested in both her construction of gender and her exploration of cultural identity (as constituted by the social determinants of race, class, gender, and religious identity) and they undoubtedly noticed that the majority of her female protagonists met the "rightful end" of typical nineteenth-century heroines. Rachel Blau DuPlessis has outlined the typical scheme of a nineteenth-century heroine's path towards bliss or doom in *Writing Beyond the Ending*: "Once upon a time, the end, the rightful end, of women in novels was social—successful courtship, marriage—or judgment of her sexual and social failure—death" (1985, 1). As DuPlessis elaborates, on their way to one of these "rightful ends," nineteenth-century heroines, as, for example, Eliot's Dorothea Brooke and Maggie Tulliver, had to endure a lot of frustration about their thwarted opportunities of acquiring education and knowledge:

> In nineteenth-century fiction dealing with women, authors went to a good deal of trouble and even some awkwardness to see to it that *Bildung* and romance could not coexist and be integrated for the heroine at the resolution, although works combining these two discourses in their main part (the narrative middle) are among the most important fictions of our tradition. (3)

Indeed, almost all of the prominent George Eliot heroines follow the patterns outlined by DuPlessis; only Romola, Gwendolen Harleth, and the Alcharisi escape the "either marriage or death conundrum," while (at least in Romola's and the Alcharisi's case) retaining their valuable talent.

Having intuited that something must be wrong with this situation, the first generations of American authors who decided to appropriate George Eliot's plots for their own fiction already attempted what DuPlessis attributes to twentieth-century women writers: to empower female protagonists by "writing beyond the ending,"[3] but they did not always succeed in doing so. Phelps, James, and Wharton all seem to have wanted to emulate Stowe's example, provided in *Oldtown Folks* (1869), of giving more agency to the George Eliot heroine. Phelps turns Eliot's singer protagonist, Armgart, who is only a "minor" heroine because she is the protagonist of a (minor) poem rather than a "major" Eliot novel, into the "major" artist protagonist of a novel. Yet in spite of being moved from a fictional margin to its center, Avis, a self-reliant American artist, remains a typical Eliot heroine in that she has to give up her vocation within the framework of a failing marriage. Henry James, in *The Portrait of a Lady* (1881, revised edition 1908),[4] and Edith Wharton, in *The House of Mirth* (1905), give agency to Isabel Archer and Lily Bart, their respective versions of Gwendolen Harleth, by seeing to it that their heroines do not necessarily have to marry in order to be financially taken care of. All three authors finally show that their self-reliant American heroines are trapped by the powerful nineteenth-century ideology of gender in the manner of George Eliot's female protagonists; Phelps's and James's heroines cannot fulfill their potential for vocational and/or financial self-reliance because they fall victim to the marriage plot. Wharton's heroine, by contrast, follows Eliot's socially unacceptable protagonists, Hetty Sorrel and Maggie Tulliver, into an untimely death.[5]

Only Harriet Beecher Stowe's independent "New England spinsters" (as Fullerian "virgins") show a "typically American" way out of the Eliotian gender conundrum. They actually achieve personal freedom because, unlike Isabel Archer and Lily Bart, they, as members of an almost classless society, manage to escape the snares of nineteenth-century gender hegemony. While Eliot's Gwendolen Harleth and her American sisters Isabel and Lily, unwittingly participate in their own victimization by allowing themselves to be objectified as social ornaments of (potential) upper class husbands, Stowe's plain New England "working women" remain in control of their own destiny. However, corroborating DuPlessis's point that education and romance cannot coexist in the nineteenth-century novel, they have to do this at the cost of forsaking personal romance.

Eliot's perhaps most influential novel, *Daniel Deronda*, inspired American authors to write beyond the ending of its culture plot as well (I am aware of "writing beyond the ending" of DuPlessis's gendered concept at this point). Both Henry James and Cynthia Ozick—who authored their books more than a century apart—were intrigued by Eliot's idea of juxtaposing the effete British internationalized leisure class culture with a healthy communal Jewish alternative. Therefore, James's *The Portrait of a Lady* and Ozick's *The Puttermesser Papers* (1997) both feature "rewrites" of *Daniel Deronda*'s cultural redemption plot. Both writers ultimately agree with Eliot that a mass market induced internationalization and globalization of culture should be resisted. James indicates in *The Portrait of a Lady* that British and American culture have already become too similar to present viable cultural alternatives to each other. And in *The Puttermesser Papers* Ozick shows that her heroine's attempts of redeeming the corrupt New York City government by means of ancient Jewish faith is bound to fail because even a golem, a kabbalistic Jewish trickster figure, cannot combat the force of twentieth-century greed and corruption. Ozick, nevertheless, seems to imply that a tradition of strong traditional "local" values still offers indispensable redemptive qualities. But it appears that both James and Ozick cannot really write beyond the ending of the cultural romance plot of Eliot's *Daniel Deronda* because they fail to conceive of a (better) alternative.

The twentieth-century writers who adapted George Eliot's marriage plot in their own fiction write beyond its ending rather unspectacularly by not having their heroines succumb to the traditional plot in a traditional manner. In *Looking for Work* (1979), Cheever presents a female protagonist who, on her way out of a conventional marriage, encounters constraints that are still quite similar to those that a typical George Eliot heroine faces when "looking for work." Gail Godwin's heroine in *The Odd Woman* (1974) longs for a relationship that resembles the "marriage of true souls" that George Eliot and George Henry Lewes had, but has to realize that (unlike Lewes) her married lover, Gabriel, will not leave his wife for her. Her fate seems to proceed in accordance with DuPlessis's observation that education and romance cannot tolerate each other within the customary romance plot. John Irving and Cynthia Ozick are the only ones among the modern writers discussed here who significantly modify the mostly realistic mode of these nineteenth-century style novels by combining the traditional form with incongruent and often grotesque subject matter. But in *A Widow for One Year* (1998), Irving, nevertheless, "enforces" Eliot's marriage ideal against all odds, whereas Cynthia Ozick, who presents the Eliot/Lewes relationship as an unreachable nostalgic ideal in *The Puttermesser Papers* (1997), deconstructs both the Eliotian marriage and death plot by relating very bizarre and grotesque versions thereof.

Back in the nineteenth century, Elizabeth Stuart Phelps was the first American author who tried to improve upon the George Eliot heroine. Like her neighbor and fellow writer Harriet Beecher Stowe before her, the writer and feminist activist Phelps[6] had become so intrigued by George Eliot—on whose work she was to lecture at Boston University[7]—that she sought personal contact with her. Thus, in February 1873, apparently dissatisfied with the unfulfilled feminist potential of *Middlemarch*, she wrote a letter to Eliot, asking her to write a novel about "the Coming Woman":

> [*Middlemarch*] is as pure as a lily and as strong as the hills. You have written the novel of the Century—but that is one matter; you have almost analyzed a woman—and that is quite another. . . . I cannot tell you how earnestly I feel that it will require a *great novel* to proclaim the royal lineage of the Coming Woman to the average mind, nor what positive personal longing it has become to me that you should write it:—if for no other reason, to prevent my writing a small one! (quoted in *George Eliot Letters* 1954–55, 5:388)

Phelps, of course, wanted Eliot to write a novel whose heroine would be endowed with more agency and opportunity than Dorothea Brooke or Maggie Tulliver. But Eliot rather lamely replied that she did not know if she could make this "really needed contribution":

> As to the "great novel" which remains to be written, I must tell you that I never believe in future books of my own, and always after finishing any work I have a period of despair that I can ever produce anything else worth giving to the world. . . . It is difficult to believe, until the germ of some new work grows into imperious activity within one, that it is possible to make a really needed contribution to the poetry of the world—I mean possible for oneself to do it. (*George Eliot Letters* 1954–55, 5:388)

Apparently not quite satisfied with Eliot's answer, Phelps set out to write the novel about the "Coming Woman" herself.[8] The result is *The Story of Avis* (1877), a novel whose storyline about a heroine who prefers being an artist to being a wife is heavily indebted to Eliot's poem "Armgart" (1873).[9]

Eliot's self-reliant artist protagonist, Armgart, most likely resembles Phelps's idea of a "Coming Woman," but as the protagonist of a poem she would, of course, not become as widely known as the heroines of Eliot's novels; therefore Phelps probably thought that a novel about a "future type of womanhood" was still needed. "Armgart" tells the story of an extremely talented, and therefore financially independent, but arrogant, opera singer who steadfastly refuses marriage to a German count, only referred to by his title, "Graf." Even after she has permanently lost her voice, Armgart holds fast to her decision not to marry her suitor. Armgart significantly influenced Phelps's conception of her heroine, Avis, who combines her personality traits with those of other, less rebellious, George Eliot heroines; the eponymous novel's storyline also combines the poem's storyline with plot aspects from Eliot's novels.

Armgart, who foreshadows the Alcharisi, is a very strong, sometimes not particularly likable heroine; she certainly can be counted as Eliot's first real feminist character. To the Graf, who wants to domesticate her and therefore asks, "Is it no offence / To wish the the eagle's wing may find repose / As feebler wings do in a quiet nest" (1873, 124), she replies rather imperiously that like his, hers is a higher nature, "I am an artist as you are a noble: / I ought to bear the burthen of my rank" (127). Moreover, she informs him that her "natural rank" sets her apart from ordinary women whose only destiny it is to procreate:

> Yes, I know
> the oft-taught Gospel: "Woman, thy desire
> Shall be that all superlatives on earth
> Belong to men, save the highest kind—
> To be a mother. Thou shalt not desire
> To do aught best pure subservience:
> Nature has willed it so!" O blessed Nature!
> Let her be arbitress; she gave me voice
> Such as she only gives a woman child
> Best of its kind. . . . (128)

The Graf retorts that he would prefer for Armgart to be an "Angel in the House": "Pain had been saved, / Nay purer glory reached, had you been throned / As woman only, holding all your art / As attribute to that dear sovereignty— / Concentering your power in home delights / Which penetrate the world" (129).

Armgart punishes the Graf's blatant sexism by not accepting his marriage proposal even after she has lost her voice due to illness. She implies to her servant, Walpurga, that the Graf wanted to marry her only in order to subdue a woman who is his equal or perhaps of even higher "natural rank" than himself. Understandably devastated after losing the talent that made her exceptional and enabled her arrogance, she complains that she has lost her place: "What am I now? / The millionth woman in superfluous herds" (137). The poem's initially conceited protagonist (by means of whom Eliot might even have intended to satirize her own penchant for looking down on "unexceptional" women) is finally subdued by her faithful, "lame" servant, Walpurga, who makes her see her arrogance. Chastised by a stroke of bad fortune and insight into her own personality, Armgart finally resigns herself to her new situation; she decides to make a living as a music teacher while at the same time benefiting the public by her talent.

Phelps brings down Eliot's famous artist heroine from her exalted position and places her into an intellectual, but still very practical, New England college community. Avis is a much toned down, less exalted, version of Armgart. Even though she shares Armgart's hatred of domesticity and "true womanhood," she does not share her contempt of "lesser" females (such as her friend and foil, the aptly named Coy Bishop). She is also more willing to give her suitor, Philip Ostrander a fair chance, but this turns out to be a bad idea since he is less sexist than the Graf only at the beginning of the novel.

From the beginning of her story, Avis is in a situation that is different from that of Armgart. Not yet an established artist, she has just returned from studying art in Europe with famous teachers and lives in her widowed father's house in a New England town. Unlike Armgart, she has not yet had a chance to reap any financial benefit from her talent. Her father, a philosophy professor, has, of course, financed her completely throughout her course of study and continues to do so afterwards. Since her mentor has told her that her artistic output over the next two years will tell whether or not she can establish herself as a famous artist on the international market, Avis devotes most of her time to painting in her studio and does not plan to engage in amorous pursuits. She is such a devoted artist that Phelps even has her imitate the debauchery associated with male artists: the vision of her one and only masterpiece, The Sphinx, occurs to Avis after she has imbibed a generous quantity of "*Eau de Fleurs d'Oranger*" ([1877] 1985, 79).

Despite her resolve not to do so, Avis falls in love with Philip Ostrander, a candidate for a professorship in geology at her father's university. For a long time she resists becoming engaged to him because marriage, as she tells him, "'is a profession to a woman. And I have my work; I have my work!'" (71). Possibly inspired by the heated exchange between Armgart and the

Graf in Eliot's poem, Phelps also has Avis explain to her future husband that love between a man and a woman is "civil war" (106).

In the courtship scene between Philip and Avis, which reenacts the courtship scene from "Armgart," Avis's words echo those of Armgart and parallel what the Alcharisi has to say about her own nature in *Daniel Deronda*:

> [God] has set two natures in me, warring against each other. He has made me a law unto myself—*He* made me so.... I do not say, Heaven knows! that I am better, or greater, or truer than other women, when I say it is quite right for other women to become wives, and not for me. I only say, If [*sic*] that is what a woman is made for, I am not like that: I am different and God did it. (107)

Avis, perhaps reflecting her creator's dislike for Armgart's arrogance, does not claim that she is greater than other women, but by stating that she is a "law unto herself," she clearly implies that she is exceptional and that she does not believe in "essentially female" gender characteristics, such as submissiveness and nurturance. (Towards the end of the novel, after her marriage has failed, she again asserts the difference of her "female nature" when she says "'*I* am nature, too. Explain me, Coy'" [249]). Unlike Armgart's suitor, Philip dispels Avis's doubts regarding the possibility of an equitable gender relationship by letting her know that he respects her exceptionality: "'I do not want your work, or your individuality. I refuse to accept any such sacrifice from the woman I love. You are perfectly right. A man ought to be above it. Let me be that man'" (107).

Avis believes him and marries him, but soon after the wedding things start to go wrong, and she immediately has to neglect her vocation—painting. She becomes the mother of two children[10] and is bogged down by household chores that she can barely manage. Philip soon forgets his promise of helping to further her career and constantly complains about her deficient housekeeping. Unfortunately, things get even worse for Avis. Like Eliot's heroine Romola, she finds out unsavory truths about her husband's moral nature: Philip not only betrayed his former fiancée but also neglected his poverty-stricken mother. When Avis is seriously ill, he finally lets her down by committing the "indecorum" of holding hands with a family friend. To make things worse, he is fired from his job as a professor because he neglects his teaching duties. Due to lung disease he has to spend the winter in the warmer climate of Europe. Avis, left behind in New England with her two children, tries to support the family, but soon finds out that she cannot even pay the creditors who turn up at her doorstep because her talent has not made her a contender in the marketplace of male competition: "the price of two portraits which she had painted—her only finished work—that winter, had gone to cover the seamstress's bills" (149). Even though Avis accomplishes a half-hearted reconciliation with her eventually reformed husband, Phelps helps her out of her unsuccessful marriage by having Philip Ostrander and their son Van, who takes after his father, die of consumption, in the manner of an Eliotian providential death. Having lost her talent as a result of too much strain on her nerves, Avis, who has to support herself and her daughter, resolves to become a teacher.

Due to its Eliotian ending, Jack H. Wilson very negatively judges *The Story of Avis* as "a feminist text that did begin to emerge and [then] fell prey to the myth of a metaphysical center" (1993, 73). He argues that

> [t]he humanization of Armgart emphasizes the primary ethical messages of George Eliot's fiction and poetry—we grow into full humanity and wisdom only with sorrow, the heroic is to be achieved in humble, commonplace endeavors, the highest moral virtue is to live altruistically for and through others—and these clearly argue that a life given to altruism and renunciation of the self is as good as or better than a merely artistic life. As the bildungsroman text unfolds in *The Story of Avis*, we see an emphasis upon the same ethical imperatives. (67)

I do not agree with Wilson's negative assessment since I am convinced that Phelps does not wholeheartedly endorse such renunciation in her novel. Avis certainly is forced into renunciation by both the patriarchal gender hegemony and financial straits (which can at least indirectly be blamed on the patriarchal social order), but does not ever truly accept her situation. Thus, towards the end of the novel, she bitterly wonders "how it would have been . . . if her feeling for that one man, her husband, had not eaten into and eaten out the core of her life, left her a riddled, withered thing, spent and rent" ([1877] 1985, 244). And she still hopes that her daughter Wait (named after her paternal grandmother Waitstill Ostrander)—or Wait's daughter, if the wait for "A WOMAN" (246) really takes three generations as Avis has come to believe—will have a better life as

> A WOMAN. A being of radiant physique, the heiress of ancestral health on the maternal side; a creature forever more of nerve than of muscle, and therefore trained to the energy of the muscle and the repose of the nerve; physically educated by mothers of her own fibre and by physicians of her own sex,—such a woman alone is fitted to acquire the drilled brain, the calmed imagination, and sustained aim, which constitute intellectual command. (246)[11]

Here it becomes clear that Phelps, rather than endorse female renunciation, expects future generations of women to implement Avis's ambitious plans. While George Eliot perhaps might not have approved of this matrifocal utopia (in spite of presenting one herself with Romola's alternative family of mothers and children), she certainly did not always suggest altruism and renunciation as better alternatives to the artistic life. Elizabeth Stuart Phelps had explicitly asked George Eliot to write a novel about a "Coming Woman"; I would argue that with the character of the Alcharisi (also based on Armgart), Eliot, at the same time that Phelps wrote *Avis*, conceived of a more radically feminist, and therefore perhaps even stronger, "Coming Woman" character than Phelps herself. While the Alcharisi is not the central female protagonist of *Daniel Deronda*, she definitely presents a viable alternative to Eliot's altruistic female protagonists, as my discussion of Eliot's most feminist character has shown.

Like Elizabeth Stuart Phelps, Henry James and Edith Wharton also engaged in trying to refashion the George Eliot heroine as "self-reliant American girl" by enlarging her opportunities in life by means of additional types of social agency. But it turns out that the young female American protagonists experience almost the same difficulties as Eliot's heroines do when faced with the overpowering male bias of nineteenth-century gender ideology; therefore, they do not really enjoy a significant enlargement of opportunity for self-realization. Both James and Wharton have selected *Daniel Deronda*'s Gwendolen Harleth as simultaneous model and foil for their own heroines. James's indebtedness to Eliot's novel was brought to the fore by F. R. Leavis's (in)famous remark in *The Great Tradition* that "Henry James wouldn't have written *The Portrait of a Lady* if he hadn't read *Gwendolen Harleth* (as I shall call the good part of *Daniel Deronda*)" (1950, 85).[12] And Henry James himself detected in Wharton's writing "the fine benevolent fingermarks of the good George Eliot—the echo of much reading of that excellent woman" (quoted in Hutchinson 1997, 315). But since it is James who is usually viewed as the most important influence on Wharton, it might be impossible to establish to what extent the impact of *Daniel Deronda* on *The House of Mirth* had to compete with influential "interferences" from James's *The Portrait of a Lady*.[13]

Important similarities between the plotlines of all three novels can be found in the personalities of the three writers' heroines, their aims in life, and how these aims are frustrated by the workings of nineteenth-century gender ideology. Gwendolen Harleth, Isabel Archer, and Lily Bart can all be described as very pretty, very ambitious, and very spoiled upper class girls who want to "remain independent" throughout their lives. Since the social constraints they are confronted with in their societies are very similar, even though James has transplanted his American heroine to England, and even though Wharton's Lily lives in New York at the turn of the twentieth century rather than mid to late nineteenth-century England, they all face the same problems in the accomplishment of this goal: independence means financial independence and this comes at a cost. Since all of them derive from the higher classes and have learned to love the finer things of life, their independence depends on the ready availability of monetary funds. These can be obtained in three different ways, which all prove to be tricky: 1) through inheritance, 2) through marriage (which might turn out to be counterproductive to maintaining independence), 3) through their own talent or even labor (which is difficult because upper class future "angels in the house" are not trained to use skills). For Gwendolen and Lily the first option eventually falls through; moreover, like Isabel Archer (who does become a rich heiress), they initially reject marriage. Option three therefore seems to present the most reasonable strategy of maintaining independence, except for the well-known facts that job opportunities were scarce for upper class ladies in late nineteenth-century Europe and America and that ladies' skills were mostly of the ornamental kind, including expertise in "looking good" and performing (singing, playing a musical instrument) for men. (Leisure class ladies apparently did not even have to fulfill the more strenuous part of the "dual feminine function" of "beauty and usefulness" that the "The Cult of True Womanhood" required of more ordinary nineteenth-century ladies [see Welter 1966, 163].)

Thus hampered by nineteenth-century gender hegemony, all three heroines encounter extreme difficulties in trying to preserve their independence. Ironically, Isabel Archer, who has been made financially independent by her cousin's gift of half of his inheritance, is the first one to sacrifice her self-reliant American independence without any pressing reason in her marriage to the sadistic Osmond, whose artificial "European" charm she succumbs to in her quest for real style.[14] The other two protagonists hold out longer. Gwendolen's independence is endangered from the start by her mother's financial difficulties. She first tries to remedy her financial situation by gambling and then tests her talent as an actress. When Klesmer tells her with a brutal honesty that defies nineteenth-century gender decorum that she has no talent as an actress, she briefly considers becoming a governess. She decides to reject that loathed possibility and, even though she does not love him, finally accepts Grandcourt's offer of marriage in order to prevent her family's and her own financial ruin. Ultimately, Gwendolen ends up having to sell herself; in Dorothea Barrett's terminology, she reverts to prostitution within marriage (see 1985, 164). Even though she initially assumes that she can win the "civil war" of the sexes because "she was thinking of him . . . as a man over whom she was going to have indefinite power" ([1876] 1995, 315), she finally has to give up all independence to Grandcourt, who likewise expresses his wish "to be completely master of this creature" (301)—and it remains debatable whether or not she gets her revenge since her ominous role in her husband's providential death does not give her satisfaction. Isabel, whom James made a little "nicer" than Gwendolen, also comes to engage in a "war of the sexes" with her husband and has similar experiences.

Wharton's Lily Bart, finally, even though she has a wider range of social possibility than both Gwendolen and Isabel, runs the whole gamut of thwarted opportunity for self-realization and independence available to (American) women at the turn of the twentieth century. As surplus of the upper class marriage market, she remains independent of a sadistic husband like Grandcourt or Osmond but also falls prey to the gambling habits of higher society. In the course of the financial gambling that she engages in to stay financially afloat, she turns down a real offer to prostitute herself with the man she is indebted to and finally decides to work for a living. Yet the price that Lily pays for her relative autonomy is too high: she actually descends to the level of the working class; due to the shame she feels about her situation, she inadvertently commits suicide.

These examples indicate the inexorable working of ideology on the three protagonists.[15] Gwendolen, Isabel, and Lily all think that they have much more choice in determining their lives' options than they actually do.[16] While within the narratives of *Daniel Deronda* and *The House of Mirth*, Gwendolen and Lily develop an understanding of the fact that their choices are not unlimited (and that they are curbed by the males who hold social power) much sooner than Isabel does in *The Portrait of a Lady*, all three of them do not realize that their social desires are constructed by the contemporary ideology of gender. According to an Althusserian understanding, the "ideological (state) apparatus," "Patriarchy," functions in these three novels in a similar way as does "Judaism" in *Daniel Deronda*. It interpellates the three protagonists into the social order by giving them the illusion that "Patriarchy's" desires are their own. Thus, Gwendolen, Isabel, and Lily assent to and collaborate with being used as essentially powerless "social ornaments" for powerful (potential) husbands.

Both James and Wharton, who stem from the "classless" U.S., put very much emphasis on their heroine's fascination with the perks that higher class life affords. Eliot, by contrast, for whom class difference is a given fact of life, exposes the danger of class consciousness in *Daniel Deronda* when she has

Deronda (and also Gwendolen) realize that true fulfillment can only be found in a communal lifestyle that transcends class boundaries—as traditional Judaism does in her novel. James and Wharton, however, do not provide their heroines with even a glimpse of a redemptive communal model of social organization, but rather have them fall for their fascination with European and New Yorkian upper class elegance. The fates of Isabel Archer and Lily Bart, ultimately, indicate that James and Wharton, as American authors, were not able to improve British gender relationships by writing beyond the customary ending of the nineteenth-century romance. Their heroines succumb to the typical plots outlined by DuPlessis: Isabel marries and Lily dies. Yet the example presented by Harriet Beecher Stowe in *Oldtown Folks* (discussed in chapter 1), nevertheless, shows that some nineteenth-century American heroines are indeed able to escape such fates that seem compulsory. But they have to be lucky enough to have been placed by their creators in a practically classless American society that spurns rather than emulates British class consciousness and social stratification; only Stowe's unfashionable rural and "pre-capitalist" Oldtown appears to be such a community.

Culture in Need of Redemption?

Europe and the U.S. in James's The Portrait of a Lady

In *The Portrait of a Lady*, his fictional answer to *Daniel Deronda*, Henry James also addressed the dangers inherent in a globalization of leisure class culture that George Eliot had already targeted in her Jewish novel. Richard Freadman observes about "James's Europe" that it "is just as rotten as the England of *Daniel Deronda* . . . [h]owever, there is no Palestine" (1986, 100). Thus, without going into much detail, Freadman hints at the fact that James follows Eliot—who promotes Zionism as a healthier cultural alternative to the leisure culture of the British upper classes—in incorporating a cultural comparison in his "rewrite" of Eliot's novel. The novel presents, of course, a variation upon James's "international theme," but the cultural comparison undertaken is much more complex and much less clear-cut than "standard" explanations of James's works as focusing on American innocents being ruined abroad would suggest (see Leavis 1950, 142; Edel 1985, 261).[17] Most importantly, it indicates that British and American culture have, in significant ways, become too similar to be able to redeem each other.

Most of James's American characters in *The Portrait of a Lady* are drawn to Europe because they seem to view the United States as culturally deprived in the way outlined by James in a February 1879 notebook entry:

> Oh yes, the United States—a country without a sovereign, without a court, without a nobility, without any army, without a church or clergy, without a diplomatic service, without a picturesque peasantry, without palaces and castles, or country seats, or ruins, without a literature, without novels, without an Oxford or Cambridge, without cathedrals or ivied churches, without latticed cottages or village ale-houses, without political society, without sport, without fox-hunting or country gentlemen, without an Epsom or an Ascot, an Eton or Rugby. (quoted in Moore 1986, 12)

Gilbert Osmond, Madame Merle, and Ned Rosier, and to some extent Ralph Touchett and Isabel Archer, choose to live in Europe because Europe offers the treasures listed in the passage above. But, European culture, specifically English culture, as Eliot presents it in *Daniel Deronda*, is in the process of becoming depleted by a consumerism that is at least partly made possible by the exploitation of overseas colonies. This incipient capitalism precludes the organic social community of Eliot's earlier novels and ushers in a "new world . . . that anticipates the alienated settings of modernism" (Barrett 1989, 163). Therefore, according to Eliot, it needs a cultural corrective such as the alternative Jewish lifestyle presented in the novel.

In addition to showing the cultural depletion of late nineteenth-century England, Eliot focuses on another important and very visible aspect of European corruption in *Daniel Deronda* that James also incorporates in *The Portrait of a Lady*: the higher classes are too leisured, and this has a number of pernicious effects. Upper-class gentlemen do not have to work; in Daniel Deronda's case this leads to a general sense of aimlessness which Daniel learns to combat only after he has met Mordecai and Mirah and has been invigorated by their—and then his own—vital Judaism. By the same token, the vicious Henleigh Grandcourt is enabled by an overabundance of money and time to cultivate a certain lifestyle that allows him to impress his peer group with his houses, hunting parties, and so forth and to devise complicated plans to ensnare and subdue other men, women, and his dog, too.

Ironically, to stay on top of this society and to maintain one's leisure requires hard work that goes into fashioning and keeping up one's style. In order not to risk descending into "poverty" (though the poverty alluded to in nineteenth-century novels seems a far cry from the real thing), both higher-class women, like Gwendolen Harleth, and even men, like Gilbert Osmond, are forced to make so-called "good marriages" if they run out of money. By juxtaposing lazy, effete, and feminized European and Europeanized men, like Osmond and Ned Rosier, with hard-working American males—and females—like Caspar Goodwood and Henrietta Stackpole, James almost seems to suggest that American values could redeem European sloth and corruption. Isabel's suitor Caspar Goodwood personifies the will to succeed and seems to be the epitome of American industriousness since "he liked to organize, to contend, to administer; he could make people work his will, believe in him, march before him and justify him" ([1908] 1986, 169–70). Isabel's American "working woman" friend, Henrietta Stackpole, actively defends such American work ethics against European high class sloth throughout the entire novel. For example, when Isabel tells Henrietta that Ralph Touchett—who actually is too sick to work—"'does nothing; . . . he's a gentleman of large leisure,'" she replies, "'[w]ell, I call that a shame—when I have to work like a car conductor. . . . I should like to show him up'" (142).

Yet, as several critics have pointed out, Henry James, due to both his feminization and his admiration for the finer things of life, is definitely not on the side of the productive Caspar Goodwoods of this world—which should effectively preclude him from proclaiming American industrialists possible agents of cultural redemption. Moreover, it seems that James had massive problems with accepting the prevalent cultural discourse on masculinity because it served to discriminate against him. As Martha Banta points out, President Roosevelt, for example (whom James met at a White House dinner three years before the New York edition of *Portrait of a Lady* was published) viewed males of James's masculine disposition as not fit for American society. Banta quotes passages from Roosevelt's writing in which he maintains that a man (like James) "who becomes Europeanized, who loses his power of doing good work on this side of the water . . . is a silly and undesirable citizen" (Roosevelt quoted in Banta 1998, 26) Moreover, he does not become European, but "only ceases being an American, and becomes nothing" (26).[18] Thus, for Roosevelt, a writer like Henry James must have represented a total failure of masculinity since

> [t]he male who does not stay in America denies his manhood; anyone who lives abroad is classified as "feminine" whatever his or her biological status. The male who stays but does not work is also condemned to be a man without a country. Since what artists do is not considered real work, the man who takes up the literary life abroad is doubly damned. (Banta 1998, 26)[19]

Banta reasons that James's encounter with Roosevelt profoundly influenced his writing and that by the time he prepared *The American Scene* for publication, "its pages were filled with his anxiety over the ruinous effect upon American life when notice was granted only to two kinds of people: the man of business and the woman of society" (24).

The same gendered and cultural anxiety can already be felt on the pages of *A Portrait of a Lady*, which was published more than twenty-five years before *The American Scene* but revised shortly after the latter book was published. James's heroine, Isabel Archer, indeed seems to reflect her creator's loathing of dominant masculinity and cultural unbelonging. She turns away from her American roots and to Europe because people like Caspar Goodwood and Henrietta Stackpole fail to live up to her cultural expectations. They lack style and refinement and are much too coarse and vulgar, direct and forceful. Isabel, for example, hates the way in which he pronounces "belong" as "belawng" ([1908] 1986, 380). Moreover, she intuits that he wants to dominate her with his masculinity and registers that "it was part of the influence he had upon her that he seemed to deprive her of the sense of freedom" (168). This impression of Goodwood as rigid and overpowering is reinforced at the end of the novel when Isabel, by then thoroughly disenchanted with Osmond, interprets Goodwood's kiss as an act of rape: "His kiss was like white lightning . . . she felt each thing in his hard manhood that had least pleased her, each aggressive fact of his face, his figure, his presence, justified of its intense identity and made one with this act of possession" (636). However, the same acquisitive "American" aggressivity displayed by Goodwood is also at work in the aesthete Osmond, who is just another side of the same coin. Yet since in Osmond's case his rapaciousness is glossed over by a European veneer that to some extent complements and feeds it, it is much less obvious that his collectorship is motivated by the same "aggressive manhood" that makes Goodwood want to own and dominate. Isabel initially overlooks this similarity. This cultural twist then, at least implicitly, also deconstructs notions of cultural difference between England and the U.S. by raising the question of whether or not greed and the hunger for power are "American," "European," or even "male" characteristics.[20]

Following Eliot's lead from *Daniel Deronda*, James has his heroine embark on a—albeit less complex—search for an identity that is both personal and collective. Like Eliot's protagonist, Daniel Deronda, Isabel Archer becomes steeped in two national (in this case both Anglo-) cultures that should suffice to provide the necessary material for her endeavor; yet she finds that neither the contemporary U.S. nor contemporary England can live up to her expectations and ultimately turns to "timeless historic Rome" for a cultural model that is able to provide more transcendent sustenance. Isabel marries the Europeanized Osmond because she initially misinterprets the attractive cultural finish that he has applied to himself and that hides his dominant, "masculine" nature from her. She wants to lead what she deems a European "aristocratic life" at his side, but does not realize that his culture is mere surface.

Isabel does not understand yet that her jaded American expatriate compatriots actually view all items of cultural representation as dispensable commodities in an ongoing procedure of self-fashioning according to whatever fashion is opportune at the moment. In an interesting and often quoted philosophical conversation about the phenomenon of identity, Madame Merle tries to enlighten Isabel about what by now has come to be known as the "socially and culturally constructed nature of the self" (and, in a way, even seems to alert her to the interpellative powers of social discourses). Yet, "[u]nable to accompany her friend into this bold analysis of the human personality" (253), Isabel retorts that she is so sure of her/self that she does not need any of the culturally available "appurtenances" to express her/self. The important exchange of ideas begins by Madame Merle rather haughtily telling Isabel that there is no "core self":

> When you've lived as long as I you'll see that every human being has his shell and that you must take the shell into account. By the shell I mean the whole envelope of circumstances. . . . [W]e're each of us made up of some cluster of appurtenances. What shall we call our 'self'? Where does it begin? where does it end? It overflows into everything that belongs to us—and then it flows back again. I know a large part of myself is in the clothes I choose to wear. I've a great deal of respect for *things!* One's self—for other people—is one's expression of one's self; and one's house, one's furniture, one's garments, the books one reads, the company one keeps—these things are all expressive. (253)

Isabel, equally haughtily, replies: "'I don't agree with you. I think it is just the other way. I don't know whether I succeed in expressing myself, but I know that nothing else expresses me. . . . My clothes may express the dressmaker, but they don't express me. To begin with it's not my own choice that I wear them; they're imposed upon me by society'" (253). Isabel might indeed speak the truth at this moment, but her self-assurance appears to be rendered in quite an ironic manner—James's readers already know at this point that she has rejected Caspar Goodwood at least partly because his way of dressing does not suit her. Isabel, however, as Madame Merle curtly observes, dresses very well. To the people she comes into contact with (as, for example, Gilbert Osmond), her way of dressing must, therefore, suggest that she knows about the social conventions that construct social/cultural identity and that she is willing to play by the rules. But her clothes certainly cannot signify to what extent she is going play by the rules and observe convention.

The trouble indeed seems to be that neither American nor British culture can supply Isabel with the cultural "appurtenances" that would provide a perfect fit. She rejects American plainness and "vulgarity" but tragically mistakes Osmond's appropriation of European aristocracy for the real thing. Recent analyses of the international theme in Henry James suggest that James meant to present cultural/national identity as something much more transitional and fluid than critics interested in the "corrupt Europe vs. innocent America" dichotomy have assumed. Joel Porte points out that cultural appearances are indeed dangerously deceptive in *The Portrait of a Lady*: "Osmond represents 'negative power,' the force of the alien 'other' that seems to be 'European'; but, as we know, he too, is an American—though one who has consented to worship at the altar of convention, propriety, whatever seems to be 'aristocratic' and nonvulgar" (1990, 3). And Jonathan Freedman argues that "James depicts a world where national and cultural identity exists as something to be made, not something given" (1998, 11) since he writes at a cultural moment

> when identities start to circulate across and through national borders and boundaries, when financial and cultural capital are being exported wholesale from an attenuating British empire or a vitiated Europe to a new kind of world power, [and when] what it is to be "English" or "Italian" or "French" is as much up for grabs as it [*sic*] what it is to be American. (8)

But James's Isabel is culturally conservative and, therefore, she cannot accept models that present identity as subject to change. Already having rejected Madame Merle's explanation of personal identity as constructed, she turns away from the cultural uncertainties of contemporary England and America to what "old Rome" has to offer. Like Daniel Deronda, she seeks and finds comfort in a conservative explanation of human identity as historically continuous. Among the ruins of Rome, Isabel feels one with all of humankind, experiencing a "haunting sense of the continuity of the human lot" ([1908] 1986, 564). As the narrator reports, "[Isabel] had grown to think of [Rome] chiefly as the place where people suffered. This was what came to her in the starved churches, where the marble columns, transferred from pagan ruins, seemed to offer her a companionship in endurance and the musty incense to be a compound of long-unanswered prayers" (564). In this context, it is interesting to note that it seems to be ancient Roman culture, "a world of ruins" (564) rather than people, that sustains Isabel. "Real

Italians" are as absent from James's novel as they are from Hawthorne's and Eliot's fiction about Italy. Isabel finds consolation in a belief in the same eighteenth-century cosmopolitanism that Eliot expresses in the proem to Eliot's *Romola*, where her narrator, in almost the same words as James's, talks about "the broad sameness of the human lot" ([1863] 1980, 43), thus asserting that humanity and its fate have remained unaltered by and throughout the centuries.

Yet while Isabel is comforted by what historical Rome can give her, James's novel ultimately does not follow Eliot's *Daniel Deronda* in presenting a cultural alternative to a corrupt and culturally depleted England. While Mordecai's ultra-traditional Jewish way of life, which enables organic identification with all of humankind in "divine unity," points towards a communal alternative to the hierarchies of English society, the American way of life depicted in *The Portrait of a Lady* has nothing to offer to Europe in that regard because it has already become highly imitative of Europe.[21] This is at least somewhat ironic since from its very beginning America has not only viewed itself as the cradle of democracy, but also, according to its national myth, presented itself as "God's own country," inhabited by a "chosen people." In addition to the national myth it devised, American religion should have much redemptive power to offer to Europe, its mother continent; the Puritans did after all leave England because they already viewed the country as spiritually corrupt. Moreover, as indicated in the previous chapter, transcendentalism, the religious philosophy that developed as a reaction to Puritanism, offers the same spiritual basis for community as Mordecai's kabbalistic Judaism since it shares the same Neoplatonic origins. Yet unlike the Judaism presented in *Daniel Deronda*, American religion and philosophy have lost their vitality in *Portrait of a Lady*. Puritanism only continues to exist in the arid Puritan work ethics represented by the industrialist Caspar Goodwood; and transcendentalism, as Richard Poirier has suggested, is made fun of through James's characterization of both Osmond and Isabel as "mock transcendentalists" (see 1967, 219-20). The pessimistic attitude regarding the possibility of cultural renewal that James displays at the threshold to literary modernism might indeed, as Freedman suggests, be grounded in his realization that the capitalist "American national subject" functions as the spearhead of a globalizing and equalizing mass culture: "[I]t becomes the very type of what we might want to call modernity (or even postmodernity). Transnational or even global, its various varieties . . . create in their turn a collective, mass identity" (1998, 10).

Interestingly, it is Edith Wharton's *The House of Mirth*, her "adaptation" of both *Daniel Deronda* and *The Portrait of a Lady* which, finally, without having much recourse to contemporaneous Europe, presents an analysis of the cultural disaster that ensues when the incipient (gendered) capitalism of her novel's pre-texts becomes a global standard. *The House of Mirth* gives a detailed description of the social hierarchies of New York at the turn of the twentieth century and provides a look at New York society from its highly differentiated top strata to its working class bottom level. Lillian Robinson details how this "new and improved" capitalism that has superseded the "naturalized" capitalism presented in Eliot's and James's novels functions to benefit both the holders of inherited wealth and financial newcomers (while exploiting the working classes as, for example, the working girls in milliner's shops whom Lilly Bart must eventually join).[22] She calls attention to the fact that Wharton incorporates a very sarcastic analysis of how capitalist society corrupts the institution of marriage: "The gendered relation to income in [the upper] class's culture is almost caricatured by the marriage of Lily Bart's parents: he earns the money, presumably by managing investments; she consumes it in such a way as exhaust his economic potency while making it look as if she has more to spend than he has" (1994, 351)[23]

Perhaps even more importantly, Wharton also shows with *The House of Mirth* that the female socialites' overabundance of leisure and their assumption of non-existent gender power has dire moral consequences along with financial ones; in the novel's upper-class New York sexual intrigue has become the accepted standard while matrimony is emptied of its meaning and ridiculed. In the process of demonstrating this, she also denounces the process of cultural appropriation. Admitting English class stratification into "classless" American society leads to social chaos, precludes social and cultural redemption, and even fails to properly emulate British social life, as Shari Benstock observes about Wharton's "grim picture of the moneyed class in America": "British reviewers . . . did not doubt her portrait of New York society (one suspects a certain gleefulness in their readiness to condemn American crassness)" (1994, 312).

By means of the social satire incorporated in *The House of Mirth*, Wharton exposes the vulgarity of the globally expanding capitalism that already lurks behind the leisured stylishness of society ladies like Gwendolen Harleth and Isabel Archer. Wharton's novel, furthermore, calls attention to the fact that Isabel Archer, who can wear her stylish clothes only because of the wealth of the males whose money has bought her these clothes, is indeed naïve to assume that her clothes do not express her. While she might feel inadequately expressed by her clothes, they still expose the unsavory fact that as display object in the international "market of female beauty and social grace" (Robinson 1994, 346) any leisure-class lady in the fictional universes of Eliot, James, and Wharton is a mere signifier of the wealth of the man who "owns" her. Within the "global fictions" of the three authors, faith might perhaps still lead to the redemption of the faithful few of the ilk of Daniel Deronda, but, unfortunately, it does not point towards any cultural alternative that could redeem the injustice of the global and globalizing gender hegemony.

A (Post)modern Cultural Redemption through Judaism?—Cynthia Ozick's
The Puttermesser Papers

The (post)modern[24] Jewish writer Cynthia Ozick follows James in looking to *Daniel Deronda* for a narrative that thematizes the possibility of cultural redemption. With *The Puttermesser Papers* (1997) she renders a tribute to George Eliot that also calls for the possibility of cultural renewal, and, at least on a cursory reading, seems to put more hope in it than James's *The Portrait of a Lady*. Like Eliot's Jewish novel, Ozick's novel dramatizes an attempt to revitalize "Anglo" culture (in this case New York) by means of ancient Jewish Kabbalah. As such it partakes of a larger cultural project that Ozick has embarked upon and that proposes to recover Jewish tradition by asserting the universality of Judaism as a world civilization.

The Puttermesser Papers, previously published in *The New Yorker, Salmagundi, Atlantic,* and the collection of stories *Levitation* (1982),[25] over roughly three decades, chronicles the life of its heroine, Ruth Puttermesser (who is exactly the same age as her creator, Cynthia Ozick)[26] from age thirty-four until her death by murder in her sixties. In her private life, Puttermesser, having "read all of Tolstoy and George Eliot" (Ozick 1997b, 14) tries to emulate George Eliot's life with George Henry Lewes, but, sadly, instead only finds Eliot's "second husband," Johnny Cross, in her lover, Rupert Rabeeno. Her career takes her from rather insignificant jobs "as token Jewish female" in a law firm and minor civil servant to its summit as mayor of New York. But then, inevitably, hubris provokes Puttermesser's political fall and her life ends in brutal rape and murder.

Ozick relates Puttermesser's futile efforts to relive Eliot's private life in the chapter "Puttermesser Paired." In "Puttermesser and Xanthippe," which deals with Puttermesser's Jewish—and Eliotian—penchant for (female) (over)achievement as mayor of New York, she tells the story of her protagonist's attempt to parallel the Kabbalah-based social-activist Zionism of Eliot's nation-building hero, Daniel Deronda. In addition to that, she carefully scatters hints at both Eliot's works and life throughout the entire novel. Thus, in a very ironic description of "Puttermesser vs. American beauty ideals" (from "Puttermesser: Her Work History, Her Ancestry, Her Afterlife") Ozick reveals that she not only resembles Eliot's dark misfit heroines, like Maggie Tulliver, but that her dark looks also favor Eliot's Jewish hero, Daniel Deronda, whose face also seems slightly oriental:

> Puttermesser had a Jewish face and a modicum of American distrust of it. She resembled no poster she had ever seen: she hated the Breck shampoo girl, so blond and bland and pale-mouthed. . . . Puttermesser's hair came in bouncing scallops—layered waves from scalp to tip, like imbricated roofing tile. It was nearly black and had a way of sometimes sticking straight out. Her nose had thick, well-haired, uneven nostrils, the right one noticeably wider than the other. Her eyes were small, the lashes short, invisible. She had the median Mongol lid—one of those Jewish faces with a vaguely Oriental cast. With all this, it was a fact she was not bad-looking. (4–5)

In her midthirties she finds herself in the predicament of many Eliot heroines: she has not found a man to marry. Fortunately, in the U.S. of the twentieth-century, female overachievers like George Eliot and her heroines have no trouble supporting themselves. And so Puttermesser works as a lawyer by day, and by night she tries to still her unquenchable thirst for knowledge[27] by reading scholarly books and studying Hebrew grammar in bed. Ozick's description of her heroine's approach to studying Hebrew recalls Eliot's ironic rendering of the convoluted windings of Casaubon's brain and his efforts to find the "Key to all Mythologies," for example, during his wedding trip to Rome and the Vatican: "The idea of the grammar of Hebrew turned Puttermesser's brain into a palace, a sort of Vatican; inside its corridors she walked from one resplendent triptych to another" (5).[28] In what might be an intended mockery of Eliot, Ozick even has Puttermesser's voracious reading habits destroy her love life. Her married lover, Morris Rappoport, leaves her because while in bed with him she prefers finishing Plato's *Theaetetus* to having sex.

Ozick presents Puttermesser's approach to the Judaic tradition as undoubtedly inspired by Eliot's tribute to Judaism in *Daniel Deronda*; Puttermesser refers to it as "Deronda's visionary Zion" (214) in the novel's final chapter, "Puttermesser in Paradise."[29] Ruth Puttermesser's family seems to have lost touch with the (religious) traditions of Judaism. At the beginning of the book she registers her Jewishness only when confronted with direct—sometimes discriminatory—reactions to her background or with her stereotypical "Jewish mother's" attitudes. But since "a Jew must own a past" (17), she wills herself back into Judaism by means of preserved textual memory much in the same way in which Daniel Deronda, who had been cut off from his Jewish roots, finds out about the tenets of the Jewish faith. She decides to take Hebrew lessons from an old uncle who represents the family's only connection to the old Jewish ways because "America is a blank, and Uncle Zindel is all her ancestry" (17):

> Poor Puttermesser has found herself in the wilderness without a past. . . . Her father is nearly a Yankee: his father gave up peddling to captain a dry-goods store in Providence, Rhode Island. In the summer he sold captain's hats, and wore one in all of his photographs. Of the world that was, there is only this single grain of memory: that once an old man, Puttermesser's mother's uncle, kept his pants up with a rope belt, was called Zindel, lived without a wife, ate frugally, knew the holy letters, died with thorny English a wilderness between his gums. To him Puttermesser clings. (17)

Twice a week, Puttermesser travels by bus to his shabby apartment in a Hispanic neighborhood so that he can teach her the Hebrew alphabet, "Mrs. Zayen pregnant in one direction, Mrs. Gimel in the other" (16). So far so good it seems, until the reader finds out (by means of a clever narrative comment which obfuscates the question of who invented the scenes with Uncle Zindel) that Puttermesser never knew her uncle in person:

> Stop. Stop, stop! Puttermesser's biographer, stop! Disengage, please. Though it is true that biographies are invented, not recorded, here you invent too much. A symbol is allowed, but not a whole scene: do not accommodate too obsequiously to Puttermesser's romance. Having not much imagination, she is literal with what she has. Uncle Zindel lies under the earth of Staten Island. Puttermesser has never had a conversation with him; he died four years before her birth. (16)

In her novel, Ozick investigates the same questions about racioreligious "authenticity" that Harriet Beecher Stowe already addressed in *Uncle Tom's Cabin* and *Dred,* and that George Eliot explored in *Daniel Deronda,* and she presents Puttermesser's Judaism as mainly "acquired" by means of intellect and imagination. Like her nineteenth-century predecessors, Ozick explores whether or not (a more or less "artificially acquired") faith can actually bring about spiritual and social reform. She finally puts this question to the test in the chapter "Puttermesser and Xanthippe," which shows how Puttermesser, with a little help from the Kabbalah and other Jewish texts, constructs a golem that will help her as mayor of New York to implement a "PLAN for the resuscitation, reformation, reinvigoration & redemption of the City of New York" (Ozick 1997, 67).

Bonnie Lyons, arguing that "the Great Tradition of Judaism, especially Hebrew and the sacred texts . . . is the real focus of the Jewish aspects of [Ozick's] work" (1998, 140), writes about "Puttermesser and Xanthippe" that it "is a Jewish text about texts, including Ozick's own earlier Puttermesser story. It is both a musing on and reconstitution of Jewish stories about golems found in "strange old texts," which supposedly Puttermesser had read so often that "she knew certain passages nearly verbatim" 144). While Lyons is certainly right about Ozick's use of the "Great Tradition of Judaism" in *The Puttermesser Papers*, it has to be added that in using this tradition, Ozick is heavily indebted to George Eliot's method of endowing her fiction with heavy doses of (religio-)philosophical background. Like Eliot, who had studied all the leading historical Kabbalah scholars prior to writing *Daniel Deronda*, Ozick uses "the noble Dr. Gershom Scholem's bountiful essay 'The Idea of the Golem,'" which Puttermesser virtually knows "by heart" (Ozick 1997, 48), to authenticate the kabbalistic Golem story in *The Puttermesser Papers*.[30] And in much the same way in which Eliot—at least according to Nurbhai and Newton—makes Daniel Mordecai's golem, who implements her plan of resuscitating the Jewish faith and building a Zionist state, Ozick makes Puttermesser's golem, Xanthippe, act out her plan for the restoration of civic order in New York. As shown in the previous chapter, Eliot presents Mordecai and Daniel's "marriage of souls" through metempsychosis as a building block towards a transcendental marriage of all human souls which, according to the Kabbalah, is the prerequisite for the reunification of the fragmented spiritual structure of mankind. Once Daniel's union with his spiritual teacher Mordecai is accomplished, Daniel moves to Palestine to help restore the unity of the Jewish nation, which is to precede the unity of mankind.

As Daniel faithfully executes Mordecai's spiritual estate, so Puttermesser's golem, Xanthippe, likewise, is supposed to act out Puttermesser's ambitious plan for New York. Here, Ozick again hints at the master texts informing the narrative of *The Puttermesser Papers*: Jewish religious historians report that Rabbi Judah Loew of Prague created a golem that "cleansed Prague of evil and infamy, of degeneracy and murder, of vice and perfidy" (46). And Puttermesser engages in daydreams about "[o]ld delicate Prague, swept and swept of sin, giving birth to the purified daylight, the lucent genius, of New York!" (64).[31] But Ozick also names George Eliot as a kindred spirit to and possible source of Puttermesser's sense of social order and justice. Puttermesser wants to put her in charge of "social services" along with other eminent, mostly nineteenth-century, writers endowed with "noble psyches and visionary hearts" (73).[32]

But, even though Ozick has Puttermesser pick out Eliot as patron saint of social services and even though Judah Loew's golem cleaned up Prague—at least for a while—Puttermesser's social program, the PLAN, is bound to fail because the figure of the golem, as particular representative of Kabbalah, usually stands for inevitable chaos following the temporary (social) order that he brings about.[33] Ozick's choice of an ultimately ineffective kabbalistic figure as her social agent suggests that she has a good measure of (post)modern ironical distance to the truth value of Kabbalah.[34] In *Daniel Deronda*, Eliot, having deliberately adopted a romantic fictional mode, focuses on the relationship of Mordecai and Daniel (who acts out Mordecai's wishes, as Xanthippe acts out Puttermesser's) as kabbalistic trope of the "marriage of true souls" and presents it as the positive organizing principle behind a Zionist society that has the potential to reform the world at large. Ozick, however, in "Puttermesser and Xanthippe," shows that the golem, as artificial human created by another human to implement a better social organization, is bound to fail miserably.[35]

Unlike the legendary creators of golems, Puttermesser fashions her golem, Xanthippe, unconsciously and inadvertently. It lies in her bed, having emerged from the clay pots and potting soil of her house plants; and it reflects her longing to have a daughter as well as her desire to get back at the city official who fired her from her job as First Bursary Officer. As Xanthippe puts it in writing, she was created "[s]o that my mother should become what she was intended to become" (65); and that is mayor of New York. In spite of her somewhat unusual creation, Xanthippe has all the characteristics of a golem and she displays all of the advantages and disadvantages, and then some, that accompany the making of an artificial human according to Jewish legend.[36] Like a historical golem, she cannot speak, but since she is an exceptional twentieth-century golem, she knows how to write. She mostly acts as a faithful servant, grows uncontrollably, and sports the Hebrew letters *aleph, mem* and *tav* (reading *emeth*, which means "truth") on her forehead. She also dies in the fashion of most historical golems: the golem becomes unmanageable, the letter aleph is removed, the inscription then spells the word *meth*, "dead," and the golem drops dead.

Xanthippe reflects the most common problem associated with human golem creation, namely that the golem, even though its creation is sanctioned by God, gets out of control and, after bringing about temporary order, causes some sort of havoc. Thus, Rabbi Loew's golem, which according to legend, was created "either to be his servant or to protect the Jews from pogroms," ran amok one Sabbath evening, "ripping up the Jewish ghetto of Prague" (Sherwin 1985, 21). The dilemma of the unruly golem is frequently mentioned in reference to various historical golems by Scholem in his essay and elaborated by Byron L. Sherwin in *The Golem Legend: Origins and Implications*. Sherwin gives a whole list of the drawbacks but also the chances inherent in golem creation:

> Creativity is a double-edge sword. . . . The creative endeavor is replete with dangers. That which we create to help insure our physical comfort or our physical security may ultimately threaten our physical comfort and/or our physical security. The creative act, by its nature, creates the potential for self-harm and for self-destruction. . . . A creature reflects back upon its creator. Human beings reflect back upon God. Golems reflect back upon human beings. Reflection upon the nature of the things we create can serve as a conduit to self-reflection, to self-understanding. . . . Adam was the first Golem. Adam is a Golem who became human. Is the converse also possible: can a human become a Golem? (1985, 24–25)

In "Puttermesser and Xanthippe," Ozick addresses all of the difficulties that accompany the use of golems. Xanthippe grows uncontrollably and evades Puttermesser's authority by developing an insatiable sexuality that is entirely foreign to a historical golem.[37] Moreover, she takes over her creator's job and assumes control over her. Puttermesser finally "sees that she is the golem's golem" (Ozick 1997, 79). By associating Puttermesser's downfall with Xanthippe's unbridled sex drive, Ozick seems to want to draw attention to the fact that when it comes to politics—at least in the twentieth century and beyond—the spirit cannot cohabit with the flesh in a peaceful manner and that any kind of possible political/social achievement must necessarily be ruined by the interference of sexuality. While Ruth Puttermesser controls her own sexual desire to the point of denying it (as in the bed scene with Morris Rappoport), Xanthippe, as her double,[38] acts out hers in a voracious manner that matches her ever growing size. Ultimately, Xanthippe's insatiable sexuality, having gone completely haywire, "infects" all the public officials that she comes in contact with as Puttermesser's campaign manager. The men, spent with lust for the golem, become unable to do their jobs, and New York finally reverts to its previous unreformed and unredeemed state.

This course of events points up an important difference between Eliot's and Ozick's presentation of the social potential of Kabbalah; both authors deal very differently with the interaction of the spirit and the flesh. In *Daniel Deronda*, Eliot, drawing on the insights of Feuerbach and Renan, very subtly shows that in the relationship of Mordecai and Daniel (albeit sublimated) fleshly desire enables the spiritual and that a communal ideal can flourish as an extension of individual relationships that are both spiritual and carnal. Unlike Eliot, who adheres to a rather nineteenth-century (sometimes even eighteenth-century) romanticized view about the possibility of social community (see chapter 1), Ozick, firmly situated in the twentieth century, obviously does not present kabbalistic and Zionist ideals as a solution to social ills or as an alternative to gentile (social) politics. One might, nevertheless, wonder about the "ethno-religious" intention behind her story about the golem and what it implies about her view of the spiritual status of traditional Judaism. Ozick has always claimed the recovery of Jewish tradition as one of her tasks as a novelist since she always intended to be a specifically Jewish writer, as Esther Frank observes:

> In her well known essay "Towards a New Yiddish," first published in 1970, she clarifies her views on how to embrace Judaism and how to establish a new literature that would be centrally Jewish. . . . Ozick's interests at that time were to create new basis [*sic*] for an American Jewish Literature to be written in English. She characterized her claims as a call for liturgical literature impregnated with the values of Judaism. What would make Jewish fiction distinctive and enduring would be the incorporation of Jewish religious and historic matter. (Frank 1999, online)

But, as Ozick said in a recent interview, this does not turn her into a spokesperson for other Jews; she in fact refuses to be a representative of contemporary Jewish identity:

> [N]o writer of stories should be expected to be a moral champion or a representative of "identity." That way lies tract and sermon and polemic. When a thesis or a framework—any kind of prescriptiveness or tendentiousness—is imposed on the writing of fiction, imagination flies out the door, and with it the freedom and volatility and irresponsibility that imagination both confers and demands. I have never set out to be anything other than a writer of stories. It disturbs me when, as sometimes happens, I am mistaken for a champion of identity in the currently fashionable multicultural sense, with its emphasis on ethnic collectivities. (Interview with Cynthia Ozick by Diane Osen, no date, online)

Ozick here emphatically denies a collective ethnic and/or didactic aim behind her presentation of Jewishness. While Eliot still explores the possibility that there might be a racial essence to Jewishness, Ozick—in line with twentieth-/twenty-first century approaches towards ethnicity—views what is unique about Jewishness as culturally constructed. Thus, when asked in an interview why she embraces the designation "Jewish writer" while disowning the label "woman writer," she indicated that she does not view

"Jewish" as biological category (whereas she regards "woman" as such): "People often ask how I can reject the phrase 'woman writer' and not reject the phrase 'Jewish writer'—a preposterous question. 'Jewish' is a category of civilization, culture, and intellect, and 'woman' is a category of anatomy and physiology" (Interview with Cynthia Ozick by Katie Bolick, 1997a, online).

Ozick's project of Jewish cultural recovery apparently eschews any preachiness or didacticism, but it still aims at the preservation "of Jewish religious and historical matter" within a specifically Jewish literature. The realization of this aim, however, seems almost impossible within the framework of a (post)modern text like "Puttermesser and Xanthippe" which in the process of deconstructing the legendary Jewish golem also appears to self-deconstruct. Unlike Eliot, Ozick, ultimately, is not able to locate a racial—or spiritual—potential for regeneration inherent in Judaism. This inability to design a revitalizing alternative cultural narrative, finally, aligns her position about the (im)possibility of revitalizing a dominant culture by a counter-culture with the cultural pessimism that Henry James shows in *The Portrait of a Lady*.

George Eliot—A "Classic" for the Twenty-First Century?

As the example of Ozick already shows, like their nineteenth-century predecessors, late twentieth-century writers have also turned to the novels of George Eliot for inspiration. With the exception of "Puttermesser and Xanthippe," which reworks Eliot's cultural criticism, the "rewrites" by twentieth-century writers Susan Cheever, Gail Godwin, and John Irving—and again Cynthia Ozick with "Puttermesser Paired" ([1990], 1997)[39]—center on Eliot's romance plots. Godwin's and Ozick's plots, while also pointing up cultural similarities between "the genteel South" (Godwin), a "Jewish culture of female overachievement" (Ozick), and Eliot's own intellectual and cultural penchants, focus on Eliot's personal romance with her partner, George Henry Lewes.

George Eliot's "classics" continue to fascinate modern writers even at a time when the notion of the timelessness of the classic has come under attack. Jane Tompkins, for example, has contested the idea that classics "speak to people in all times and places" (1985, 36) by calling attention to the fact that the supposedly universal ideas incorporated in each classic derive their "timelessness" from the circumstance that they are preserved by various cultural interest groups.[40] Yet Eliot's novels apparently still speak to contemporary American writers, who do, of course, know that their female protagonists are a continent and at least a hundred years removed from hers. Therefore, the fact that Susan Cheever's, Gail Godwin's, and Cynthia Ozick's protagonists face some of the same gender-related problems as George Eliot's do is a bit surprising—if not downright depressing.

While still embracing Eliot's ideal of "everlasting love" (within a "marriage of true souls") along with her caveat against patriarchal cultural scripts, the modern authors attempt, with varying success, to "write beyond the ending" of the traditional female plots presented in her fiction: marriage, death, and quest for *Bildung*. They do this by modifying the plot itself—and to some extent also its narrative presentation—as outlined by Rachel Blau DuPlessis:

> In the work of twentieth-century women, the marriage plot, with its high status in novels, and the quest plot of punishment for female aspiration were displaced, eroded, or removed from the center of the novel. This project I have called writing beyond the ending, taking ending as a metaphor for conventional narrative, for a regimen of resolutions, and for the social, sexual, and ideological affirmations these make. (1985, 21)

The modification of conventional narrative along with conventional content is important for DuPlessis because in the twentieth century "a new and unconventional view of woman" called for an adaptation of "essentially conservative narrative conventions" (Greene 1991, 169).[41] The realistic text, George Eliot's preferred mode of writing, is often viewed by poststructural criticism as a form of "ideological closure," which reproduces "a single and uniform ideological position of a set of hierarchised discourses of which one is always a controlling 'truth-voice'" (Boumelha 1987, 19). Therefore, by naturalizing meaning, realistic texts purportedly delay change.

The twentieth-century writers discussed here all "wrote beyond" Eliot's endings by changing her plots to indicate the social change that has taken place since the nineteenth century; to some extent they also tried to modify Eliot's narrative form, but as they all are committed realists, their experimentation with narrative form remains rather limited. Since it makes sense to group together the two pieces that deal with Eliot's personal life, Gail Godwin's *The Odd Woman* (1974) and Cynthia Ozick's "Puttermesser Paired" (1997), I will begin my discussion of twentieth-century adaptations of Eliot's romance plot with Susan Cheever's *Looking for Work* (1979), even though the book was published five years after Godwin's novel. Salley Gardens, the protagonist of Susan Cheever's novel, is something like an updated American version of Rosamond Vincy (with a tad of Dorothea Brooke—minus the character's altruism) for the late sixties and early seventies. In a departure from the typical narrative perspective of George Eliot's fiction, but not its customary realism, Susan Cheever lets her heroine tell her own story, thus forgoing the hegemonic narrative control that an omniscient narrator, who in Eliot's novels often appears to be male, has over the character s/he describes. But even this first person perspective—as Eliot's third person perspective often does—makes the protagonist reveal herself as rather shallow and vapid, but, nevertheless, professionally ambitious.

As the daughter of a renowned college professor, Salley decides to look for a job in journalism despite her "gentlewoman's C- average" (1979, 11) in her college work and also despite the female Dean of Women's age-old question "'What does a girl like you want a job for? . . . All our *best* girls are engaged'" (31). After a short stint as a student activist registering black voters in Alabama, and a reporter for a small town paper in far away Wyoming, Salley decides to "do the right thing." She marries Jason Gardens, a somewhat older fellow journalist, and follows him to San Francisco, where he has found a job as the editor of an already floundering magazine.

From the beginning, Salley, heiress to Gwendolen Harleth's and Lily Bart's penchant for "finery," feels displaced in California because she does not fit the scenery due to her Eastern social and sartorial aspirations: "Sometimes I think if you aren't wearing the California Girl uniform—faded jeans and a T-shirt, clogs and long straight hair—you don't really exist. . . . I'd flee, wandering through the strange bright streets in my neat little Banlon dresses with my matching high-heeled sandals and handbag" (53). She also becomes bored because she does not have anything to do and fails to find a job because she does not know how to and is not overly qualified to boot. Thus, she simply attempts to charm her possible employers with her social accomplishments but does not succeed. Moreover, having decided not to invest her life in men as her mother-in-law had done before her, she feels limited by her husband's demands: "'Giving dinner parties for Jason's piggy colleagues violates my autonomy. Following Jason wherever his professional ambitions take him violates my autonomy'" (53). However, in spite of having become infatuated with the Italian painter Max Angelo, who wins her heart at a party by making the sensitive comment, "'I know it's very hard for a woman here'" (64), she follows her husband, Jason, back to the East Coast where, with the help of the "good old boy network," he finds a job in no time at all.

Back in Cambridge, George Eliot comes into the picture when Salley—for no immediately discernable reason—compares her husband, Jason, to Casaubon, the epitome of all bad husbands, after she has found a copy of *Middlemarch* in a rental apartment:[42]

> In the kitchen cupboard, next to a moldy jar of brown rice, I found a dog-eared student's copy of George Eliot's *Middlemarch*. All day long I read it, huddled in the bathroom, my ears stopped with pink plastic plugs against the noise from the vacant lot. All day long I dreamed its romantic dreams. Was Ladislaw coming to save me? At seven o'clock Jason/Casaubon would come back to the stifling apartment, old and stony and cold. (69)

Reading Eliot's novel does not immediately activate Salley's gender politics since indeed a creative, sensitive Ladislaw-stand-in in a black velvet suit (if not on a black steed) comes to her rescue. It is, of course, the painter Max, who now completely conquers her heart by making the simple observation, "' hear you're still looking for work'" (75). They become lovers, but Salley, politicized by her reading of both Wharton's *The House of Mirth* and the *Village Voice,* soon comes to realize that her dependence on men is no longer politically correct: "In the *Village Voice* I read a story about how marriage is really just a form of prostitution. . . . I think that maybe I stay with Jason since he supports me. I remember that when I first met him, how impressed I was by the fact that he had his own trust fund" (103). Salley, in a way, also realizes that she is like Eliot's and Wharton's "ornamental" leisure-class ladies because due to her social conditioning she cannot really give up her social perks for either feminism or a vocation:

> [t]here's a whole generation of women . . . not feminists exactly, but feminists in a way. Women who want to stay inside that golden circle society describes, who want to love men, and have pretty dresses and learn to cook and bear children in peace, but who can't help being a little different. And that makes them want to change things. (162)

Thus, love, social aspirations and feminist ideas about female autonomy contend for Salley's attention. Eventually, her persistent "looking for work" pays off. As a result of successful professional networking with her own and Jason's college friends, regardless of her poor journalistic credentials, she is commissioned to write a story for the *Village Voice* on "Being Single." But this work interferes with her relationship with Max Angelo, who finally, even though he is still in love with Salley, marries his "other girlfriend" since Salley refuses to join him in California. Salley misses his companionship, but pats herself on the shoulder and rejoices, "The *Voice* even paid me, after all. Strong Salley" (166). The novel ends with a continuation of her professional fairy-tale; she receives a phone call from somebody at *Newsweek* and eventually even becomes the successful editor of the magazine's society pages.

With *Looking for Work*, Cheever succeeds in writing beyond the ending of *Middlemarch* and other George Eliot novels by presenting a late twentieth-century heroine who gets divorced rather than married, achieves her goal of "looking for work," and also does not die. But Cheever's book, nevertheless, leaves a strange and unsatisfying taste since, compared with Eliot's female protagonists, neither Salley's life story nor her personality seem particularly interesting. Except for reporting a few unfavorable comments about women who are looking for work, Cheever does not give a real depiction of the social constraints that make this activity so difficult for her protagonist. In spite of being compared to Casaubon, Salley's husband, Jason, is nothing like Eliot's patriarchal villain. Jason neither encourages nor discourages Salley's job search, nor does he pursue an "important" scientific project to which his wife could apprentice herself. Salley herself is not particularly endearing, either, since she presents a curious twentieth-century mix of the nineteenth-century social climber (of the ilk of Rosamond Vincy or Lily Bart) and Eliot's vocation-seeking heroines, Dorothea Brook and Maggie Tulliver. Her upper-class ennui as well as her supposedly emancipatory promiscuity seem rather vapid in comparison with the toils of her fictional forebears, and her successful job search is diminished by the fact that, by becoming an editor of *Newsweek's* lifestyle section she does not transcend her shallow social ambition.[43] She does, however, transcend the limits of both Eliot's marriage and quest plot in that she remains single and accomplishes her goal of "looking for work."

The protagonist of Gail Godwin's also firmly realistic novel *The Odd Woman* (1974), an exact contemporary of Cheever's heroine, has already solved the problem of "looking for work" at the outset of the novel. Jane Clifford, assistant professor at a Midwestern state school, has found not only work but actually a vocation. Having been brought up in a traditional society by a genteel Southern grandmother, Jane, as a college professor and literary woman of sorts, reads her own life as an unmarried woman in the mid-to-late-twentieth century against both George Eliot's life story (which culminated in a happy "marriage" with Lewes) and the plot of her Aunt Cleva's nineteenth-century-type very early twentieth-century romance (which ends in the heroine's death since her unfortunate great aunt was seduced by a villain and died shortly after giving birth to an illegitimate child).

From childhood, where she briefly went to a "finishing school" (of the sort to be found in George Eliot or Charlotte Brontë) that taught "Diction and the deadly Poise" (1974, 137), to graduate school, where she started living "more in the nineteenth century than in her own" (35), she sees herself as a historical rather than modern female protagonist. While writing her dissertation on "The Theme of Guilt in George Eliot" (213), "Her topic absorbed her. It suited her perfectly. The woman Marian Evans gave her courage. She had not found her love till she was thirty-five, nor her life's work till she was thirty-seven" (214).

In addition to becoming intrigued by Eliot's novels beyond what seems to be professional interest, Jane, being an "odd" (read unmarried) woman in her own society, also becomes absorbed in the fates of George Gissing's "odd women" heroines—from the 1890 novel *The Odd Women*. Since to her the lives of Gissing's heroines seem to suggest possible blueprints for her own life, in spite of the difference in historical time, she meticulously records their "ends":

> *Monica Madden* . . . COMPROMISE-REBELLION AGAINST ONE'S OWN COMPROMISE-DEATH . . . *Virginia Madden* . . . ESCAPE THROUGH DRINK-PARTIAL REHABILITATION TO "A USEFUL MEMBER OF SOCIETY". . . *Alice Madden* . . . STARTING ALL OVER IN A CHILD . . . *Mary Barfoot* . . . FINDING FULFILLMENT THROUGH OTHERS . . . *Rhoda Nunn* . . . SUBLIMATION OF PERSONAL DESIRES AND FURIES INTO A "CAUSE." (293)[44]

As antidote against these disagreeable late nineteenth-century fates, which deny romantic and sexual fulfillment to the "odd," unmarried women, she imagines a "perfect idyllic relationship" (279) with her lover, Gabriel, a married art professor, who lives "in the next state over" (5). During a conversation with her mother, Jane, fortified by her relationship with Gabriel, states that against all odds she is collecting evidence of the possibility of everlasting love between men and women. Not very surprisingly, considering her literary penchants, she does find proof in the personal life of George Eliot:

> Look at George Eliot and George Henry Lewes. *They* completed each other. They were passionate, but neither of them exploited the other. They met in the middle of their lives when both were on their way to being disappointed people, and they gave each other back the birthrights of their best selves. . . . She was afraid to write fiction before he told her she could. They were outrageously happy, and they were all to each other for twenty-five years." (167–68)

Jane's mother, more firmly ensconced in the twentieth-century, plainly tells her that she is trying to live in some idealized, inaccessible past, "'Can anyone *living* look me in the eye and tell me they have lived with a man for twenty-five years and been *outrageously happy*? You're living in myths, Jane, to expect such things!'" (168–69).

When she thinks about the fact that Lewes had left his wife when he went to Germany with Eliot, whereas Gabriel just proposes "nine months of secrecy in London" (245) during a Guggenheim fellowship that he might win, Jane herself reluctantly realizes that her relationship with Gabriel is far from the perfect one that Eliot had with Lewes. Moreover, Gabriel's project of interpreting the "entire art collection of the Western world as expressions and manifestations of various kinds of love, which he has enumerated, with true Procrustean economy, as being six in number" (256), unfortunately, in "a moment of horror," reminds her of "George Eliot's Mr. Casaubon and his worthless lifetime project, The Key to All Mythologies" (261).

Twentieth-century reality with its increasing disbelief in any certainties invades Jane's thoughts at several points in the novel, for example, when she wonders about Northrop Frye's perfect system for categorizing literature, or when she asks herself if the art historian Panofsky in talking about "*essential tendencies of the human mind . . . wasn't limiting things, too*" (258). But she carefully avoids letting such thoughts gain precedence until she reads an interview with "a new, revolutionary psychiatrist" (268) who claims that "'*all of life is a fight, a competition, a ceaseless and disastrous attempt to make permanent what is so obviously only a process, a flow, an event*" (269). The interviewer's disbelieving question, "'[A]re you saying that there is no ego? . . . That there is only "a process, a flow, an event," where we have always thought the ego was'" (269) is also Jane's. She balks at the thought that there is no essential core self and immediately shields herself with "experience" to the contrary gleaned from nineteenth-century novels:

> And Jane thought of all her friends and family and even her favorite characters in novels, which were also friends and family; she thought of their painful strivings, their absolute certainty that they were who they were: "Dorothea," or "Isabel" or "Jude," or "Ivan," working so hard to make sense of that "entity," with all its disharmonies and conversations and conflicts and love affairs and failures and ultimate death, perhaps not thinking once during the course of their whole life that the "entity" was only a process. (271)

Yet in light of my discussion in the previous chapters, it becomes clear that the psychiatrist quoted by Jane Clifford is not particularly revolutionary and that Godwin has her "romantic heroine" Jane misread what nineteenth-century authors like George Eliot or Henry James actually say about the ego. While James's Isabel might believe in the ego as "entity," like Godwin's Jane, his Madame Merle does not seem to be particularly bothered by the view of the self as "only a process"; and while Eliot's Dorothea and perhaps even

Daniel Deronda also think of the self as "entity," the philosophical meditation on personal as well as cultural identity that Eliot incorporated in *Daniel Deronda*, along with her refraction of narrative perspective, suggests that Eliot herself took a much less monolithic view of the self.

Gayle Greene concedes that Godwin presents Jane and her mother as people who can live in neither the present nor in the past because they have "both fallen 'in the interstices of the *Zeitgeists*'" (1991, 176), but criticizes Godwin for not breaking out of the novelistic form of the nineteenth-century. In Greene's view, Godwin, like her protagonist, does not "[follow] through on [her incipient] analysis of the ideology of forms" (177). Therefore, she strongly voices her disappointment with Godwin's failure to write beyond the formal ending of the nineteenth-century novel:

> [H]aving so skillfully suggested [a] sense of uncertainty and flux, Godwin's narrative rigidifies to so sure and fixed a form. . . . [T]he sequence of events leading to the end of the affair [with Gabriel] moves her inexorably from the possible to the probable to the necessary, according to the Aristotelian principles that Godwin has described as "a good plot." (180)

Greene's dissatisfaction with Godwin's refusal to transcend the realistic fictional mode might be understandable, but I would like to point out that Greene herself (and also Rachel Blau DuPlessis) misreads George Eliot's fictional effort when she views her as a diehard realist, who controls her discourses by congealing them into one fixed meaning to be assigned to a certain story.[45] As previously discussed, George Eliot does not qualify as an author who writes exclusively in the realistic mode. Thus, her final novel, *Daniel Deronda*, gestures back to "American" romantic indirection, but also points forward towards modernism in both its formal and thematic open-endedness. It is precisely the experiment with form, the masterful indirection and refraction of perspective, that makes it impossible to tell what exactly brings about Daniel's identification with Judaism. The novel's thematic open-endedness, moreover, sees to it that Gwendolen does not find closure; she is one of the two or three George Eliot heroines that do not get married or die.

At any rate, the encounter that Godwin's protagonist has with "modern" psychology ruins her "perfect idyllic relationship" with her lover and forces her to face reality. Having read the interview, Jane decides to confront him with her view of both "the ego" and "eternal love" and asks him, "'Can two selves . . . after they have cleaned themselves up, got their 'egos' in hand, can they then have a permanent love relationship?'" (1974, 277). He replies immediately by giving her an unreflected version of the psychologist's wisdom,

"'A relationship by its very nature, is transient, because it is made between people, and people change'" (277). This answer, which indicates to Jane that Gabriel is not inclined to think about their relationship as permanent, motivates Jane's decision to end it.⁴⁶ At the end of the novel, Jane is not left with much besides her belief in eternal love. Her relationship with Gabriel is over by her own choice; she has had a falling out with her best friend Gerda, an ardent feminist whom she turned to immediately after leaving New York and Gabriel; and even the (still living) old man, who supposedly ruined her Aunt Cleva and whom she has located in New York, seems to have turned out to be the wrong villain. Thus, both standard nineteenth-century "women's ends" (Eliot's and Cleva's) have failed in Jane's reenactment of them. But, if she wants to, Jane can still comfort herself by means of "sublimation of personal desires," like Gissing's heroines; and she can also identify with at least one George Eliot heroine—like Gwendolen Harleth she has one choice left that really is not one: to go on with her life.⁴⁷

George Eliot's life and ideal of marriage also inform the gender relationships of two pieces of fiction published in the 1990s; while John Irving's⁴⁸ *A Widow for One Year* (1998) seems to express the wish that George Eliot's ideal of "everlasting love" should still be valid, Cynthia Ozick's "Puttermesser Paired" (1997) suggests that it might not be. Critics have often called attention to the fact that John Irving, who claims Dickens as his favorite writer (see Pritchard 1998, online), is indebted to the form of the nineteenth-century novel to tell his very modern, very violent stories, which relate tales of terrorism, horrible accidents, bizarre sexual encounters, and bloody abortions.⁴⁹ As Michiko Kakutani observes, *A Widow for One Year* is "a sprawling 19th-century production, chock full of bizarre coincidences, multiple plot lines, lengthy digressions and stories within stories" (1998, online). Yet Irving's use of the traditional form feels experimental because of the incongruity between it and his bizarre, often absurd, subject matter. Thus, since in all of his novels "he writ[es] about—without feeling he can really change—the universal wrongness of life" (Harter and Thompson 1986, 16), his fictional endeavor sometimes seems like a quixotical type of "writing beyond the ending" by having the "wholesome form" clash with its "unwholesome content."

A Widow for One Year tells (most of) the life stories of Eddie O'Hare and Ruth Cole. Both characters are novelists; their choice of writing as a profession is possibly occasioned by a mutual need to try to explain the unsettling events that happened over the summer during which their lives became strangely entangled. Eddie is sixteen when he is hired by Ruth's father as driver, literary assistant, diversion for his wife, and babysitter for four-year-old Ruth. When he joins the family, Ted Cole and his wife, Marion, are in the process of splitting up due to insurmountable marital difficulties, mostly resulting from the tragic deaths of their teenage sons in a car accident. Ruth, who was conceived as "replacement," cannot keep her parents' perennially shaky marriage together (her father is a notorious philanderer and heavy drinker, while her mother has emotionally closed herself off after the death of her sons). One day, while Eddie is still around, Marion decides to leave her husband and daughter—mainly for fear of losing her daughter Ruth, whom she has also come to love against her resolution not to do so. Before she leaves, Marion, who is thirty-nine at the time, has an affair with Eddie, who reminds her of both her sons. Eddie, deeply affected by this first love, cannot get her off his mind for the thirty-seven years that it takes until they meet again. In the meantime, he authors five novels about love affairs between older women and younger men. In spite of Eddie's deep attachment to Marion, it is Ruth, the female protagonist, who (having grown up in a house where there were only vacant picture hooks left to remind her of her dead brothers and lost mother) introduces George Eliot's ideal of "eternal love" to the novel. She tells Scott Saunders (a man who will later abuse her and resurface in one of her novels as "the bad boyfriend" of its title), about a statement George Eliot made about undying love: "'How does that passage from George Eliot go? . . . I once liked it so much I wrote it down,' Ruth told him. 'What greater thing is there for two human souls, than to feel that they are joined for life'" (1998, 322). Scott's reaction, however, immediately suggests that he is not the right man for Ruth: "'Did he stay married?' Scott asked her. 'Who?' Ruth said. 'George Eliot. Did he stay married?'" (322).

Like all of the other female protagonists in Irving's novel, Ruth has completely transcended the nineteenth-century *Bildungs* plot by being meaningfully employed; her vocation as a writer does not interfere in any way with her love relationships.[50] Yet having always longed for permanence in her life, she decides to get married to her literary agent, Allan Albright. She asks Eddie about the origin of the Eliot passage because she wants to have it read at her wedding; Eddie, having consulted his father Minty (an English teacher), reports that the passage is from *Adam Bede*. Her best friend Hannah reads it, even though she is personally unenthusiastic about marriage:

> At Ruth's wedding, Hannah read from George Eliot with a lack of conviction, but the words themselves were alive for Ruth. "What greater thing is there for two human souls, than to feel that they are joined for life—to strengthen each other in all labor, to rest on each other in all sorrow, to minister to each other in all pain, to be one with each other in silent unspeakable memories at the moment of the last parting?" (444)

It looks as if at this point Ruth has indeed succumbed to the more pleasurable nineteenth-century "female end"—marriage—but since *A Widow for One Year* is a typical John Irving novel, Ruth has to give it another try before she will achieve permanent happiness. Allan Albright dies unexpectedly of a heart attack, but after a few more plot convolutions Ruth Cole does find wedded bliss with retired police sergeant Harry Hoekstra of Amsterdam.

And, as the novel advances, Eddie O'Hare, who "wasn't a George Eliot fan" (323), also turns to Eliot for advice on gender relations. But he selects for himself and his relationship with Marion, Ruth's mother, a more pessimistic passage from *Middlemarch*, in which Casaubon reflects on his relationship with Dorothea:

> There then came the last sentence of Chapter 44 of *Middlemarch*, which the old schoolteacher had underlined in red, and which his son read aloud in a gloomy voice. Eddie was thinking that George Eliot's sentence might apply to his feelings for Marion or Ruth—not to mention their imagined feelings for *him*. "He distrusted her affection; and what loneliness is more lonely than distrust?" (523)

Yet, in spite of his pessimism, and against all odds, Eddie also recovers his soulmate in a typical, improbable John Irving happy ending. When Marion reappears unexpectedly after thirty-seven years, Eddie and Marion resume their relationship almost as if nothing had happened, thus apparently affirming the validity of Eliot's concept of "the marriage of true souls." The novel's "conventional ending" indeed seems to endorse the nineteenth-century marriage plot. But as stated above, the incongruity between the multiple happy endings and the novel's grotesque descriptions of incestuous longings, of a dead son's body with a severed leg, and of the murder of a prostitute—along with the rather tasteful description of fifty-three-year-old Eddie having sex with seventy-six-year-old Marion—throw a strange light on Irving's adaptation of the romance plot. Irving's adherence to it thus seems quite incongruous and untimely, but the fact that he relies on the marriage/romance plot in almost every novel, nevertheless, suggests that it still holds a strong, perhaps nostalgic, fascination for him and his characters.

In light of so much veneration for George Eliot and her romance plot, it is almost refreshing that Cynthia Ozick—who once, in all seriousness, tried to write a Henry Jamesian novel[51]—reserves for herself the privilege of "killing" the common literary foremother, albeit with a good measure of nostalgia, too. With "Puttermesser Paired," she deconstructs the notion that original art can or should be reenacted and she ridicules the idea that another person's life can be used as a model for one's own. Moreover, within the framework of the predominantly realistic form of *The Puttermesser Papers* (employing a similar strategy as Irving by "marrying" the traditional form to bizarre content), she ironizes the two customary nineteenth-century female endings—marriage and death—by rendering them completely grotesque.

In the "Puttermesser Paired" section of the book, Puttermesser has taken "a year off to live on her savings and think through her fate" (1997b, 105). It occurs to her, "[a]t the unsatisfying age of fifty-plus, . . . that what she ought to do was marry" (105). One day, while studying personal ads in the newspaper and considering the fates of unhappily married nineteenth-century heroines (Isabel Archer, Gwendolen Harleth, Anna Karenina, and Dorothea Brooke), she is roused from her thoughts by a pizza delivery boy, who has rung the wrong doorbell. Puttermesser delivers the pizza to the right apartment; there is a party going on, and, to her great amazement, in the process of daydreaming about spending an afternoon with George Eliot at the Priory instead of attending a noisy party in New York, she suddenly sees a man who looks exactly like George Henry Lewes. This comes in particularly handy since she is reading "her third or fourth, or perhaps fifth or sixth, George Eliot biography" (112). The next day, after having contemplated passages from George Eliot's letters that deal with Eliot's relationship with Lewes, Puttermesser goes to the Metropolitan museum. There she sees the Lewes-lookalike, copying a picture entitled "The Death of Socrates." When she accuses him of copying, of failing to make up anything new "that never existed before" (126), he replies, "'Whatever I do is happening for the first time. Anything I make was never made before'" (127). She becomes intrigued by Rupert Rabeeno, the copyist, because "[s]he understood that she had happened on an original. A mimic with a philosophy! A philosophy that denied mimicry!" (127). Soon she gushes that she has "Found! George Henry Lewes, George Henry Lewes in New York! He had a kind of thesis, a life's argument" (127).

Puttermesser and Rupert Rabeeno soon take to each other and read to each other from *Middlemarch* and George Eliot's letters. Puttermesser remains slightly worried about his profession as a copyist—she has found out that he copies original art and that his copies are then photographed to be sold as postcards of the originals—but rationalizes her doubts away by telling herself that they have a common goal: "Wasn't her dream of having George Lewes again—a simulacrum of George Lewes—exactly the same as Rupert Rabeeno's wanting to make things happen again? Wasn't she, all on her own, a mistress of reënactment?" (132). Puttermesser and Rupert thus proceed to reenact the relationship of "the two Georges" (139), and she is absolutely elated when Rupert finally suggests that they get married.[52]

Convinced that she has found her version of George Henry Lewes, she overlooks several facts that foreshadow an unexpected fate: 1) Rupert is an expert copyist, 2) George Eliot's only marriage was to Johnny Cross, a man who was twenty years younger and who had lost his mother, 3) Cross and Eliot rather than Lewes and Eliot developed their romantic relationship by reading passages from Dante to each other, 4) Rupert in spite of being "well into the thirties" (124) is at least fifteen years younger than she is, and his mother died when he was a boy, and 5) he did not propose marriage to her until they had stopped reading the Lewes scenes and had moved on to the ones with Johnny Cross. When Rupert starts to focus on Cross rather than Lewes in his reenactment of George Eliot's love life, Puttermesser is not particularly happy about his thesis that Cross was not really in love with George Eliot. According to Rupert, Cross tried to transform himself into George Henry Lewes "[i]n another packet of flesh" (144) because he was infatuated with him rather than George Eliot. Puttermesser still plays along with his story even though she intuits that he is making Cross into a version of himself: "'You're making him into Johnny Cross, Reënactments. . . . You're making him into a copyist!'" (145).

Blinded by taking her own superior cleverness for granted, Puttermesser also fails to guess what is behind his reenactment of what happened during the honeymoon night when Johnny Cross (whom Eliot had married roughly a year after Lewes's death) threw himself into the Grand Canal in Venice. But she tells him to get his story over with quickly: "'You don't have to milk it'" (148). And thus Rupert tells about "the honeymoon's secret shock" from his perspective, turning the venerable George Eliot into a geriatric succubus and Johnny Cross into a helpless animal about to be killed:

> "Johnny dear," she said. He did not answer. She was alarmed and faintly shamed: she removed her foot from his calf, and put her hand to the thigh of the other leg. It was cold, cold. Despite the trail of wind, the night was warm. It was growing warmer and warmer. The grooves flowing from her nose to the corners of her mouth, an old woman's creases, ran with sudden sweat; her armpits were sweated. She was not doing what he wished. She was too immodest, there was some muted direction he intended which she could not interpret. . . . He turned to her then, and showed her his eyes. They were unrecognizable—the rims of the lids as raw and bloody as meat, stretched apart like an animal's freshly slaughtered throat. Only the whites were there—the eyeballs had rolled off under the skin. . . . They were entombed in a furnace. . . . A tremendous swipe—the scream of a huge bullwhip or instant cyclone—cut through naked space. A projectile of some kind—she had seen the smudge of it fly past her own back. . . . The projectile was Johnny. (153–54)[53]

Puttermesser should be warned, but even at this point, in spite of being highly intelligent, highly educated, and very much like the learned George Eliot, she still does not guess that she has become engaged to Johnny Cross rather than George Henry Lewes. Moreover, she does not fathom that she herself is the inferior copyist, whereas Rupert is the master reenactor who produces reenactments of "real things" with a difference of his own, as he has explained. Puttermesser and Rabeeno do get married in a paltry mock version of the traditional Jewish wedding;[54] afterwards they return to Puttermesser's apartment. Rupert announces that he cannot stay and opens the window, but instead of jumping, he simply turns around and leaves: "Puttermesser squinted into the snow. It was pointless to call down to him as George Eliot had called down into the Grand Canal, but anyhow she called and called; the snow blew into her mouth. She leaned into the wetness until her hair was all white with snow. A copyist, a copyist!" (165).

While Puttermesser, like some other twentieth-century literary people, might assume that nineteenth-century plots still apply, Ozick, by means of this ingenious ending, sends out a word of warning to all of those who think that they can naively reenact "the real George Eliot," either in writing or by emulating her personal life. If reenactments of venerable models are to make any sense at all, she seems to say, they have to be artful and original and they might even have to break the original mold. Puttermesser, perhaps like the young Cynthia Ozick who tried to imitate Henry James, has failed to copy George Eliot's life and plots. Yet Rupert Rabeeno, the supposed copyist, has made something that nobody made before: by humiliating Puttermesser in a similar but not exactly the same way in which George Eliot was (presumably inadvertently) humiliated by Johnny Cross, he has created an original reenactment. Thus, very obviously, her marriage is exposed as a farce in "Puttermesser Paired." And in the final section of *The Puttermesser Papers*, "Puttermesser in Paradise," her death, which could be viewed as the typical nineteenth-century death of the rebellious misfit heroine, is described in such a drastic and grotesque manner that it immediately becomes clear that Puttermesser can in no way properly emulate the nineteenth-century heroine—not even in death. Her New York-style rape and subsequent murder by a burglar (who surprises her while she is thinking about Thomas Mann, *Middlemarch*, *Daniel Deronda*, John Updike, and Joyce Carol Oates) are rendered in a thoroughly (post)modern fashion that does not spare the readers any vomit, gore, and seminal fluid. Even Puttermesser's ascent into paradise is a total letdown. While Eliot's Maggie, for example, transcends earthly worries by being reunited in death with the brother whom she had lost in life, "Puttermesser in Paradise" is exposed to endless ambiguity and loss. She is given the things that she longed for in life—a lover and a child, for example—but as soon as she gets used to having them, they are taken away from her and she discovers the cruel secret of paradise: "Timelessness does not promise the permanence of any experience. . . . Paradise is a dream bearing the inscription on Solomon's seal: this too will pass. . . . The secret meaning of Paradise is that it too is hell" (234). Thus, in Ozick's fictional universe even the last things are not what they were once made out to be. By having Puttermesser marry and die in a rather bizarre fashion, Cynthia Ozick seems to try to "overachieve" Eliot's endings for women's life stories. But in light of the fact that she substantially changes both the marriage and the death plot, one can argue that among the modern George Eliot adaptors discussed in this study she is the one who best fulfills DuPlessis's requirement for properly handling nineteenth-century plots in the twentieth-century—while she does not put George Eliot to rest, she certainly writes beyond the ending.

Notes

INTRODUCTION

1. Throughout this book, I will refer to Mary Anne (sometimes also spelled Marian) Evans by the pen name she chose for herself—George Eliot. Critics have suggested various reasons for Eliot's adoption of this particular pseudonym. Standard explanations include the speculation that Eliot wanted to empower her "feminine" writing through her choice of a masculine synonym as well as the suggestion that Evans called herself George in an attempt to legitimize her union with George Henry Lewes. For a discussion of the scholarly debate about Eliot's pen name see Kristin Brady (1992, 47–48).

2. See John Rignall's (ed.) *George Eliot and Europe* (1997) and Andrew Thompson's *George Eliot and Italy: Literary, Cultural and Political Influences from Dante to the Risorgimento* (1998).

3. Adams revised her stance in her 2001 book *Our Lady of Victorian Feminism: The Madonna in the Work of Anna Jameson, Margaret Fuller, and George Eliot*, where she reads Dinah in terms of a Jamesonian rather than a Fullerian Madonna.

4. Significant short contributions are Catherine Civello's "From Middlemarch to Manhattan" (1989), which briefly discusses Susan Cheever's *Looking for Work* (1979) and Gail Godwin's *The Odd Woman* (1974), as well as Gayle Greene's "An 'Old Story': Gail Godwin's *The Odd Woman*" (1991).

5. I discuss Henry James as an American writer because his upbringing was predominantly American. James was born in New York, lived more than half of his life in Europe, and became a British citizen in 1915, a year before his death.

6. Even though Hawthorne lived in England from 1853–58 (and in Italy until 1860), he never met George Eliot. Edward Stokes speculates about Hawthorne's admitted interest in Eliot (gleaned from a journal entry):

> Although it includes no implicit comment on her work, Hawthorne's interest, and the wish to meet her (which was probably somewhat qualified by his apparent concern about "all that may have been amiss or awry in the conduct of her life," even though he somehow gained the impression that she was now married to Lewes) make it virtually certain that he must have read *Adam Bede* at least. (1985, 89)

7. After graduation from high school, Hawthorne isolated himself in a bedroom in his mother's house for roughly twelve years in order to apprentice himself as a writer (see Miller

1991, 85–165). Eliot served as her father's housekeeper after her mother's death in 1835 until his death in 1850 (see Rignall [ed.] 2000, 473–74).

8. For a critical overview of works comparing British and American literature see Giles (2001, 1–16).

9. My use of the term "postcolonial" for U.S. Americans in reference to Britain results from the fact that the original American settlements in New England were British colonies. I am aware of the fact that in recent critical idiom the term "postcolonial" also implies a certain resistance to the former colonizer.

10. Since Comte's *Cours de philosophie positive* (1830–42) comprises six volumes of stylistically difficult material in the French language, I will cite from Harriet Martineau's (still standard) condensed three-volume translation *The Positive Philosophy of Auguste Comte* (1896).

11. The term "religion of humanity" was coined by David Friedrich Strauss, who called for a "carrying forward of the Religion of Christ to the Religion of Humanity" (see Graver 1984, 57).

12. David Hawkes criticizes the appropriation of the term ideology by postmodernism:

> [Postmodernism] challenges the pertinence of the term "ideology." The notion of false consciousness becomes redundant if the concept of an independent consciousness is itself illusory. All consciousness then becomes artificial, and therefore "false" only in the sense that an artificial limb is false. (1996, 5)

13. Hawkes, who in his book *Ideology* tries to save the "most venerable" definition of ideology "as a system of thought which propagates systematic falsehood in the selfish interest of the powerful and malign forces dominating a particular historical era" (1996, 12) from the ravages of postmodernism, calls Althusser's influence on contemporary thought "malign" (129) because he has invented the "objectified subject celebrated by the postmodernists" (123) and "blithely accepts it as the correct and inevitable state of affairs" (124).

14. Althusser describes the subjecting of subjects within the dual mirror structure as follows:

> We observe that the structure of all ideology, interpellating individuals as subjects in the name of a unique and Absolute Subject is *speculary* i.e. a mirror-structure, and *doubly* specular: this mirror duplication is constitutive of ideology and ensures its functioning. . . . [I]t *subjects* the subjects to the Subjects, while giving them in the Subject in which each subject can contemplate its own image (present and future) the *guarantee* that this really concerns them and Him, and that since everything takes place in the Family . . . , "God will *recognize* his own in it," i.e., those who have recognized God, and have recognized themselves in Him, will be saved. ([1970] 1984, 54)

15. Hall regards this passage as the beginnings of a theoretical account of the subject in Foucault, though "Foucault would, of course, not commit anything so vulgar as to actually deploy the term 'identity'" (1996, 13).

16. In *Gender Trouble* (1990), Butler indeed seems to suggest that gender performativity can achieve resignification (but in *Bodies that Matter* [1993] she takes care to stress the contingent nature of this process):

> In the place of the law of heterosexual coherence, we see sex and gender denaturalized by means of a performance which avows their distinctness and dramatizes the

cultural mechanism of their fabricated unity. . . . [G]ender parody reveals that the original identity after which gender fashions itself is an imitation without an origin. To be more precise, it is a production which, in effect—that is, in its effects—postures as an imitation. This perpetual displacement constitutes a fluidity of identities that suggests an openness to resignification and recontextualization; parodic proliferation deprives hegemonic culture and its critics of the claim to naturalized or essentialist gender identities. (1993, 138)

17. Domestic ideology functioned very similarly on both sides of the Atlantic despite the terminological difference: in Britain the "true woman" of Victorian literature was deemed the "Angel in the House," whereas in American literary criticism, following Barbara Welter's eponymous landmark article, the prevailing gender ideology became known as "The Cult of True Womanhood."

18. Teresa de Lauretis observes that the definition of "True Womanhood" is subject to change. At different times and in different cultures, "Woman with the capital letter, the *representation* of an essence inherent in all women" has been defined as "Nature, Mother, Mystery, Evil incarnate, Object of (Masculine) Desire and Knowledge, Proper Womanhood, Femininity, et cetera" (1987, 9-10).

19. Nineteenth-century feminists, however, apparently did not think that domestic ideology necessarily had detrimental effects on women. Levine argues that

> for many women committed to the fight for women's rights, the most effective weapon was not the total rejection of that ideology but rather a manipulation of its fundamental values. After all, if women's purity made them the natural custodians of religious teachings and values, then their effect in public life could only be uplifting. . . . The sentiment of moral superiority became the leading edge of many women's rights campaigns in this period. (1987, 13)

20. For a brief overview of transcendental philosophy see D. Wyatt Aiken's *The Search for Truth: A Textbook for Transcendental Philosophy* (1988).

21. For a discussion of how Ralph Waldo Emerson's work incorporates ideas that anticipate deconstructionist thought and thus run counter to its Romantic impulse see Richard Poirier's *The Renewal of Literature: Emersonian Reflections* (1987).

22. Sally Shuttleworth observes about the wide range of Lewes's theory that

> [organicism as] guiding principle affects his epistemology, psychology and social theory. Organicism is an approach, he argues, that transcends the traditional oppositions of subject and object, mind and body, spiritualism (or vitalism) and materialism, and the political stances of Toryism and Radicalism. It reconciles the Tory demands for continuity with the radical demands for change "by showing that Progress is the development of Order." (1984, 18)

23. In his book *Postethnic America*, David Hollinger draws attention to the fact that it is a common problem of cosmopolitan/universalist approaches "to have confused the local with the universal: to have made claims on behalf of all humankind for which the salient referent was later said to be but a fragment of that elusive whole" (1995, 52).

24. Bhabha explains the possible accomplishments of such a "Third Space of enunciation" as follows:

> [T]he theoretical recognition of the split-space of enunciation may open the way to conceptualizing an *inter*national culture, based not on the exoticism of multicultur-

alism or the *diversity* of cultures, but on the inscription and articulation of culture's *hybridity*. To that end we should remember that it is the "inter"—the cutting edge of translation and negotiation, the *in-between* space—that carries the burden of the meaning of culture (1994, 38).

25. In *An Autobiography* (1904) Spencer explains this mechanism of "use-inheritance" of "habits" very succinctly while summarizing the main arguments from his *Principles of Psychology* (1855):

> The familiar doctrine of association here undergoes a great extension; for it is held that not only in the individual do ideas become connected when in experience the things producing them have repeatedly occurred together, but that such results of repeated occurrences accumulate in successions of individuals: the effects of associations are supposed to be transmitted as modifications of the nervous system. ([1904] 1966, 470)

26. Luther S. Luedtke has located oriental plots in Hawthorne's works (1989); Judie Newman has devoted an article entitled "Spaces In-Between: Hester Prynne as the Salem Bibi in Bharati Mukherjee's *The Holder of the World*" (1999) to showing how Indian American writer Bharati Mukherjee, in her rewrite of *The Scarlet Letter*, actually describes the exploitative Indian trade of the Salemites that Hawthorne's novel only hints at. Jay Grossman argues rather unconvincingly about race in *The Scarlet Letter* that because "in 1850, in hyper-racialized America . . . blackness never appears inconspicuously" (1993, 16), the frequent references to "the Black Man" hint at a subtext of miscegenation in the novel and that Pearl is the mixed-race offspring of Hester's sexual encounter with "the Black man" (18).

27. Christina Zwarg cites George Catlin's *Letters and Notes on the Manners, Customs, and Condition of the North American Indian* (1841) as Fuller's theoretical source on race (1995, 109).

28. Zwarg attributes Fuller's daydream of "naked savages" threatening her with a tomahawk to culturally constructed "protocols of reading she had brought with her to the falls" (1995, 102) whereas Rosowski argues that Fuller, "cast[ing] herself in a . . . comic role of a lady, carrying a sunshade among Indians at Mackinaw Island" (1990, 132), might be using irony in her descriptions of encounters with Native Americans.

29. Stowe might have derived her racialist view about blacks from lectures delivered in 1837 and 1838 by Alexander Kinmont in Cincinnati, where she lived (see Nuernberg 1992, 260).

30. By means of her narrator Theophrastus Such, Eliot, in line with her customary social conservatism, argues for a very gradual "mixing of races" so that the distinctive English national character might be preserved:

> All we can do is to moderate [the] course [of racial fusion], so as to hinder it from degrading the moral status of societies by a too rapid effacement of those national traditions and customs which are the language of the national genius, the deep suckers of healthy sentiment. Such moderating and guidance of inevitable movement is worthy all effort. ([1879] 1894, 206)

31. Eliot's investigation of racial/ethnic identification seems to anticipate issues raised in recent cultural studies. Thus, in *Postethnic America: Beyond Multiculturalism* David Hollinger describes a postmodern, postethnic evaluation of cultural affiliation as follows:

A postethnic perspective favors voluntary over involuntary affiliations, balances an appreciation for communities of descent with a determination to make room for new communities, and promotes solidarities of wide scope that incorporate people with different ethnic and racial backgrounds. A postethnic perspective resists the ground of knowledge and moral values in blood and history. . . . A postethnic perspective builds upon a cosmopolitan element prominent within the multiculturalist movement and cuts against its equally prominent pluralist element. (1995, 3).

32. Beer points out that Eliot here seems to be indebted to Comte: "In notebook 707 George Eliot quotes Comte's Definition of Humanity: 'The continuous whole formed by the Beings which converge'" (1983, 193–94).

33. This "Third Space" enabled by the relationship of Mordecai and Daniel is very slight indeed. Since Daniel's constitutive "English" history is never entirely displaced, he might not achieve hybridity in the sense outlined by Homi Bhabha in the "Third Space" interview (conducted by Jonathan Rutherford):

[F]or me the importance of hybridity is not to be able to trace two original moments from which the third emerges, rather hybridity to me is the "third space" which enables other positions to emerge. This third space displaces the histories that constitute it, and sets up new structures of authority, new political initiatives, which are inadequately understood through received wisdom. (Rutherford 1990, 211)

Chapter 1. George Eliot's "English" Novels and American Literature

1. The chapter title is inspired by Bob Dylan's 1965 album, "Bringing it all Back Home."

2. Henry James and Edith Wharton, in *The Portrait of a Lady* ([1881] 1908) and *The House of Mirth* (1905), their "re-writes" of Eliot's *Daniel Deronda* (1876), drastically reverse this impression of the American heroine as independent "working woman." Following Eliot's example of Gwendolen Harleth, they portray their own female protagonists as "ornamental" leisured upper class ladies rather than empowered Fullerian "virgins."

3. See especially Kimberly vanEsveld Adams's "Feminine Godhead, Feminist Symbol" (1996) and *Our Lady of Victorian Feminism* (2001), Armin Paul Frank's "Amerikanische und britische Erzählliteratur im Vergleich: Der Fall Hester gegen Hester" (1983), Gilbert and Gubar's discussion of Eliot's work in *Madwoman in the Attic* (1980), and Nicolaus Mills's *American and English Fiction in the Nineteenth Century* (1973).

4. Michael Dunne also detects a critical attitude on Hawthorne's part towards transcendentalist philosophy in *The Scarlet Letter*. He reads Hawthorne's remark about Puritan aptness to "interpret all meteoric appearances, and other natural phenomena . . . as so many revelations from a supernatural source" (135) as comment about "the interpretive dispositions of Hawthorne's romantic contemporaries" (1995, 133).

5. Following the publication of Richard Chase's seminal *The American Novel and Its Tradition* (1957), American critics have argued that American nineteenth-century writers veered rather far away from the English tradition by devising a romance tradition of their own. Michael Davitt Bell modifies this view by proposing that the American romance tradition is not as clearly defined and distinct as critics often maintain (see Bell 1985, 32–34).

For a similar discussion see also Armin Paul Frank's "Amerikanische und britische Erzählliteratur im Vergleich" (1983).

6. Bell also stresses the similarities rather than differences between *The Scarlet Letter* and Eliot's writing:

> *The Scarlet Letter* is, in the most fundamental respects, a significantly realistic work of fiction. Its greatest importance to the history of fiction in English is probably its development of analytical, psychological realism, especially in its probing and elaboration of the conscious and unconscious motives and feelings of Hester Prynne and Arthur Dimmesdale. In this respect, it foreshadows (as it also influenced) the work of such later psychological realists as George Eliot and Henry James. (1985, 46)

7. According to MacCabe, in *Middlemarch*, for example, this "meta-language" invariably imposes George Eliot's view of reality on her readers: "The claim of the narrative prose to grant direct access to a final reality guarantees the claim of the realist novel to represent the invariable features of humanity" (1978, 17).

8. There is almost no criticism on Hawthorne and class; Nicholas Bromell's article "'The Bloody Hand' of Labor: Work, Class, and Gender in Three Stories by Hawthorne" (1990) focuses almost exclusively on work and gender.

9. Ingham observes that the shift to speaking about "classes" rather than social "ranks" occurred between 1800 and 1830 (see Ingham 1996, 6).

10. Daniel Cottom provides a reasonable analysis of Eliot's attitude towards class difference as gleaned from her novels:

> This is the vision of class difference controlling Eliot's aesthetics: on the one hand, a perception of a genteel class with no warrant for its assumption of superiority and, on the other, of a lower class that increasingly demanded moral attention but was impossible to reach through forms of discourse identified with the traditional power of the upper classes. . . . Gentility of a traditional sort was demeaned in Eliot's fiction because she identified her art with the common people, who were garnering more attention as England gradually became more democratic in its political system and in its public values. (1987, 84)

11. Ingham writes that during the late eighteenth and early nineteenth century, "the interpretation of society and its meaning was based on a grading largely dependent on inherited status at birth, ownership or non-ownership of land, and profession or occupation. It provided the individual with a personal identity, a role to play, a status and a set of social mores" (1996, 5).

12. A typical mid-eighteenth century "chain of ranks" in a preindustrial society consisted of "Nobility, Gentry, Mercantile or Commercial People, Mechanics and Peasantry" (Ingham 1996, 5).

13. Cottom observes about Eliot's attitude towards education and social mobility: "In place of a hierarchy of classes—so the liberal intellectual believes—education makes degrees of enlightenment available. Individuals do not receive their place in society as a birthright or as the fruit of patronage; instead they rank themselves according to their ability to receive enlightenment" (1987, 27).

14. For a discussion of the philosophical basis of Eliot's idea of sympathy see Ellen Argyros's *"Without Any Check of Proud Reserve": Sympathy and Its Limits in George Eliot's Novels* (1999).

15. This scene certainly adds dramatic effect to the story, but it is theologically untenable since Puritan belief in predestination precludes the idea that salvation can be positively or negatively influenced by a person's conduct.

16. In light of the cultural comparison that is central to this chapter, it might be worth noting that, in a scene pointing out that the Puritan dignitaries were not averse to all sensual comforts, Hawthorne calls attention to the fact that John Wilson, the most "Anglican" Puritan, is less stern than his colleagues:

> The old clergyman, nurtured at the rich bosom of the English Church, had a long established and legitimate taste for all good and comfortable things; and however stern he might show himself in the pulpit, or in the public reproof of such transgressions as that of Hester Prynne, still, the genial benevolence of his private life had won him warmer affection than was accorded to any of his professional contemporaries. ([1850] 1986, 96)

Conversely, Mr. Ryde, the clergyman who is presented in a negative light in *Adam Bede*, behaves a bit like Hawthorne's Puritans: "Mr. Ryde insisted strongly on the doctrines of the Reformation, visited his flock a great deal in their own homes, and was severe in rebuking the aberrations of the flesh" ([1859] 1985, 225).

17. Charles Swann draws attention to the "public" nature of Hester and Dimmesdale's "private" sin: "Hester's and Dimmesdale's adultery must be seen as wrong. Adultery destroys the possibility of the fulfilment of private relationships and of wider public relationships. For Hawthorne it is only when the two are brought together that there is the possibility of sustained authentic life" (1991, 83).

18. At least Eliot's narrator seems to be critical of Mr. Irwine's attitude since Arthur's behavior is severely castigated in the following quote:

> Our deeds determine us as much as we determine our deeds.... There is a terrible coercion in our deeds which may first turn the honest man into a deceiver, and then reconcile him to the change; for this reason—that the second wrong presents itself to him in the guise of the only practicable right. ([1859] 1985, 359)

19. As Hester becomes more and more respected as a capable nurse within her community, the letter's meaning shifts for her fellow Puritans from "adultery" to "able."

20. The fact that Hetty's "outer beauty" does not correspond to "inner beauty" might also represent Eliot's criticism of Herbert Spencer's thesis that in most cases spiritual beauty also manifests itself in physical beauty. Spencer writes in "Personal Beauty": "It is a common opinion that beauty of character and beauty of aspect are unrelated. I have never been able to reconcile myself to this opinion" ([1854] 1996, 387).

21. As Bell Gale Chevigny observes, Fuller's active modification of nineteenth-century conceptions of gender went beyond mere "literary achievement" because of its performative nature:

> Her exaggerated behavior and diction are not so much affected or unnatural as they are performative, experimental rehearsals of the authentic.... Nature and character are both given and made through desiring and defiant performances. Fuller's performances of her "problem" of gender identification were endeavors to resolve her problem, to escape it, or to throw it in the face of the public—or perhaps all at once. In short, Fuller often made her own kind of "gender trouble"—in Judith Butler's arresting phrase—to disrupt the social notion and expose the construction of gender

by performing gender "badly," through exaggeration and contradiction. (1994, xxxiii)

22. In *The Subjection of Women*, John Stuart Mill refutes the idea that larger brain size equals higher intelligence: "But (it is said) there is anatomical evidence of the superior mental capacity of men compared with women: [T]hey have a larger brain. . . . A tall and large-boned man must on this showing be wonderfully superior in intelligence to a small man, and an elephant or whale must prodigiously excel mankind" ([1869] 1983, 119).

23. Flavia Alaya notes that John Stuart Mill (and later the German socialist August Bebel) successfully debunked this sort of "falsely scientific" argument with a valid counter-argument:

> Mill's one essential scientific argument, eventually to be adapted by socialists like August Bebel, that *no* conclusions on the question of sexual capabilities could be called scientific without parallel analysis of a control group under different conditions (which did not exist), went unheeded. (1991, 237)

24. Comte changed his mind regarding women for personal reasons. His marriage was unsuccessful and rather devoid of love, but he later "experienced a moral regeneration caused by the influence of Clothilde de Vaux" (Paxton 1986, 145), with whom he had platonic love relationship shortly before her expected death.

25. In a letter to her friend Barbara Bodichon, which predates the publication of Mill's *The Subjection of Women*, Eliot also seems to have taken the position that women should not exercise their right to work: "What I should like to be sure of as a result of higher education for women . . . is, their recognition of the great amount of social unproductive labour which needs to be done by women, and which is now either not done at all or done wretchedly" (*George Eliot Letters* 1954–55, 4:425). A first reading of this passage certainly suggests that Eliot sanctions the conservative ideology of separate spheres; a closer look at the entire letter, however, shows that her argument takes a slightly different slant by asking for a different, higher valuation of the "social unproductive labour" done by women.

26. As late as 1874, five years after the publication of Mill's *The Subjection of Women*, Darwin wrote in the second edition of *The Descent of Man*:

> The chief distinction in the intellectual powers of the two sexes is shewn by man's attaining to a higher eminence, in whatever he takes up, than can woman—whether requiring deep thought, reason or imagination, or merely the uses of the senses and hands. If two lists were made of the most eminent men and women in poetry, painting, sculpture, music (inclusive both of composition and performance), history, science, and philosophy, with half-a-dozen names under each subject, the two lists would not bear comparison. ([1874] 1906, 858)

Moreover, women's "powers of intuition" and of rapid "perception" suggested female atavism to Darwin since as he argues "these faculties are characteristic of the lower races, and therefore of a past and lower state of civilization" (858).

27. Eliot stresses repeatedly in her novels that surrogate motherhood can be as rewarding as biological motherhood. This might perhaps be a reflection of her positive experience with being a "second mother" to George Henry Lewes's three sons (see Bodenheimer 189–231).

28. For a discussion of gender shifts in the narrative perspective of novels by Stowe and Eliot see Robyn Warhol's *Gendered Interventions* (1989).

29. Hutcheon gives an account of the naturalizing, "doxifying" power of literary discourse in the following passage:

> Lennard Davis describes the politics of novelistic narrative representation in this way: "Novels do not depict life, they depict life as it is represented by ideology." Ideology—how a culture represents itself to itself—"doxifies" or naturalizes narrative representation, making it appear as natural or common-sensical; it presents what is really *constructed* meaning as something *inherent* in that which is being represented. (1989, 49)

30. Hester, according to Hawthorne's narrator, has become "masculinized" by forsaking "feminine" passion for "masculine" thought: "Much of the marble coldness of Hester's impression was to be attributed to the circumstance that her life had turned, in a great measure, from passion and feeling to thought" ([1850] 1986, 143).

31. Charles Swann, quoting the final passage of *The Scarlet Letter*, in which Hester reasons that "[t]he angel and apostle of the coming revelation [about a different future of gender relationships] must be a woman" ([1850] 1986, 128), even argues that Hawthorne here speculates about the second coming of a female Christ (see 1991, 92).

32. Hawthorne also made a few equally notorious, devastating remarks about his one-time friend Margaret Fuller on the occasion of her tragic death by drowning after he found out that her child might have been illegitimate. His description of Fuller's conduct in his *French and Italian Notebooks* shows that in his estimation, Fuller had "prostituted" herself by means of her choice of a sexually alluring dunce for her partner and her decision to make a work of art out of her own life. By denying the authority of a "proper husband," Fuller also denied "The Cult of True Womanhood," male authority, and—by implication—the Law of the Father as God's authority. Hawthorne's final judgment of Fuller's character reveals that he felt that Fuller deserved to die because she had dared to violate the bounds of female decency (see *French and Italian Notebooks* [1858–59] 1980, 156–57).

33. Adams's claim that her reading of "Fuller's Virgin Mother, as I have described her, helps us to see how the Madonna functions in Eliot" (1996, 60) might be a bit presumptuous and also slightly off if one considers that Fuller's Madonna figure is a feminist prototype rather than a character in a novel:

> I have urged on woman independence of man, not that I do not think the sexes are mutually needed by one another, but because in woman this fact has led to an excessive devotion, which has cooled love, degraded marriage, and prevented either sex from being what it should be to itself or the other.... I wish woman to live, *first* for God's sake. Then she will not make an imperfect man her god, and thus sink into idolatry.... By being more a soul, she will not be less a woman, for nature is perfected through spirit.... A profound thinker has said, "no married woman can represent the female world, for she belongs to her husband. The idea of woman must be represented by a virgin." ([1845] 1994, 330)

34. In *Our Lady of Victorian Feminism* (2001), published five years after the above discussed article, Adams corrects her initial stance of describing Dinah as a Fullerian Madonna. She views the figure of Dinah as more indebted to Anna Jameson's *Legends of the Madonna* (1852) than to Fuller's *Woman in the Nineteenth Century* (1845), calls her "a Jamesonian Madonna-figure" (152), and stresses similarities "between Jameson's Madonnas and Eliot's character Dinah Morris" (156).

35. Nancy Armstrong provides yet another clue by pointing to larger cultural implications when she calls attention to the fact that character splitting—like the "Hester"—splitting into Hetty and Dinah—was absolutely common in Victorian literature, which in general denied their virtuous heroines "desire":

> Desire rarely comes in its pure form, at least not in a flesh and blood Englishwoman. It takes such forms as Jane Eyre's nemesis Bertha Mason, the ghost of the first Catherine Earnshaw, May Barton's near-dead Aunt Esther who collapses into an unrecognizable heap outside her window . . . or Estella's murderous working class mother. (2001, 110)

36. Dorothea Barrett, refreshingly, views Dinah as the more unsympathetic, "evil" half of the Hetty/Dinah pair:

> Is Dinah an admirable woman with a vocation who works selflessly and with positive results for the community? Or is she a repressed egoist who unconsciously disguises her egoism as altruism, her sexuality and vanity as religious vocation, and her desire for ascendancy over Hetty, both in the affections of the man, Adam Bede, and the battle for centrality in the novel, *Adam Bede*, as a sincere and disinterested desire to help? Similarly, is Hetty a vain and heartless opportunist who meets with condign punishment, or a blameless 18 year-old-girl who is crucified for the sins of others, not least of women like Dinah who falsify their own, and by extension their gender's, true motives and desires? (1989, 46–47)

37. For a discussion of Maggie's association with demonism see Nina Auerbach's "The Power of Hunger: Demonism and Maggie Tulliver" (1975).

38. Alicia Carroll discusses the racial overtones of Maggie's darkness, when she writes that Eliot "relies on . . . this constructed image to 'wash' her English or European characters free of a compulsory sexual innocence" (2003, 25). Carroll makes an important observation about Eliot's presentation of racial and sexual otherness by arguing that Eliot employs ethnic otherness in order to be able to speak about desire in her novelistic work:

> Transposing elements of the Orient or Moorish Spain into English narratives and literally into the "blood" of English characters allows Eliot to attempt to resist sometimes successfully, sometimes unsuccessfully, a pervasive "cultural frigidity" which affects the representation of both men's and women's experiences of desire and sexual pleasure in the English novel. (20)

39. Keeping in mind Gilbert and Gubar's famous opening question from *The Madwoman in the Attic*, "Is a pen a metaphoric penis?" (1980, 3), Johnson reads Dimmesdale's authoring of the election day sermon as a last creative outburst, which, ultimately, "fathers" the novel (see 1993, 609–10).

40. As Richard Ellmann points out, Eliot here uses the image of "the seed" as metaphor for sexuality, fertility, and creativity, as she had done in *Adam Bede* (see 1977, 756).

41. Gordon Haight writes in his Eliot biography that Stowe initiated her correspondence with Eliot after having read *The Mill on the Floss* (among other Eliot novels): "Out of the blue in May 1869 [Stowe] sent 'a really noble letter,' full of admiration of *Silas Marner*, and *The Mill on the Floss*, and *Adam Bede* . . . and wondering about George Eliot's religious views" ([1968] 1992, 412).

42. Frederick Karl discusses Maggie's situation of not being able to acquire the education that she yearns for against a background provided by "nineteenth-century science and pseudo-science" (1995, 324):

> We cannot fully comprehend Maggie's frustration without the following medical context. She is doomed not by Eliot but by how medical "evidence" determined women's destiny; the argument being that because of the female sexual and reproductive systems, women's cerebral evolution had been arrested at a certain undeveloped point. . . . These were the conclusions of Darwin and, in time, of Spencer. (324)

43. In *Our Lady of Victorian Feminism* Adams distinguishes between two types of self-reliant women in Fuller's *Woman in the Nineteenth Century*: the Fullerian independent "virgin" and the "Madonna," "not only a virgin but also a wife and mother, both an independent self and a companion to man" (2001, 128).

44. Miss Nervy's adventures as "almost a sea-captain" are described as follows:

> In the earlier part of her life, she had gone on a Mediterranean voyage with her brother Zachariah Randall, who was wont to say of her that she was a better mate than any man he could find. And true enough, when he was confined to his berth with a fever, Miss Minerva not only nursed him, but navigated the ship home in the most matter-of-fact-way in the world. ([1869] 1982, 1293)

45. Kathryn R. Kent provides a thought-provoking reading of Asphyxia as an antilesbian fantasy on Stowe's part:

> The central fantasy of at least the first third of *Oldtown Folks* is that Miss Asphyxia, as a representative of the evils of both slavery and mechanical reproduction, will, through her "unnatural" influence, make Tina, the emblem of white, middle-class femininity, into a black, nonfemale (and, by extension, not heterosexually productive) slave. (1997, 53)

46. In contrast, Harry's "masculine" character traits are entirely positive:

> He was naturally one of those manly, good-natured, even-tempered children that are the delight of nurses and the staff and stay of mothers. Early responsibility and sorrow, and the religious teachings of his mother, had awakened the spiritual part of his nature to a higher consciousness than usually exists in childhood. There was about him a steady, uncorrupted goodness and faithfulness of nature, a simple, direct truthfulness, and a loyal habit of prompt obedience to elders, which made him one of those children likely, in every position of child-life, to be favorites, and to run a smooth course. ([1869] 1982, 990)

47. For an in-depth discussion of Spencer's attitude towards women see Nancy L. Paxton's *George Eliot and Herbert Spencer* (1986).

48. Eliot invokes social organicism throughout her career as a novelist. She gives a description of a relatively integrated and functioning hierarchical society in *Adam Bede* (1859), her first full-length novel. In her later novels, as for example *Middlemarch* (1871–72) and *Daniel Deronda* (1876), she still professes her belief in the organic ideal, but focuses on individuals who struggle against unjust social structures and conditions.

49. In *The Principles of Sociology* (1870–72), Spencer actually compares workers and the organizations of the work force to bodily organs:

> It is the same in a society. The clustered citizens forming an organ which produces some commodity for national use, or which otherwise satisfies national wants, has within it subservient structures substantially like those of each other organ carrying on each other function. Be it a cotton-weaving district or a district where cutlery is made, it has a set of agencies which bring the raw material, and a set of agencies which collect and send away the manufactured articles; it has apparatus of major and minor channels through which the necessaries are drafted out of the general stocks circulating through the kingdom. ([1898] 2002, 1.2:478)

50. Suzanne Graver comments on this as follows:

> Committed both to pioneering new modes of social existence and to preserving a social organism based on inviolable laws of nature, *Social Statics* suffered from a self-contradictory ideal. A piece Lewes wrote for the *Leader* offers a striking example of this dual orientation, for while he insists that "society is a growth, not a transplantation," he also opposes taking this admission to mean "a rigorous abstinence of all radical changes" (1984, 156).

51. In a short article entitled "Virgin Saint, Mother Saint" (1999), Patricia Marks calls attention to a few parallels between Dorothea as St. Theresa in *Middlemarch* (1871–72) and Hawthorne's Marian/Madonna figure Hilda in *The Marble Faun* (1860).

52. *Oldtown Folks* is perhaps Stowe's most ambitious project, both in terms of content and style. Hedrick argues that Stowe wanted the rather laborious *Oldtown Folks* to be her "magnum opus, her claim to being a 'classic' writer" (1994, 332). She also points out that Stowe experimented with a more sophisticated narrative technique:

> Horace Holyoke's resolve to be a passive mirror, a mere "observer and reporter," is a step toward the objective, omniscient narrative voice of the late nineteenth-century novel that Henry James perfected. This checking of Stowe's opinionated, funny, whimsical narrative voice considerably narrowed the register of expressiveness available to her, and the beginning of *Oldtown Folks* reads as if she is casting about in a tight place. (333)

53. In her letter to Stowe, Eliot did not comment on the very evident anti-Europeanism of *Oldtown Folks*. This might be due to the fact that Eliot agreed with at least some of Stowe's positions on the "old world."

54. Apparently not all Puritan descendants held such stern beliefs. Miss Mehitable's brother Jonathan, belonging to the milder "Arminian wing of the Church" ([1869] 1982, 1264), does not believe in this doctrine, unlike Esther's father. In regard to Tina's spiritual well-being, he advises his sister Mehitable:

> Plant the footsteps of your child on the ground of the old Cambridge Platform, and teach her as Winthrop and Dudley and the Mathers taught their children,—that she "is already" a member in the Church of Christ, that she is in covenant with God, and hath the seal thereof upon her, to wit, baptism; and so, if not regenerate, is yet in a more hopeful way of attaining regeneration and all spiritual blessings. (1263)

55. In an allegorical statement invoking the American Revolution against British rule, she likens the Puritan descendents' religious rebellions against what she perceives as the monarchical, anti-democratic aspects of religious doctrine to the revolutionary war:

> It was inevitable that a people who had just carried through a national revolution and declared national independence on the principle "that governments owe their just power to the consent of the governed," and who recognized it as axiom to be held in view in all governments, should very soon come into painful collision with forms of theological statement, in regard to God's government, which appeared to contravene all these principles, and which could be supported only by referring to the old notion of the divine right and prerogative of the King Eternal. ([1869] 1982, 1247)

56. Stowe, apparently believing that any sincere believer should have access to God's grace, also "saved" other characters in her New England fiction by relying on New Testament theology, which stresses God in his function as a savior rather than Jonathan Edwards's "angry God." As Edward Tang points out, in *The Minister's Wooing*

> it is [the freed slave] Candace . . . who rewrites religious doctrine to emphasize the New Testament theology of a God so loving that He entered the world and humbled himself to redeem an errant humanity. She calms Mrs. Marvyn by declaring that James is clearly among the elect, not because Candace has any visible proof of his particular case, of which there is none, but simply because Christ's protective love extends to all. (1998, 81)

57. Racial alterity, which is not allotted a great deal of space in *Oldtown Folks*, is presented as a type of alterity that can be contained in a community that takes a decidedly paternalistic attitude towards Native and African Americans. Thus, after Aunt Nancy Prime's "stolen children" are restored by Ellery Davenport, the whole family is given "the relics of the Thanksgiving feast" ([1869] 1982, 1229) by Horace's grandmother.

Chapter 2. Fuller's, Hawthorne's, Stowe's, and Eliot's Italy

1. Unification was not fully accomplished until 1870 when, after the French surrender at Sedan, Rome was restored as the Italian capital. For a discussion of the political situation in nineteenth-century Italy see Lucy Riall's *The Italian Risorgimento* (1994).

2. For an overview of Comte's philosophy see Mary Pickering's *Auguste Comte: An Intellectual Biography* (1993). For a discussion of Comtean influence on Eliot's work see in particular David Maria Hesse's *George Eliot and Auguste Comte* (1996) and Felicia Bonaparte's *The Triptych and the Cross* (1979).

3. Eliot did not keep a journal of another trip to Italy in 1861 which was undertaken with the purpose of doing research for *Romola*.

4. *Agnes of Sorrento* was serialized in *Cornhill Magazine* from April 1861 to May 1862. *Romola* followed from July 1862 to August 1863. Lewes became the magazine's consulting editor in April 1862 (see Sheets 1997, 323). Eliot does not mention *Romola* in her letters, but since George Henry Lewes, as he reported, "read *Agnes* while Eliot 'was deep in her researches' for Romola" (Sheets 1997, 323) it is to be assumed that Eliot was in some way familiar with the novel's content, even if she might not have read it.

5. Hawthorne's biographer Miller writes "Hawthorne took the post at Liverpool with two purposes in mind: to accumulate enough money in four years to make an extended stay on the Continent possible for the following year or two and, more important, to leave Europe with substantial savings that, combined with royalties from his books, would guarantee the family's security" (1991, 401).

6. The writers discussed here, two Americans and one English woman, are "Anglocentric"—they assert the cultural superiority of their own native country over Italy.

7. In *Orientalism*, Edward Said describes this process for the "cultural production" of the Orient:

> Everyone who writes about the Orient must locate himself vis-à-vis the Orient; translated into his text, this location includes the kind of narrative voice he adopts, the type of structure he builds, the kinds of images, themes, motifs that circulate in his text—all of which add up to deliberate ways of addressing the reader, containing the Orient, and finally, representing it or speaking in its behalf. (1995, 20)

8. While Hawthorne's and Eliot's travel notes were not meant for publication, Margaret Fuller's dispatches were published; as "reports from the front" they were of public interest and thus met the first one of the requirements that Sara Mills lists for "publishable travel writing" in the nineteenth century:

> Travellers normally only write (and are published) under the following circumstances: firstly, if they travel to well-established places (in this case, the writer has to produce something which is novel, witty or erudite to compensate for the fact that they are writing about the well-known); secondly, if they write about travel to non-places (the Gobi desert, Tibet, that is, places which have not been written about before); or thirdly, if they describe travelling by a difficult means of transport. (1991, 84)

9. Jeffrey Steele, apparently drawing a different conclusion from Fuller's "patriotic tone," argues that it is her fellow Americans whom she wants to teach a political lesson:

> With one eye on her nation back home, she recorded a series of political lessons that she hoped might cure the moral and political disease that had corrupted the American body politic. Ultimately, in Italy, Fuller encountered an enthusiastic upwelling of political fervor and democratic sentiment that seemed to be missing in America, which had grown complacent since the nationalistic passion of its own revolutionary birth. (2001, 263)

His argument follows that of Bell Gale Chevigny, who views Fuller's distancing herself from her home country as "Freudian" precondition to rapprochement: "Perhaps Fuller saw divorce as the precondition of superior remarriage" (1986, 190).

10. Von Mehren reports that Fuller alienated Mazzini by publicly advising him to seek a reconciliation with the Pope (see 1994, 273).

11. The Triumvir, of which Mazzini was a member, was the executive branch the Roman Republic, which only lasted for six months, from January until July 1849.

12 The astounding number of references in the dispatches to Protestantism as "the right faith" invite speculation as to whether Fuller did not mention her "life's philosophy" because she assumed that the *Tribune* readers did not have any transcendentalist sympathies or whether "Catholic superstition" renewed her appreciation of New England Protestantism. Larry Reynolds even suggests that in Europe, Fuller began to distance herself from transcendentalism's individualism (which, as I argue in the next chapter, she had already modi-

fied towards more of a communal ideal in her own writings) and her mentor, Emerson: "[Emerson] convinced her of the primacy of individualism and ineffectiveness of cooperative reform efforts, two convictions she would eventually reject in Europe" (1988, 57).

13. In this respect, Hawthorne's demeanor in Italy almost corresponds to Margaret Fuller's acerbic remarks about the American traveler who passes "through the great cities, escorted by cheating couriers and ignorant *valets de place*, unable to hold intercourse with the natives of the country, and passing all his leisure hours with his countrymen, who know no more than himself" (1856, 250).

14. Hawthorne rather amusedly reports in his May 24, 1858, journal entry:

> We left Rome this morning, after troubles of various kinds, and a dispute in the first place with Lalla, our female servant, and her mother. . . . Mother and daughter exploded into a livid rage, and cursed us plentifully, wishing that we might never come to our journey's end, and that we might all break our necks, and that we might die of the apoplexy—the most awful curse that an Italian knows how to invoke upon his enemies, because it precludes the possibility of extreme unction. However, as we are heretics, and certain of damnation anyhow, it does not much matter to us. . . . (*French and Italian Notebooks* [1858–59] 1980, 231)

15. Mills remarks rather laconically about the subject of "foreignness and filth": "There are several other constraints on writing about other nations: one of these is portraying the other nation in terms of abhorrent smells and filthiness" (1991, 90). Lucy Riall's description of sanitary conditions in nineteenth-century Italy, however, suggests that travelers' reports of unsanitary sights might not have always have been exaggerated: "Few, if any, towns possessed adequate sanitary facilities. People disposed of their rubbish in the streets which became open sewers, slept in the same damp rooms as their animals and defecated in front of their houses" (1994, 44).

16. In *Agnes of Sorrento*, Harriet Beecher Stowe, who must have observed similar sights in Italian towns when she traveled in Italy at exactly the same time as Hawthorne, gives a much more relaxed description of the way in which poor Italians lived (at the end of the fifteenth century), which even incorporates some social analysis:

> Meek dwellers in those dank, noisome caverns, without any opening but a street-door, which are called dwelling-places in Italy, they lived in uninquiring good-nature, contentedly bringing up children on coarse bread, dirty cabbage-stumps, and other garbage, while all they could earn was sucked upward by capillary attraction to nourish the extravagance of those upper classes on which they stared with such blind and ignorant admiration. ([1862] 1967, 274)

17. As Kristeva explains:

> The abject has only one quality of the object—that of being opposed to *I*. If the object, however, through its opposition, settles me within the fragile texture of a desire for meaning, which, as a matter of fact, makes me ceaselessly and infinitely homologous to it, what is *abject*, on the contrary, the jettisoned object, is radically excluded and draws me toward the place where meaning collapses. (1982, 1–2)

18. Kristeva locates the origin of abjection in faulty early childhood development:

> Essentially different from "uncanniness," more violent, too, abjection is elaborated through a failure to recognize its kin; nothing is familiar, not even the shadow of a

memory. I imagine a child who has swallowed up his parents too soon, who frightens himself on that account, "all by himself," and to save himself, rejects and throws up everything that is given to him—all gifts, all objects. He . . . has a sense of the abject. . . . What he has swallowed up instead of maternal love is an emptiness, or rather, a maternal hatred without a word for the words of the father; that is what he tries to cleanse himself of, tirelessly. What solace does he come upon within such loathing? Perhaps a father, existing but unsettled, loving but unsteady, merely an apparition, but an apparition that remains. (1982, 6)

In this context, it might be tempting to provide some information about Nathaniel Hawthorne's psychological make-up: Hawthorne's father died when Nathaniel was still a small child; as a result of this, Hawthorne's mother, who due to financial reasons had to move back into her father's house, became more and more distant and reclusive (see Miller 1991, 25–29).

19. In her elaboration on the origin of the abject, Kristeva calls it "a repulsive gift from the Other":

And, as in jouissance where the object of desire, known as object *a* [in Lacan's terminology], bursts with the shattered mirror where the ego gives up its image in order to contemplate itself in the Other, there is nothing either objective or objectal to the abject. It is simply a frontier, a repulsive gift that the Other, having become *alter ego*, drops so that "I" does not disappear in it but finds, in that sublime alienation, a forfeited existence. (1982, 9)

20. Bhabha explains that "racial fetishism" actually prevents a recognition of difference and arrests the culturally other in the negative stereotype:

What is denied the colonial subject, both as colonizer and colonized, is that form of negation which gives access to the recognition of difference. It is that possibility of difference and circulation which would liberate the signifier *skin/culture* from the fixations of racial typology, the analytics of blood, ideologies of racial and cultural dominance or degeneration. "Wherever he goes," Fanon despairs, "the Negro remains as Negro"—his race becomes the ineradicable sign of *negative difference* in colonial discourses. (1994, 75)

21. Hawthorne had some rather strange reactions to his ancestors' country of origin. His seemingly unmotivated vituperations against English women, advocating their murder because they are too fat, have acquired a sad fame:

[M]y experience is that an English lady of forty or fifty is apt to become the most hideous animal that ever pretended to human shape. No caricature could do justice to some of their figures and features; so puffed out, so huge, so without limit, with such hanging dewlaps, and all manner of fleshly abomination. . . . They are gross, gross, gross. . . . Surely, a man would be justified in murdering them—in taking a sharp knife and cutting away their mountainous flesh, until he had brought them into reasonable shape, as a sculptor seeks for the beautiful form of woman in a shapeless block of marble. (*English Notebooks* [1853–56] 1987, 133)

22. Piedmont had wanted Lombardy and Venetia, whereas France claimed Nice and Savoy. In 1859 Napoleon III signed an armistice with Austria, according to which Pied-

mont received only Lombardy. Cavour, angry about this development, resigned as prime minister (see Riall 1994, xiii).

23. In his campaign biography for Franklin Pierce, Hawthorne comments on slavery:

> [Slavery is] one of those evils which divine Providence does not leave to be remedied by human contrivances, but which, in its own good time, by some means impossible to be anticipated, but of the simplest and easiest operation, when all its uses have been fulfilled, it causes to vanish like a dream. (quoted in Miller 1991, 383)

24. This diary entry, "Arezzo, May 30, 1858," has been omitted from the *French and Italian Notebooks* but is part of Sophia Hawthorne's first edition of Hawthorne's notebooks.

25. Hawthorne gives a rather funny description of the early Madonnas of the Sienese school of art: "It is remarkable that all the early faces of the Madonna are especially stupid, and all of the same type; a sort of face such as one might carve on a pumpkin, representing a heavy, sulky, and phlegmatic woman, with a long and low arch of the nose" (*French and Italian Notebooks* [1858–59] 1980, 451).

26. In 1861 a kingdom of Italy was declared and Vittorio Emanuele II of Piedmont became King of Italy (see Riall 1994, xiii).

27. Harris and Johnston go to great lengths explaining that the inattention to current affairs and the emotional paucity of Eliot's *Recollections of Italy. 1860* can be attributed to the fact that "the journal is written with due regard to genre" (330), and Paul Fussell writes about the genre that "it is true that the Grand Tour very seldom encouraged original inquiry or fresh perceptions" (1987, 131), but to me this still does not entirely explain the feeling of disappointment that Eliot's Italian journal leaves her readers with.

28. Hawthorne's narrator in *The Marble Faun* also refers to his Italian character Donatello in terms of animal imagery, calling him "a pet dog" ([1860] 1990, 14) and "gentle and docile as a pet spaniel" (43).

29. Eliot often endows her "positive foreign characters" with musical abilities. Will Ladislaw from *Middlemarch* and Herr Klesmer from *Daniel Deronda* are prime examples of this.

30. Geertz asks the rhetorical question "Can this halfway house [of human nature as both "universal" and constructed] between the eighteenth and twentieth centuries really stand?" ([1973] 1993, 39) and then answers it negatively:

> Whether it can or not depends on whether the dualism between empirically universal aspects of culture rooted in subcultural realities and empirically variable aspects not so rooted can be established and sustained. And this, in turn, demands (1) that the universals proposed be substantial ones and not empty categories; (2) that they be specifically grounded in particular biological, psychological, or sociological processes, not just vaguely associated with "underlying realities"; and (3) that they can convincingly be defended as core elements in a definition of humanity in comparison with which the much more numerous cultural particularities are of clearly secondary importance. On all three of these counts it seems to me that the *consensium gentium* approach fails; rather than moving toward the essentials of the human situation it moves away from them. (39)

31. A mere look at Eliot's chapter epigraphs which derive from countless "multicultural" sources substantiates Seeber's claim.

32. In keeping with this idea, Hollinger endorses a "situated cosmopolitanism" that he labels "postethnic":

> The term postethnic marks an effort to articulate and develop cosmopolitan instincts with a new appreciation for the ethnos. Cosmopolitanism itself is more generic. It is an impulse toward worldly breadth associated especially with the Enlightenment of the eighteenth century but found also in antiprovincial intellectuals in a host of times and places. As "citizens of the world," many of the great cosmopolitans of history have been proudly rootless. But postethnicity is the critical renewal of cosmopolitanism in the context of today's greater sensitivity to roots. "Rooted cosmopolitanism" is indeed a label recently adopted by several theorists of diversity whom I take to be moving in the direction I call postethnic. (1995, 5)

33. As already mentioned above, Fuller, curiously enough, did not establish any links between transcendentalism, democracy, and the Italian revolution.

34. In "The Modern Hep! Hep! Hep" Eliot also presents Italian nation building, which was based on shared memory, as a model for Jewish nation building:

> Half a century ago, what was Italy? An idling place of dilettantism or of itinerant motiveless wealth, a territory parceled out for papal sustenance, dynastic convenience, and the profit of an alien Government. . . . Thanks chiefly to the divine gift of a memory which inspires the moments with a past, a present, and a future, and gives the sense of corporate existence that raises man above the otherwise more respectable and innocent brute, all that, or most of it has changed. ([1879] 1894, 185–86).

35. Thompson suggests that there is even some physical resemblance between Deronda and Mazzini: "It is quite possible . . . that Eliot had in mind her own memories of Mazzini or accounts of his appearance in creating Daniel" (1998, 176).

36. Margaret Fuller's political radicalism, however, is apparent. On Mazzini's return to Italy, she comments on Mazzini's shortcomings as a truly "radical" politician:

> And yet Mazzini sees not all: he aims at political emancipation; but he sees not, perhaps would deny, the bearing of some events, which even now begin to work their way. Of this, more anon. . . . Suffice it to say, I allude to that of which the cry of Communism, the systems of Fourier, &c., are but forerunners. (1856, 320)

37. Eliot uses an uncharacteristically forceful and irreverent vocabulary here: "Certainly, our decayed monarchs should be pensioned off: we should have a hospital for them, or a sort Zoological garden, where these worn-out humbugs may be preserved" (*George Eliot Letters* 1954–55, 1:254).

38. In *George Eliot: Her Mind and Her Art* Joan Bennett lists parallels between the intellectual climate in Renaissance Italy and nineteenth–century England:

> In both periods there was strong hope and belief in the expansion of human knowledge and power; there was also, among Christian believers in both periods, the recognition of a relaxation and even corruption in Church teaching and of a consequent deterioration in human conduct, resulting in zealous desire to reform the Church. (148–49)

39. Fuller's final and rather generous evaluation of Pius IX clearly shows her disappointment:

> There can be no doubt that all his natural impulses are generous and kind, and in a more private station he would have died beloved and honored; but to this he was unequal. . . . However that may be, I cannot forgive him some of the circumstances of this flight. To fly to Naples; to throw himself in the arms of the bombarding monarch, blessing him and thanking his soldiery for preserving that part of Italy from anarchy; to protest that all his promises at Rome were null and void . . . when Rome was thus left without any government, to refuse to see any deputation, even the Senator of Rome, whom he had so gladly sanctioned,—these are acts of either a fool or a foe. . . . No more of him! His day is over. He has been made, it seems unconsciously, an instrument of good his regrets cannot destroy. (1856, 343)

40. Bonney MacDonald draws attention to Hawthorne's preoccupation with the "pagan roots of Catholicism" with an astute comment: "Catholic Rome, he recalls, is planted in the very citadel of Paganism, and the resulting moral tension is rarely far from his view" (1990, 16).

41. The narrator of *The Marble Faun* states his protestant bias strongly when he relates Hilda's thoughts upon entering St. Peter's in order to pray there: "She felt as if her mother's spirit somewhere within the Dome, were looking down upon her child, the daughter of Puritan forefathers, and weeping to behold her ensnared by these gaudy superstitions" (351).

42. In *Hawthorne: Calvin's Ironic Stepchild*, a book devoted to Hawthorne's religious views, Donohue argues that Hawthorne's stay in Italy and his critical discussion of Catholicism in *The Marble Faun* ultimately caused him to lose faith both in God and in his art. Associating Protestantism with virility and Catholicism with sterility—impotence and abortion—Donohue, who does not focus on gender in her book, inscribes an interesting (and apparently not intended) gendered evaluation of Hawthorne's art in her succinct summary of her main thesis:

> Europe destroyed for Hawthorne the Calvinist conviction of an exigent Fall. His experiences there challenged his Puritanism, for if there were a way back into Eden, especially if good could come from evil, and the Fall could be fortunate (the *felix culpa*), then Hawthorne's moral and dramatic center was gone. His art was emasculated of its primal terror and instress; the heart of his mystery had been plucked out. The faltering final attempts at writing a romance, made during the last four years of his life after his return for America, were aborted—a tragic revelation of his impotence. (1985, 339)

43. As Donohue—quoting Roman Catholic liturgy for Holy Saturday—insists, Hawthorne is entirely indebted to Catholic rather than Protestant theology in his depiction of Donatello's development. Through his reenactment of his murder of the model by throwing a "destructive worm" over the parapet of his tower, Donatello experiences a second, this time "fortunate fall":

> The reading of the second Fall cannot be understood in a Calvinist context, as can the first Fall, but only as the Catholic fortunate fall. Donatello sins and through his suffering and anguish allows the seeds of the Word to grow in his heart and is moved to atonement, penance, and penitence. Through sin he has become truly human; through his agony and remorse he will be able to "work out his *salvation* with diligence," confined in prison, even if it takes on the rest of his life: "O inaestimabilis dilectio caritatis: ut servum redimeres, filium tradidisti! O certe necessar-

ium Adae peccatum, quod Christi morte deletum est. *O felix culpa*, quae talem ac tantum meruit habere Redemptorum!" (1985, 277)

44. When Kenyon visits Donatello after the murder, he tells him that he is the "last of [his] race" and that "there is a secret [surrounding] . . . the quick extinction of [his] kindred" ([1860] 1990, 221).

45. Kemp himself repeatedly qualifies his statements, for example, when he remarks about his argument that the figure of Donatello corresponds to Fanon's "decolonized other": "Of course, this allegory does not "work" insofar as the text does not overtly allegorize the nationalist movement in Italy" (1997, 228).

46. Coincidentally, the protagonist of E. T. A. Hoffmann's story "Der Sandmann," (1816) which Freud uses as main example in his discussion about the uncanny, is also named Nathaniel.

47. The German word "unheimlich" is usually translated as uncanny; "unhomely" would be a more literal, if rather strange sounding, translation.

48. Even though Hawthorne's presentation of Italy more often deals with cultural rather than racial difference, it still makes sense also to apply Abdul JanMohamed's insights about "imaginary" and "symbolic" (post)colonialist fiction to his writing. Hawthorne's depiction of the country and its "natives" corresponds to what JanMohamed in his landmark essay, "The Economy of Manichean Allegory," labels the first category of "symbolic" texts. In his discussion of "the function of racial difference in colonialist literature" (as his essay is subtitled), JanMohamed distinguishes between "imaginary" representations of people, which equate "native" with "evil," and "symbolic" texts, which at least to some extent "thematize the problem of the colonialist mentality and its encounter with the racial Other" (1985, 65–66). The discussion of Hawthorne's works has clearly shown that they belong to the first order of "symbolic" texts.

49. Udo Nattermann even includes the other "foreign" figures in *The Marble Faun* in his list of "atavistic characters": "Donatello, Miriam, and the model are history come alive; they are touristic wish fulfillments performing different historical roles on an Italian stage" (1994, 57).

50. In the postscript to *The Marble Faun* Hawthorne, referring to himself as "the Author," refers to Cuvier only to deny having wanted to classify Donatello scientifically:

> He had hoped to mystify this anomalous creature between the Real and the Fantastic, in such a manner that the reader's sympathies might be excited to a certain pleasurable degree, without impelling him to ask how Cuvier would have classified poor Donatello. ([1860] 1990, 463)

51. In *The Marble Faun*, Hawthorne shies away from presenting the visionary aspects of Catholicism. Unlike the Puritans in *The Scarlet Letter* who interpret "supernatural" manifestations of the A, his Catholics are not prone to visions. This might be due to the fact that Hawthorne preferred to think of Catholicism as a faith of "small superstitions" rather than grand visions.

52. There are a few other aspects of *Romola* that clearly show that Eliot was inspired by both *The Scarlet Letter* and *The Marble Faun*. Savonarola's desperate attempt to hold on to his power, for example, recalls Dimmesdale's spiritual vanity about preaching the election day sermon, and Dino's and Tessa's fake wedding performed by a false priest seems to be modeled on Donatello's and Miriam's false carnival wedding.

53. In a very insightful article on feminism and positivism in *Romola*, Nancy Paxton discusses which aspects of the Positivist ideology of gender that can be discerned in *Romola* might have appealed to Eliot and which ones might not (see 1986, 143–47).

54. According to Hesse, this scene shows that Romola has reached the highest stage of Comtean development: "Romola, having ascended the scale of cultural evolution up to the present, is the center of a nucleic family" (1996, 301).

55. I agree with Mary Wilson Carpenter's assessment that "[t]he narrative constructs ambivalence toward Romola, but it develops a carefully calculated, sadistic rage towards Tito and Savonarola" (1990, 120). For a discussion of the various ways in which the ending of *Romola* has been read see Robin Sheets's "History and Romance: Harriet Beecher Stowe's *Agnes of Sorrento* and George Eliot's *Romola*" (1997).

56. Donatello's "civilizing" fall is usually referred to as a "fortunate fall" in criticism about the novel. However, I agree with Richard Brodhead who has difficulties in perceiving anything particularly fortunate about it. In his introduction to the Penguin edition of *The Marble Faun*, Brodhead states: "Kenyon says that suffering guilt has led to the birth of higher faculties in Donatello, but Donatello never displays the faculties Kenyon names" (1990, xxiv).

Chapter 3. From *Uncle Tom's Cabin* to *Daniel Deronda*

1. For a discussion of the discriminatory presentation of African Americans in *Uncle Tom's Cabin* see also Sarah Smith Ducksworth's article "Stowe's Construction of an African Persona and the Creation of White Identity for a New World Order" (1992) and Sophia Cantave's "Who Gets to Create the Lasting Images? The Problem of Black Representation in *Uncle Tom's Cabin*" (2000).

2. Rachel Bowlby has argued persuasively that Stowe, in spite of believing in the effectiveness of education, does not concede that the "raw, or human material" is the same for whites and blacks (1992, 200). Michael J. Meyer, however, tries to—in my opinion rather unsuccessfully—end "the Stowe debate" by suggesting that Stowe actually achieves an egalitarian presentation of blacks and whites through her "reflective and refractive" images and characters (1992, 236).

3. Arthur Riss argues that—perhaps a bit paradoxically—"Stowe generates the 'progressive' politics of *Uncle Tom's Cabin* by means of racial essentialism" (1994, 536).

4. In *In My Father's House: Africa in the Philosophy of Culture* Appiah distinguishes between "racialism," the view "that there are heritable characteristics, possessed by members of our species, which allow us to divide them into a small set of races, in such a way that all the members of these races share certain traits and tendencies with each other that they do not share with members of any other race" (1992, 13) and "racism" which justifies the belief that "members of different races differ in respects that *warrant* the differential treatment—respects, like honesty or courage or intelligence, that are uncontroversially held . . . to be acceptable as a basis for treating people differently" (13).

5. Jan Nederveen Pieterse points out that it was common to associate "lower races" with women and children: "Like Africans and blacks, the Irish have been referred to as 'savages' and likened to 'apes,' to 'women' and to 'children,' just as the Celts were often described as a 'feminine' race, by contrast with the 'masculine' Anglo-Saxons" (1992, 214). It seems that

through her positive application of the term "childlike" to women and non-white races, Stowe is trying to debunk the negative stereotype.

6. Gayle Kimball—who does not acknowledge the discriminatory politics underlying Stowe's views on gender and race—states a bit naively that "Stowe explained that [women] did not have the sexual temptations that men had; HBS took her own case to be the norm, writing to Calvin that she had no sexual passion and therefore felt no jealousy.... She asserted the chaste purity of woman, contrasting it with the baser male inclinations, and identifying men with the physical body and women with the spirit" (1982, 72). This position was not altogether uncommon in the nineteenth century, as Barbara Welter describes similar attitudes in "The Cult of True Womanhood" (1966).

7. Ducksworth poses the question "how could [the nineteenth-century reading audience] have read the passages dealing with [Tom and Eva's] mawkish display of affection without a mustard seed of suspicion that Tom, though simple-minded, could have been a dangerous pedophile?" (1992, 227). Spillers views Little Eva's affection for Tom as a manifestation of Stowe's displaced sexual desire for black men (see Spillers 1989, 42–43). P. Gabrielle Foreman, however, locates "illicit desire" in *Uncle Tom's Cabin* in the homoerotic relationship of Tom and St. Clare (see Foreman 1993, 64).

8. Eliot had not always been positively inclined towards Jews, as an 1848 letter to John Sibree, written almost thirty years before the publication of *Daniel Deronda*, indicates:

> My Gentile nature kicks most resolutely against any assumption of superiority in the Jews.... Their stock has produced a Moses and a Jesus, but Moses was impregnated with Egyptian philosophy and Jesus is venerated and adored by us only for that wherein he transcended or resisted Judaism.... Everything *specifically* Jewish is of a low grade. (*George Eliot Letters* 1954–55, 1:246–47)

In the same letter Eliot also voices her "puzzlement" over the black race (one has to concede that Eliot seems to have changed her view of racial alterity considerably in her later years):

> The negroes certainly puzzle me—all the other races seem plainly destined to extermination or fusion not excepting even the "Hebrew-Caucasian." But the negroes are too important physiologically and geographically for one to think of their extermination, while the repulsion between them and the other races seems too strong for fusion to take place to a great extent. (246)

9. In retrospect Eliot's Zionist repatriation efforts were not appreciated by Edward Said. He deplores that Eliot, who could only "sustain her admiration of Zionism ... by seeing it as a method for transforming the East into the West" (1992, 65), completely disregards the fate of the Palestinian Arab population—which would be displaced by a Zionist state in Palestine. Said accuses Eliot of assenting to contemporary "Gentile and Jewish versions of Zionism" which viewed "the Holy Land as essentially empty of inhabitants, not because there were no inhabitants ... but because their status as sovereign and human inhabitants was systematically denied" (66).

10. In *Reuben Sachs*, Levy's characters mock Eliot's decision to send her Jewish characters to Palestine; one of them calls *Daniel Deronda*'s idealism an "elaborate misconception" because "ours is the religion of materialism" (116): "'I wonder,' cried Rose, throwing herself into the breach, 'what Mr. Lee-Harrison thought of it all.' 'I think,' said Leo, 'that he was shocked to find us so little like the people in *Daniel Deronda*.' 'Did he expect,' cried Esther, 'to see our boxes in the hall, ready packed and labeled *Palestine*?'" ([1888] 1973, 115)

11. It might also be worthwhile noticing in this context that the eminent contemporary Jewish critic Bryan Cheyette does not take offense at Eliot's presentation of Jews in *Daniel Deronda*. In his book *Constructions of "The Jew" in English Literature and Society*, Cheyette also identifies Eliot's inability to engage with cultural difference pointing out that she depicts Judaism as an "unknowable racial other-realm," yet he nevertheless commends her purpose of "positioning 'the Jew' at the centre of her hopes for the future renewal of England" (1993, 49).

12. Following a recent critical tendency to recover George Eliot for feminism, Eileen Sypher makes a very similar argument about Gwendolen: "Eliot resists Gwendolen's subjection, her insertion into any ideological system." Thus Gwendolen, who exhibits "latent powers of agency" (1996, 514), at least according to Sypher, escapes patriarchal interpellation as subjected female. (Sypher's critical position can be argued with, however.)

13. According to Harold Bloom, "'Kabbalah' has been, since about the year 1200, the popularly accepted word for Jewish esoteric teachings concerning God and everything God created" (1975, 15). Gershom Scholem, in *On the Kabbalah and Its Symbolism*, points out that Kabbalah first "surfaced" in twelfth-century France (it remained a vital form of Judaism until the seventeenth century) and reached its zenith in thirteenth-century Spain with the publication of the *Zohar*, the kabbalists' holy book, by Rabbi Moses de Leon (see Scholem [1960] 1996, 89).

14. In the first chapter of his book *In my Father's House*, Appiah discusses at some length W. E. B. DuBois's rather frustrating attempts "to make sense of racial identity" (1992, 32) by finding points of correspondence between different cultural groups of the same racial origin such as African Americans and Africans. Appiah further explains that it was easier for Diaspora Jews than for Pan-Africanists to define a communal identity:

> It seems to me . . . that Judaism—the religion—and the wider body of Jewish practice through which the various communities of the Diaspora have defined themselves allow for a cultural conception of Jewish identity that cannot be made plausible in the case of Pan-Africanism. (43)

15. Lynn Wardley hints at voodoo when she identifies Stowe's description of "the 'fine damask tablecloth' in which 'some raw meat' is wrapped" (1992, 203) in *Uncle Tom's Cabin* as an indication of "the suspicion of occult practices in the slave's domain" (203–4). She points out that "the mesmerism and spiritualism practiced by Stowe and others in her middle-class milieu resonated with West African religious beliefs introduced in the slave population" (209). She reaches the inevitable conclusion that Stowe ultimately rejected African culture and spirituality: "[E]ven as she invests in African survivals, Stowe posits Africanization itself as a problem to be solved by repatriation" (212).

16. Stowe's reluctance in accepting cultural and ethnic alterity can also be detected in those scenes in which she makes George a mouthpiece for white racial prejudice, as, for example, in the scene in which he explains his rationale for escaping from slavery to Mr. Wilson, his former employer, and by doing so presents Native Americans as a violent race of potential enslavers:

> I wonder, Mr. Wilson, if the Indians should come and take you a prisoner away from your wife and children, and want to keep you all your life hoeing corn for them, if you'd think it your duty to abide in the condition in which you were called. I rather think that you'd think the first stray horse you could find an indication for Providence—shouldn't you? ([1852] 1981, 184)

17. Irwin speculates that Eliot's Hebrew teacher Emanuel Deutsch might have been a model for Mordecai (1996, xxviii) whereas the Jewish historian Salomon Maimon might rather have served as a foil for him (102).

18. George Eliot excerpted and translated Heinrich Graetz's explanation of metempsychosis in her *Pforzheimer Notebook 711*:

> Starting from the doctrine that all souls have been pre-existent from the beginning of the Spiritual world, the Kabbala taught that they are all destined to an earthly career in corporeal form. . . . But if the soul becomes stained it must once & again, but at most only thrice, return into corporeal life, till by repeated trials it can ascend in purity. On this transmigration of souls was founded the theory of retribution. The sufferings of the righteous serve simply to purify them. Seth's soul passed into Moses. . . . Marriage in general was a mystical institution, being the means of bringing souls into corporeality. (quoted in Irwin 1996, 174)

While Irwin is the first scholar to publish an edition of Eliot's *Daniel Deronda* notebooks, pioneering work was done by William Baker, who first called attention to the kabbalistic sources of *Daniel Deronda* in "The Kabbalah, Mordecai and George Eliot's Religion of Humanity" (1973). Saleel Nurbhai and K. M. Newton provide an in-depth discussion of Kabbalah and metempsychosis in *George Eliot, Judaism and the Novels* (2002).

19. David Carroll—who views Deronda as directionless and "egoless" before his encounter with Judaism—identifies this moment as identity-constituting for Daniel:

> This is the pre-hermeneutic moment to which Deronda's state of suspension, his negative capability, his habitual self-emptying or *kenosis*, enables him to respond. This is the primal religious experience, the divine influx, the spirit breathing upon the waters, not only before interpretation gets to work but even before there is a vision to interpret. . . . Deronda is able to respond because he has the correct form of pre-understanding, that of a man whose life is the open hypothesis which hasn't yet crystallized into a theory or a character. (1992, 289)

Tony Jackson argues similarly that with Daniel, Eliot presents an initially "egoless" protagonist, but cannot sustain this mode of characterization and reassigns "a self-secured, what we would now call Cartesian, self" (1996, 482) to Daniel after he has landed in the secure haven of Judaism.

20. Frank Lentricchia gives a more explanatory definition of the term ideology: "The political synonym for belief is 'ideology' in the particular sense of a constructed thing which nevertheless feels natural and is never (or is only rarely) experienced as a thing bearing interested intention" (1988, 137).

21. Stuart Hall calls attention to a seeming inconsistency in Althusser's theory of interpellation: Althusser models the doubly specular aspect of interpellation on Lacan's mirror stage, yet he apparently does not take into consideration "Lacan's somewhat sensationalist proposition that *everything* constitutive of the subject not only happens through this mechanism but happens in the same moment [at the resolution of the Oedipal crisis]" (1996, 8). Hall criticizes Lacanian "hot-gospellers" who adopt this notion because "the more complex notion of a subject-in-process is lost in these polemical condensations" (8). Althusser seems to present the interpellation of an adult in his "policeman" example. Eliot's Daniel Deronda is also interpellated as an adult of approximately twenty-five years.

22. Here, Eliot again anticipates concerns of recent cultural theory. According to David Hollinger, identification with one's less "obvious" roots is possible only in a postethnic society:

> And postethnicity would enable [Alex] Haley and [Ishmael] Reed to be both African American and Irish American without having to choose one to the exclusion of the other. Postethnicity reacts against the nation's invidiously ethnic history, builds upon the current generation's unprecedented appreciation of previously ignored cultures, and supports on the basis of revocable consent those affiliations by shared descent that were previously taken to be primordial. (1995, 21)

Thus, in a postethnic society Eliot's Daniel Deronda could as easily identify with both his English and his Jewish roots as Stowe's George Harris could with both his African American and his white heritage.

23. Anthony Appiah describes a "post-Romantic" shift in attitudes about the self:

> Authenticity speaks of the real self buried in there, the self one has to dig out and express. It is only later, *after romanticism* that the idea develops that one's self is something that one creates, makes up, so that every life should be an artwork, whose creator is, in some sense, his or her greatest creation (1996, 96).

The tension between different models for the construction of identity in *Daniel Deronda* suggests that the novel was written at the time when the paradigm for "selfhood" started to shift.

24. Lawrence Grossberg adds a new dimension to the theorization of cultural identity by invoking "space" as an identity-constituting category. Grossberg introduces space because "people's access to knowledge is determined in part by the places—of conception, birth, death and residence—from and by which they speak" (1996, 101). It seems indeed that in Daniel Deronda's case "being in the right place at the right time" is decisive for the constitution of his personal identity.

25. Appiah's suggestion to change negative racial ascriptions into more positive ones seems to allow for a large margin of individual and collective "agency," considering that he describes his critical stance as postmodern (1996, 104).

26. In the *Hand and Banner* scene Eliot's narrator seems rather skeptical about the notion of "pure blood" when s/he comments: "In fact, pure English blood (if leech or lancet can furnish us with the precise product) did not declare itself predominantly in the party at present assembled" ([1876] 1995, 523).

27. Richard Freadman provides a more definite and conservative description of Eliot's view of the self: "What in fact did Eliot assume about the self? Very generally, she pictures it as possessing a genetic essence which interacts intricately, instinctively and integratively with culturally specific conditions" (1986, 64). Unfortunately, Freadman, while tracing Eliot's view of the self as "integrative" in her adoption of Feuerbachian ideas, does not provide any further information about Eliot's assumptions about the self and its genetic essence.

28. Bernard Semmel provides a different evaluation of Eliot's depiction of nationalism in *George Eliot and the Politics of National Inheritance*. He argues that Eliot does not show any assimilationist tendencies in *Daniel Deronda*. Quite to the contrary, he views her as a racial essentialist who "put a stress in romantic fashion on blood and the effect of inheritance upon temperament, character, and appearance" (1994, 118) and that her characters "Daniel

and Mordecai's [separatist] views" (129) reflect her own views about racial and national separatism.

29. In "The Modern Hep! Hep! Hep!," in which Eliot's narrator speaks positively about Jews and refers to "a common descent as a bond of obligation" ([1879] 1894, 188), references to a genetic "racial core" cannot be found, either.

30. For a discussion of homoeroticism in *The Blithedale Romance* in light of the Melville/Hawthorne relationship see Monika Mueller, *"This Infinite Fraternity of Feeling": Gender, Genre, and Homoerotic Crisis in Hawthorne's* The Blithedale Romance *and Melville's* Pierre (1996).

31. Shaffer furthermore argues that in *Daniel Deronda*, Eliot puts much emphasis on the I-thou relationship, the social component of religious feeling. According to the kabbalistic philosophy underlying the social philosophy of *Daniel Deronda*, "The mystical basis of the I-Thou unity is the gnostic-cabbalistic notion of Adam as the soul that contained all souls" (1975, 255). While the Neoplatonic origins of the kabbalistic notion of the "soul that contains all souls" will be discussed later at greater length, it might be worthwhile to point out here that Hawthorne's *The Blithedale Romance*, which also focuses on idealized relationships between humans within a religious community, provides a similar philosophic background for the social and religious experiment by couching it in the transcendental philosophy that views human beings as parts of the all-encompassing oversoul.

32. To suggest that the homoerotic attraction between Mordecai and Daniel need not necessarily result in sexual activity, Callanan refers to the (by now standard) theoretical model of locating male-male desire on a continuum between homosocial and homosexual desire—which was introduced by Eve Kosofsky Sedgwick in *Between Men* (1990) for explaining homosexual desire before homosexuality became a subject of medical inquiry (see Callanan 1996, 180).

33. Since Eliot still wrote at a time when "male-male desire [was] widely intelligible primarily by being routed through triangular relations involving a woman" (Sedgwick 1990, 15), the marriage of Daniel and Mirah can be viewed as an instance of a homoerotic exchange of a woman between Mordecai and Daniel.

34. The fact that Fuller included the marriage of the faultless Flying Pigeon to a "barbarous Indian chief" among her examples of more or less "ideal" marriages attests to her democratic transcendentalist spirit:

> The Flying Pigeon (Ratchewaine) was the wife of a barbarous chief, who had six others, but she was his only true wife, because the only one of a strong and pure character, and, having this, inspired a veneration, as like the mind of the man permitted. . . . She died when her son was only four years old, yet left on his mind a feeling of reverent love worthy the thought of Christian chivalry. Grown to manhood, he shed tears on seeing her portrait. ([1845] 1984, 273)

35. The passage in which Mordecai repeatedly employs the word "fuller" reads as follows:

> It has begun already—the marriage of our souls. It waits but the passing away of this body, and then they who are betrothed shall unite in a stricter bond, and what is mine shall be thine. Call nothing mine that I have written, Daniel; for though our Masters delivered rightly that everything should be quoted in the name of him that said it . . . yet it does not exclude the willing marriage which melts soul into soul, and makes thought fuller as the waters are made fuller, where the fulness is inseparable and the clearness is inseparable. For I have judged what I have written, and I

desire the body that I gave my thought to pass away as this fleshly body will pass; but let the thought be born again from our fuller soul which shall be called yours. ([1876] 1995, 751)

36. Fuller gives an account of her understanding of the "soul" in her recollection of a "conversion experience" that she had as a twenty-two year old in 1831:

I saw how long it must be before the soul can learn to act under these limitations of time and space, and human nature, but I saw, also that it MUST do it. . . . I saw that there was no self; that selfishness was all folly, and the result of circumstance; that it was only because I thought self real that I suffered; that I had only to live in the idea of the ALL, and all was mine. ([1840] 1992, 10–12)

37. For a discussion of Emerson's understanding of the Swedenborgian notion of "correspondence" between mind and nature see Steele (1987, 24–25) and Packer (1982, 38–39).

38. As Frederic Ives Carpenter explains in his 1930 book *Emerson and Asia*: "If Emerson's discussion of *Nature* is often Neoplatonic—his doctrine of the Over-Soul practically *is* Neoplatonism. It is the theory of spiritual emanation—the theory that, from an Absolute source, the living water . . . streams down into all creatures below, imparting to them the divine energy" (1930, 75).

39. Cameron furthermore points out that Emerson, who acquired most of his knowledge about Neoplatonism from Ralph Cudworth's *The True Intellectual System of the Universe* (1820), was pleased to find correspondences between his own works and those of "the old philosophers" because it seemed to have confirmed his belief in the accessibility of "absolute truth": "He confessed that it encouraged his self-reliance by pointing out in the works of old philosophers exact parallels to his own thoughts, and thereby convinced him that truth was accessible to him in the present as it had been to others in the past" (1971, 57).

40. George Eliot's comment to her friend Sara Hennell on meeting Ralph Waldo Emerson was highly enthusiastic: "I have seen Emerson—the first *man* I have ever seen" (*George Eliot Letters* 1954–55, 1:270–71).

41. The epigraph to chapter 47, "And you must love him ere to you / He will seem worth of your love" ([1876] 1995, 578) is taken from Wordsworth's "A Poet's Epitaph" and refers to Daniel's relationship with Mordecai. Chapter 68—in which Daniel proposes to Mirah—is introduced by four lines ("All thoughts, all passions, all delights / Whatever stirs this mortal frame / All are but ministers of Love, / And feed his sacred flame" [787]) from Coleridge's poem "Love."

42. According to Barbara Packer, Emerson does not understand the "fall of man" and his consequential fragmentation as a result of sin or disobedience, but rather, as his writings show, as "a consequence of 'self-distrust,' the self's ignorance or denial of its own divinity" (1982, x).

43. Even though Emerson only mentions the male gender in the following, his readers would have to assume that he is including women in his "One Man" since he is speaking about all of society.

44. Both Jeffrey Steele and Harold Bloom understand the oversoul and Kabbalah, respectively, as psychological theories of identification (see Steele 1987, 25–31; Bloom 1975, 28). Jonathan Bishop also discusses Emerson's concept of the oversoul as a psychological concept in his book *Emerson on the Soul* (1964).

45. Eliot characterizes the kabbalistic restoration through metempsychosis as follows:

> Starting from the doctrine that all souls have been pre-existent from the beginning in the Spiritual world, the Kabbala [*sic*] taught that they are all destined to an earthly career in a corporeal form. Now as most souls are stained by their union with the body, forget their heavenly origin, & are subjected to repeated transmigrations, it is chiefly old souls, i.e. such as have already been on earth, that come into physical existence, & only seldom does a *new soul* come on earth. Through the sinfulness of men which causes the same souls continually to re-enter earthly bodies, the great deliverance is delayed. For the new souls cannot come into existence because the world is almost entirely peopled with old souls. (quoted in Irwin 1996, 174)

46. Dieter Schulz discusses the differences between Fuller's and Emerson's view of the self as "social self" in light of the dynamics of their personal relationship and argues that for Fuller the self is to a great extent constituted relationally through "the other," whereas Emerson cherishes solitude and would prefer to be "alone with the Alone" (see Schulz 1997, 16).

47. In the "Discipline" chapter of *Nature,* Emerson elaborates his thoughts on the elusiveness of friendship:

> When much intercourse with a friend has supplied us with a standard of excellence, and has increased our respect for the resources of God who thus sends us a real person to outgo our ideal; when he has, moreover, become an object of thought, and, whilst his character retains all his unconscious effect, is converted into the mind into solid and sweet wisdom,—it is a sign to us that his office is closing, and he is commonly withdrawn from our sight in a short time. ([1836] 1983, 31)

48. Elsewhere, Emerson argued very similarly: "Marriage (in which is called the spiritual world) is impossible, because of the inequality between every subject and object. . . . There will be the same gulf between every me and every thee as between the original and the picture" (quoted in Packer 1982, 175).

49. Richard Poirier argues in *The Renewal of Literature* that Emerson partakes of a tendency in "writing off" (and thus "dissolving" the unified self) that can also be observed in the writing of William James and Friedrich Nietzsche. He concludes that Emerson's view of the self to some extent anticipates deconstructionist thought (see Poirier 1987, 203). I, nevertheless, agree with Christina Zwarg, who deems it wrong to assume that Emerson actually is an early deconstructionist, since "Poirier also identifies a quality of action in Emerson's thinking which supersedes the terms of deconstruction as they are generally understood" (1995, 16).

Chapter 4. Writing Beyond the Ending?

1. This chapter obviously cannot include all reactions by American writers to Eliot's work, due to space limitations. For an in-depth discussion of James's indebtedness to Eliot see Richard Freadman, *Eliot, James and the Fictional Self: A Study in Character and Narration* (1986). In his endeavor to show that Eliot and James instrumentalize narrative technique in order to present autonomous "fictional selves" that are not entirely socially constructed, as Freadman insists, he compares *Daniel Deronda* (1876) with *The Portrait of a Lady* ([1881]

1908); *Middlemarch* (1871-72) with *The Golden Bowl* (1904); and *Romola* (1863) with *The Wings of the Dove* (1902).

2. James wrote a well-known critical piece, "*Daniel Deronda*: A Conversation" (1876), about Eliot's novel. In "A Conversation" three amateur literary critics, Pulcheria, Theodora, and Constantinius, discuss *Daniel Deronda*. Constantinius, who complains that especially the Jewish characters seem too artificial, supposedly reflects James's own criticism of the novel (see [1876] 1984, 978).

3. Rachel Blau DuPlessis outlines "writing beyond the ending" as follows:

> It is the project of twentieth-century women writers to solve the contradiction between love and quest and to replace the alternate endings in marriage and death that are their cultural legacy from nineteenth-century life and letters by offering a different set of choices. They invent a complex of narrative acts with psychosexual meanings, which will be studied here as "writing beyond the ending." (1985, 4)

4. Henry James's *The Portrait of a Lady* was first published in book form by Macmillan (London) in 1881. James revised the novel for the 1908 New York edition. All quotes are from the text of this edition (reprinted by Penguin in 1986).

5. DuPlessis calls attention to the fact that the "quest plot," which demanded female education, often added a subversive aspect to the "ending in death": "Th[e] nineteenth-century ending in death had offered muted yet resonant elements of symbolic protest, often referring back to brief moments of social integration, expressed energy, and personal triumph, from Maggie Tulliver like a great maternal spirit to Lily Bart" (142).

6. For a discussion of Phelps's feminist journalistic activities see Susan Ward's "The Career Woman Fiction of Elizabeth Stuart Phelps" (1986). Phelps was a very prolific writer; she published a total of fifty-seven novels as well as numerous serializations, articles, and uncollected stories (see Kessler 1982, 121).

7. In *Elizabeth Stuart Phelps*, Carol Farley Kessler points out that Phelps was the first woman to lecture to undergraduates at Boston University, which offered the first B.A. degree to women: "Phelps . . . discussed George Eliot in a series of four lectures on 'Representative Modern Fiction'" (1982, 53). Unfortunately, Kessler does not report which aspects of Eliot's work Phelps focused on in her lectures.

8. Phelps's estimate that she herself could not author a "great novel" seems to have proven true. While contemporaneous critics often commended her for her choice of subject matter, they almost customarily pointed out the "stylistic inconsistencies" of her novels (see Kessler 1982, 125–26).

9. The second important source of *The Story of Avis* is Elizabeth Barrett Browning's *Aurora Leigh* (1857), a blank-verse novel that tells a story of female success. As Kessler points out in a footnote to the novel, unlike Eliot's "Armgart," *Aurora Leigh* "presents the dilemma of the creative woman . . . —how to live and work creatively in a society that claims she cannot—and permits both Aurora's resolution of this dilemma and her successful achievement" (Kessler in Phelps [1877] 1985, 253).

10. Phelps takes care to show that even as a mother Avis does not succumb to the demands of "The Cult of True Womanhood." Having children of her own has not made Avis "naturally" sentimental about children. Thus, when something is wrong with one of Coy's children, she remarks rather dryly: "Coy was busy: it was something about the mosquitos; but whether they had killed the baby, or the baby had killed the mosquito [*sic*], Avis did not distinctly understand, and did not offer to stay and discover" ([1877] 1985, 159).

11. This "Coming Woman" will be accompanied by a "Coming Man" who will finally be able to "[surprise] her nature by the largest abnegation of which his own is capable" ([1877] 1985, 246). The empowering of a "Coming Woman" rather than a contemporary protagonist is also a typical feature of the nineteenth-century love/death plot, as DuPlessis points out: "Sometimes the ends of novels were inspirational, sublimating the desire for achievement into a future generation, an end for female quest that was not fully limited to marriage or death" (1985, 1).

12. F. R. Leavis takes the Jewish part of *Daniel Deronda* to be the "bad half" of the book because it expresses Eliot's "generous moral fervour" (1950, 81). Like many more recent commentators, I do not share his assessment since I very much appreciate the interpretative possibilities arising from the ambiguity and indirection of the meditation on identity in the book's "Jewish half."

13. For more in-depth discussions of the influence of *Daniel Deronda* and *The Portrait of a Lady* on *The House of Mirth* see Stuart Hutchinson's "From *Daniel Deronda* to *The House of Mirth*" (1997) and Mary Nyquist's "Determining Influences: Resistance and Mentorship in *The House of Mirth* and the Anglo-American Realist Tradition" (2001).

14. There are quite a few—intended—parallels in the relationships between Gwendolen and Grandcourt and Isabel and Osmond. Both women not only have to endure their husbands' sadistic actions in everyday life, they also both find out that their husbands have former lovers who are still involved in their lives (Mrs. Glasher and Madame Merle) and illegitimate children from these previous relationships. Both Mrs. Glasher and Madame Merle interfere negatively with their ex-lovers' marriages; in *A Portrait of a Lady* Isabel's ultimately successful relationship with Madame Merle's daughter Pansy alleviates the situation.

15. Karen C. Gindele argues that in George Eliot's work (and, I would add, by extension also in Henry James's *The Portrait of a Lady*), marriage functions as a type of "ideological apparatus" (see 2000, 257) that places human subjects within society. As part of a larger argument that suggests that in *Middlemarch* Eliot developed "a theory to invent 'necessity' as ideology, which she locates in the 'medium,' metaphors, and 'minutiae' (everything small)" (2000, 257), Gindele develops the interesting idea that while Eliot's fictional characters pursue lofty, idealistic, "far-away" aims (like altruism and freedom) their efforts are hampered by what is close by—like unsuitable spouses and the "something awful in the nearness [marriage] brings" (267).

16. Patricia E. Johnson, who compares James's and Eliot's "framing" of their female characters, suggests that James's female protagonists are more trapped by the masculinist gender hegemony than Eliot's:

> Both James and Eliot question, or allow their characters to question, the power of the male gaze, but Eliot's questioning is both more direct and more broadly challenging to Western cultural assumptions. James frequently authorizes the male gaze by conflating the scopic positions, even while he denies or criticizes its power. Isabel alternates between positions of interiorizing the male gaze, producing herself as its object, and of confronting it with her desire to see life for herself. . . . Unlike James who returns Isabel to her prison, Eliot tries to find an alternative to a life organized by an all-powerful male gaze. (1997, 53)

17. F. R. Leavis, for example, refers to the corrupting influence of Europe when he says about Madame Merle that she is "the complete expatriate who has none of the American virtues" (1950, 151).

18. Madame Merle's comments suggest that she also thinks of idle American men as "good for nothing":

> The worst case, I think, is a friend of mine, a countryman of ours, who lives in Italy.... He's Gilbert Osmond—he lives in Italy; that's all one can say about him or make of him.... No career, no name, no position, no fortune, no past, no future, no anything. (James [1908] 1986, 249)

19. Delia da Sousa Correa similarly speculates that James's negative attitude towards "capitalist" productivity and his "defence of the significance of psychological 'incident' can be read as a defence of the work of the novelist as opposed to materially productive work" (2001, 118).

20. Jonathan Freedman makes a valid point about the "European" roots of "American" collectorship:

> [I]n *The Golden Bowl* when the millionaire Adam Verver carries the cultural riches of Europe to a palace of art in American City, America ... the novel is clear to note that this act of appreciative appropriation places him, and the booming American capital he represents, in the position of the imperial projects that preceded him—those of Greece, Rome, and England. (1998, 7)

21. In *Daniel Deronda*, Eliot, perhaps not always successfully, descends into the nitty-gritty of Jewish working class culture to show the environment in which vital faith and possible redemption reside. James, in spite of criticizing upper class British and American life, does not follow her in locating the possibility for cultural redemption in the American or even Italian working classes. He apparently did not view them as equipped with possibility for spiritual revitalization.

22. Robinson provides a valuable analysis of how money is made and spent in the upper echelons of New York society:

> The Penistons and their ilk are the descendants of Dutch and English merchants, whose fortunes have been long invested in New York real estate and the kinds of stocks and bonds that gave these holdings the generic name "securities." The work of a male in this class is to oversee the protection of an inheritance.... Although it may take place right on Wall Street, this work is as far removed from the rough and tumble of stock market speculation as it is from the ancestral enterprises.... The Trenor-Dorset axis of the very rich also includes "old money," although it need not be quite as hard to qualify for membership in that group. It is this circle that the social climbers seek to penetrate.... The economic basis of this class is inherited wealth, but the males work at increasing their patrimonies through investment in that speculative market from which the fortune of a man like Simon Rosedale derives. (1994, 343)

23. Montgomery makes a similar point when she writes that Thorstein Veblen put forth in his *The Theory of the Leisure Class* (1899)

> that leisure was intentionally displayed to others because it connoted gentility, refinement, specialized knowledge, civilization, cultivation, wealth, and breeding. He also argued that it was by and large the responsibility of leisure-class women and their servants to convey these things to the public at large. (1998, 9)

24. While Ozick lives in "postmodern" times, she aligns herself with "high modernism" rather than postmodernism. In "The Muse, Postmodern and Homeless," she eloquently defends the values of modernism against those of postmodernism. Arguing against the notion of a "critical egalitarianism" (1991, 137) that holds that all texts are of equal value, she voices as her main complaint against postmodernism its devaluation of the "real artist" (see 138). However, the complete deconstruction of Puttermesser's life and life's aims—and Puttermesser is an artist of sorts and a creator—that Ozick effects in *The Puttermesser Papers* suggests to me that she is not a stranger to the more pronounced skepticism of postmodernism.

25. Cynthia Ozick's *Levitation: Five Fictions* (1982) includes "Puttermesser and Xanthippe" and Puttermesser: Her Work, Her Ancestry, Her Afterlife" along with "From a Refugee's Notebook," "Levitation," and "Shots."

26. Critics tend to view Puttermesser as Ozick's double because incidents in her life parallel incidents in her creator's life and also because she reflects Ozick's intellectualism (see Pinsker, 2002, online).

27. Ozick gives a very funny description of Puttermesser's Jewish/George Eliotian thirst for knowledge and how she imagines it to be quenched in Eden:

> Eden is equipped above all with timelessness, so Puttermesser will read at least all of Balzac, all of Dickens, all of Turgenev and Dostoevsky (her mortal self has already read all of Tolstoy and George Eliot); at last Puttermesser will read Kristin Lavransdatter and the stupendous trilogy of Dmitri Merezhkovsky, she will read *The Magic Mountain* and the whole *Fairie Queene* and every line of *The Ring and the Book*, she will read a biography of Beatrix Potter and one of Walter Scott in many entrancing volumes and of Lytton Strachey, at least, at last! In Eden insatiable Puttermesser will be nourished, if not glutted. She will study Roman law, the more arcane varieties of higher mathematics, the nuclear composition of the stars, what happened to the Monophysites, Chinese history, Russian, and Icelandic. (Ozick 1997b, 14)

28. Eliot's narrator reports Dorothea's disappointment with finding that "the large vistas and wide fresh air which she had dreamed of finding in her husband's mind were replaced by ante-rooms and winding passages which seemed to lead nowhere" ([1871–72] 1994, 195).

29. In an interview, Ozick remarked, "[w]hen I am looking for moral principle and virtuous dedication to historical justice, I am filled with admiration for the Zionist half of *Daniel Deronda*" (interview with Cynthia Ozick by Diane Osen, no date, online).

30. According to Gershom Scholem, the creation of the golem first surfaced in Kabbalah between the third and the sixth century in a text called *Book of Creation* or *Book Yetzirah* (see Scholem [1960] 1996, 167).

31. Byron L. Sherwin views parallels between the legend of the Golem as protector of the Jews and the function of the state of Israel: "Like the Golem, as [Jay] Gonen observes [in *Psychohistory of Zionism*], Israel was created as a means of protecting the physical safety of Jews through the use of physical power" (1985, 2).

32. Ozick's slightly ironic description reveals Puttermesser's—and probably also her own—respect for the listed writers' social concern:

> How she would like to put Walt Whitman himself in charge of the Bureau of Summary Sessions, and have Shelley take over Water Resource Development—Shelley whose principle is that poets are the legislators of mankind! William Blake in the

Fire Department. George Eliot doing Social Services. Emily Brontë over at Police. Jane Austen in Bridges and Tunnels, Virginia Woolf and Edgar Allan Poe sharing Health. Herman Melville overseeing the Office of Single Room Occupancy Housing. (1997, 74)

33. The golem supposedly is flawed because his creator is flawed (see Sherwin 1985, 24–25); if Daniel Deronda, as Nurbhai and Newton suggest, represents a golem that actually achieves his goal, then this reflects positively on the flawless nature of his creator, Mordecai.

34. When asked in an interview about her response to mysticism, Ozick replied:

> The mystic believes that the Godhead can enter the human soul, that the human being can be filled with the Godhead. Quite aside from this hubris, I don't think we ought to live under such a delusion. . . . I think of Gershom Scholem's famous comment about his work on Kabbalah, the mystical current in Judaism . . . : Kabbalah, he said, is nonsense, but the study of Kabbalah is scholarship. For me, mysticism is foolish self-deception, but the use of it in fiction is inspiration (interview with Cynthia Ozick by Diane Osen, no date, online).

35. Elaine M. Kauvar points out that passages from Plato's *Theaetetus* included in "Puttermesser and Xanthippe" also hint at the fact that Puttermesser's intellectual offsprings are "'wind-eggs,' . . . falsehoods which in their fruitlessness are like unfertilized eggs." She takes this to indicate that "in adverting to that passage in the *Theaetetus*, Ozick implies the risk inherent in Puttermesser's activities" (1991, 133).

36. As already indicated, Ozick acknowledges her indebtedness to Gershom Scholem's essay "The Idea of the Golem" (see Ozick 1997, 48), which is faithfully reflected in "Puttermesser and Xanthippe."

37. A footnote to Gershom Scholem's essay reports that it was said about Rabbi Loew's golem that

> [t]he golem had to be made without generative power or sexual urge. For if he had had this urge, even after the manner of animals in which it is far weaker than in man, we would have had a great deal of trouble with him, because no woman would have been able to defend herself against him. ([1960] 1996, 194)

Ozick mentioned in an interview that she deliberately turned Xanthippe into a "dangerous" sexual creature in spite of being aware of the fact that "in Jewish folklore the golem is, as I expressed in that story, a sort of savior. And not an erotic creature at all. And it's true that Xanthippe does turn into a Greek goddess of Eros or lust" (Interview with Cynthia Ozick by David Wiley, 1997c, online).

38. Xanthippe presents herself to Puttermesser as her double: "I am your amanuensis. . . . I express you. I copy and record you. Now it is time for you to accomplish your thought" (Ozick 1997, 67).

39. Ozick's "Puttermesser Paired" was first published in the 8 October 1990 issue of the *New Yorker*. All quotations are from the story as printed in *The Puttermesser Papers* (1997).

40. In *Sensational Designs*, Tompkins argues that the "durability of a text" relies to a large extent on "publishing practices, pedagogical and critical traditions, economic structures, [and] social networks":

> The "durability" of the text is not a function of its unique resistance to intellectual obsolescence; for the text, in any describable, documentable sense, is not durable at

all. What endures is the literary and cultural tradition that believes in the idea of the classic, and that perpetuates that belief from day to day and from year to year by reading and rereading, publishing and republishing, teaching and recommending for teaching, and writing books and articles about a small group of works whose "durability" is thereby assured. (1985, 36–37)

41. In *Writing Beyond the Ending*, DuPlessis presents various types of narrative modification introduced by twentieth-century women writers. Thus, Virginia Woolf, for example, sometimes replaces gendered individuals by "androgynous" communal protagonists or "breaks the sentence," which DuPlessis explains as follows:

To break the sentence rejects not grammar especially, but rhythm, pace, flow, expression: the structuring of the female voice by the male voice, female tone and manner by male expectations . . . female writing by existing conventions of gender—in short any way in which dominant structures shape muted ones. (1985, 32)

And, according to DuPlessis, Dorothy Richardson, author of *The Pilgrimage*, a series of novels published between 1915 to 1967, introduces the concept of "liminality": "Liminality—constant transition that does not crystallize into any 'state' (married or single, male or female, one opinion versus another)—ends gender scripts by dissolving alternative, polarized either/or possibilities into infinite potentiality" (150).

42. In *Looking for Work* there is a second reference to gender relations in George Eliot's work, which indicates that at least Salley (if not Cheever herself) is not a very attentive reader: "After lunch I usually lie in bed and read, and one afternoon just as Daniel Deronda is losing my sympathy by falling for the prim goody-goody Miriam [*sic*] instead of regal and troublesome Gwendolyn [*sic*], the telephone rings" (130).

43. With her shallow protagonist Salley, who does not seem to experience much personal growth throughout the novel, Cheever, at least in my estimation, fails to present a very compelling twentieth-century adaptation of a George Eliot heroine. This impression of Cheever's *Looking for Work* (1979) as a rather minor twentieth-century novel seems to be corroborated by the fact that there is only one MLA citation (MLA bibliography 1963–2003) for the novel. In this one reference, Catherine Civello does not comment much on the novel beyond observing that "Salley, 'looking for work' . . . must have responded to Dorothea, who 'longed for work,' according to Eliot" (1989, 54). Dorothea, unlike Salley, is, of course, looking for socially beneficial and meaningful work.

44. Elaine Showalter points out that George Gissing was attracted by feminism and devised alternative opportunities for "odd women" out of self-interest:

"My demand for female 'equality,' " he wrote to his friend Edouard Bertz, "simply means that I am convinced there will be no social peace until women are intellectually trained as much as men. More than half the misery of life is due to the ignorance and childishness of women . . . I am driven frantic by the crass imbecility of the typical woman. That type must disappear, or at all events become altogether subordinate." (1991, 30)

45. In the first chapter of *Writing Beyond the Ending* (1985), "Endings and Contradictions," which addresses nineteenth-century marriage and death plots, DuPlessis does not analyze the form (narrative perspective, etc.) of the nineteenth-century novels she discusses.

46. Curiously enough, even after Jane has realized that Gabriel is not the nineteenth-century husband she seeks, she still cannot refrain from thinking of him in terms of the George

Eliot/George Henry Lewes relationship and permanence (unfortunately, her thoughts now center on his relationship with his wife):

> And yet when Eleanor went on to say, "I have often thought recently that childless couples remain truer to each other longer, because they are more things to each other," Jane's heart stung with another connection she would rather not have made: Ann and Gabriel Weeks, Marian Evans and George Henry Lewes—childless couples. (393)

47. Elaine Showalter also concludes a bit pessimistically about Godwin's novel that "Godwin seems to be indicating that despite the success of women novelists, women professors, feminist journals, and women's studies, little has changed" (1991, 34).

48. According to DuPlessis, male authors can also write beyond the ending because writing itself is not male or female: "there is nothing exclusively or essentially female about the sentence of the feminine gender" (1985, 32); besides that, Irving has shown his sensitivity towards gender relationships by means of his penchant and sympathy for transgendered characters such as Roberta in *The World According to Garp* (1978) and the hijras in *A Son of the Circus* (1994).

49. Irving has often been criticized for his sensationalism, but as Harter and Thompson suggest, he clearly transcends the limits of sensational topics and "their treatment by those writers who would exploit them merely for easy commercial success" (1986, 7).

50. The nineteenth-century "female end" in death fails to work for Irving's *A Widow for One Year* since all the people who die in the novel are male.

51. Elaine M. Kauvar comments on Ozick's reverence for James and her subsequent effort to gain independence from her artistic master:

> When she wrote "The Lesson of the Master" and divulged her mistaken apprehension of his advice—how as a young woman she chose art over life—Cynthia Ozick did not claim Henry James as the artistic model whose path she followed in writing *Trust*. Instead her essay laments an idealization common to the young, an identification with an older artist, a young writer's desire to achieve what an elderly writer had attained over a lifetime. (1986, 2–3)

52. In describing Puttermesser's enthusiasm for Rabeeno, Ozick might also have wanted to ridicule Eliot for presenting her courtship with Cross "as a kind of miraculous romance tale, in which the heroine, rescued from death and restored to life at the last minute, is still too dazed to know quite what has happened to her" (1994, 116), as Rosemarie Bodenheimer puts it.

53. Eliot's biographer Frederick Karl describes the situation almost as drastically:

> [A] younger man on his honeymoon, finding himself in the footsteps of his predecessor, with a fixation on a woman he worships as a divine presence, is confronted by this woman in a state of undress, or naked, and all his inhibitions, anxieties, confusions come to haunt him in a sudden expression of impotence. Unable to face the pressure on him, he leaps into the Grand Canal, the most romantic of places, but in actuality one of the most pestilent places on earth. The honeymoon turns into a nightmare. (1995, 632)

54. Ozick's description of the Puttermesser's and Rupert Rabeeno's wedding ceremony is hilarious:

Puttermesser had retrieved her mother's wedding ring from an old felt wallet she kept inside an empty plastic margarine container at the back of the vegetable bin in the refrigerator. . . . In Puttermesser's apartment afterward Harvey Morgenbluth and Raya Lieberman each drank a Styrofoam cup of champagne (Harvey's present) and ate a piece of wedding cake—Puttermesser made do with Entenmann's chocolate layer from the supermarket on Third—and then the two witnesses went off together. (1997, 162)

Works Cited

Adams, Kimberly VanEsveld. 1996. "Feminine Godhead, Feminist Symbol: The Madonna in George Eliot, Ludwig Feuerbach, Anna Jameson, and Margaret Fuller." *Journal of Feminist Studies in Religion* 12:41–70.

———. 2001. *Our Lady of Victorian Feminism: The Madonna in the Work of Anna Jameson, Margaret Fuller, and George Eliot.* Athens: Ohio University Press.

Aiken, D. Wyatt. 1988. *The Search for Truth: A Textbook for Transcendental Philosophy.* Frankfurt: Peter Lang.

Alaya, Flavia. 1991. "Victorian Science and the Genius of Woman." In *Race, Class and Gender in Nineteenth-Century Culture,* edited by Maryanne Cline Horowitz, 231–50. Rochester: University of Rochester Press.

Althusser, Louis. 1984. *Essays on Ideology.* Thetford, U.K.: The Thetford Press.

Ammons, Elizabeth. 1986. "Stowe's Dream of the Mother-Savior: *Uncle Tom's Cabin* and American Women Writers before the 1920s." In *New Essays on* Uncle Tom's Cabin, edited by Eric J. Sundquist. 155–95. Cambridge: Cambridge University Press.

Appiah, Kwame Anthony. 1992. *In My Father's House: Africa in the Philosophy of Culture.* New York: Oxford University Press.

———. 1996. "Race, Culture, Identity: Misunderstood Connections." In *Color Conscious: The Political Morality of Race,* edited by K. Anthony Appiah and Amy Gutmann, 30–105. Princeton: Princeton University Press.

Argyros, Ellen. 1999. *"Without Any Check of Proud Reserve": Sympathy and Its Limits in George Eliot's Novels.* New York: Peter Lang.

Armstrong, Nancy. 2001. "Gender and the Victorian Novel." In *The Victorian Novel,* edited by Deirdre David, 97–125. Cambridge: Cambridge University Press.

Asad, Talal. 1986. "The Concept of Cultural Translation in British Social Anthropology." In *Writing Culture: The Poetics and Politics of Ethnography,* edited by James Clifford and George E. Marcus, 141–64. Berkeley: University of California Press.

Auerbach, Nina. 1975. "The Power of Hunger: Demonism and Maggie Tulliver." *Nineteenth-Century Fiction* 30:150–71.

Baker, William. 1973. "The Kabbalah, Mordecai, and George Eliot's Religion of Humanity." *Yearbook of English Studies* 3:216–21.

Banta, Martha. 1998. "Men, Women, and the American Way." In *The Cambridge Companion to Henry James*, edited by Jonathan Freedman, 21–39. Cambridge: Cambridge University Press.

Barrett, Dorothea. 1989. *Vocation and Desire: George Eliot's Heroines*. London: Routledge.

Beebee, Thomas O. 1994. *The Ideology of Genre: A Comparative Study of Generic Instability*. University Park: Pennsylvania State University Press.

Beer, Gillian. 1983. *Darwin's Plots: Evolutionary Narrative in Darwin, George Eliot and Nineteenth-Century Fiction*. London: Routledge.

Bell, Michael Davitt. 1985. "Arts of Deception: Hawthorne, 'Romance,' and *The Scarlet Letter*." In *New Essays on* The Scarlet Letter, edited by Michael J. Colacurcio. 29–56. Cambridge: Cambridge University Press.

Benhabib, Seyla, Judith Butler, Drucilla Cornell, and Nancy Fraser. 1995. *Feminist Contentions: A Philosophical Exchange*. New York: Routledge.

Bennett, Joan. 1948. *George Eliot: Her Mind and Her Art*. Cambridge: Cambridge University Press.

Benstock, Shari. 1994. "A Critical History of *The House of Mirth*." In Wharton, Edith, *The House of Mirth: Complete, Authoritative Text with Biographical and Historical Contexts, Critical History, and Essays from Five Contemporary Critical Perspectives*, edited by Shari Benstock. 309–23. Boston: Bedford Books.

Bentley, Nancy. 1995. *The Ethnography of Manners: Hawthorne, James, Wharton*. Cambridge: Cambridge University Press.

Bercovitch, Sacvan. 1991. *The Office of the Scarlet Letter*. Baltimore: Johns Hopkins University Press.

Bhabha, Homi K. 1994. *The Location of Culture*. London: Routledge.

Bishop, Jonathan. 1964. *Emerson on the Soul*. Cambridge: Harvard University Press.

Bloom, Harold. 1975. *Kabbalah and Criticism*. New York: The Seabury Press.

Bodenheimer, Rosemarie. 1994. *The Real Life of Mary Ann Evans: George Eliot, Her Letters and Fiction*. Ithaca: Cornell University Press.

Bonaparte, Felicia. 1979. *The Triptych and the Cross: The Central Myths of George Eliot's Poetic Imagination*. Brighton: Harvester Press.

Boumelha, Penny. 1987. "George Eliot and the End of Realism." In *Women Reading Women's Writing*, edited by Sue Roe, 15–35. Brighton, U.K.: The Harvester Press.

Bowlby, Rachel. 1990. "Breakfast in America: Uncle Tom's Cultural Histories." In *Nation and Narration*, edited by Homi K. Bhabha, 197–212. London: Routledge.

Brady, Kristin. 1992. *Women Writers: George Eliot*. Houndmills, U.K.: Macmillan.

Brennan, Timothy. 1990. "The National Longing for Form." In *Nation and Narration*, edited by Homi K. Bhabha, 44–70. London: Routledge.

Brodhead, Richard. 1990. Introduction to the *The Marble Faun*, by Nathaniel Hawthorne, ix–xxix. New York: Penguin.

Bromell, Nicholas K. 1990. "'The Bloody Hand' of Labor: Work, Class, and Gender in Three Stories by Hawthorne." *American Quarterly* 42:542–64.

Bullen, J. B. 1975. "George Eliot's *Romola* as a Positivist Allegory." *Review of English Studies* 26:425–35.

Butler, Judith. 1990. *Gender Trouble: Feminism and the Subversion of Identity.* New York: Routledge.

———. 1993. *Bodies That Matter: On the Discursive Limits of "Sex."* New York: Routledge.

Callanan, Laura. 1996. "The Seduction of Daniel Deronda." *Women's Writing* 3:177–88.

Cameron, Kenneth Walter. 1971. *Young Emerson's Transcendental Vision: An Exposition of His World View with an Analysis of the Structure, Backgrounds, and Meaning of* Nature, *1836.* Hartford, CT: Transcendental Books.

Cantave, Sophia. 2000. "Who Gets to Create the Lasting Images? The Problem of Black Representation in *Uncle Tom's Cabin*." In *Approaches to Teaching Stowe's* Uncle Tom's Cabin, edited by Elizabeth Ammons and Susan Belasco, 93–103. New York: The Modern Language Association of America.

Carpenter, Frederic Ives. 1930. *Emerson and Asia.* Cambridge: Harvard University Press.

Carpenter, Mary Wilson. 1990. "The Trouble with Romola." In *Victorian Sages and Cultural Discourse*, edited by Thaïs Morgan, 105–28. New Brunswick: Rutgers University Press.

Carroll, Alicia. 2003. *Dark Smiles: Race and Desire in George Eliot.* Athens: Ohio University Press.

Carroll, David. 1992. *George Eliot and the Conflict of Interpretations: A Reading of the Novels.* Cambridge: Cambridge University Press.

Cave, Terence. 1995. Introduction to *Daniel Deronda*, by George Eliot, ix–xl. Harmondsworth: Penguin.

Chase, Richard. 1957. *The American Novel and Its Tradition.* Garden City, N.Y.: Doubleday.

Cheever, Susan. 1979. *Looking for Work.* New York: Simon and Schuster.

Chevigny, Bell Gale. 1986. "To the Edges of Ideology: Margaret Fuller's Centrifugal Evolution." *American Quarterly* 38:173–201.

———. 1994. *The Woman and the Myth: Margaret Fuller's Life and Writings.* Boston: Northeastern University Press.

Cheyette, Bryan. 1993. *Constructions of "The Jew" in English Literature and Society: Racial Representations, 1875–1945.* Cambridge: Cambridge University Press.

Christ, Carol. 1976. "Aggression and Providential Death in George Eliot's Fiction." *Novel* 9:130–40.

Civello, Catherine. 1989. "From Middlemarch to Manhattan." *The George Eliot Fellowship Review* 20:52–56.

Clayton, Jay, and Eric Rothstein, eds. 1991. *Influence and Intertextuality in Literary History.* Madison: University of Wisconsin Press.

Colacurcio, Michael J. 1985. "'The Woman's Own Choice': Sex, Metaphor, and the Puritan 'Sources' of *The Scarlet Letter*." In *New Essays on* The Scarlet Letter, edited by Michael J. Colacurcio. 101–35. Cambridge: Cambridge University Press.

Comte, Auguste. 1865. *A General View of Positivism*, translated by J. H. Bridges. London: Trübner and Co.

Comte, Auguste, and Harriet Martineau. 1896. *The Positive Philosophy of Auguste Comte,* freely translated and condensed by Harriet Martineau. 3 vols. London: Bell.

Corbett, Mary Jean. 1988. "Representing the Rural: The Critique of Loamshire in *Adam Bede.*" *Studies in the Novel* 20:288–301.

Correa, Delia da Sousa. 2001. "*The Portrait of a Lady*: Identity and Gender." In *The Nineteenth-Century Novel: Identities*, edited by Dennis Walder, 116–36. London: Routledge.

Cottom, Daniel. 1987. *Social Figures: George Eliot, Social History, and Literary Representation.* Minneapolis: University of Minnesota Press.

Daniel, Janice B. 1993. "'Apples of the Thoughts and Fancies': Nature as Narrator in *The Scarlet Letter.*" *American Transcendental Quarterly* 7:307–19.

Darwin, Charles. [1874] 1906. *The Descent of Man and Selection in Relation to Sex.* London: John Murray.

de Lauretis, Teresa. 1987. *Technologies of Gender: Essays on Theory, Film, and Fiction.* Bloomington: Indiana University Press.

Donohue, Agnes McNeill. 1985. *Hawthorne: Calvin's Ironic Stepchild.* Kent, OH: Kent State University Press.

Ducksworth, Sarah Smith. 1992. "Stowe's Construction of an African Persona and the Creation of White Identity for a New World Order." In *The Stowe Debate: Rhetorical Strategies in* Uncle Tom's Cabin, edited by Mason I. Lowance, Jr., Ellen E. Westbrook, and R. C. De Prospo, 205–35. Amherst: University of Massachusetts Press.

Dunne, Michael. 1995. *Hawthorne's Narrative Strategies.* Jackson: University of Mississippi Press.

DuPlessis, Rachel Blau. 1985. *Writing Beyond the Ending: Narrative Strategies of Twentieth-Century Women Writers.* Bloomington: Indiana University Press.

Easton, Alison. 1996. *The Making of the Hawthorne Subject.* Columbia: University of Missouri Press.

Edel, Leon. 1985. *Henry James: A Life.* New York: Harper and Row.

Edwards, Lee R. 1977. "Women, Energy, and Middlemarch." In Eliot, George, *"Middlemarch": An Authoritative Text, Backgrounds, Reviews and Criticism*, edited by Bert G. Hornback. 683–93. New York: Norton.

Eliot, George. 1856. "Margaret Fuller's Letters from Italy." *The Leader*, May 17:475.

———. [1856] 1894. "The Natural History of German Life." In *Impressions of Theophrastus Such/Miscellaneous Essays*, 272–317. Boston: Estes and Laureat.

———. [1879] 1894. "The Modern Hep! Hep! Hep!" In *Impressions of Theophrastus Such/Miscellaneous Essays*, 184–213. Boston: Estes and Laureat.

———. 1954–55. *The George Eliot Letters*, edited by Gordon S. Haight. 7 vols. New Haven: Yale University Press.

———. [1858] 1973. *Scenes of Clerical Life.* Harmondsworth, U.K.: Penguin.

———. [1860] 1979. *The Mill on the Floss.* Harmondsworth, U.K.: Penguin.

———. [1863] 1980. *Romola.* Harmondsworth, U.K.: Penguin.

———. [1859] 1985. *Adam Bede.* Harmondsworth, U.K.: Penguin.

———. [1861] 1985. *Silas Marner: The Weaver of Raveloe.* Harmondsworth, U.K.: Penguin.

———. [1873] 1989. "Armgart." In *Collected Poems*, edited by Lucien Jenkins. 114–54. London: Skoob Books.

———. 1990. *Selected Essays, Poems and Other Writings*, edited by A. S. Byatt and Nicholas Warren. Harmondsworth, U.K.: Penguin.

———. [1871–72] 1994. *Middlemarch*. Harmondsworth, U.K.: Penguin.

———. [1876] 1995. *Daniel Deronda*. Harmondsworth, U.K.: Penguin.

———. [1866] 1995. *Felix Holt: The Radical*. Harmondsworth, U.K.: Penguin.

———. 1998. "Recollections of Italy. 1860." In *The Journals of George Eliot*, edited by Margaret Harris and Judith Johnston. 327–68. Cambridge: Cambridge University Press.

Ellmann, Richard. 1977. "Dorothea's Husbands." In George Eliot, *"Middlemarch": An Authoritative Text, Backgrounds, Reviews, and Criticism*, edited by Bert G. Hornback. 750–65. New York: Norton.

Emerson, Ralph Waldo. 1983. *Essays and Lectures*. New York: The Library of America.

Feuerbach, Ludwig. [1841] 1989. *The Essence of Christianity*, translated by George Eliot. Amherst: Prometheus Books.

Fields, Annie, ed. 1898. *Life and Letters of Harriet Beecher Stowe*. Boston: Houghton, Mifflin, and Co.

Foreman, P. Gabrielle. 1993. "'This Promiscuous Housekeeping': Death, Transgression, and Homoeroticism in *Uncle Tom's Cabin*." *Representations* 43:50–72.

Foucault, Michel. 1990. *The Use of Pleasure: Volume 2 of the History of Sexuality*. New York: Vintage Books.

Frank, Armin Paul. 1983. "Amerikanische und britische Erzählliteratur im Vergleich: Der Fall Hester gegen Hester." In *Anglistentag 1981: Vorträge*, edited by Jörg Hasler, 266–80. Frankfurt: Peter Lang.

Frank, Esther. 1999. "Reading Jewish Women's Writing." http://www.arts.mcgill.ca/programs/Jewish/30yrs/frank (accessed 8 August 2002).

Franzosa, John. 1983. "Locke's Kinsman, William Molyneux: The Philosophical Context of Hawthorne's Early Tales." *ESQ* 29:1–15.

Freadman, Richard. 1986. *Eliot, James and the Fictional Self: A Study in Character and Narration*. New York: St. Martin's Press.

Freedman, Jonathan. 1998. "Introduction: The Moment of Henry James." In *The Cambridge Companion to Henry James*, edited by Jonathan Freedman, 1–20. Cambridge: Cambridge University Press.

Freud, Sigmund. 1999. "Das Unheimliche." In *Der Moses des Michelangelo: Schriften über Kunst und Künstler*, 137–72. Frankfurt: Fischer.

Fuller, Margaret. 1856. *At Home and Abroad, or Things and Thoughts in America and Europe*. Boston: Crosby, Nichols, and Company.

———. 1992. *The Essential Margaret Fuller*, edited by Jeffrey Steele. New Brunswick, NJ: Rutgers University Press.

———. [1844] 1994. *Summer on the Lakes*. In *The Portable Margaret Fuller*, edited by Mary Kelley, 69–227. New York: Penguin.

———. [1845] 1994. *Woman in the Nineteenth Century*. In *The Portable Margaret Fuller*, edited by Mary Kelley, 228–362. New York: Penguin.

Fussell, Paul, ed. 1987. *The Norton Book of Travel*. New York: Norton.

Gatens, Moira. 1991. *Feminism and Philosophy: Perspectives on Difference and Equality*. Cambridge: Polity Press.

Geertz, Clifford. [1973] 1993. *The Interpretation of Cultures: Selected Essays*. London: Fontana Press.

Gilbert, Sandra M., and Susan Gubar. 1980. *The Madwoman in the Attic: The Woman Writer and the Nineteenth-Century Literary Imagination.* New Haven: Yale University Press.

Giles, Paul. 2001. *Transatlantic Insurrections: British Culture and the Formation of American Literature, 1730–1860.* Philadelphia: University of Pennsylvania Press.

Gilman, Sander. 1991. *The Jew's Body.* New York: Routledge.

Gindele, Karen C. 2000. "The Web of Necessity: George Eliot's Theory of Ideology." *Texas Studies in Literature and Language* 42:255–89.

Godwin, Gail. 1974. *The Odd Woman.* New York: Alfred A. Knopf.

Goshgarian, G. M. 1992. *To Kiss the Chastening Rod: Domestic Fiction and Sexual Ideology in the American Renaissance.* Ithaca: Cornell University Press.

Graver, Suzanne. 1984. *George Eliot and Community: A Study in Social Theory and Fictional Form.* Berkeley: University of California Press.

Greene, Gayle. 1991. "An 'Odd Story': Gail Godwin's *The Odd Woman.*" In *Old Maids to Radical Spinsters: Unmarried Women in the Twentieth-Century Novel,* edited by Laura L. Doan, 169–92. Urbana: University of Illinois Press.

Greenwald, Elissa. 1991. "Hawthorne and Judaism: Otherness and Identity in *The Marble Faun.*" *Studies in the Novel* 23:128–38.

Grossberg, Lawrence. 1996. "Identity and Cultural Studies: Is That All There Is?" In *Questions of Cultural Identity,* edited by Stuart Hall, and Paul du Gay, 87–107. London: Sage Publications.

Grossman, Jay. 1993. "'A' is for Abolition?: Race, Authorship, *The Scarlet Letter.*" *Textual Practice* 7:13–30.

Haight, Gordon. [1968] 1992. *George Eliot: A Biography.* Harmondsworth, U.K.: Penguin.

Hall, Stuart. 1996. "Introduction: Who Needs 'Identity'?" In *Questions of Cultural Identity,* edited by Stuart Hall, and Paul du Gay. 1–17. London: Sage Publications.

Hamilton, Kristie. 2002. "Fauns and Mohicans: Narratives of Extinction and Hawthorne's Aesthetic of Modernity." In *Roman Holidays: American Writers and Artists in Nineteenth-Century Italy,* edited by Robert K. Martin and Leland S. Person. 41–59. Iowa City: University of Iowa Press.

Hannaford, Ivan. 1996. *Race: The History of an Idea in the West.* Baltimore: Johns Hopkins University Press.

Harris, Margaret. 1997. "What George Eliot Saw in Europe: The Evidence of Her Journals." In *George Eliot and Europe,* edited by John Rignall. 1–16. Aldershot, U.K.: Scolar Press.

Harris, Margaret, and Judith Johnston, eds. 1998. *The Journals of George Eliot.* Cambridge: Cambridge University Press.

Harter, Carol C., and James R. Thompson. 1986. *John Irving.* Boston: Twayne Publishers.

Hawkes, David. 1996. *Ideology.* London: Routledge.

Hawthorne, Nathaniel. 1903. *Notes of Travel IV,* edited by Sophia Hawthorne. Cambridge: Houghton, Mifflin, and Co.

———. 1941. *The English Notebooks,* edited by Randall Stewart. New York: Modern Language Association.

———. 1980. *The French and Italian Notebooks. Centenary Edition XIV,* edited by Thomas Woodson. Columbus: Ohio State University Press.

———. [1851] 1984. *The Blithedale Romance.* Harmondsworth, U.K.: Penguin.

———. [1851] 1986. *The House of the Seven Gables.* New York: Penguin.

———. [1850] 1986. *The Scarlet Letter.* New York: Penguin.

———. 1987. *The English Notebooks, 1853–1856. Centenary Edition XXI,* edited by Thomas Woodson. Columbus: Ohio State University Press.

———. 1987. *The Letters, 1853–1856. Centenary Edition XVII,* edited by Thomas Woodson, James A. Rubino, L. Neal Smith, and Norman Holmes Pearson. Columbus: Ohio State University Press.

———. [1860] 1990. *The Marble Faun.* New York: Penguin.

———. 1994. *Miscellaneous Prose and Verse. Centenary Edition XXIII,* edited by Thomas Woodson, Claude M. Simpson, and L. Neal Smith. Columbus: Ohio State University Press.

Hedrick, Joan D. 1994. *Harriet Beecher Stowe: A Life.* Oxford: Oxford University Press.

Henry, Nancy. 1994. Originating Fictions: Harriet Beecher Stowe and George Eliot. Ph.D. diss., University of Chicago.

———. 2002. *George Eliot and the British Empire.* Cambridge: Cambridge University Press.

Hesse, David Maria. 1996. *George Eliot and Auguste Comte: The Influence of Comtean Philosophy on the Novels of George Eliot.* Frankfurt: Peter Lang.

Hollinger, David A. 1995. *Postethnic America: Beyond Multiculturalism.* New York: Basic Books.

Hutcheon, Linda. 1989. *The Politics of Postmodernism.* London.

Hutchinson, Stuart. 1997. "From *Daniel Deronda* to *The House of Mirth.*" *Essays in Criticism* 47:315–31.

Ingham, Patricia. 1996. *The Language of Gender and Class: Transformation in the Victorian Novel.* London: Routledge.

Irving, John. 1998. *A Widow for One Year.* New York: Ballantine Books.

Irwin, Jane. 1996. *George Eliot's* Daniel Deronda *Notebooks.* Cambridge: Cambridge University Press.

Jackson, Tony E. 1996. "George Eliot's 'New Evangel': *Daniel Deronda* and the Ends of Realism." In *George Eliot: Critical Assessments,* edited by Stuart Hutchinson, 476–93. Mountfield, U.K.: Helm Information.

James, Henry. [1876] 1984. "*Daniel Deronda*: A Conversation." In *Literary Criticism: Essays on Literature, American Writers, English Writers,* 974–92. New York: The Library of America.

———. [1908] 1986. *The Portrait of a Lady.* Harmondsworth, U.K.: Penguin.

JanMohamed, Abdul. 1985. "The Economy of Manichean Allegory: The Function of Racial Difference in Colonialist Literature." *Critical Inquiry* 12:59–87.

Johnson, Claudia Durst. 1993. "Impotence and Omnipotence in *The Scarlet Letter.*" *The New England Quarterly* 66:594–612.

Johnson, Patricia E. 1997. "The Gendered Politics of the Graze: Henry James and George Eliot." *Mosaic* 30: 39–54.

Kakutani, Michiko. 1998. "*A Widow for One Year:* Randomness and Luck, but Whew, No Bears." www.nytimes.com/books/98/04/26/daily/irving-book-review.html (accessed 21 September 2002).

Karl, Frederick. 1995. *George Eliot: A Biography*. London: HarperCollins.

Kauvar, Elaine M. 1991. *Cynthia Ozick's Fiction: Tradition and Invention*. Bloomington: Indiana University Press.

Kemp, Mark A. R. 1997. "*The Marble Faun* and American Postcolonial Ambivalence." *Modern Fiction Studies* 43:209–36.

Kent, Kathryn R. 1997. "'Single White Female': The Sexual Politics of Spinsterhood in Harriet Beecher Stowe's *Oldtown Folks*." *American Literature* 69:39–65.

Kessler, Carol Farley. 1982. *Elizabeth Stuart Phelps*. Boston: Twayne Publishers.

Kolodny, Annette. 1984. Introduction to *The Blithedale Romance*, by Nathaniel Hawthorne, vii–xxx. Harmondsworth, U.K.: Penguin.

Kristeva, Julia. 1982. *Powers of Horror: An Essay on Abjection*, translated by Leon S. Roudiez. New York: Columbia University Press.

———. 1991. *Strangers to Ourselves*, translated by Leon S. Roudiez. New York: Harvester Wheatsheaf.

Leavis, F. R. [1948] 1950. *The Great Tradition: George Eliot, Henry James, Joseph Conrad*. London: Chatto and Windus.

Lefkovitz, Lori. 1987. "Delicate Beauty Goes Out: *Adam Bede's* Transgressive Heroines." *The Kenyon Review* 9:84–96.

Lentricchia, Frank. 1988. *Ariel and the Police: Michel Foucault, William James, Wallace Stevens*. Madison: University of Wisconsin Press.

Lesjak, Carolyn. 1996. "Labours of a Modern Storyteller: George Eliot and the Cultural Project of 'Nationhood' in *Daniel Deronda*." In *Victorian Identities: Social and Cultural Formations in Nineteenth-Century Literature*, edited by Ruth Robbins and Julian Wolfreys. 25–42. Houndmills, U.K.: Macmillan Press.

Levine, Philippa. 1987. *Victorian Feminism, 1850–1900*. Tallahassee: Florida State University Press.

Levy, Amy. [1888] 1973. *Reuben Sachs: A Sketch*. New York: AMS Press.

Lewes, George Henry. 1874. *Problems of Life and Mind*. Vol. 1. London: Trübner and Co.

———. [1853] 1996. *Comte's Philosophy of the Sciences*. London: Routledge/Thoemmes Press.

Lewis, Reina. 1996. *Gendering Orientalism: Race, Femininity and Representation*. London: Routledge.

Lodge, David. 1973. Introduction to *Scenes of Clerical Life*, by George Eliot, 7–32. Harmondsworth, U.K.: Penguin.

———. 1992. "'Middlemarch' and the Idea of the Classic Realist Text." In *George Eliot: Middlemarch*, edited by John Peck, 45–64. Houndmills, U.K.: Macmillan.

Luedtke, Luther S. 1989. *Nathaniel Hawthorne and the Romance of the Orient*. Bloomington: Indiana University Press.

Lyons, Bonnie. 1998. "Faith and Puttermesser: Contrasting Images of Two Jewish Feminists." In *Talking Back: Images of Jewish Women in American Popular Culture*, edited by Joyce Antler, 139–49. Hanover, NH: Brandeis University Press.

MacCabe, Colin. 1978. *James Joyce and the Revolution of the Word*. London: Macmillan.

MacDonald, Bonney. 1990. *Henry James's Italian Hours: Revelatory and Resistant Impressions*. Ann Arbor: UMI Research Press.

Makarushka, Irena S. M. 1994. *Religious Imagination and Language in Emerson and Nietzsche*. New York: St. Martin's Press.

Manuel, Frank E. 1991. "From Equality to Organicism." In *Race, Class and Gender in Nineteenth-Century Culture*, edited by Maryanne Cline Horowitz, 3–18. Rochester: University of Rochester Press.

Marks, Patricia. 1999. "Virgin Saint, Mother Saint: Hilda and Dorothea." In *Hawthorne and Women: Engendering and Expanding the Hawthorne Tradition*, edited by John L. Idol, Jr., and Melinda M. Ponder, 151–58. Amherst: University of Massachusetts Press.

Martin, Robert K. 2002. "An Awful Freedom: Hawthorne and the Anxieties of the Carnival." In *Roman Holidays: American Writers and Artists in Nineteenth-Century Italy*, edited by Robert K. Martin and Leland S. Person, 41–59. Iowa City: University of Iowa Press.

Mazzini, Giuseppe. 1852. "Europe: Its Conditions and Prospects." *The Westminster Review* (New Series) 1:442–67.

Meyer, Michael J. 1992. "Toward a Rhetoric of Equality: Reflective and Refractive Images in Stowe's Language." In *The Stowe Debate: Rhetorical Strategies in* Uncle Tom's Cabin, edited by Mason I. Lowance, Jr., Ellen Westbrook, and R. C. De Prospo, 236–54. Amherst: University of Massachusetts Press.

Meyer, Susan. 1996. *Imperialism at Home: Race and Victorian Women's Fiction*. Ithaca, N.Y.: Cornell University Press.

Mill, John Stuart. [1869] 1983. *The Subjection of Women*. London: Virago.

Miller, Edwin Haviland. 1991. *Salem is My Dwelling Place: A Life of Nathaniel Hawthorne*. Iowa City: University of Iowa Press.

Mills, Nicolaus. 1973. *American and English Fiction in the Nineteenth Century: An Antigenre Critique and Comparison*. Bloomington: Indiana University Press.

Mills, Sara. 1991. *Discourses of Difference: An Analysis of Women's Travel Writing and Colonialism*. London: Routledge.

Mitchell, Judith. 1994. *The Stone and the Scorpion: The Female Subject of Desire in the Novels of Charlotte Brontë, George Eliot, and Thomas Hardy*. Westport, CT: Greenwood Press.

Moore, Jeffrey. 1986. Introduction to *The Portrait of a Lady*, by Henry James, 7–37. Harmondsworth, U.K.: Penguin.

Mueller, Monika. 1996. "*This Infinite Fraternity of Feeling*": *Gender, Genre, and Homoerotic Crisis in Hawthorne's* The Blithedale Romance *and Melville's* Pierre. Madison, N.J.: Fairleigh Dickinson University Press.

Myers, William. 1984. *The Teaching of George Eliot*. Leicester: Leicester University Press.

Nattermann, Udo. 1994. "Dread and Desire: 'Europe' in Hawthorne's *The Marble Faun*." *Essays in Literature* 21:54–67.

Newman, Judie. 1999. "Spaces In-Between: Hester Prynne as the Salem Bibi in Bharati Mukherjee's *The Holder of the World*." In *Borderlands: Negotiating Boundaries in Post-Colonial Writing*, edited by Monika Reif-Hülser, 69–87. Amsterdam: Rodopi.

Nuernberg, Susan Marie. 1992. "The Rhetoric of Race." In *The Stowe Debate: Rhetorical Strategies in* Uncle Tom's Cabin, edited by Mason I. Lowance, Jr., Ellen E. Westbrook, and R. C. De Prospo, 255–270. Amherst: University of Massachusetts Press.

Nurbhai, Saleel, and K. M. Newton. 2002. *George Eliot, Judaism and the Novels: Jewish Myth and Mysticism*. Houndmills, U.K.: Palgrave.

Nyquist, Mary. 2001. "Determining Influences: Resistance and Mentorship in *The House of Mirth* and the Anglo-American Realist Tradition." In *New Essays on* The House of Mirth. 43–106. Cambridge: Cambridge University Press.

Offen, Karen. 1988. "Defining Feminism: A Comparative Historical Approach." *Signs*. 14:119–57.

Ozick, Cynthia. 1982. *Levitation: Five Fictions*. New York: Alfred Knopf.

———. 1991. "The Muse, Postmodern and Homeless." In *Metaphor and Memory*. 136–39. New York: Vintage.

———. 1997a. "The Many Faces of Cynthia Ozick." Interview by Katie Bolick. *www.theatlantic.com/unbound/factfict/ozick.htm* (accessed 10 August 2002).

———. 1997b. *The Puttermesser Papers*. New York: Knopf.

———. 1997c. "Things Fall Apart." Interview by David Wiley. www.mndaily.com/ae/Print/1997/st/csint.html (accessed 31 August 2002).

———. no date. "A Conversation with Cynthia Ozick." Interview by Diane Osen. 209.67.253.214/NBF/docs/www_curri_COZick.htm (accessed 10 August 2002).

Packer, B. L. 1982. *Emerson's Fall: A New Interpretation of the Major Essays*. New York: Continuum.

Paxton, Nancy L. 1986. "Feminism and Positivism in George Eliot's *Romola*." In *Nineteenth-Century Women Writers of the English Speaking World*, edited by Rhoda B. Nathan. 144–50. Westport, Conn.: Greenwood Press.

———. 1991. *George Eliot and Herbert Spencer: Feminism, Evolution, and the Reconstruction of Gender*. Princeton: Princeton University Press.

Phelps, Elizabeth Stuart. [1877] 1985. *The Story of Avis,* edited by Carol Farley Kessler. New Brunswick: Rutgers University Press.

Pickering, Mary. 1993. *Auguste Comte: An Intellectual Biography*. Vol. 1. Cambridge: Cambridge University Press.

Pieterse, Jan Nederveen. 1992. *White on Black: Images of Africa and Blacks in Western Popular Culture*. New Haven: Yale University Press.

Pinsker, Sanford. 2002. "Cynthia Ozick, Aesthete." www.bu.edu/partisanreview/archive/2002/2/pinsker.html (accessed 8 August 2002).

Poirier, Richard. 1967. *The Comic Sense of Henry James: A Study of the Early Novels*. Oxford: Oxford University Press.

———. 1987. *The Renewal of Literature: Emersonian Reflections*. New York: Random House.

Porte, Joel. 1990. "Introduction: *The Portrait of a Lady* and 'Felt Life.'" In *New Essays on* The Portrait of a Lady, edited by Joel Porte, 1–31. Cambridge: Cambridge University Press.

Pratt, Mary Louise. 1992. *Imperial Eyes: Travel Writing and Transculturation*. London: Routledge.

———. 1996. "Arts of the Contact Zone." In *Ways of Reading: An Anthology for Writers*, edited by David Bartholomae and Anthony Petrosky, 528–42. Boston: Bedford Books.

Press, Jacob. 1997. "Same Sex Unions in Modern Europe: *Daniel Deronda, Altneuland,* and the Homoerotics of Jewish Nationalism." In *Novel Gazing: Queer Readings in Fiction*, edited by Eve Kosofsky Sedgwick, 299–329. Durham: Duke University Press.

Pritchard, William H. 1998. "No Ideas! It's a Novel!" www.nytimes.com/books/98/05/24/reviews/980524.24pritcht.html (accessed 21 September 2002).

Reynolds, Larry J. 1988. *European Revolutions and the American Literary Renaissance.* New Haven: Yale University Press.

Riall, Lucy. 1994. *The Italian Risorgimento: State, Society and National Unification.* New York: Routledge.

Rignall, John, ed. 1997. *George Eliot and Europe.* Aldershot, U.K.: Scolar Press.

———. 2000. *Oxford Reader's Companion to George Eliot.* Oxford: Oxford University Press.

Riss, Arthur. 1994. "Racial Essentialism and Family Values in *Uncle Tom's Cabin.*" *American Quarterly* 46:513–44.

Robinson, Lillian S. 1994. "The Traffic in Women: A Cultural Critique of *The House of Mirth.*" In Wharton, Edith, *The House of Mirth: Complete, Authoritative Text with Biographical and Historical Contexts, Critical History, and Essays from Five Contemporary Critical Perspectives,* edited by Shari Benstock, 340–58. Boston: Bedford Books.

Rose, Jacqueline. 1986. *Sexuality in the Field of Vision.* London: Verso.

Rosowski, Susan. 1990. "Margaret Fuller, an Engendered West, and *Summer on the Lakes.*" *Western American Literature* 25:125–44.

Rutherford, Jonathan. 1990. "Interview with Homi Bhabha: The Third Space." In *Identity: Community, Culture, Difference,* edited by Jonathan Rutherford, 207–21. London: Lawrence and Wishart.

Saglia, Diego. 1998. "Looking at the Other: Cultural Difference and the Traveller's Gaze in *The Italian.*" *Studies in the Novel* 28:12–37.

Said, Edward W. 1992. *The Question of Palestine.* New York: Vintage Books.

———. [1978] 1995. *Orientalism: Western Conceptions of the Orient.* Harmondsworth, U.K.: Penguin.

Scholem, Gershom. [1960] 1996. *On the Kabbalah and Its Symbolism.* New York: Schocken.

Schulz, Dieter. 1997. *Amerikanischer Transzendentalismus: Ralph Waldo Emerson, Henry David Thoreau, Margaret Fuller.* Darmstadt: Wissenschaftliche Buchgesellschaft.

Sedgwick, Eve Kosofsky. 1985. *Between Men: English Literature and Male Homosocial Desire.* New York: Columbia University Press.

———. 1990. *Epistemology of the Closet.* Berkeley: University of California Press.

Seeber, Hans Ulrich. 1997. "Cultural Synthesis in George Eliot's *Middlemarch.*" In *George Eliot and Europe,* edited by John Rignall, 17–31. Aldershot: Scolar Press.

Semmel, Bernard. 1994. *George Eliot and the Politics of National Inheritance.* New York: Oxford University Press.

Shaffer, Elinor S. 1975. *Kubla Khan and the Fall of Jerusalem: The Mythological School in Biblical Criticism and Secular Literature.* Cambridge: Cambridge University Press.

Sheets, Robin. 1997. "History and Romance: Harriet Beecher Stowe's *Agnes of Sorrento* and George Eliot's *Romola.*" *CLIO* 26:323–46.

Sherwin, Byron L. 1985. *The Golem Legend: Origins and Implications.* Lanham: University Press of America.

Shires, Linda M. 1992. "Afterword: Ideology and the Subject as Agent." In *Rewriting the Victorians: Theory, History, and the Politics of Gender,* edited by Linda M. Shires, 185–90. New York: Routledge.

Showalter, Elaine. 1991. *Sexual Anarchy: Gender and Culture at the Fin de Siècle.* London: Bloomsbury.

Shuttleworth, Sally. 1984. *George Eliot and Nineteenth-Century Science: The Make-Believe of a Beginning.* Cambridge: Cambridge University Press.

Spencer, Herbert. 1859. "Physical Training." *The British Quarterly Review.* April 1859: 362–97.

———. [1904] 1966. *An Autobiography I. The Works of Herbert Spencer XX.* Osnabrück: Otto Zeller.

———. [1854] 1996. "Personal Beauty." In *Essays: Scientific, Political, and Speculative.* 387–99. London: Routledge/Thoemmes Press.

———. [1851] 1996. "The Rights of Women." In *Social Statics,* 155–171. London: Routledge/Thoemmes Press.

———. [1860] 1996. "The Social Organism." In *Essays: Scientific, Political, and Speculative.* 265–307. London: Routledge/Thoemmes Press.

———. [1898] 2002. *The Principles of Sociology.* 3 vols. New Brunswick, NJ: Transaction Publishers.

Spillers, Hortense J. 1989. "Changing the Letter: The Yokes, the Jokes of Discourse, or, Mrs. Stowe, Mr. Reed." In *Slavery and the Literary Imagination,* edited by Deborah E. McDowell and Arnold Rampersand. 24–61. Baltimore: Johns Hopkins University Press.

Spurr, David. 1993. *The Rhetoric of Empire: Colonial Discourse in Journalism, Travel Writing and Imperial Administration.* Durham: Duke University Press.

Steele, Jeffrey. 1987. *The Representation of the Self in the American Renaissance.* Chapel Hill: University of North Carolina Press.

———. 2001. *Transfiguring America: Myth, Ideology, and Mourning in Margaret Fuller's Writing.* Columbia: University of Missouri Press.

Stocking, George W., Jr. 1987. *Victorian Anthropology.* New York: The Free Press.

Stokes, Edward. 1985. *Hawthorne's Influence on Dickens and George Eliot.* St. Lucia, Australia: University of Queensland Press.

Stowe, Harriet Beecher. [1862] 1967. *Agnes of Sorrento.* New York: AMS Press.

———. [1854] 1968. *The Key to Uncle Tom's Cabin.* New York: Arno Press.

———. [1856] 1970. *Dred.* New York: AMS Press.

———. [1852] 1981. *Uncle Tom's Cabin.* New York: Penguin.

———. 1982. *Uncle Tom's Cabin, The Minister's Wooing, Oldtown Folks.* New York: The Library of America.

Swann, Charles. 1991. *Nathaniel Hawthorne: Tradition and Revolution.* Cambridge: Cambridge University Press.

Sypher, Eileen. 1996. "Resisting Gwendolen's 'Subjection': *Daniel Deronda*'s Proto-Feminism." *Studies in the Novel* 28:507–24.

Tang, Edward. 1998. "Making Declarations of Her Own: Harriet Beecher Stowe as New England Historian." *The New England Quarterly* 71:77–96.

The Concise Oxford Dictionary. 1995. 9th ed. CD-ROM. Oxford: Oxford University Press.

Thompson, Andrew. 1998. *George Eliot and Italy: Literary, Cultural and Political Influences from Dante to the Risorgimento.* Houndmills, U.K.: Macmillan.

Tompkins, Jane. 1985. *Sensational Designs: The Cultural Work of American Fiction, 1790–1860.* New York: Oxford University Press.

Urbanski, Marie Mitchell Olesen. 1980. *Margaret Fuller's Woman in the Nineteenth Century: A Literary Study of Form and Content, of Sources and Influence.* Westport,CT: Greenwood Press.

von Mehren, Joan. 1994. *Minerva and the Muse: A Life of Margaret Fuller.* Amherst: University of Massachusetts Press.

Ward, Susan. 1986. "The Career Woman Fiction of Elizabeth Stuart Phelps." In *Nineteenth-Century Women Writers of the English-Speaking World*, edited by Rhoda B. Nathan, 209–19. Westport, CT: Greenwood Press.

Wardley, Lynn. 1992. "Relic, Fetish, Femmage: The Aesthetic of Sentiment in the Work of Stowe." In *The Culture of Sentiment: Race, Gender, and Sentimentality in Nineteenth-Century America*, edited by Shirley Samuels, 203–220. Oxford: Oxford University Press.

Warhol, Robyn R. 1986. "Poetics and Persuasion: *Uncle Tom's Cabin* as a Realist Novel." *Essays in Literature* 13:283–97.

———. 1989. *Gendered Interventions: Narrative Discourse in the Victorian Novel.* New Brunswick, NJ: Rutgers University Press.

Weisbuch, Robert. 1986. *Atlantic Double-Cross: American Literature and British Influence in the Age of Emerson.* Chicago: University of Chicago Press.

Welter, Barbara. 1966. "The Cult of True Womanhood: 1820–1860." *American Quarterly* 18:151–74.

Westra, Helen Petter. 1992. "Confronting Antichrist: The Influence of Jonathan Edwards's Millennial Vision." In *The Stowe Debate: Rhetorical Strategies in Uncle Tom's Cabin*, edited by Mason I. Lowance, Jr., Ellen E. Westbrook, and R. C. De Prospo, 141–58. Amherst: University of Massachusetts Press.

Wharton, Edith. [1905] 1994. *The House of Mirth,* edited by Shari Benstock. Boston: Bedford Books.

Wiesenfarth, Joseph. 1982. "*Middlemarch*: The Language of Art." *PMLA* 97:363–77.

Wilson, Jack H. 1993. "Competing Narratives in Elizabeth Stuart Phelps' *The Story of Avis.*" *American Literary Realism, 1870–1910* 26:60–75.

Winnifrith, Tom. 1994. *Fallen Women in the Nineteenth-Century Novel.* New York: St. Martin's Press.

———. 1997. "Renaissance and Risorgimento in *Romola.*" In *George Eliot and Europe*, edited by John Rignall, 166–78. Aldershot: Scolar Press.

Wood, Mary E. 1993. "'With Ready Eye': Margaret Fuller and Lesbianism in Nineteenth-Century American Literature." *American Literature* 65:1–18.

Yarborough, Richard. 1986. "Strategies of Black Characterization in *Uncle Tom's Cabin* and the Early Afro-American Novel." In *New Essays on* Uncle Tom's Cabin, edited by Eric J. Sundquist, 45–84. Cambridge: Cambridge University Press.

Young, Robert. 1995. *Colonial Desire: Hybridity in Theory, Culture and Race.* London: Routledge.

Zimmerman, Bonnie. 1986. "George Eliot and Feminism: The Case of *Daniel Deronda.*" In *Nineteenth-Century Women Writers of the English-Speaking World*, edited by Rhoda B. Nathan, 231–37. Westport, CT: Greenwood Press.

Zwarg, Christina. 1995. *Feminist Conversations: Fuller, Emerson, and the Play of Reading.* Ithaca: Cornell University Press.

Index

abjection, 42, 112, 117–18, 127, 137, 142, 148, 249 n. 17, 249 n. 18, 250 n. 19
Adams, Kimberly VanEsveld, 15, 27, 74–75, 83, 235 n. 3, 239 n. 3, 243 n. 33, 245 n. 43
Aiken, D. Wyatt, 237 n. 20
Alaya, Flavia, 242 n. 43
alterity: cultural, 14, 16, 20, 23–24, 37, 39–43, 48, 96–97, 101–3, 114, 122, 137, 141, 143, 148–50, 179, 257 n. 16; gendered, 20, 37; racial, 16, 20, 37, 47–49, 137, 142, 170, 247 n. 57, 256 n. 8, 257 n. 16; religious, 40–42, 143, 170
Althusser, Louis, 29–36, 71, 173, 236 n. 14, 258 n. 21
Ammons, Elizabeth, 47, 153, 158
Angel in the House, 70, 146, 197, 237 n. 17
Anglicanism, 60, 99–104, 241 n. 16
Appiah, Kwame Anthony, 32–33, 155–57, 167, 176–77, 255 n. 4, 257 n. 14, 259 n. 23, 259 n. 25
Argyros, Ellen, 63, 240 n. 14
Armstrong, Nancy, 244 n. 35
Asad, Talal, 108
Auerbach, Nina, 244 n. 37

Baker, William, 182, 258 n. 18
Banta, Martha, 206
Barrett, Dorothea, 76, 202, 205, 244 n. 36
Beebee, Thomas O., 31

Beer, Gillian, 49, 94, 174–75, 178, 239 n. 32
Bell, Michael Davitt, 239 n. 5, 240 n. 6
Benhabib, Seyla, 21
Bennett, Joan, 134, 252 n. 38
Benstock, Shari, 211
Bentley, Nancy, 45, 137
Bercovitch, Sacvan, 58
Bhabha, Homi K., 42–43, 49, 119, 150, 237 n. 24, 239 n. 33, 250 n. 20
Bishop, Jonathan, 261 n. 44
Bloom, Harold, 22, 186, 188–89, 257 n. 13, 261 n. 44
Bodenheimer, Rosemarie, 242 n. 27, 269 n. 52
Bonaparte, Felicia, 148–49, 247 n. 2
Boumelha, Penny, 57, 220
Bowlby, Rachel, 255 n. 2
Brady, Kristin, 235 n. 1
Brennan, Timothy, 178
Brodhead, Richard, 255 n. 56
Bromell, Nicholas, 240 n. 8
Bullen, J. B., 106, 145, 148
Butler, Judith, 21, 32–33, 71, 236 n. 16

Callanan, Laura, 181, 260 n. 32
Calvinism, 28, 99–104
Cameron, Kenneth Walter, 185–87, 261 n. 38
Cantave, Sophia, 255 n. 1
Carpenter, Frederic Ives, 186, 261 n. 38
Carpenter, Mary Wilson, 255 n. 55

285

Carroll, Alicia, 50, 244 n. 38
Carroll, David, 175, 258 n. 19
Catholicism, 23, 40–41, 107–8, 111–15, 120–22, 125, 131, 135–36, 139–50, 253 n. 40, 254 n. 51
Cave, Terence, 153, 161–62
Chase, Richard, 239 n. 5
Cheever, Susan, 25, 193, 195, 219, 220–21, 223, 235 n. 4, 268 nn. 42 and 43
Chevigny, Bell Gale, 241 n. 21, 248 n. 9
Cheyette, Bryan, 163, 257 n. 11
Christ, Carol, 74
Civello, Catherine, 235 n. 4, 268 n. 45
class, 19, 20, 23–24, 38–39, 94–95, 99, 170, 193, 205–6, 211, 240 n. 8, 265 n. 21, 265 n. 23; differences between G.B. and the U.S., 51–52, 58–59, 83, 87, 99, 102, 195, 204, 206, 265 n. 21; and gender, 19, 23–24, 193, 195, 201–4
Clayton, Jay, 20–21
Colacurcio, Michael, 62
Comte, Auguste, 25–27, 34, 38, 67–69, 91–93, 143–45, 147–48, 160, 190, 236 n. 10, 238 n. 32, 242 n. 24, 247 n. 2
Corbett, Mary Jean, 54
Correa, Delia da Sousa, 265 n. 19
cosmopolitanism, 19, 24, 40, 124, 129, 149–50, 210, 237 n. 23, 238 n. 31, 251 n. 32; as eighteenth-century discourse, 24, 129, 149, 210, 251 n. 32
Cottom, Daniel, 56–58, 79, 240 n. 10
Cult of True Womanhood, 33, 68, 71–72, 88, 93, 202, 237 n. 17, 243 n. 32, 256 n. 6

Daniel, Janice B., 54
Darwin, Charles, 34, 44, 67, 91–92, 94, 155, 174, 242 n. 26, 245 n. 42
de Lauretis, Teresa, 29–30, 32–33, 71, 101, 237 n. 18
Donohue, Agnes McNeill, 136, 253 nn. 42 and 43
Ducksworth, Sarah Smith, 158, 255 n. 1, 256 n. 7
Dunne, Michael, 239 n. 4

DuPlessis, Rachel Blau, 193–95, 204, 220, 226, 233, 263 n. 3, 263 n. 5, 264 n. 11, 268 n. 41, 268 n. 45, 269 n. 48

Easton, Alison, 29
Edel, Leon, 17, 204
Edwards, Lee R., 98
Eliot, George: *Adam Bede*, 13, 15, 23, 34, 51–65, 69, 73–78, 81, 86, 228, 235 n. 6, 241 n. 16, 241 n. 18, 241 n. 20, 244 nn. 35–38, 244 n. 40, 244 n. 41, 245 n. 42, 245 n. 48; "Armgart," 17, 196–200, 263 n. 9; *Daniel Deronda*, 15–20, 23–24, 27, 29–30, 34–36, 47–49, 57–58, 69, 78, 103, 118, 125, 131, 149–63, 166, 168, 170, 172, 174–76, 178, 181, 183–95, 199, 201, 203–5, 207, 209–17, 226, 232, 239 n. 2, 245 n. 48, 251 n. 2, 256 n. 8, 256 n. 10, 257 nn. 11 and 12, 258 nn. 17, 18, and 19, 257 n. 21, 259 nn. 22, 23, and 24, 259 n. 26, 259 n. 28, 260 n. 29, 260 nn. 31, 32, and 33, 260 n. 35, 262 n. 45, 262 n. 1, 263 n. 2, 264 nn. 12, 13, and 14, 265 n. 21, 266 n. 29, 267 n. 33, 268 n. 42; *Felix Holt*, 58, 92, 135; "Margaret Fuller's Letters from Italy," 123; *Middlemarch*, 14, 18, 51, 57, 80–82, 86, 88–89, 91, 94–99, 103–4, 109, 125, 127, 129, 193, 196, 221–23, 229–30, 232, 240 n. 7, 245 n. 48, 246 n. 51, 251 n. 29, 262 n. 1, 264 n. 15; *The Mill on the Floss*, 23, 79–80, 82, 193, 244 nn. 37 and 38, 244 n. 41; "The Modern Hep! Hep! Hep!," 48, 118, 260 n. 29; "The Natural History of German Life," 39; "Recollections of Italy. 1860.," 106, 122, 124–25; *Romola*, 14, 23, 27, 40–41, 65, 69, 81, 106–7, 109, 122, 124–25, 128–30, 132–36, 141, 143–50, 153, 160, 194, 199, 201, 210, 247 n. 4, 254 n. 52, 255 nn. 53, 54, and 55, 262 n. 1; *Scenes of Clerical Life*, 125–26; *Silas Marner*, 34, 244 n. 41
Ellmann, Richard, 244 n. 40

Emerson, Ralph Waldo, 20, 22, 24–27, 35, 151, 185–86, 188–92, 237 n. 21, 248 n. 12 , 261 nn. 38–44, 262 nn. 46–49
Enlightenment, 41, 43, 128, 149, 251 n. 32
ethnicity, 19, 143, 218

feminism: contemporary, 71, 76, 78, 222, 227; and ideology, 30; ninteenth-century, 15, 19, 47, 66, 69, 74–75, 77, 80, 84, 86, 103–4, 145–46, 165, 196–97, 200–201, 243 n. 29, 255 n. 53, 257 n. 12, 263 n. 6, 268 n. 44
Feuerbach, Ludwig, 15, 27, 60–61, 74, 147, 181, 189–90, 217
Fields, Annie, 17
Foreman, P. Gabrielle, 256 n. 7
Foucault, Michel, 32, 35, 71, 236 n. 15
Fourier, Charles, 38, 110, 252 n. 36
Frank, Armin Paul, 239 n. 3, 239 n. 5
Frank, Esther, 218
Franzosa, John, 28
Freadman, Richard, 16–17, 204, 259 n. 27, 262 n. 1
Freedman, Jonathan, 209–10, 265 n. 20
Freud, Sigmund, 119, 141–42, 170, 254 n. 46
Fuller, Margaret: *At Home and Abroad*, 23, 105, 109, 112; *Summer on the Lakes*, 45–46; *Woman in the Nineteenth Century*, 27, 51–52, 66, 69–70, 74, 86, 183–84, 190–91, 243 nn. 33 and 34, 245 n. 43
Fussell, Paul, 251 n. 27

Gatens, Moira, 84
Geertz, Clifford, 128–29, 251 n. 30
gender: and identity, 30, 32–33, 37, 85, 236 n. 16, 237 n. 18; and ideology, 15, 19–20, 29–37, 68–71, 74, 88–93, 165, 194, 201–3, 237 n. 19, 242 n. 25, 255 n. 53; influence of Eliot on U.S. writers' presentation of, 193–204, 211–12, 219–24, 227–33; influence of U.S. writers on Eliot's presentation of, 14–20, 23–24, 51–52, 64–99, 133–34, 146, 151, 193; nineteenth-century discourse on gender, 39, 64–75, 87–91, 191, 202, 241 n. 21, 242 nn. 22–25, 243 n. 32, 256 n. 6; and race, 46, 157–59, 164–65, 169–70. *See also* Angel in the House; Cult of True Womanhood; homoeroticism; homosexuality; feminism; masculinity; technology of gender
Gilbert, Sandra, 14–15, 51, 73–74, 187, 239 n. 3, 244 n. 39
Giles, Paul, 22–23, 236 n. 8
Gilman, Sander, 155
Gindele, Karen C., 264 n. 15
gnosticism, 186, 190, 260 n. 31
Godwin, Gail, 20, 25, 193, 195, 219–20, 223, 225–26, 235 n. 4, 269 n. 47
Goshgarian, G. M., 31
Grand Etre, society as, 19, 25–29, 190; correspondences between the positivist Grand Etre and the transcendentalist oversoul, 19, 25–29, 190
Graver, Suzanne, 69, 92–93, 246 n. 50
Greene, Gayle, 220, 226, 235 n. 4
Greenwald, Alissa, 142
Grossberg, Lawrence, 259 n. 24
Grossman, Jay, 238 n. 26
Gubar, Susan, 14–15, 51, 73–74, 187, 239 n. 3, 244 n. 39

Haight, Gordon, 244 n. 41
Hall, Stuart, 32–33, 36, 175, 236 n. 15, 258 n. 21
Hamilton, Kristie, 45
Hannaford, Ivan, 155, 160
Harris, Margaret, 109, 122–24, 251 n. 27
Harter, Carol C., 227, 269 n. 49
Hawkes, David, 35, 236 n. 12
Hawthorne, Nathaniel: *The Blithedale Romance*, 24, 28, 77–78, 80, 180–81, 260 nn. 30 and 31; *The House of the Seven Gables*, 55; *The Marble Faun*, 14, 28, 40, 42, 45, 106, 109, 116, 120, 124–25, 128, 135–50, 246 n. 51, 251 n. 28, 253 nn. 40–43 , 254 n. 44, 254 nn. 49–52, 255 n. 56; *The Scarlet Letter*, 13, 23, 28, 35, 51–65, 72–73, 78, 80–81, 125, 144, 238 n. 26, 239 nn. 3 and 4, 240 n. 6, 243 nn. 30 and 31, 254 n. 51 and 52

Hedrick, Joan, 98–99, 246 n. 52
Henry, Nancy, 15, 163, 166–69, 175
Hesse, David Maria, 25–26, 144, 247 n. 2, 255 n. 54
Higher Criticism, 143
Hollinger, David A., 129, 150, 237 n. 23, 238 n. 31, 251 n. 32, 259 n. 22
homoeroticism, 36, 49, 57, 70, 180–81, 256 n. 7, 260 n. 30, 260 n. 32
homosexuality, 180–82, 260 n. 32
Hutcheon, Linda, 70–71, 243 n. 29
Hutchinson, Stuart, 201

identity: cultural/collective, 16, 29–33, 35–37, 40, 48–49, 82, 101, 117, 151, 160, 162, 168–193, 207–10, 218, 226, 259 nn. 22–27; ethnic/racial, 19, 23, 37, 48–49, 57–58, 151–52, 154, 160, 162, 166–79, 187–93, 218, 226, 257 n. 14; gender, 30, 32–33, 37, 85, 236 n. 16; national, 15, 19, 22, 151–55, 161, 164, 166–67, 176–79, 191; personal/individual, 16, 19, 21, 29–33, 117–19, 171–84, 187–93, 207–10, 226, 236 n. 15, 259 n. 27; and self, 16, 29, 86, 175, 178–79, 191–92, 208, 225–26, 259 n. 27, 262 nn. 46, 47, and 48
ideology, 236 nn. 13 and 14, 237 n. 17, 243 n. 29, 258 nn. 20 and 21; and gender identity, 15, 19–20, 29–37, 68–71, 74, 88–93, 165, 194, 201–3, 237 n. 17, 255 n. 53, 264 n. 15; and racial identity, 165, 173–77. *See also* interpellation; technology of gender
influence, literary, 13, 16–17, 20–25, 51–54
Ingham, Patricia, 58–59, 240 n. 9
interpellation, 29–30, 35–37, 165, 173–75, 257 n. 12, 258 n. 21
intertextuality, 20–21
Irving, John, 16, 20, 25, 193, 195–96, 219, 227–30, 269 nn. 49 and 50
Irwin, Jane, 170, 172, 182, 258 nn. 17 and 18
Italy: and abjection, 14, 23, 42, 116–19, 127, 137, 249 nn. 17 and 18; and Catholicism, 107, 111–15, 120–22, 125, 127, 130, 135–36, 140, 141, 143–44, 146–50, 247 n. 55, 248 n. 12, 253 nn. 40–43, 254 n. 51; as "evolutionarily backward," 14, 23, 41, 135, 137, 139, 141–44, 146–50; italianness as alterity, 16, 23, 40, 114, 122, 137, 141, 143, 150; nineteenth-century political situation of, 40–41, 105–6, 108–11, 121–33, 140, 247 n. 55, 247 n. 1, 251 n. 26, 252 nn. 33 and 34, 252 n. 36; as tourist attraction, 19, 105, 107, 109, 116, 122, 248 n. 8, 249 nn. 13–16

Jackson, Tony E., 258 n. 19
James, Henry: "Daniel Deronda; A Conversation," 263 n. 2; *The Portrait of a Lady* 16, 24, 40, 194–95, 201–5, 209–12, 219, 239 n. 2, 262 n. 1, 263 n. 4, 264 nn. 13, 14, and 15
JanMohamed, Abdul, 254 n. 48
Johnson, Claudia Durst, 80, 244 n. 39
Johnston, Judith, 109, 122–24, 251 n. 27
Judaism: and androgyny, 36, 182; correspondences between Kabbalah and the transcendentalist oversoul, 24, 27, 36, 185–86, 191, 210, 261 n. 44; golem, 187, 195, 214–19, 266 nn. 30 and 31, 267 n. 33, 267 nn. 36 and 37; and identity, 36–37, 48–49, 57–58, 151–52, 54, 160, 162, 166, 168, 172–84, 187–93, 218, 226, 258 n. 19; Kabbalah, 27, 151, 171, 182, 186–88, 212, 214–17, 257 n. 13, 258 n. 68, 261 n. 44, 266 n. 30, 267 n. 34; and metempsychosis, 171, 182, 190, 215, 258 n. 18, 262 n. 45; Neoplatonic origins of Kabbalah, 19, 24, 27, 36, 151, 171, 185–86, 210, 260 n. 31; and race, 47–49, 138, 151–55, 159, 160–79, 191; and women, 164–65, 178; Zionism, 162–63, 168, 178, 204, 212, 215–16, 218, 256 n. 9

Kakutani, Michiko, 227
Karl, Frederick, 76–77, 245 n. 42, 269 n. 53
Kauvar, Elaine M., 267 n. 35, 269 n. 51
Kemp, Mark R., 140, 254 n. 45

Kent, Kathryn R., 245 n. 45
Kessler, Carol Farley, 263 nn. 7 and 8
Kolodny, Annette, 180
Kristeva, Julia, 39, 117–18, 141–42, 149, 249 nn. 17 and 18, 250 n.19

Leavis, F. R., 16, 201, 204, 264 n. 17
Lefkovitz, Lori, 75
Lentricchia, Frank, 258 n. 20
Levine, Philippa, 33, 237 n. 19
Levy, Amy, 161, 256 n. 10
Lewes, Henry: *Problems of Life and Mind*, 91, 93
Lewis, Reina, 48, 154, 162–63
Lodge, David, 57
Luedtke, Luther S., 238 n. 26
Lyons, Bonnie, 215

MacCabe, Colin, 57, 240 n. 7
MacDonald, Bonney, 253 n. 40
Makarushka, Irena S. M., 189–90
Manuel, Frank E., 37, 39
Marks, Patricia, 246 n. 51
Martin, Robert K., 45
Martineau, Harriet, 236 n. 10
masculinity, 66, 74, 84–85, 154, 156, 206–7, 245 n. 46
Mazzini, Giuseppe, 41–42, 105, 111, 125, 130–32, 248 nn. 10 and 11, 252 nn. 35 and 36
Meyer, Michael J., 255 n. 2
Meyer, Susan, 162–63
Mill, John Stuart, 38, 67–68, 87–88, 91, 242 nn. 22 and 23
Miller, Edwin Haviland, 107, 235 n. 7, 248 n. 5, 251 n. 23
Mills, Nicolaus, 239 n. 3
Mills, Sara, 42, 248 n. 8, 249 n. 15
Mitchell, Judith, 64, 76
Moore, Jeffrey, 205
Mueller, Monika, 260 n. 30
Myers, William, 136

Nattermann, Udo, 254 n. 49
Neoplatonism, 185–87, 261 n. 39
Newman, Judie, 238 n. 26
Newton, K. M., 182, 187, 215, 258 n. 18, 267 n. 33

nineteenth-century social discourses. *See* alterity; class; ethnicity; gender; positivism; race; religion; religion of humanity; social organicism; transcendentalism
Nuernberg, Susan Marie, 238 n. 29
Nurbhai, Saleel, 182, 187, 215, 258 n. 18, 267 n. 33
Nyquist, Mary, 16, 264 n. 13

Offen, Karen, 69–70
oversoul, 19, 24–28, 185–86, 190–91, 260 n. 31, 261 n. 36, 261 n. 38, 261 n. 44; correspondences between the transcendentalist oversoul and the positivist Grand Etre, 19, 25–29, 190
Ozick, Cynthia: *Levitation*, 212, 266 n. 25; *The Puttermesser Papers*, 25, 195–96, 212, 215, 230, 232, 266 n. 25, 266 n. 27, 266 n. 32, 267 nn. 35–39

Packer, B. L., 191, 261 n. 42, 262 n. 48
Paxton, Nancy L., 90, 242 n. 24, 245 n. 47, 255 n. 53
Phelps, Elizabeth Stuart, 16–17, 19–20, 193–201, 263 nn. 6–10
Pickering, Mary, 247 n. 2
Pieterse, Jan Nederveen, 160, 255 n. 5
Pinsker, Sanford, 266 n. 26
Poirier, Richard, 210, 237 n. 21, 262 n. 49
Porte, Joel, 209
positivism, 14, 25–27, 41, 68, 92, 106, 146–48, 236 n. 10, 255 nn. 53 and 54
postcolonial, attitude of American writers toward Europe, 23, 42, 99–100, 103, 107–8, 115, 119, 124, 137, 140–41, 143, 236 n. 9
Pratt, Mary Louise, 43, 108, 150
Press, Jacob, 49, 152, 177–79, 181
Pritchard, William H., 227
Protestantism: 23, 28, 40, 42, 112–15, 125, 127, 135–36, 248 n. 12, 253 n. 43
Puritanism: 23, 28, 52–53, 58, 61–64, 79, 85, 99–101, 104, 113, 136, 190, 210, 241 nn. 15 and 16, 246 n. 54, 253 n. 41

race: and gender, 46, 157–59, 164–65, 169–70, 242 n. 26, 256 nn. 6 and 7; and identity, 19, 23, 37, 48–49, 57–58, 151–52, 154, 160, 162, 166–79, 187–99, 218, 226, 257 n. 14, 258 n. 19; and ideology, 29, 35–37, 173–77; and Judaism, 47–49, 138, 151–55, 159–79, 191; and national identity, 15, 19, 151–55, 161, 164, 166–79, 191; nineteenth-century race theory, 43–49, 93, 137–40, 142–43, 156–57, 160, 238 nn. 26–31; and religion, 168–77; as socio-biological determinant, 23, 155, 157, 167–68, 193

realism, literary, 19–20, 23, 51, 55–58, 172, 187, 221, 240 n. 7; "American romance" vs. "British realism," 53, 55–57

relationship between George Eliot and U.S. writers: personal, 14–20, 22–25, 193–96

religion: Anglicanism compared to Calvinism, 99–104. *See also* Anglicanism; Catholicism; Protestantism; Puritanism

religion of humanity, 25, 60, 79, 97, 130, 145, 147–48, 236 n. 11

Reynolds, Larry J., 110–12, 248 n. 12

Riall, Lucy, 130, 247 n. 1, 249 n. 15, 250 n. 22

Rignall, John, 235 n. 2, 235 n. 7

Riss, Arthur, 255 n. 3

Robinson, Lillian S., 211, 265 n. 22

romance, literary, 14, 19, 51, 53, 55–57, 172, 194–95, 204, 219–20, 223, 229, 239 n. 5, 269 n. 52; "American romance" vs. "British realism," 53, 55–57

Rose, Jacqueline, 89

Rosowski, Susan, 238 n. 28

Rothstein, Eric, 20–21

Rutherford, Jonathan, 239 n. 33

Saglia, Diego, 111

Said, Edward W., 248 n. 7, 256 n. 9

Saint-Simon, Henri de, 38

Scholem, Gershom, 188, 215, 217, 257 n. 13, 266 n. 30, 267 n. 34, 267 nn. 36 and 37

Schulz, Dieter, 191, 262 n. 46

Sedgwick, Eve Kosofsky, 260 n. 32

Seeber, Hans Ulrich, 129, 251 n. 31

Semmel, Bernard, 259 n. 28

Shaffer, Elinor S., 181, 190, 260 n. 31

Sheets, Robin, 247 n. 4, 255 n. 55

Sherwin, Byron L., 216–17, 266 n. 31, 267 n. 33

Shires, Linda M., 21

Showalter, Elaine, 268 n. 44, 269 n. 47

Shuttleworth, Sally, 38, 237 n. 22

Spencer, Herbert: *An Autobiography I*, 238 n. 25; "Personal Beauty," 241 n. 20; "Physical Training," 67; *The Principles of Sociology*, 67, 92, 246 n. 49; "The Rights of Women," 67, 87; "The Social Organism," 91

Spillers, Hortense, 158, 256 n. 7

Spurr, David, 42, 108, 118

Steele, Jeffrey, 27, 185, 189, 191, 248 n. 9, 261 n. 44

Stokes, Edward, 13–14, 146, 180, 235 n. 6

Stowe, Harriet Beecher: *Agnes of Sorrento*, 40, 65, 106–7, 114–15, 124–25, 133–34, 247 n. 4, 249 n. 16, 255 n. 55; *Dred*, 17, 23, 28, 47–48, 114, 151–53, 156–59, 166–172, 214; *Oldtown Folks*, 18, 23, 28, 51, 81–86, 91, 98–103, 194, 204, 245 n. 45, 246 n. 53, 247 n. 57; *The Key to Uncle Tom's Cabin*, 168–69; *Uncle Tom's Cabin*, 15, 23, 28, 47–48, 114, 134, 151–61, 165–70, 214, 255 n. 1, 256 n. 7, 257 n. 15

Swann, Charles, 241 n. 17, 243 n. 31

Sypher, Eileen, 257 n. 12

Tang, Edward, 247 n. 56

technology of gender, 29, 33, 71

Third Space, 43, 49, 150, 237 n. 24, 239 n. 33

Thompson, Andrew, 105, 124, 126–27, 132, 143, 235 n. 2, 252 n. 35

Thompson, James R., 227, 269 n. 49

Tompkins, Jane, 219, 267 n. 40

transcendentalism, 15, 20, 24–25, 28–29, 36, 41–42, 55, 75, 112–13, 130, 147, 151, 181, 185–87, 210, 239 n. 4, 248 n. 12, 252 n. 33, 260 n. 31; correspondences between the transcen-

dentalist oversoul and Kabbalah, 24, 27, 36, 185–86, 191, 210, 261 n. 44; Neoplatonic origins of, 24, 27, 36, 151, 185–89, 210
travel writing, 108, 122, 124, 248 n. 8

universalism, 37, 39–41, 43, 45, 49, 149, 237 n. 23
Urbanski, Marie Mitchell Olesen, 190

von Mehren, Joan, 18, 105, 107, 111

Ward, Susan, 263 n. 6
Wardley, Lynn, 257 n. 15
Warhol, Robyn R., 242 n. 28
Weisbuch, Robert, 22

Welter, Barbara, 33, 202, 237 n. 17, 256 n. 6
Westra, Helen Petter, 28, 152
Wharton, Edith, 16, 19–20, 24, 193–94, 201–4, 210–12, 222, 239 n. 2
Wiesenfarth, Joseph, 128
Wilson, Jack H., 200
Winnifrith, Tom, 64–65, 123, 132
Wood, Mary E., 70

Yarborough, Richard, 48, 154, 156
Young, Robert, 43–44, 46

Zimmerman, Bonnie, 165
Zwarg, Christina, 238 n. 27, 262 n. 49